DUBLIN PAPERS, and their Rates of Subscription.

DAILY MORNING.

	Per Annum. £	s.	d.
Saunders's News-Letter, . }	5	4	0
Freeman's Journal, . . }			
Daily Express, . . .	5	0	0
,, 2nd Edition, .	3	0	0

MONDAY, WEDNESDAY, AND FRIDAY EVENINGS.

	£	s.	d.
Evening Mail, ...	3	0	0
Telegraph, ...	2	10	0

MONDAY AND THURSDAY.

	£	s.	d.
Evening Herald, ...	3	0	0

TUESDAY THURSDAY, AND SATURDAY EVENINGS.

	Per Annu £	s.	
Evening Packet, . . . }			
Evening Post, . . . }	3	0	
Evening Freeman, . . }			

WEEKLY.

Wednesday.

	£	s.	d.
Medical Press, ...	1	5	
Advocate, ...	1	6	

Friday Evening.

	£	s.	d.
Mercantile Advertiser, . .	1	0	0

WEEKLY—*continued.*

	£	s.	d.
Weekly Telegraph, . .	0	13	0
Commercial Journal, . .	1	0	0

LONDON NEWSPAPERS.

And the Prices for which they are forwarded to all parts of the World, including Envelopes, Directions, &c., corrected to December, 1850.

DAILY MORNING.

	Price per Quarter. £	s.	d.
The Times, ... }			
Morning Chronicle, . . }			
Morning Herald, . . . }			
Morning Post, . . . }	1	15	0
Morning Advertiser, . . }			
Daily News, . . . }			
Public Ledger, ...	1	2	6

DAILY EVENING.

	£	s.	d.
Globe, ... }			
Standard, ... }	1	17	6
Sun, ... }			
Shipping Gazette, . . .	2	0	0
Express, ...	0	19	6
Lloyd's List, ...	0	18	6
Packet List, ...	0	8	0
Bill of Entry, ...	1	6	6

MONDAY, WEDNESDAY, AND FRIDAY.

	£	s.	d.
Evening Mail, ...	0	17	6

TUESDAY, THURSDAY, AND SATURDAY

	£	s.	d.
St. James's Chronicle, . .	0	17	6

MONDAY AND THURSDAY.

	£	s.	d.
†Record, ... }			
Patriot, ... }	0	12	6
†May Supplements included, }			

TUESDAY AND FRIDAY.

London Gazette, per Sheet, 8*d*.
Course of the Exchange, £3 3*s*. per annum.

MONDAY EVENING.

	£	s.	d.
Mark-lane Express, . . .	0	8	0
Bell's Messenger, . . . }			
John Bull, ... }	0	6	6
Observer, ... }			
County Chronicle, . . . }			
Magnet, ...	0	5	0
Wesleyan Times, ...	0	5	6

TUESDAY EVENING.

	£	s.	d.
Mercantile Journal, . . .	0	13	0
Mercantile Price Current, . .	0	19	6
London New Price Current, £3 3*s*. per annum.			
Trade List, £3 per annum.			
Merchant, ...	0	6	6

WEDNESDAY EVENING.

	£	s.	d.
Guardian and Supplements, .	0	8	6
Nonconformist, ...	0	6	6
Watchman, ... }	0	5	6
British Banner, ... }			

THURSDAY EVENING.

	£	s.	d.
English Churchman, . . .	0	6	6
Cottage Gardener, . . . }	0	4	0
,, Sup. once per Mo. }			
Punch, ...	0	4	6

FRIDAY MORNING.

	£	s.	d.
Lady's Newspaper, . .	0	6	6

FRIDAY EVENING.

	Price per Quarter. £	s.	d.
Prince's Price Current, . .	0	13	0
Medical Gazette, ...	0	10	0
Lancet, ... }	0	9	0
Medical Times, . . . }			
British Army Despatch, . }			
Church and State Gazette, . }			
County Herald, . . . }			
Christian Times, . . . }			
Catholic Standard, . . . }			
Deutsche Londoner Zeitung, }			
*Illustrated London News, . }	0	6	6
*Weekly News, . . . }			
Gardeners & Farmers' Jour., }			
*Bell's Messenger, . . . }			
*Britannia, ... }			
*Leader, ... }			
Justice of Peace, . . . }			
*Northern Star, . . . }			
Builder, ... }			
London Commercial Record, }	0	5	6
*Standard of Freedom, . . }			
Architect, ... }			
Jewish Chronicle, . . . }			
*Lloyd's Weekly Newspaper, }			
*News of the World, . . }	0	3	3
Household Words, . . . }			
*Weekly Times, . . . }			
London New Price Current, per annum, . . .	3	3	0
Lady's Companion, . . .	0	4	6
Notes and Queries, . . .	0	4	6
Reynolds's Newspaper, . .	0	2	9
Chambers's Edinburgh Journal,	0	2	9
Law Times, exclusive of Supps.	0	13	0

* *Signifies that a later edition is published on Saturdays.*

SATURDAY MORNING.

	£	s.	d.
Economist, ...	0	10	0
*Atlas, ... }			
*Britannia, ... }			
*Dispatch, ... }			
Herapath's Railway Journal, }			
Journal of Commerce, . . }			
Railway Times, . . . }			
*Weekly Chronicle, . . }	0	6	6
Railway Record, . . . }			
*Bell's Life in London, . }			
Courier de l'Europe, . . }			
Gardiners' Chronicle, . . }			
John Bull, ... }			
Court Journal, . . . }			
Sunday Times, . . . }			
Athenæum, ... }	0	5	6
Literary Gazette, . . . }			
Naval and Military Gazette, }	0	8	0
United Service Gazette, . }			

* *Signifies that a later edition is published on Saturday Evenings.*

SATURDAY EVENING.

	£	s.	d.
Legal Observer, . . . }	0	10	0
Spectator, ... }			
Patent Journal, ...	0	8	0
Inquirer, ... }			
Era, ... }	0	6	6
Mining Journal, . . . }			
Mechanics' Magazine, . . }	0	4	6
Musical World, . . . }			
Perry's Bankrupt List, per an.,	2	12	6
Jurist, ...	varies.		

SATURDAY EVENING—*continued.*

	Price per Quarter. £	s.	d.
Homœopathic Times, . .	0	4	6
Examiner, ... }			
Nautical Standard, . . }	0	6	6
Railway Gazette, . . . }			

Every other Saturday.

	£	s.	d.
New Zealand Journal, . .	0	3	6
Universal Emigration Messen.	0	1	9

1st & 15th of each Month.

	£	s.	d.
Chemical Gazette, . . .	0	3	6
Publishers' Circular, . .	0	2	0
Critic, ...	0	3	3

7th & 24th of every Month.

	£	s.	d.
Atlas for India, (exclusive of Postage,) . . . . }	0	4	0
Home News, . . . }			

MONTHLY.

	£	s.	d.
Colonial Church Chronicle (1*st*),	0	1	9
The Friend, . . . ,,	0	1	6
Educational Times, . ,,	0	1	6
Anti-slavery Reporter, . ,, }	0	1	3
South Australian News, ,, }			
Eng Presbyterian Messenger,,	0	1	0
Labourers' Friend, . ,,	0	1	6
National Temperance Chron.,,	0	0	8
Teetotal Times, . . ,,	0	0	6
Parish Choir, . . ,, }			
Bradshaw's Time Tables, ,, }	0	0	6
Bradshaw's Railway Guide,, }			
Herald of Peace, . . ,,	0	0	9
Eng. Journal of Education, ,,	0	1	9
Evangelical Christendom, ,,	0	1	6
County Courts' Chronicle, ,,	0	4	9
Gazette of Fashion, . ,,	0	6	0
,, Annual Subscription, ,,	1	0	0
Musical Times, . . ,,	0	0	8
Primitive Church Magazine,,	0	1	3
Botanical Gazette, . ,,	0	3	3
London Review, . . ,,	0	1	9
Freeholder, . . . ,,	0	1	0
Vegetarian Advocate, . ,,	0	0	9
Church Miss. Intelligence, .	0	1	6
Magistrate . . (15*th*),	0	3	3
,, Supp., ...	0	1	6
Ecclesiastical Gaz. (2*nd Tues.*)	0	1	6
Bent's Advertiser, (10*th*) & an Annual Supplement, 1*s*. extra,	0	1	9
Willis's Price Current of Literature, ...	0	0	9
Monthly Digest, . . .	0	3	3
Medical Examiner, . .	0	1	9
Household Narrative, . .	0	0	9
Law Students' Magazine, .	0	5	3
Natal Journal, . . .	0	0	9
Reporter, ...	0	1	3
Journ. of Gas Lighting (10*th*),	varies.		

Arrival of Overland Mail.

	£	s.	d.
Indian Mail, ...	0	6	0
Indian News, ...	0	3	0

Occasionally.

Racing Calendar, with Book, per an. 35*s*.

Eason & Son
A History

Eason & Son
A History

L.M. CULLEN

Professor of Modern Irish History
Trinity College
Dublin

EASON & SON LTD
MIDDLE ABBEY STREET,
DUBLIN 1

ISBN 0-900346-87-6

First published 1989 by
Eason & Son Ltd,
Middle Abbey Street
Dublin 1
Ireland

Disk Editing: Tony Farmar
Index: Helen Litton
Design: Jacques Teljeur
Production: Tony Farmar
Setting: Printset & Design Ltd
Printing and Binding: Billings & Sons Ltd

Contents

List of Tables

Preface

THIS HISTORY OF EASON & SON has had a long gestation, for research for the present volume began in 1979. The distribution of newspapers, magazines and books is a complicated affair, and changes in structure and technique often occur with great rapidity. They are often by no means obvious to the outsider, nor fully documented in the written record.

Without a constant dialogue over many years with present and recent directors, many errors would have been committed and some important aspects of the business's history in the twentieth century left unexplored. Indeed, some of the picture presented here has been influenced or shaped imperceptibly by casual conversations, without either party being aware at the time of their significance for the story.

The obligations accumulated in the course of a long-drawn-out task of research and writing — and re-writing profiting from comments — are many, and I hope that none of them are overlooked. The greatest single obligation is to James Walmsley: he took a keen interest in the project at every stage, encouraged and facilitated it in every way possible, and commented at length on the entire text. I am greatly indebted also to Robert Eason who from his profound knowledge of the book trade provided me with a large amount of information on its development from the 1890s and made available a number of records which he had brought together. He also made available the common place book of Charles Eason I and the letters received by Benjamin MacFarlane Eason from his brother Charles II, at the time in the possession of his sister the late Caroline Vause Eason in Sheffield. Another major contribution has been by Basil Walmsley who provided access and guidance to the large volume of records in Belfast, also arranged for the transfer of some of them to Dublin, and as well as commenting on the Belfast chapter provided some important lore about the Belfast house. Sydney Carpenter, the previous managing director, Eddie Kelliher the former chairman, and Harold

Clarke, the present chairman, have also provided much assistance over the years, and informal comments from other directors, have often been helpful both in regard to recent history and the Eason family. The greater part of the book was in first draft when Charles Wilson's history of W.H. Smith's *First with the News,* appeared in 1985. The two histories overlap in the period 1850-86. Where they do, the W.H. Smith history affords a glimpse of the Irish business from the perspective of the Smith partners, and the Eason records provide an insight into the views of Smith's senior staff at the time.

Mrs Leslie Whiteside did an invaluable report on a visit by her to the Smith archives in Britain, and Mr T.W. Baker-Jones gave me much assistance when I visited the archives in 1981. At all times, Mrs O'Halloran, secretary to the Directors has been helpful. Mr Evan Hassell helped with keeping the records of the house in order, and retrieving items. Mrs O'Halloran, Mrs Joanna Crooks, Ms Muriel Saidlear, Department of Modern History and Mrs Alice Tunney and members of the Central Secretariat, T.C.D., have patiently typed what appeared to be endless chapters of an apparently interminable enterprise. I am grateful also to Ms Jean Harrison, librarian, All Hallows College, for access to the collection of prayer books published by the firm and deposited in the library in 1972, and to Mr Michael Hewson, then Director of the National Library, for help with one small but intricate point.

Mrs Joan Hall and Mrs Molly Walmsley, daughters of J.C.M. Eason, the remarkable man who guided the destinies of the firm through three decades of great adversity and yet had time to play a role in government commissions, Chamber of Commerce and Statistical and Social Enquiry Society of Ireland have provided some useful comments on his family life. Professor R.B. Kershner of the English Department, University of Florida, Gainesville, kindly provided me with an interesting and exhaustive list of the references to magazines and newspapers in James Joyce's *Ulysses:* the range of such items which could occur in the account of one day, 16 June 1904, is a striking illustration of the extent to which news had penetrated deeply into middle-class life by the outset of the twentieth century. Dr Fergus Darcy of the Department of History, University College, Dublin, kindly brought to my attention a diary of an employee of the firm in 1864, which rests in the library of the University of Kansas.

A special obligation exists to Tony Farmar who was appointed by the Board of Eason's as editor to see the volume through the press. He has made numerous helpful comments on the text, and in particular has made suggestions for restructuring the chronological presentation of the chapters for which the reader will have every reason to be grateful.

I have been given freedom to express my own views, and the views expressed in the volume are therefore those of the author, not necessarily those of the Board of Eason's. However, I have benefited by drawing on the information and recollections of many members of the Board. In some regards, as for other firms in keeping with modern trends, Eason's records for recent decades are less informative than are older records, and personal recollection and reminiscences are invaluable.

On one issue, indeed, they rather graphically illustrate the pitfalls inherent in the historian's reliance on the written record. For the development of the retail trade from the end of the 1950s, I had provided originally an interpretation in which the firm anticipated the new trends. From the perspective of recollections within the house, however, the impetus for the growth of the retail side simply resulted in the first instance from the release of space as some operations were moved elsewhere, although undoubtedly as opportunity in retail custom rose, the firm's response was positive and immediate.

L.M. Cullen
Trinity College, Dublin
January 1989

Chapter 1 Introduction

DURING THEIR HISTORY, EASON'S HAVE been involved with retailing and wholesaling many products. They have sold almanacs, books, Christmas cards, diaries, health foods, magazines, newspapers, prayerbooks and stationery, to name only a few of the more prominent. They have been printers, stationery manufacturers, publishers and advertising agents. But the core of the business has always been the retailing and wholesaling of newspapers and magazines in Ireland. The servicing of this 'news' business (to use the wholesaler's term) gave Eason's a structure through which the other products could profitably be channelled. At different times non-news products, such as books, stationery or railway advertising have made a greater contribution to profits than news, but selling news remained the central rationale of the business.

News in this sense is a comparatively recent product in the wholesale and retail trade. In the seventeenth century news, as purveyed in newspapers, was not only a novelty but also an elite form of communication, which scarcely existed outside a handful of capital cities. Newspapers were bought by a small number of individuals either living in metropolitan centres, or having close contacts with them. Intermediaries, except in a city on the scale of late eighteenth century London, were not required for distribution. Readers bought direct from the publishers. As a result print runs were small, and newspapers often proved short-lived. In Ireland, only Dublin and Belfast had achieved a stable press by 1750. By that time 157 newspaper ventures had been started in Dublin, of which only 8 were still in existence.[1]

Early newspapers were prized largely for their advertising. They contained advertisements and London news, in that order. Local news was given sparingly and haphazardly. The space allotted to advertising

1 R.L. Munter *A Handlist of Irish Newspapers* (London, 1960)

was a measure of its importance, both to the publisher, for whom it supplemented the revenue from the cover price as it does today, and also to the reader. Advertising was a selling point for the press and early Dublin newspapers sold in the provinces as much for their advertisements as for their news, if not more. In the middle decades of the eighteenth century, land and leases were extensively advertised. Only from the 1760s did the news content, especially coverage of Irish events, grow significantly, and because of this the newspapers began to be politicised. Increasingly the press was manipulated, bribed or maintained by the government, and political censorship had become a fact by the onset of the nineteenth century.[2]

As news content increased, the scope for a successful local or provincial press, as opposed to a metropolitan press, became much larger. From the 1770s or 1780s the vigour of the provincial press began to become evident. The number of provincial newspapers and their news content grew even more strikingly in the early decades of the nineteenth century. The appearance of a healthy provincial press provided scope for specialisation between local and metropolitan newspapers. Even for Ireland, a metropolitan press increasingly meant a London press, because London was close to the organs of power which controlled foreign policy and war. The trend was powerfully reinforced by the Act of Union which made London the parliamentary capital of Ireland. During the politicisation process after 1760, reports of Irish parliamentary debates had received prominence in the Dublin press, and after the Union this interest switched to reports from Westminster.

The channels of newspaper distribution, however, were still narrow. Sales were to subscribers, usually paying a quarter or a half year's subscription in advance, and subscribers away from the publisher's office were supplied through the mails. This explains why the Clerks of the Road, officials in the London headquarters of the Post Office were able to organise a distribution service of sorts. Many readers, even well-off readers, consulted the press simply through subscribing to newsrooms or the grander clubs, which were as late as the 1850s the most prestigious customers of the early newspaper wholesalers. In the countryside newspapers were frequently read to wider audiences by a literate person; in general, due to the newsrooms, newspaper buying was in its infancy, even among the literate and well-off.

The wholesalers' emergence was a consequence firstly of improved

2 B. Inglis *The Freedom of the Press in Ireland, 1784-1841* (London, 1954)

coach services in the 1820s, and then of the railway age. If newspapers had continued to be delivered through the mails, there would have been little scope for the growth of a news distribution empire. Coach and railway schedules enabled newspapers to be delivered to Dublin and to the English provinces more quickly than through the post. To achieve this, the wholesaler took supplies as soon as they were printed from the publisher to the coach or railway terminus, and ensured that they were whisked away at the other end without loss of time to the distributor's shop or to other customers. If necessary, W.H. Smith's even hired special trains to ensure distribution. The motto, as Smith himself expressed it in 1861, was 'the mails must *never* beat us'. Success in this new entrepreneurial role depended on two factors. The first was a high degree of organisation and painstaking attention to detail both in the despatch and delivery of papers. The second was the negotiation of carriage rates at attractive levels with the railway companies. Because of their success in both of these aspects, W.H. Smith and Son began to outdistance their rivals in London in the 1840s and 1850s.

As wholesaling developed, the distribution of London papers became dominated by metropolitan wholesalers: the publishers dealt in bulk only with wholesalers who could take delivery from the publishing house directly. This meant that provincial wholesalers were forced to draw supplies from one of several London houses. The first newspaper wholesaler in Dublin, J.K. Johnston & Co., which had been founded in 1819, was in this position. The London papers, which were more important to the Dublin wholesale business than the local press, were supplied to Johnston's by W.H. Smith's, who eventually took over the company as the largest creditor when Johnston's collapsed in 1850.[3] Because both retailers and readers alike could obtain supplies of the local press directly from the publisher, this dimension of the wholesale trade was not very important. There is no evidence that 'newswalks'[4] existed in Dublin. The London press, therefore, created the need for a Dublin wholesaler; the Dublin press itself remained independent of wholesale intermediaries. In the north of England, local wholesalers grew, and in the case of Scotland, the Edinburgh house of Menzies gradually

3 Smith's manager in Dublin from 1856 was Charles Eason I; he eventually bought the company from W.H. Smith in 1886.

4 The Smith's business had started in 1792 as a newswalk, based in Berkeley Square. This business was basically that of a newsround, based on a territory of three or four square miles (see C. Wilson *First with the News* (London, 1985) p. 9).

established a dominance of the Scottish market from 1855 onwards.[5] In Ireland itself, Smith's branch in Dublin remained much more independent of London control than did the branches of the house in the north of England.

The market for newspapers, and hence the emergence of news wholesaling was greatly stimulated from the 1850s by a change in the quality of the news itself. The telegraph from 1850 revolutionised the dissemination of information, and indeed was more instrumental than the express railway in enhancing the freshness of news. In Ireland, the use of the telegraph enabled the Dublin press to regain ground lost over the first half of the century. Local newspapers could receive information as quickly as London papers, and could put it into the hands of the reader a day ahead of the arrival in Dublin of the London press. In other words, for the first time since London newspapers had become popular in Ireland after the Union, a Dublin paper was a near-perfect substitute for its London rivals. As a result Dublin papers gradually gained a new vigour in the 1850s, and began to push the London dailies out of significance in circulation.

However, there were problems for the wholesaler. While the news-hungry public was expanding rapidly for the first time, it was not doing so rapidly enough to cover all the costs of distribution. This was particularly so for the new penny papers, which began to appear after the abolition of stamp duty in 1855. The extra sales did not compensate for the loss in wholesaler's revenue as customers transferred from high-priced dailies to penny dailies. One response was for the wholesaler to develop advertising and book sales, whose price and therefore profit margin was much larger. Another response was to sell a wider range of 'news', particularly the weeklies and fortnightlies whose number was rapidly increasing. The volume of such material exceeded that of daily newspapers, and its carriage costs — as it was available ahead of the day of sale and delivered at non-express rates — were significantly lower. This weekly 'news' market, typified in the 1850s by the *Illustrated London News*, provided the mainstay of news wholesaling, made the business profitable and financed the prestigious but limited and costly distribution of national dailies across these islands. The growth in the volume and profitability of news distribution depended more and more on this literature.

Every year between 1861 and 1877/8, W.H. Smith's in Dublin recorded annual growth in wholesale news turnover (which in the firm's

5 *The Menzies Group* (Edinburgh, 1965) pp. 12-13

classification included sales at the railway bookstalls). This uninterrupted expansion was due to many circumstances. The first was certainly the combination of cheap publications and growing literacy. The advent of penny newspapers in Dublin in 1859 was one factor. The abolition of the tax on paper itself was a further contributor, reflected in the appearance of many kinds of cheap publication. In the struggle to find markets, publishers were increasingly receptive to the distribution arrangements which were offered by a house such as W.H. Smith & Son. As early as 1861, the Irish Census Commissioners, noting that knowledge of reading was more widespread than knowledge of writing, attributed it in part to: '.... the ready access which the present low prices afford to newspapers and other cheap publications.'[6] Schooling and literacy were rising rapidly. The proportion of children aged nine who were attending school rose from 34 per cent in 1851 to 65 per cent in 1881, and literacy rose sharply as well during the period. In 1841, 47 per cent of the population aged five and upwards were described as literate, and by 1881 this figure had risen to 75 per cent.

As people became more literate, newspapers and other publications entered more into their lives. Four out of the five Dublin morning daily newspapers were conservative in politics in the 1860s, but as time went on the number and circulation of other papers increased relatively, particularly from the 1870s. Circulation outside Dublin widened during the 1860s and 1870s. The cheap Dublin papers created a taste for news, and this was sustained by the emergence of provincial papers, which were mainly weekly. A large number of weekly newspapers made their first appearance in the 1870s and 1880s, with nationalist papers appearing in addition to unionist papers, in response not only to changing politics but also to a widening market. Many who could not afford to buy dailies, and those who had no access to a retailer except in the course of a weekly visit to market or to Mass on Sunday, supported the new weeklies. As well as provincial weeklies, weekly editions of the Dublin papers, especially of the nationalist *Freeman's Journal* began to circulate widely. The circulation of the *Weekly Freeman* outside Dublin probably equalled the total sales of the daily *Freeman's Journal*, and certainly reached a wider audience than the daily. For example, in the late nineteenth century in the tiny shop of the Brownes at Ballymockler on the slopes of Slievenamon, one hundred copies of the *Weekly Freeman* were distributed

6 L.M. Cullen *Life in Ireland* (London, 1968) p. 159

to country people who did their shopping after Mass on Sunday. No daily paper was sold in the parish at all.[7]

Increased literacy ensured that letter writing increased in volume also. Emigrants created a vast correspondence with relatives at home, and every letter required a response. Within Ireland both personal and commercial correspondence grew also. Between 1843 and 1857 the number of letters delivered rose from 23.4 million to 42.0 million. The rural and village post office was becoming a focal point of life, and the fact that the post office was often linked to other commercial pursuits illustrates how much it was sought after in retail business as a magnet for the local population. A large demand came into existence for stationery and writing requisites. Although W.H. Smith & Son in England did not service this demand, in Ireland, at the personal initiative of Charles Eason, the firm became wholesalers to this trade in or before 1870. In a distinctive way, the Dublin house was built around the revolution in literacy — through the organisation of the nationwide distribution of newspapers and magazines by bookstalls and agents, and the distribution of stationery by commercial travellers who carried samples throughout the island.

Another important factor was the development of the railway network. In Ireland, the development of the railway system was a phenomenon of the 1850s and the early 1860s. In 1849, 428 miles had been laid, by 1866 1,909 miles. Using techniques evolved from the firm's experience in England in the 1840s, W.H. Smith and his Irish manager Charles Eason rapidly achieved a virtual monopoly of bookstall and advertising sites on Irish lines, apart from some minor lines in the north east, and the local companies in Cork. This enabled them to negotiate favourable bulk carriage rates with the companies. The bookstalls were also a perfect focus for the development of news wholesaling in their area.

When Smith took over Johnston's business in 1850, the Irish economy was still facing the aftermath of the Great Famine. Between 1841 and 1851 the population had fallen by 20 per cent to 6.55 millions. Although the direct effects of the Famine were slight as far as the better-off regions and the middle and upper classes were concerned, curtailed purchasing of consumer goods, arrears in rents and the impact of the English business recession of 1847 did however mean a deep and prolonged recession in Dublin. It is not fanciful to see the collapse of Johnston's business in 1850 as resulting from these circumstances. The bank note issue, reflecting the consumer crisis, fell from £7.3 million to £4.3 million between 1846 and

7 J. Brady *The Big Sycamore* (Dublin, 1958) p. 181

1849; bank deposits, a better indicator of the effect on a wholesale business than note issue, fell less sharply from £8.4 million in 1846 to £6.5 million in 1847, but began to recover in the following year. Railway building, which had slowed down in 1847, quickened, and the most important main lines serving Cork, Belfast, Galway and Limerick were all complete by 1851. All the indices of business prosperity were positive in the 1850s: agricultural prices, bank deposits and wages rose, rent arrears fell. However emigration, though less than its Famine peak, remained high. Political resentment at the landed classes, who were held responsible, if not for the Famine, at least for emigration, sharpened.

Paul Cullen's long administrative dominance of the catholic church began in 1850, with his archepiscopacy of Armagh and his subsequent translation to Dublin two years later. Though a bitter foe of the Fenians, in his own way he reflected, as much as the Fenians did, a resurgent catholic nationalism which presented an implacable face to the Anglo-Irish establishment which had bitterly opposed its rise in the first instance. From the point of view of the news business, Cullen's greatest achievement was the creation of a vigorous network of catholic secondary schools. This both enlarged the catholic readership and sustained the rise of a broader catholic middle class. In consequence the rising flood of English weeklies, sustained though it was, did not engulf national feeling in Ireland. Indeed, quite the reverse: a more aggressive nationalism was quickly reflected in the press. In fact in a politically divided island there was a systematic duplication of sources of news. Local conservative papers had liberal or nationalist rivals. The Dublin press was similarly duplicated, with the nationalist *Freeman's Journal* being read by quite different people from those who read the conservative *Irish Times*.

There is no gainsaying the vigour of the Irish press in the second half of the century. Newspaper editors, authors and reporters accounted for a mere 259 persons in the 1861 census, and 388 in 1881. In the agitated decade of the 1880s they rose to 651, and to 807 by 1901 and 1108 by 1911. Irish bookprinting was falling off, but a slow rise in the number of printers seems to point to the success of newsprinting. The shorthand writers who are included with reporters in the census from 1881 reflect the appearance of those patient men who dutifully recorded the proceedings of public meetings and public bodies at interminable length. Politicisation, reflected in the extraordinary attention given to such detail was unquestionably a potent feature in giving a distinctive image to the Irish press both local and national, and in ensuring a growing demand for its products. The national scale of such bodies as the Land League and the Parliamentary

Party and their tight organisation by contemporary British and continental standards rested on the creation and homogenisation of public opinion through the press as much as if not more than through the numerous public meetings. The role of the press is reflected ultimately in the number of newspaper proprietors and reporters — quite disproportionate to the number in the profession — who made a mark as politicians in the Irish party.[8]

No retail channels for newspapers and magazines existed at the outset of the 1840s or 1850s. No separate occupational data for newsagents as opposed to newsvendors appeared until the 1861 census, and in that year they amounted to a mere 14 persons. Newsrooms met much of the demand, so circulations were small, but readership per copy comparatively high. The retail trade in news grew only slowly. In the railway bookstalls of the 1840s, books rather than news were the basis of the business (hence the name). Later, newspapers and magazines became the mainstay of their turnover, and almost half of the wholesale news turnover in the Dublin house was actually retailed through the firm's own bookstall network. Indeed the success of the railway bookstalls, a precocious feature in Britain and Ireland, may help to explain why the metropolitan press, no longer constrained by the limits of the postal subscription service of the pre-1850 decades, played so much greater a role in provincial Britain and Ireland than in continental Europe or America. The smallness of the retail market was especially marked in Ireland. The number of newsagents went up very slowly from 349 in 1871 to 412 in 1891, 477 in 1901 and 494 in 1911.[9] Even as late as the 1880s, a retail market in depth did not exist. Only the weekly editions of the Dublin dailies sold widely outside the cities. Between the 1860s and the 1890s the *Weekly Freeman*, because it responded to the political aspirations of nationalists occupied a unique place in Ireland. No other newspaper, Irish or English, equalled it in circulation and in particular no paper could match its rural readership. It was the great innovator in the countryside, creating in many households for the first time the habit of regular purchase of a newspaper.

Since Eason's bookstall network numbered over a hundred at its peak, their importance as a vehicle of retail distribution is clear. Further, the number of newsagents supplied by Eason's does not differ greatly from

8 For an introduction, see C.C. O'Brien *Parnell and his Party* (Oxford, 1957), and S. Clark, 'The social composition of the Land League', *Irish Historical Studies* vol XVII, no. 68 (Sept. 1971)

9 Census returns in *Parliamentary Papers*.

the number in the census.[10] Since few shopkeepers confined themselves to newsagency, the fact that they picked out this element as a description for the census suggests that not only was the business producing significant turnover, but it was also acquiring prestige. Newsagents were still exceeded in number in the second half of the nineteenth century by both booksellers and stationers. In 1901 however newsagents for the first time exceeded booksellers, a pointer to the higher profile of the retail newsagent. The newsagent proper was now beginning to appear in country towns where previously newsagency had been a mere adjunct to other businesses. News was seen to bring custom into the shop. The rise of newsagency is also reflected in beginnings of resentment of the retail role played by the wholesaler, and in the first attempt at retail association by newsagents. However even with these changes sales per agent were still much lower than in Britain. Unlike Smith's after 1905, Eason's did not open 'High Street' shops, until the 1960s. The publishers of Sunday papers in search of a mass market pushed sales through new channels, street and church door sellers were much more widespread than in Britain, and their numbers grew with the effort to achieve mass circulation. A mass market for news developed in the first two decades of the twentieth century, led by the growing number of popular weeklies with an emphasis on entertainment and illustrations. By 1910, the *News of the World* was the clear market leader and pace-setter, and cross-channel Sundays may have been selling between 80,000 and 120,000 copies. Even this figure was short of the sales achieved in the 1920s. Widespread retailing of dailies — in the sense of a mass market — came only in the 1920s, when their price fell back to the pre-war level of 1d, while money wages almost doubled. In real terms, therefore, the daily newspapers were being sold at about one-eighth of the cost of the papers of the 1840s, and about half the cost of the penny papers that took their place after 1859.

As a business, Eason's was a mirror image of the much larger W.H. Smith operation in England. This followed both from its origins as a branch of Smith's and from its possession of a similar niche, albeit in a much smaller, much less densely populated market, with a rural population whose incomes and reading habits were much more limited. In one respect Smith's Irish business differed widely from the English business. As a result of the character and drive of the first Charles Eason,

10 This understates Eason's relative importance, as newsagent in the census returns represents a profession, not a firm. In a few cases more than one member of a firm may have returned themselves as a newsagent.

stationery sales had been developed in Ireland, and then gradually stationery manufacture as well. At the outset of the 1870s, book and stationery sales together exceeded newspapers and magazines in turnover. Through the travelling representatives, stationery sales helped to secure orders for news products, and to build up the small town newsagent, who was usually a bookseller and stationer or a general retailer.

Smith's business in its essentials was the creation of W.H. Smith the elder (1792-1865) and was turned by his son into one of the great enterprises of Victorian England: a mammoth organisation, national in scale and of substantial profitability. His direct involvement in Ireland was forced on him by circumstances, though he seized the opportunity to take over Johnston's failing business as part of his grand strategy for securing his dominant place in London wholesaling. He had no more real interest in Ireland than he had in Scotland, where he contented himself with opening a short-lived bookstall in Edinburgh.[11] A passing comment in later years suggests that Smith may even not have attached any deep importance to retaining the ownership of the Dublin house, as long as it drew its London supplies from his house. Once the strategy of dominating supplies from London to Dublin was assured, Smith was content to leave a wide measure of discretion to his Dublin manager, Charles Eason. This was characteristic of his management style: the business both in England and in Ireland depended for its success on senior staff he had appointed — such as Charles Eason in Dublin, John White, head of the Newspaper Department and the Counting House, and Jabez Sandifer, head of the Book Department in London — all of whom had a remarkable degree of expertise and devotion which in their respective spheres could successfully meet the day-to-day demands of running a vast and intricate business.

Charles Eason, who was born in Somerset, was one of many Scots and Englishmen who played a large part in the story of Victorian business in Dublin. Some were manufacturers, like several of the whiskey distillers; some, like Findlaters, were spirit retailers. Others came as managers, such as Charles Eason, or the Scots who, serving below him in the business, provided much of the administrative capacity of the house in the early decades. These men are frequently lumped together in Dublin's protestant and unionist business class, but they were as varied in outlook as they were in temperament. Dissenters like Eason himself did not necessarily

11 Wilson, op. cit., p. 145.

share the political outlook of the ruling Anglican ascendancy in the city. They tended to be liberal rather than conservative in politics. Only in the 1880s did something like a political consensus emerge among protestant businessmen, when the land agitation and a more radical home rule movement began to frighten the propertied classes. Charles Eason was a confirmed, not to say eccentric dissenter, with a distinctive and independent outlook that led him, for instance, into being trusted by the catholic archbishop as a publisher. In the increasingly sectarian wilderness that Dublin represented he was accepted by catholic clergy and people as a publisher of prayerbooks.

The semi-independence of the Irish house, Charles Eason's anxiety to do something for his family, the unrest among the senior managers in W. H. Smith's, and Smith's rise in conservative politics combined in the 1880s to bring the relationship between the Dublin and London houses to the fore. The association of the house with catholic prayerbook publishing had already led to a celebrated onslaught by Tim Healy on Smith in the House of Commons in 1884. Smith's short-lived term as Chief Secretary in January 1886, amid growing political excitement as British governments moved towards the introduction of home rule, brought the whole issue of the Dublin house to a head. Smith made his mind up quickly, and sold the Dublin house to Eason. The ease with which the decision was taken was of course helped by the close relationship with London, and the knowledge that the new owner would continue to acquire news through the London house.

After becoming independent in 1886, Dublin became a provincial house in the same way as wholesalers in the north of England or Scotland were, in the sense of reliance for most of its news purchases on a London wholesaler. Eason's continued to buy all its news through Smith's until 1905, and continued to obtain small circulation magazines through them until the 1960s. The direct link between Smith's and Eason's had been severed in 1886, but the good spirit in which the decision was then taken, the personal links between Eason and Smith and between Eason and Smith's senior staff ensured that a bond of goodwill and communication continued, which it does to this day.

Chapter 2 The Dublin Newspapers Business before 1856

NEWSPAPER CIRCULATIONS WERE SMALL IN the early nineteenth century and, outside London, were made up moreover largely of subscriptions rather than casual sales. Nor did newspaper distributors as such in either Dublin or London have the trade to themselves. They had to compete with the 'Clerks of the Road' in the Post Offices in both cities. These officials took advantage of their central position in the postal system to build up a private business in the transmission of newspapers through the mails.

Though the growth in newspaper reading was modest, the newly emerging emphasis on punctuality and speed in life generally gave the independent news distributors of the early nineteenth century an opportunity to develop a distinctive service to the public. They made use of the improving coach services, which ran as fast as and at more convenient times than the mail coaches, to deliver their papers. The day coaches of private contractors setting out from London in the mornings, introduced in the 1820s, were not only an alternative to the night mail coaches but more importantly made possible the delivery of morning editions in the provinces on the same day. In this way distributors were able to guarantee delivery ahead of the mails, and thus to offer a real service, whose benefits were felt at once by the newsreaders of a less leisurely age.

It was this expanding market, requiring rapid delivery, that provided the opportunity for the rise of newspaper distributors, and for keen competition between them. The Smith family ran a news-walk business in London from at least 1792, but it was only after 1816, when the widow of the first Smith passed the business to her two sons, that the firm began to grow in earnest. Through the energy of the younger brother, W.H. Smith the first, it expanded greatly. By 1828 the business had become his sole property. The firm, which used the day coach services to beat the mails in the distribution of newspapers, made early use of the railways for the same purpose. By 1846 the house even hired special newspaper trains. In 1848 Smith's son, W.H. Smith the second, succeeded in making the first contract for sole rights for the operation of bookstalls on the London & North-Western Railway.[1] For the remainder of the century, the railway station bookstalls were to be the firm's chief contact with the public.

Long before the retirement of the elder Smith in 1857, W.H. Smith the younger had become the driving force in the firm. His coup in 1854 of obtaining the privilege of having, for an annual charge of £4,000, the first copies off the press of *The Times* of London was the vital step in assuring the ascendency of the firm in wholesale news distribution to the provinces.[2] At this time, Smith's, though leaders, did not yet have the field to themselves: no less than ten or twelve agents in London sent newspapers to the provinces by the first railways.[3] During the 1850s securing the firm's position became its major objective; the process of realising this aim made the decade one of the most decisive in the history of the firm.

In Ireland newspaper distribution was likewise tending to become centred in the hands of a single firm, that of Johnston & Co., established by Capt. Johnston of the 25th regiment, the King's Own Borderers,[4] at 1 Eden Quay, Dublin in June 1819. He was later succeeded by two sons, John Kent and Alexander. There is no evidence of an earlier Dublin wholesaler; the Dublin press sold few copies outside the capital and it was only the new-found importance of London newspapers which made possible the rise of a Dublin wholesaler. In an advertisement in the *Almanack & Post Office Directory* of 1833, the firm drew the attention of their customers to the

> Unprecedented and decided advantage by dealing with Johnston & Co. which they cannot obtain through any other channel — UNPRECEDENTED in expeditious transmission and delivery; they being enabled to deliver their newspapers in Dublin by their own messengers, a full hour at least, EARLIER than the Post Office Delivery, and to anticipate in many of the Principal Towns in Ireland the regular Post by 14 or 18 hours, in consequence of getting their papers daily by Express direct from London, INDEPENDENTLY OF THE POST OFFICE.

1 C. Wilson *First with the news* (London 1986) p. 102.
2 Wilson op. cit. p. 176.
3 Wilson op. cit. p. 48.
4 This detail is given in Alexander Johnston's advertisement in *Thom's Directory* 1856.

Johnston's advertised heavily, a reflection of the existence of a market which could be solicited in this way, and evidence, in the absence of comparable advertising by rivals, of their prominence in the business. The privileges of the Clerks of the Road were finally cancelled in 1834, and the newsagents had the field to themselves. In advertisements which appeared during the following year, Johnston's were able to refer 'with pride to the success attending their exertions during the several past Sessions of Parliament', and promised their subscribers the continuance of their express system which guaranteed delivery in Dublin an hour before the postal delivery.

The largest circulation of a Dublin published paper was less than 2,000 copies per issue in the early 1820s,[5] and even as late as 1857 the circulation of the largest Dublin daily probably did not greatly exceed that number. The confines of the market are reflected also in the fact that the successful newspapers were protestant and conservative. But the small scale of newspaper circulation should not lead to an underestimation of the importance of newspapers as vehicles of news and opinion. A minor catholic notable, Humphrey O'Sullivan of Callan, frequently noted foreign news from the newspapers in his diary in the late 1820s and early 1830s.[6] In the same county a decade earlier, the compiler of the statistical memoir of the neighbouring parish of Tullaroan on the western borders of Co. Kilkenny noted that *Cox's Hibernian Magazine* had formerly been sold every year to some farmers 'by fellows who had hawked it about' but that at the time of writing no newspaper was to be met with in the parish. While it was received, it was often read to a crowd of villagers on a Sunday evening.[7] Somewhat later a painting attempted to catch the atmosphere of a gathering of this kind, with a central figure reading the *Nation* to an audience around him.[8]

The better-off did much of their reading in newsrooms, to which they subscribed as members. The significance of the newsroom can be seen fleetingly in the accounts of a Dundalk newsagent, John Lee, who was supplied with his papers by Johnston's of Dublin.[9] Of total sales of newspapers from 7 October 1846 to 10 February 1847 amounting to £49 7s 8d, no less than £34 0s 2d consisted of sales to the town's two

5 B. Inglis *The Freedom of the Press in Ireland 1780-1841* (London, 1954).

6 *Diaries of Humphrey O'Sullivan* ed. M. McGrath (Dublin, 1936-7) 4 volumes.

7 W.S. Mason *Statistical Account or Parochial Survey of Ireland,* vol. III (Dublin, 1819), pp. 628, 639.

8 H. McManus, painting in the National Gallery of Ireland, Dublin

9 Public Record Office of Northern Ireland, D.2458/2

newsrooms, the Guildhall Newsroom, and the Commercial Newsroom. The Guildhall had the larger bill, and catered for a more upper-class clientele. Its subscriptions included *The Times*, the *Naval and Military Gazette*, and the *United Services Gazette* in addition to other London, Liverpool and Dublin newspapers. John Lee supplied both newsrooms, so it is likely that he was the most successful local newsagent. Even so the January/February accounts of 1847 included only 25 accounts apart from the newsrooms. Among them were a captain, two 'doctors', an officer's mess and four 'reverends', including the Rev. Sir T. Foster of Beaulieu. When the *Nation* appeared, it gained a single individual subscriber. The Commercial, the more liberal of the two newsrooms, also subscribed. All this illustrates how limited the market was. While other customers floated through the accounts over the years, it seems clear not only that the newsrooms were the mainstay of the agent's business, but that to a large extent they were the focal point of newspaper reading in an entire town.

In post-union Ireland, London had a new significance, and the London press encroached increasingly on Dublin. In their advertisements, Johnston's referred with an emphasis that varied somewhat from time to time to the 'nobility and gentry of Ireland, proprietors of news-rooms, reading-rooms, libraries, institutions, hotels etc.' This was a market bound by many political and business ties to England, whose members consequently looked to the London papers, delivered rapidly, as the fullest and most reliable source of parliamentary news and business intelligence. References to parliamentary news and to parliamentary sessions crop up repeatedly in Johnstons' advertisements, and emphasise the basic advantage which made it possible for the London papers to increase their sales at the expense of local newspapers. Up to 1836 Irish newspapers had enjoyed the advantage of a lower stamp duty than in England — two pence as against four pence — but in that year the reduction of the stamp duty to a common level of one penny eliminated this differential, to the advantage of the English newspapers.

London papers were more in demand in Dublin, the centre of wealth and social life, than in small towns and the countryside, where readers were relatively remote from the outside world. But everywhere army garrisons — sergeants' and officers' messes — were an important element in newspaper readership. Many if not most of the commissioned and non-commissioned ranks were from England, and favoured English news and newspapers. The records of surviving accounts with the London parent house in the Dublin branch of W.H. Smith & Son for 1853-56 contain a number of payments made directly to London in respect of individual officers, regiments and messes, sergeants' as well as officers'.[10] The opening of a shop at the Curragh Military Camp as late as the 1860s, and the relatively large turnover of that outlet, shows the continuing importance of army business.

Johnston's do not seem to have conducted either a bookselling business or a news reading-room, both of which were important to W.H. Smith in London. However they were agents for advertisements in the newspapers. The bulk of advertisements no doubt came from the ranks of the 'professional gentlemen, surveyors, land agents, and booksellers', from whom they solicited business. Johnston's claimed in 1833 that they kept files of most papers in the United Kingdom for twelve years for inspection by advertisers.[11] John Lee in Dundalk handled some local advertising for them on one occasion. A statement of November 1838 referred to an advertising account for the Trustees of the Turnpike Road.

Johnston's had the largest newspaper wholesaling business in Dublin, and apparently most of the Irish business of W.H. Smith & Son was in their hands. The small number of Irish entries in the so-called 'Coach Book' of Smith's for 1840-42,[12] the only surviving newspaper record in the London house for the early years, relate to changes in address, principally of subscribers such as army officers, gentry and peers, who moved a great deal, and whose papers were dispatched by coach. Only three of these customers are identified as clients of Johnston's, whose importance is probably understated, as they would as a rule have catered for the needs of their customers from Dublin, including their changes in address. The number of clients in Ireland served directly by W.H. Smith & Son, if measured by the narrow criteria of change of address, is small, at most a few dozen. Apart from Johnston's, only five agents can be identified. One of these is Henderson, a Belfast bookseller, the only one for whom more than one subscriber is recorded in this restricted list. Henderson survived into the era following Smith's acquisition of Johnstons' business. But his business cannot have been very significant as his association with W.H. Smith & Son was terminated in a peremptory letter from Smith in London on 4 January 1853:

> It is your fault and not ours, whatever may happen. We have no kind of responsibility after sending off the papers correctly according to

10 In Eason's, Dublin

11 The fact that their files went back precisely twelve years suggests that their advertising dated from twelve years previously, i.e. from 1821.

12 W.H. Smith & Son, London, A 16

> the instructions given to us.... As you have thought it right to indulge in remarks which are quite at variance with the truth, we give you notice that your account will be closed after Saturday 8th next.
>
> We give value in goods and labour for all that we ever receive from you, and no obligation exists which entitles you to use language to us which no respectable house would permit a man to address to them for a single day.[13]

The fact that Smith's dominated Johnstons' supply of London news is confirmed by their heavy indebtedness to Smith's at the outset of 1850. A letter from Smith to his sister Gussie in January 1850 gives the impression that Smith's initiated the proceedings which culminated in the bankruptcy of the firm and Smiths' acquisition of the business by the sale in the Bankruptcy Court later in the same year.[14]

The new manager, Barker, seems to have been dispatched to Dublin in June 1850. John Kent Johnston was given employment, although he appears to have died later in the year.[15] Some provision for the widow was made out of the proceeds of the Dublin house, and, as far as one can judge from a virtually illegible damp-press copy of a letter, for a daughter of Johnston's as well, when she reached her twenty-first year. As late as 1855 Smith was in correspondence with Dublin regarding the sum actually paid to Mrs Johnston, and expressed the thought that they might make her a small annual allowance. At the same time, he wrote to Mrs Johnston, explaining that the business had not yielded any profit, and informing her of his instructions to his manager, Barker. Smith was frequently very generous in money matters with individuals, and even when the financial issues with the Johnstons had come to a head, he was clearly quite well disposed towards them, despite the large sums of money involved.

In the letter to his sister in January 1850, Smith described how distasteful was the task he had in hand in Dublin:

> to spend nearly a week in Dublin in such weather, your occupation being the agreeable[16] one of taking the means of subsistence in the

13 W.H. Smith & Son, letter book, 1852-3, A1

14 W.H. Smith, London, B/16. The Irish bankruptcy records were destroyed in 1922, but a reference to the proceedings survives in the Index of old files bankruptcy 1778-1857. Public Record Office of Ireland, SR5/3/4. See also W.H. Smith & Son London, A 1, letter book, 1852-3 letter dated Dublin 12 February 1853.

15 He is mentioned as 'deceased' in *Thom's Directory* 1851 which would suggest that he had died by 31 December 1850.

16 An ironic usage

> most complete and legal manner from the head of a family — probing his necessities, his home secrets, the affairs of his connections as well as his own — and then making as a gratuity and on certain conditions an allowance per week, as to a servant .... and the agreeable task of giving his brother and his nephews to understand that I being master in the place of Johnston, and things being as they are, they must look for another shelter and make or find a home for themselves.
>
> Every possible accident had had to be guarded against, just as if, which is very nearly the case, all mankind were rogues, but it is not pleasant to take over and settle these contingencies before the face of a man like Johnston, 'for our legal security', who really shows himself willing to do all he can to repair the evil he has done us. However these are things which become a matter of necessity and can no more be avoided than the necessity of submitting to a medical treatment in illness can be....[17]

Johnston's brother set up, apparently in 1850, a separate newsagency at 34 Batchelor's Walk 'trusting that the patronage expended over a period of 31 years will still be continued to him as the *Survivor*. He hopes it is unnecessary that he should refer more particularly to any peculiar claims he may have upon the *Irish Public*'.[18] He ran a series of advertisements almost identical with those which Johnston & Co had run before, so the odd position was created in the 1850s *Thom's Directories* of Alexander Johnston and W.H. Smith & Son having almost identical advertisements side by side, for newsagencies with broadly similar titles. Smith's clarified the position of their 'Johnston's Newspaper and Advertising Office' in the 1853 *Thom's Directory* by specifying that they were 'successors to J.K. Johnstons & Co (deceased).' Alexander Johnston's advertisement last appeared in the 1856 *Thom's Directory*. His gesture of challenge seems to have been a pathetic rather than determined one: Smith did not advert to it in any of his surviving letters, and the house does not seem to have eaten into Smith's turnover. Significantly, Smith was able to note in February 1853 that 'old customers of the house are still in the habit of writing and rewriting to the Messrs J.K. Johnston, and to individuals who conducted the correspondence in his life time.'[19]

The substantial indebtedness of Johnston's to W.H. Smith & Son

17 W.H. Smith & Son, London, B/16
18 *Thom's Directory* 1851
19 W.H. Smith & Son, London, A 1, letter book 1852-3 letter dated 12 February 1853

reflects Smith's success in supplying the Dublin market. Clearly Johnston's had long forfeited the freedom to turn to other London wholesalers, which may well have been why Smith's tolerated the increasing indebtedness. Through the link with Johnston's, Smiths were the major supplier of news to the Dublin market, a position they sought in the London market. The Smiths attached a good deal of importance to Dublin in those early years. When George IV died in 1830, for instance, Smith senior chartered a special boat and delivered the news in Dublin a full twenty-four hours ahead of the royal messengers,[20] let alone any rivals. Smith junior, who was now becoming the driving force in the house, did not think differently. It was he who was in charge of the dealings with Johnston, and he seems not to have involved his father in the full details.

In the early 1850s Smith's still did not dominate the wholesale news market in London. Other houses, such as Dawson's, supplied news to Dublin, and Clayton's even had a house in Dublin, although its position was precarious. But Smith's were a potent force in Dublin, and it was the London end of the business, not the local market, which gave Dublin its significance in the eyes of the younger Smith. A business in Ireland which was dependent on Smith's was helpful to the London strategy of the firm. It deprived London rivals of a market they might capture if a non-dependent Dublin business, supplied by Smith's from London, should collapse. It was this circumstance that led Smith to open a branch in Dublin in 1850 by taking over J.K. Johnston, seven years before the establishment in Birmingham of their first wholesale branch in England. The significance of the step is reflected in the fact that this is the only time in the history of Smith's that the Dublin house was the focus of strategic innovation by the firm.

After the detailed attention he gave in 1850 to affairs in Dublin, by 1852 Smith had relaxed his attention, as he wrote to his sister on 20 July 1852: 'If you are in Dublin, be civil to Barker, Johnston, and our people there. They don't see much of us, and a little kindness goes a long way'. Unfortunately the new Dublin house did not prosper financially, although it seems to have maintained or even expanded the turnover of Johnston & Co.[21] This was largely the fault of the manager, John Barker, who had been appointed in 1850. In February 1853 Smith wrote to him, drawing

20 *The Story of W.H. Smith* (London, 1949) pp. 8, 13.

21 The story can be made out principally from W.H. Smith and Son London. A 1, letter book, 1852-3; A 2, letter book, 1852-6; A 41, solicitors' bills of cost, 1846-73. Some letters from Smith in the Dublin house also amplify the latter stages of the story of the years 1850-6.

his attention to the balance of £2,300 due from the Dublin house at the end of 1852. As the annual turnover between Dublin and London amounted at this time to just over £7,000, this was a very substantial figure. Smith remonstrated:

> This is really a very serious matter. Indeed, something must be done to prevent the continuing drain of capital which has been going on with increased rapidity during the last six months.
>
> We were quite prepared to relinquish all hope of profits for some time and even to make a slight advance, but we did not at all contemplate such a balance against the concern in our London books.

In March 1853 he visited Dublin himself to try to put things right, but no improvement followed. By June, when the outstanding balance was larger than at the end of 1852, the thought of ridding himself of the Dublin house was on Smith's mind: 'unless the drain of capital can be checked and turned the other way, we must consider the policy of maintaining the business. Pray think over it and let me know'. The situation continued to deteriorate. The date of the last balance sheet from Dublin was June 1852; none followed in the next two years, and in September 1854 Smith was pressing for a statement 'which will show how the business has been going on since 1852'. By March 1855 the account with London, the only index available to Smith of how affairs were progressing, was £1,000 worse than in August 1854. Feeling that the house was sinking, Smith offered the business to Barker, and wanted to 'know at once what probability there is of your finding sufficient capital to avail yourself of the offer we were disposed to make: viz. to give the business up to you'. Smith's visit projected at the outset of 1855 was put off. By this stage, some £5,000 was estimated to have been sent over to the Dublin house, and only the prospect of sale to Barker had deferred action. Indeed Barker seems to have been able to protract this affair, and even to presume on it. A sharp rebuke was issued to him by Smith on 16 July 1855:

> In the *Telegraph* appear the names of Messrs Smith and Barker as our firm's agent for the paper in Dublin. Who authorised the publication in that shape — and if not authorised how has it come to pass?
>
> It is neither to your advantage nor to ours that a thing which is not should be held out to the world as a fact.

In March 1855 Smith intimated that an accountant would be sent to Dublin if there was any delay in recovering debts, to make up the books and to ensure a flow of funds to London, which would more than cover the current supply of newspapers. As nothing improved, an accountant was eventually sent over, and the conditions of the bond which had been signed by Barker's guarantor in June 1850 were examined. By the end of 1855 the evidence was mounting against Barker on all sides, even in the crucial area of newspaper dispatch. An exasperated Smith wrote to a customer, Dr Adams, in December 1855, to apologise for 'any want of the attention to your orders on the part of our Dublin house. In order to prevent any extention of the irregularity, we have placed your name as a sure customer for the *Evening News* on our London books....' Barker and his surety, a Mr Pope, seem to have met Smith's solicitor in London. Smith went to Dublin on 30 January 1856. By 4 February Barker had disappeared, but his brother promised to find him in time for an appointment on 8 February. This meeting apparently took place, as the solicitor's bill of cost in the London house includes a reference dated 9 February to a written statement from Barker, and on 20 February Barker's surety, Pope, sent on a cheque for £1,000 to discharge the amount of his forfeited bond.

At this time the total outstanding against the Dublin house was £8,000. It had long been evident, from the growing balance against the branch and the lax accounting procedures, that the systems in the Dublin house left a lot to be desired. Smith himself can be regarded as partly responsible for the situation which developed, having failed to act sooner despite evidence pointing to problems. From an early date Barker had departed from the standard practice of regular weekly remittances to London, and when money was forwarded, it was sometimes in a slapdash fashion. Smith wrote in September 1854 that: 'We were rather surprised to receive a remittance last week from the Dublin house without any note of the amount or any remark at all from you. We think it hardly safe and it is anything but satisfactory, as we have nothing to refer to, to show the amount received is the same as that sent'. How casual some of the management was, in fact, is shown in Smith's solicitor's bill of costs, where one item on 4 March 1856 refers to a request from Smith for information from Barker 'in reference to a period of some months during which there were no entries in the pass book and apparently no banking account'.

Smith believed that some of the balance due was attributable to excessive credit given to solicitors for Encumbered Estates Courts advertisements.[22] Certainly, after Smith took charge of the accounts in

22 The Encumbered Estates Act, 1849, made it easier for landlords bankrupted during the Famine to sell their entailed estates. Some five million acres were sold under this Act, mostly to Irish purchasers.

1856, such instances came to light. In one case the publishers were paid by Smith's in 1853, but Smith's were still out of pocket in July 1856. Similar evidence came to light in accounts with retailers. Smith wrote in June 1856, 'Almost the only good agents are Worrall and Gordon, all the others should be made to agree their accounts, pay up or close'. In fact, there was more to the losses. There was a real deficiency, quite apart from excessive credit and risky debts. An alarming estimate was drawn-up, based on the inspection of the books, after Barker confessed to 'the origin of his deficiencies — purchase of carriage, horses and action(?), mining speculation, Castle's hotel and Barry's loan — also the misconduct of a clerk — in whom he had reposed confidence'. It suggested that the deficiency might amount to £6,000, not £2,000. One of Barker's interests had included some investment in hotels. In October 1853 Smith had poured cold water on a proposal from Barker for a *Hotels Guide*. Barry's loan seems, from a later letter, to have been intended for Radly of the Gresham Hotel, who in Smith's view 'used him (Barker) to obtain money, he cared not how — or who it might be. He *knew* it was not Barker's'. By April 1856 the solicitors had obtained details from Barker on his connection with mining speculations at Barravore, Ballygoneen, Clonkeen and Llandillo, and had secured his authority to dispose of his interest.

More intensive examination of the books brought to light the extent of credit outstanding, much of which could be recovered. By December 1857 the total deficiency was down to £2,861, and by 1858 to £1,892. For all practical purposes this represented the final state of affairs. A letter from the Dublin house in July 1859 accompanying the accounts for the year 1858 fills in some of the details of the situation at that time:

> In presenting this summary I am quite sensible that it does not equal what may be expected from this business, but I am seriously of the opinion that the Dr. side of the account in 1857 was not fully up to the mark and that the deficiency was really greater than it looked. A year adds something to one's experience in the getting up of these statements and I am pretty sure that if there was any omission on the Dr side now it is more than counterbalanced by the Crs. not taken as of any worth. The stopt papers and unsettled accounts in the bad debts ledger are worth £40 and £50 and are not yet taken into account.

The deficiencies had been contributed to by an employee, Atkinson, and it is possible that another employee was also at fault. Smith had noted from London in July 1856 a payment post-entered into the accounts with the *Dublin Daily Express*, and thought that if one payment had been omitted there may have been many. He felt it likely that one of the employees, Flaherty, was 'seriously compromised in the business'. In fact, Flaherty had resigned on 7 May, to become (as he stated in a letter to Smith,) 'a partner in and have the management of a newspaper agency establishment in Dublin', on what he claimed were more liberal terms than he enjoyed under Smith. Flaherty's became the third agency in Dublin, after Smith's and the one run by Clayton, whom Smith did not think of as a serious competitor, as 'he does his work irregularly and without the punctuality which we try to ensure'.

Smith's involvement in the affairs of the house in Ireland was not from choice. The relationship with Johnston had already led to the opening of a Dublin house in 1850. Barker's mismanagement brought on the second crisis in Smith's Irish affairs, which came to a head at the same time as the Tipperary Bank, run by the Irish speculator, Sadlier, had failed, creating a notorious scandal in London. Its failure caught Smith's attention. In February he referred to it in a letter in which he sent a cutting with a bit of distasteful Irish news to his sister.[23] It can only have added to his growing caution about all things Irish.

Despite Barker's negligence, Smith's had held on to their place in the Dublin agency business. Smith observed that 'our late manager had robbed us very extensively and had also neglected his duties, but the business is a very good one, and the reputation of the house stands high'. For the first eleven month period of the years 1853, 1854 and 1855, the total of the London account rose: £6,538 in 1853, £6,711 in 1854 and £7,411 in 1855. Smith had little interest in taking over his rivals. Clayton's seems to have been offered for sale to him, but Smith's advice to his new manager in October 1856 was almost contemptous: 'If they sell cheaply it is worthwhile — but I doubt whether we shall not prosper quite as much with two very weak competitors as without any'. He did not fear any competition from Flaherty, who had not the resources to expand his business. As things turned out, Flaherty was in difficulties by the end of the year. His supply of London papers came through one of Smith's London rivals, Dawson's. But they were failing to supply him by the beginning of December, and he was reduced to trying to get copies from Smith's. The small number of dailies which he sought — 38 copies, a figure which he divulged in seeking to obtain them from Smith's — was itself a comment on the minute scale of his business. He also wrote to Smith expressing a hope of returning to his old place in the firm. He had served for six years with Smith's in Dublin, and for eighteen years prior to that

23 W.H. Smith & Co., London, B/27

with Johnston's. He assured Smith that he had been unaware of Barker's irregularities, but Smith, although sympathetic to his plight, did not feel that he could allow him to return.

All these problems necessitated Smith's only long business stay in Ireland. He seems to have spent almost a fortnight in Dublin in February 1856, and he returned in March again to continue his work. It was in the course of this later stay that he telegraphed to Charles Eason, then manager of Smith's railway bookstall in Manchester, to join him with a view to discussing a proposal that Eason should run the Dublin house.

Chapter 3 The Easons and their Family Circle

CHARLES EASON MOVED TO DUBLIN from Manchester, but in fact he was born in Somerset, and lived there throughout his formative years. The Eason family came from the comfortable, literate and devout Baptist circle of Yeovil and Chard in south Somerset. George, the first male Eason, is identified in the will of his father, Richard Taylor of Yeovil, a glover.[1] (Details of the Eason family tree are given in Appendix 1).

George was born in 1782, apparently Richard Taylor's illegitimate son, for he was given the name of his mother, Eleanor Eason, a spinster. At this time dissenter marriages, if not performed by an Anglican clergyman, lacked full legal validity, but the fact that the son bore his mother's name suggests that a full family unit did not exist. From his will, Taylor himself seems to have been unmarried. Apart from the bequest to his son, George, the only other bequest was to a nephew bearing the Taylor name. George Eason's mother was already dead at the time that Taylor made his will, but the son was acknowledged and provided for handsomely.

The value of Taylor's estate was in the region of £1,500. It consisted of the house in which he had lived and worked, an orchard and garden, another house divided into two tenements, with a gloving business attached, and one and a half acres of land elsewhere in Yeovil. George Eason took over Taylor's business as a going concern in 1817, and seems to have been able to expand it, with the support of relatives. The second of the two gloving establishments in the estate he had inherited was occupied in 1825 by a relative — Ely Whitney. Provision for Whitney in George Eason's will suggests that the relationship had been a close one, and the connection between the families continued, so that in 1862 George's son and grandson called on the Whitney family during the course of a visit from Dublin to Somerset.

George Eason's resources were probably increased by a dowry in what

1 The will was drawn up on 12 June 1817 and proved on 30 June of the same year.

was for him a socially successful marriage with Rebecca Tucker. This marriage took place on 15 July 1821. Rebecca was the daughter of Charles Tucker, the postmaster at Chard, and the granddaughter of William Taylor, a gentleman of Yeovil. According to family tradition, Rebecca's father carried on a thriving business as a printer. Rebecca's sister, Mary, married John Toms, a son of the Baptist minister in Chard. John Toms was first apprenticed as a printer to Charles Tucker, and later set up in Chard as a printer and bookseller on his own account. The Toms were also connected by marriage with the Bagster family, another family of dissenters in the area, who were to build up a publishing and bookselling business for themselves as Samuel Bagster & Sons of 15 Paternoster Row, London. They were noted in particular as the publishers of *Bagsters' Bible.*

After George Eason's marriage in January 1821 to Rebecca Tucker, children followed in quick succession: George, was born in November 1821, Charles, on 11 May 1823, William Tucker, who did not live long, in 1824, and two girls, Mary, in March 1826, and Emma, in January 1828, shortly before her father's death. Marriage to Rebecca Tucker, along with success in business, confirmed the position of George Eason in the life of Yeovil. He took his place among the ranks of the respected small and middle sized business families, who relied on their own abilities and the support of their co-religionists for advancement in the not altogether benign world dominated by Anglican society and religion. His will, made three years before his death, was proved for £3,000, a larger figure than his father's.

Rebecca, who was aged 33 when she was widowed in 1828, survived until January 1856. In later years she opened a school at Banbury. It may have been necessity — although not dire — which led her to start the school, but she had capital to invest in enlarging her school on a more ambitious scale. John Toms wrote to her in 1854: 'I hope you are more comfortable in a house of your own planning. In going into it I dare say you knew at once the plan of everything. I hope you have a good addition to the number of your pupils. If this should continue for a few years, you will be remunerated for your extra outlay'. There were two assistants in the school, and Emma, the younger daughter of George and Rebecca, also taught in the school. In November 1855 Rebecca was said to be working harder because of 'Miss Marsh's illness'. A surviving letter from the older daughter, Mary, to Charles' wife after her marriage, reveals her as a devout and highly literate person.

Charles Eason was sent away to school at the age of seven. He spent the second half of 1830 at school in Weymouth and remained there until the end of 1832. In 1833 he transferred to a school in Bath. The first letter from Charles in September 1831 is in a child's hand, thanking his mother for a cake, and describing the capsizing of a yacht at a regatta with the loss of the captain. From a letter in August 1832 it appears that Mary was also at school with him; he asked after his brother George, who was at home. In December he described the funeral of the mistress of the girls' section of the school, and was looking forward to the holidays. The next letter, almost a year later, comments on his studies and acknowledges his mother's advice in a much more adult tone, suggesting that at ten he had left boyhood aside, and that the change of school in 1833 marked a step forward in his education. Other schools followed. In 1834 he attended Hoskin's school in London, and in 1836 he attended Dawson's school.

Charles' father had died when he was a boy of five years, long before the secrets of the gloving business could have been passed on to him. So although Yeovil was the centre of glove-making, and his Whitney relatives remained engaged in it, in 1838, aged fifteen, he was apprenticed for seven years to a printer in Colchester, Joshua Brackett. It is safe to assume that John Toms and the Bagsters were consulted on the son's choice of career, and that they helped to place him with a good firm. Thus, Charles Eason was steered into the world of printing and bookselling represented by his mother's relations the Tuckers, Toms and Bagsters.

The Toms were less successful than the Tuckers, and from a more modest background. The grandfather of John Toms, the printer, had had a limeburning business. John Toms' own business, at least in his later years, was not a very flourishing one, and he consoled himself with the thought that his sons 'William and George have, I believe, got hold of something superior to shopkeeping'. In fact, Toms had been a grocer as well as a printer and bookseller, which had been necessary in order to maintain a family in the poor milieu of Chard. His 'stock in trade, printing, books, stationery, grocery', in the estimate of Charles Eason's shrewd mother, amounted to £1,000 in 1854.

If a single influence on Charles has to be isolated as the dominant one, it must be that of Rebecca Eason, his mother, who had been presented with the task of bringing up her four children when she was widowed after only seven years of marriage. She was shrewd in a business sense, she was devout and she was intensely interested in education. In fact she had all the characteristics which were to be evident in the family over the three following generations, and it was she, supported by her relations, who shaped the career of her son, Charles. Even the longevity which has characterised the family seems to have originated on her side.

Charles, of course, was only the second son, but he was to become the eldest resident son, and as such the main centre of interest to the family. His older brother, George, had gone to Australia in 1840 when Charles was seventeen. We do not know why he went, though his mother later referred somewhat ambiguously to his being 'banished to a distant land'. At any rate, although George maintained some contacts with home, and with John Toms, who used to keep him supplied with copies of the *Illustrated London News* and *The Times*, there is no evidence that the contact was close, and it probably became increasingly remote as years passed.[2]

All these families — Easons, Tuckers, Toms and Bagsters — were active in the Baptist church. George Eason the elder had been a deacon in the community in Yeovil. This family and religious environment was a great influence on Charles. His venture into religious publishing — catholic as well as protestant — while due in part to fortuitous circumstances, was also certainly influenced by the example of the Bagsters in London, with whom Charles Eason long continued to have contact.

Charles Eason spent the last half year of his apprenticeship in 1844 in the business of John Toms in Chard. He then moved to Paternoster Row, London, to work for five years with John Shaw, a bookseller, who was connected by marriage to the Bagsters. In 1850 he ventured for the first time outside the circle of family contacts. W.H. Smith's business in the railways was now growing rapidly. In October 1850, aged twenty-seven, Charles Eason became clerk in charge of the bookstall at Victoria Station in Manchester.

His Commonplace Book has some scraps of information written up from articles and writings, read or collected at a much earlier date, as well as other clues to his outlook at this time. Religious observations and biblical

2 On arrival in Australia in 1840, George Eason worked on the *Sydney Morning Herald*. He later became the owner of a sheep station at Geegullalong, near Burrowa, and he also owned and edited until his death the *Burrow News*. After the drought of 1878 he lost his entire sheep property. Nevertheless a newspaper cutting sent home in 1880 by the Birks family described him as 'a magistrate of the colony, and a sterling and honourable man.' George's venture into the world of news confirmed that he had the literate qualities of all the Easons, and remained faithful to the tradition of the Tuckers, Toms and Bagsters. However his remoteness from the Dublin branch of the family is evident. When one of Charles Eason's own sons — also a George — was sent aboard in disgrace in 1876, it was to the Birks, relatives of his mother's, that he was sent, not to his uncle. Charles Eason junior recalled later that about 1890-95 he had had news of him from a catholic priest who was acquainted with the family in Australia, and called at the offices in Dublin while visiting Ireland. The family only learned of the collapse of the sheep property forty years afterwards, when a distant relative, Daphne Clare, began a regular correspondence in 1914.

extracts suggest that he was a religious man. There are also some poems, and extracts from poems, some possibly by himself, and not all on religious themes. In addition, there is evidence of interests beyond the narrow themes of business and religion that had always obsessed his family circle. The Commonplace Book contains a lecture entitled, 'Power of Phrenology in discriminating character', which he read to a meeting of the Phrenological Club of the London Mechanics Institute in 1846. A few extracts from periodicals of that time tentatively suggest an interest in wider issues, some moral in content, and others, like phrenology, fashionable intellectual topics of the day. Many years later, in a letter of 20 December 1885, he stated to Smith that 'I have all my life since 1842 been a student of Irish questions, and after I went to business in London in November 1844, I have read and followed up by study every Irish debate and every bill introduced into parliament for the remedy of Irish grievance'. This was written in a moment of growing exasperation with Smith's lack of sensitivity on Irish issues, and possibly somewhat exaggerated his early interest in Ireland. But if he was interested in current affairs when a young man in London, he would certainly have been informed on Irish affairs, which, as the tragedy of the Famine began to unfold, were about to bear more heavily on British public opinion than at any time since the Union. On the other hand, the absence of any extracts relating to Ireland among the topics written into the Commonplace Book from earlier notes, suggests that it did not absorb his attention as, for instance, did phrenology, to which there are several references in the book.

Up to 1850, Charles Eason's whole life had revolved around printing and bookselling. In 1854 he had an opportunity of returning to Chard. John Toms, who was now growing old, offered the mixed printing bookselling and grocery business to him through his mother. Two of Toms' own sons had done better for themselves, and the others were not up to its demands. Rebecca Eason, in a remarkably concise and articulate letter, advised her son against accepting the offer: 'The business does not now pay the family expenses, but were you inclined to entertain it for yourself it would then become a first question whether or not it would do under different management and different expenses.' Since £2,000 of the capital had come from the dowry of Toms' wife, Charles could have found himself paying interest charges of £150 per annum, which the business had not to bear under Toms' direction, 'before there would be anything towards carrying it on'. John Toms himself had to admit that Chard 'at present is not in a flourishing state', though he held out the prospect of the beneficial influence of an imminent railway extension, which, combined with 'adopting the advantages of the modern system of business might increase the present business one third at least'. But it is clear that the business in fact relied on the grocery side, remote from all Charles Eason's trade experience, and his mother concluded cautiously, from the example of Banbury, that 'the grocers about here go around to the villages and farm houses for orders. This involves horse and jig. I suppose they make it pay or they would not continue it.' It is obvious that mother and son had already discussed the narrow prospects in Chard:

> Your sisters say they should think you would not go and shut yourself up in such a poor place as Chard. You know the wear and tear of a large place now.... I know you think a churchman [i.e. an Anglican] would get on much better than a dissenter in the business: of this too perhaps you can judge, remembering that there is much more of bigotry in small places than in large ones.

Charles was never to reconsider living in Yeovil or Chard. There is no surviving correspondence with his relatives there, although he made a sentimental journey in the early 1860s, as his own eldest son was later to recall:

> I think it must have been in the summer of 1862 that my father took me to London with him .... we went to Yeovil — my father's birth place — and he visited the Whitneys. My grandfather was a deacon of the Baptist Chapel, and a memorial tablet was put up in the Chapel.... We then went to Chard where the Toms family lived.... At Chard I remember the service in the Baptist chapel — minister Mr. Edwards and his text....

Friendly links with the Toms family survived,[3] although it must be said that the Toms were more drawn to their successful relative in Dublin, than Charles Eason was to Chard. There were Toms in the Dublin business in the early 1860s and in the 1870s. One of them, John Toms, was destined to become virtually a country-wide institution as a traveller for the company. It seems likely that they all came from Chard. At the time of the visit in 1862 of Charles Eason and Charles junior from Dublin, the precarious grocery business seems to have been a thing of the past,

3 Charles Eason junior was familiar with the Toms, recalling Kate 'as the one I remembered best.' They took the Cambridge Local examination in the same year, 1868. Another of the Toms girls, Edith, married Ernest Gunn, who became Treasurer of Mill Hill School. Later on, Charles Eason junior, who had maintained his links with the Toms family after the visit of 1862, sent two of his sons, Keith and Alec, to Mill Hill.

and the Toms were running a brewery in which the Bagsters had shares.

After eight months in Manchester, on 2 May 1851, Charles Eason married Caroline Birks. There is no evidence of previous contact between the two families. A letter from Charles' sister Mary as late as 1855 shows that she had not yet met her brother's wife. Charles probably became acquainted with Caroline Birks either while he was in London or after he arrived in Manchester. By then he was twenty-eight years old i.e. around the age at which it was usual for young men of the Victorian middle class to marry. The background of the Birks and Eason families is similar. They were both in trade — Caroline's father was a draper — and the family was as literate and pious as the Easons.

One of the Birks sons continued the family business. Another son, George Vause Birks, qualified as a medical doctor, which was an indication of the financial ease within the family circle, as well as providing a good example of the dissenter trait of combining business, education and the professions in the same family, a trait which the Eason family followed in the future. A probate document of 1864 throws some light on the Birks family. The predominant location of the beneficiaries suggests the likelihood that the family came from Misson in Lincolnshire, although Caroline herself was born in Thorne in Yorkshire. The background was a comfortable one. Simon Birks' brother was a gentleman at Laughton-en-le-Morthen in Yorkshire, and the executors, who were members of the family, were a glass merchant and a hairdresser, respectively. Other nieces and nephews among the beneficiaries included a yeoman, and a grocer, both in Misson, a carman in Sheffield, a draper near Manchester, and a Birks in Oxfordshire, who was a Roman Catholic priest.

In August 1853 Caroline's doctor brother, George Vause Birks, emigrated with his family to Australia. He kept a diary during the voyage, which he wrote up on arrival, with a view to sending it back home. The diary gives the flavour of the family's religious outlook. On the second Sunday out, the captain requested him to hold a service for the second-class passengers:

> We got on very well until in the first prayers we came to a full stop, and could only get on by passing them by with a few words of supplication for general blessings. We had a nice attentive little company, which I spoke to them from the incidents in the 15th Luke. In the evening, being by then requested to speak again, we had a more numerous assembly — and I spoke from the parable of the sower.

The diary gives an interesting picture of shipboard life. The passengers were well fed, but their life was made miserable by the humours of the captain:

> We had an irritable tyrant in the shape of Captain Tadman, who possessing a little brief authority took care to play the despot to perfection: physical force was the only power he knew, and oaths and angry threats were plentifully used, not a passenger in the cuddy but what had been personally insulted by him.

George Vause Birks did well in Australia. He took over two medical practices and was the only medical practitioner in Augusta, 170 miles south of Perth in West Australia. He displayed the trading instincts of his family. A relative in England sent him out goods which he sold in the chemist's shop, which he combined with his medical practice. He died prematurely in 1858 after a fall from a horse while visiting a patient. His son, George Napier Birks, was a regular correspondent of Caroline Eason. He set up a business of his own at Waterloo, Kadiuna, and from 1861 he was a semi-invalid, and required two assistants to help him run it. He opened a branch in Glenely in 1868, and moved there to live himself in 1876. In that same year, he received the son of Charles and Caroline Eason, George, who was in disgrace, and employed him as an assistant. The nature of Birks' business is not completely clear, but seems to have involved sales to the agricultural community. In the fashion characteristic of both families, Charles Eason in Dublin had taken advantage of the close links between the two families to open up a market in Australia for goods supplied through W.H. Smith & Son in Dublin. No less than eighteen consignments were dispatched from Dublin to George Napier Birks and his brother William between January 1868 and June 1869, and as the first consignment for which we have a record in January 1868 was numbered 45, it suggests that this business was initiated around 1865. The outstanding account in July 1869 amounted to £743. Summaries of a few letters in 1873 contain complaints about the unsatisfactory execution of orders by the Dublin house. The goods seem to have been stationery. The amount supplied to Australia in 1872 totalled £395, from a 'summary of stationery sales' for the year ending 29 June 1872. Eason was clearly supplying stationery to the Birks in Australia before the general stationery business began at W.H. Smith & Son in Dublin, and experience derived in buying stationery for the Birks house in Australia could have prompted Charles Eason to go into the wholesale stationery business in 1870.

Like the Easons the Birks laid a heavy emphasis on education in bringing up their family. This is brought out explicitly in the surviving correspondence, quite apart from the highly literate tone of the letters.

Hannah Vause, a relative aged 80 at the time, wrote to Caroline Eason from Thorne in 1874: 'I am glad to hear all your dear (ones) were well and advancing in education which I hope will be for their future advantage'. George Vause Birks wrote reassuringly to Dublin about the disgraced George Eason: 'For a young man possessing the business ability, the education, and the manners that he does, success here is a certainty, if only he will bring to bear half the energy and perseverance displayed by his father'. The family aspirations to success were strong, and George Napier Birks bears testimony to them in 1884 when he wrote to Caroline Eason that: 'Poor William has had a grievous trial in his eldest son who has disappointed all his hopes and will never according to present appearance be much more than a common station hand'. The links with Dublin continued into the twentieth century. Descendants of the first Birks in Australia visited Dublin in 1894, in 1916, and again in 1959.

From all this a clear profile of the Eason family emerges — business acumen, an emphasis on advancement, and an interest in education. Children were well educated, but not with a view to leaving business. Two of Charles Eason's sons and his grandchildren in turn went to university. The marriages of sons and daughters conformed to the same pattern. Some of the daughters married churchmen or teachers, and the wives of Eason sons came from the same milieu. The wife of Charles Eason junior was a strong supporter of women's equality, and the wife of John Charles Malcolm Eason, grandson of Charles Eason, was one of the first women scholars and graduates of Trinity College, Dublin. With the perspective of a more secular age, we tend to stress the educational and business aspects of the family ethos; but in the middle decades of the nineteenth century, the strong dissenter religious fervour would have been the obvious characteristic, and the one which the family would have liked to stress. In fact, it seems to have been the religious nature of Charles Eason that had led his evangelical employer W.H. Smith to choose him for preferment, in offering him the management of the problem-ridden Dublin house, Smith wrote to Eason in March 1856:

> Probably the strongest reason I had for making the offer to you was my conviction that you were under the influence of real and true religion. I am not in the habit of speaking or writing commonly about such matters, and I did not therefore say as much to you; but as I know for myself that a man cannot derive the strength he requires to perform even his duties to his fellow man, from any other source,

> so I am glad to place trust in those whom from my own quiet observations I believe to live a Christian life.

There is no exaggeration in what Smith stated to be the case. It is borne out elsewhere by other evidence.

Eason was at that time manager of the railway bookstall in Manchester, and his experience was limited. He was not really equipped by training for the complex demands of a wholesale house. But after the experience with Barker, it was his honesty that recommended him to Smith. Smith himself envisaged simply a well-ordered house, not a novel experiment. His letters show that as late as October 1856 he was still undecided as to whether Dublin should be run as an independent branch, or as a department within the London firm. As things turned out, he was not disappointed in Eason's honesty, and the confidence of Smith and the other principals within the London house is reflected in the fact that for ten years from 1873 to 1883 no one from the London house set foot for business reasons in the Dublin branch. But Smith got a great deal more. Eason was not content simply to manage a Dublin house, visualised as a passive link in a news distribution empire. He set out to expand the Dublin business, and in doing so eventually developed a wider range of activities within the branch than existed in the parent house in London.

Chapter 4 The Early Years of the New House

THE FIRST TASK THAT CONFRONTED Charles Eason, when he arrived in Dublin from Manchester in 1856, was to sort out the tangled finances of the house. This took some two years. His achievement in doing this was crucial, not only to the survival of the house, but to its character. In 1856 Smith was still undecided as to whether to continue it as an independent branch of W.H. Smith & Son, or as a simple department firmly within the control of the London house. He took a very close interest in the Dublin business at this time. Only when the finances were sorted out was Eason free, in association with Smith, to set out on the path of sustained growth.[1]

The Irish business in 1856 was very similar to the Johnston business of the pre-1850 era. Apart from the trade based on the shop, a large part of which consisted of servicing Dublin subscribers, it involved a limited distribution by mails of newspapers to subscribers in Dublin and the country, largely gentry, military, clubs and hotels. Agents as opposed to subscribers were few, a mere handful, who distributed the papers to a narrow circle of reading rooms, gentry and other individuals. The advertisement agency business was confined to placing advertisements in newspapers. Its clientele was small and closely related to newspaper readership. It is impossible to disentangle the wholesale from the retail elements of the early W.H. Smith & Son's business in Dublin, but many years later, in 1870, harking back to the state of affairs on his arrival in Dublin, Charles Eason recalled that 'the retail was our chief business'. Including Eason himself, there were 23 employees in 1857.

1 A number of letters from Smith, isolated from more routine correspondence because of their significance, survive in the Dublin house together with copies of some of Charles Eason's letters to Smith. A small number of Charles Eason's letters to Smith in the 1850s and 1860s survive in W.H. Smith & Son, London. The London house has also some early copy letters (file 16) from Smith to Eason or to other parties about the Dublin business. No accounts for Dublin survive on the London side; the surviving accounting data are all in Dublin.

TABLE 1 *The Components of the Business — the company's view*

Description	*The Wholesale side*
Railway	
Bookstalls	Sales from stalls on railway stations
Advertising	Advertising space sales on railway stations
Wholesale News	Sales, particularly of newspapers and magazines, to retail newsagents
	The Retail side
Advertising agency	Commission income from advertisements placed in newspapers
Retail sales	Sales from Dublin shop

In analysing the business the firm always tended to use the terms 'retail' and 'wholesale' in a special and idiosyncratic way. In normal commercial parlance, the railway bookstalls that were to be such a prominent part of the business are clearly retail establishments. However, because they were supplied, like the wholesale orders, through the railway network, they were always classed by the firm as part of the wholesale side. The sale of advertising space on stations to commercial firms, a wholesale activity by its nature, may also have helped to ensure the inclusion of bookstall receipts in wholesale turnover, since both aspects of railway business were kept together. Bookstall rents and advertising rents were in fact as a rule negotiated as a package with the railway companies. The 'retail' classification always included the newspaper advertising agency business in addition to direct sales to Dublin readers and subscribers.

Unfortunately it is normally impossible to reclassify the data in more orthodox terms, but if the bookstall sales are included with retail sales, the retail component of the house was very much more prominent than meets the eye at first glance. For instance in 1871/2, the company's categories show that the retail side made up only 22.3 per cent of the total turnover. In more conventional terms, however, adding the bookstall receipts to retail turnover, it made up 37.9 per cent. There is some evidence to suggest that this classification (which was after all of a pragmatic, 'home and abroad' kind) did in the long run affect the company's vision of the business they were in, by disguising the essentially retail nature of the bookstalls.[2]

2 Hereafter the special use of the terms will be signalled by the use of initial capitals.

Information on the breakdown of the Wholesale side business into its component parts before 1872 is difficult to get. Even then, separate figures are lacking for the wholesale news department.[3] These have to be estimated as the residue of total sales after the deduction of figures for other departments. The first year for which a full breakdown on these lines can be attempted is 1871/2.

TABLE 2: *Components of turnover, Dublin 1871/2*

	£	%
Railway Advertising (Cash Receipts)	1,267	1.5
Bookstalls	12,923*	15.6
Books	22,312	26.9
Stationery	7,536	9.1
Catholic Prayerbooks	(2,000)**	2.4
Wholesale news (residual)	18,441	22.2
Total Wholesale side	*64,479*	*77.7*
Total Retail side	*18,513*	*22.3*
Total Turnover	*82,992*	*100.0*

* *Includes sales at the Curragh hut (£1,208) and by the Kingstown boys (£827).*
** *Estimated.*

The initial steps towards building up the business were taken simultaneously with the necessary measures to order the finances. From the time of his arrival Eason opened up negotiations which were to model the house, as in England, around newspapers and railways. The records in both London and Dublin of the business during these years are few. Some accounts from the London house provide an estimate of the scale of the Dublin business, especially as so much of it consisted of English papers. The papers were priced in the accounts at the same rate as to wholesale houses in London, and in the case of *The Times*, which did not

3 Such figures did exist, although they no longer survive. An isolated profit and loss account for the wholesale news department for four weeks ending 27 October 1877 gives sales as £2,753, the equivalent of £35,887 on an annual basis.

allow a discount to W.H. Smith & Son, the price was marked up by 10 per cent. The London accounts give an impression of a static volume of business: £7,258 in 1853, £7,567 in 1854, and £7,966 in 1857. Some definite upturn was evident in later years. The volume had risen to £9,270 in 1860, and £11,881 in 1861.[4] This upturn reflects some buoyancy in business, although as newspaper prices came down, not all the upturn can be attributed to newspapers. These figures do not include the business in Irish papers, apart from some accounts which were settled through London intermittently, or the business in newspaper advertising, which was probably well below £2,000 per annum in cash receipts at this stage. In 1856 newspaper sales would have been almost totally Retail. The main change in the following years was the growth of railway bookstall sales (included in Wholesale, but by nature retail) and of true wholesale sales to the retail trade. Wholesale sales, despite the fall in prices in 1859 were the most expansive side of the business, and showed in the early years more capacity to expand than the bookstalls, whose turnover did not grow until the mid-1860s. Retail sales, benefitting from a wider range of dailies and the reduction in price of many of them to 1d, also expanded rapidly. Retail sales greatly exceeded wholesale sales as late as the outset of 1857. Thereafter wholesale sales grew sharply: of the order of £6,000 or £7,000 in 1861, they must have been £10,000 in 1863. (This figure is derived by netting £6,000 bookstall receipts from the £16,862 Wholesale side turnover.) In 1863, deducting library and newspaper advertising, retail sales would have been roughly £16,000. They thus still exceeded wholesale sales. However agreement with the railway companies in 1860 on rates for the carriage of the cheap newspapers was quickly reflected in the growth of the wholesale business, whereas retail sales failed to grow further. Country demand was met by the wholesale trade; Dublin demand either by newsagents or by Smith's own bookstalls (which were lumped in the accounts with the wholesale side).

Business connected with the railways now made up more than half of the Wholesale side, with the bulk coming from bookstall sales. Other

4 The modern scale of these figures can be assessed by the wages the company paid. In 1857, a year after Charles Eason took over the managership, the total employed was 23, including Eason himself, and the total wage outlay was about £1,200 that year. By 1861 this had increased to 34 employees and an annual outlay of £1570 (£2,281 if the railway bookstall staff and the newspaper selling 'Kingstown boys' were included). In 1859, the highest paid employee after Eason himself earned £150 a year. One of the boy clerks recruited in 1867 started at 6s a week; ten years later he was second in command of the Retail department, earning £2 10s a week.

familiar aspects of Eason's activities were to be added in the course of this decade: a library in 1860, printing in 1863, book wholesaling in 1864, publishing in or after 1866, stationery wholesaling by 1870 or perhaps earlier.

THE START OF THE RAILWAY BUSINESS

The railway age, which Smith's had begun to exploit in England in the 1840s, hit Ireland at least a decade later. By 1856, when the disordered finances of the Dublin house forced Smith to turn his attention in that direction, the railway age in Ireland was sufficiently advanced to make a modern news business possible. The six mile line from Dublin to Kingstown, opened in 1834, was not followed by the opening of another line until 1842. By 1845 there were still only 65 miles of railway open. Four years later this had increased to 428 miles, and by 1854 to 865. The line to Cork was completed in 1849, Limerick had been linked to it in 1848, and the line to Galway was completed in 1851. With the completion of the great viaduct over the Boyne in Drogheda in 1855, a through service to Belfast was at last possible. Tralee was reached in 1859, the last link in a through service from Dublin to Derry was completed in 1861, and Sligo was reached in 1862. By that year all the most obviously attractive main lines were in place, and the major centres of population were at the end of trunk lines. A sustained railway building programme brought the mileage to 1,909 by 1866, and by this time a substantial network connected all the main proposed railway heads apart from Wexford. The line along the east coast made slow progress; it reached Enniscorthy by 1863, and Wexford was brought into the system only in 1872. After 1866 the pace of railway building fell off. Only 461 new miles were added to the network between 1866 and 1880.

As the network grew, advertising sites were developed at all the stations, and at some, bookstalls were established. Eventually, W.H. Smith & Son achieved a virtual monopoly of both for the greater part of the second half of the century. The development of the railway bookstalls and display advertising sites on railway stations was the main focus of attention in the Dublin house from 1856. Smith's were by no means the first in this field, but they were the first to develop it successfully. Eason advised the manager of the Dublin/Belfast Junction Railway in 1858 that 'the railway book and advertising business is still in an underdeveloped state in this country, and we have learned that other parties who have tried it have done it at but little profit to themselves.' Some other entrepreneurs, small and ineffective, lingered on through the 1860s. The last outside the Cork area was Mrs Buckle in the north: her orders and bookstalls were valued in 1873 at a mere £100. At the start of the 1890s, Eason & Son held all the contracts in Ireland apart from some minor lines in the north west, and the local companies in Cork. The only significant breach in the near monopoly was the temporary loss of the Great Northern Railway and of the Belfast and Co. Down Railways in the 1890s.

The first negotiations with Mr Ilberry, the general manager of the Great Southern & Western Railways (GSWR), had begun in late 1856. The contract for railway bookstalls and advertising was effective from 1 April 1857, and contracts followed with the Dublin & Wicklow Railway in June, and with the Dublin & Drogheda in August. Receipts from the GSWR began to accrue in the first half of 1857 and a few receipts from the Dublin & Wicklow before the middle of the year. Advertising revenue on the Dublin & Belfast Junction Railway flowed in by 1859, and the first bookstall income was earned a year later. Twelve bookstalls were open at the end of 1857, and four more were added in 1858. As early as 14 July 1857, Smith wrote to Eason, observing that, 'I do not see at a glance the weekly receipts of the bookstalls in your weekly statement. Could that be given easily?' The first account in response to this survives, detailing the five existing bookstalls on the GSWR and three on the Dublin & Wicklow. The Dublin & Drogheda contract was finalised soon after this, and some of the four bookstalls which opened in the second half of the year must have been on its stations. Four more bookstalls appear to have been opened in 1858: Newry, Roscrea Junction (i.e. Ballybrophy), Dundalk and Salthill. Limerick followed in 1861. The Killarney line was added to the GSWR contract in 1859, originally for its prospective advertising income. After this the spread of bookstalls slowed down, because of disappointing results, and it was only after consolidation that new openings were resumed in the second half of the 1860s.

TABLE 3 *The first railway receipts*

	Advertising	*Bookstalls*	*Total*
1857	—	£2,947	£2,947
1858	£983	£5,090	£6,073
1859	£849	£5,993	£6,842
1860	£979	£6,243	£7,222

The fact that the early bookstall business, essentially retail in its nature and drawing most of its sales from a few bookstalls, equalled the entire wholesale news business at that time underlines the still limited scale of the newspaper market. Unfortunately the railway business had been started on the eve of a severe economic depression and the bookstalls outside Dublin had poor results at first. During the first years, once the initial build-up of business in 1857 is allowed for, there was little growth in cash receipts. Even in Dublin, a number of problems had to be overcome before the business as a whole could grow in a sustained fashion. Real growth took place only in the early 1860s, when good back-up in Dublin coincided with the return of better economic conditions in the country as a whole. Total cash receipts began to grow again after 1859, but the growth concealed two diverging trends in the first half of the 1860s: stagnation in income from railway bookstalls and advertising, and expansion in wholesale sales of newspapers to local retailers. The emphasis shifted in these years from the railway bookstalls to wholesale newspaper distribution, primarily though not exclusively in the Dublin area.

As the number of bookstalls grew, the average income per bookstall fell heavily, and many of them were run at a loss. Over half of the total income of the eight book stalls then open in one week in July 1857 came from the two big Dublin stalls at Kingsbridge and Kingstown, which supplied thirty-four and twenty-four per cent respectively of the £85 total. On 25 July 1859, reviewing the results after several bookstalls had been added to the network, Eason wrote that 'there had been a falling off at two or three stations, and on the six months just ended we are a few pounds behind last year'. Smith had left it to Eason to open negotiations in April 1859 with the Ulster Railway, but it proved impossible to agree on the terms of a contract. By 1860, the firm considered giving up the Dublin & Drogheda contract, and Smith advised Eason to 'be very moderate indeed both in the manner and the matter of your demands. If we retire, let us do so with great apparent regret.' Bookings of display advertising and bookstalls sales were both a source of concern, and in 1861 losses on the Dublin & Wicklow line were a further cause of preoccupation. In a comment on the bookstall business Eason noted: 'Though at present working on a small profit it has been conducted throughout the year at much disadvantage and at much loss part of the time. I have had to train the hands and to superintend other matters as well, and it is not surprising that loss should have arisen'. Eason and Smith both believed at this stage that further expansion should be avoided.

The records of wage payments to clerks, which survive for these early years, show no growth, and even fall on the GSWR and the Dublin and Wicklow lines in the early 1860s. Smith agreed in October 1860 in a letter to Eason that 'your view about thoroughly working up present ground is quite my own. I do not wish to take extensions which are not forced upon us and Ulster can wait'. One of the few departures from this policy was the establishment of a retail shop at the Curragh.[5] The business at the Curragh was conducted in a simple wooden structure, which in the preliminary correspondence with the District Royal Engineer's Office at the Curragh, and for many decades in the internal accounts of the firm, was referred to as 'the Curragh hut'. The military clientele was already an important one, and in the 1860s the Curragh had a larger turnover than any of the railway station bookstalls with the exception of Kingsbridge. In the 1880s it was exceeded only by Westland Row.

Bookstall revenue grew very slowly, if at all. The annualised rate of the sales in the week ended 25 July 1857 would have been £4,390 or, based on the week ended 3 August 1857, £5,044. Despite a doubling in the number of bookstalls, plus the addition of significant income from the 'Curragh hut', the bookstall income in 1860 was only £6,243.

The revenue from advertising sites on the railway system had if anything been even more depressing. The results in both 1859 and 1860, despite an extension of the number of railway contracts, were down on the first year's figures. In 1862, in spite of the fact that new railway lines had opened up, the value of railway advertising orders, which was usually larger than cash receipts in the same year, was only £1,267, which suggests no growth, and the figure actually fell back in 1863 to £1,132. The main reason for this poor showing in advertising and in bookstall receipts was the economic depression of these years. Wet summers, which played havoc with fodder for pastoral farming, and poor harvests in 1859 and 1860 had induced severe economic depression in Ireland in 1860 and 1861, and indeed these proved to be the harshest years between the Famine and late 1870s[6]. Eason informed Smith in November 1861 that: 'This [year] and last year will long be remembered for the great dullness in trade generally, with declining sales at the stations, and diminished advertising on the railways...'. There was no real upturn in 1862. Writing in the autumn of that year, at a time when the state of the harvest and

5 This was closed in January 1981, and the business was taken over by a member of the staff.
6 For a discussion, see J. S. Donnelly, Jr. 'The Irish Agricultural Depression of 1859-64' *Irish Economic & Social History*, Vol. III (1976)

of the significant summer business in bookstall sales was evident, Eason reported once more in dismal tones to his employer: 'Money has not come in quite so well during the last two months, but I trust that now the harvest is gathered in we shall find the payments better. The tourists have been few this season and as a consequence our railway business exhibits much falling off.'

This was the end of depression. A better harvest was already in prospect in 1862, and recovery got under way. In 1864 advertising orders for railway sites rose to £2,083, new orders as opposed to renewals accounting for almost half the total. The steam packet companies, the Royal Dublin Society, some hotels, stores such as Pims and Todd Burns, and Lawrence, the photographer, were already regular advertisers. In that year, when an employee, Ferguson, absconded from the railway advertising department, Eason was able to console himself and Smith with the thought that in the light of the defalcation, the results had been better than they had appeared. Indeed, in late 1863 Smith received what was the first optimistic report ever from his Dublin manager, and responded to it in November 1863 with the observation that 'I am glad to have your generally good account of the business'.

THE CHANGING NEWS MARKET

Major changes in the news market coincided with the depression of the early 1860s. The abolition of stamp duty in 1855 ended the dominance of *The Times*, which in 1851 had sold four times as many copies as all its 'quality' rivals put together. Up to then, Smith's business in Britain had largely been built on the increasingly nationwide circulation of this paper, which sold at a price well beyond the pockets of the man-in-the-street. Almost immediately the stamp duty was abolished newspaper prices came down, and in late 1855 the *Daily Telegraph* was relaunched at 1d. Its circulation quickly overtook that of *The Times*. But the change from dearer newspapers with a larger profit margin to penny papers left wholesalers a very slight profit, though the change did give some buoyancy to sales. In the depth of depression the growth of newspaper sales numbers was the one bright element in the Dublin business. This buoyancy was caused by growing retail sales in the city and suburbs, rather than from the railway bookstalls. It also stimulated the development of street selling. Eason took advantage of this market and expanded the sale of papers by boys at stations on the Kingstown line, and by a vigorous canvas of the retail newsagents. In October 1862 Eason advised Smith that railway receipts had fallen off, in part because of the scarcity of tourists, and continued:

> The newspaper sales have increased and are likely further to grow. In June last I began to sell the Dublin papers by means of a staff of boys at the various stations on the Kingstown line and forward to Bray under the direction of a responsible superintendent. This has now grown to be an important auxilliary (sic) and the attempt is well received by the newspapers. We have 11 boys at work and at wages from 4/6 to 6/- per week.

In the three years 1866 to 1868 the average sales by the 'Kingstown boys' were twice the sales at the Kingstown bookstall, and larger than receipts from any other bookstall, not even excluding Kingsbridge. These sales were by no means confined to the vicinity of the railway. They seem to have included some distribution in Cabinteely and Stillorgan. The total number of papers handled in the week ending 5 December 1862 was 198 dozens. This number doubled in the first quarter of 1863, and by the end of June 1863 it reached 483 dozen per week. This latter figure represented an average of 966 copies per day.

But this did not solve the problem of the railway bookstalls themselves, whose business continued to languish. In Dublin, where the attractions of penny papers and forceful distribution were evident, news sales expanded to a middle-class market outside the bookstalls. Beyond the metropolis there was only a small market for daily newspapers at any price. Not a single new railway bookstall was opened between 1862 and 1865. In November 1863, when the first railway contract came up for renewal, Smith was against paying higher rent, because as he confided to Eason: 'The condition of the country and the alteration in our own business — penny papers for the dearer old papers — have seriously affected our business and prospects'. He was even more emphatic when he wrote to Ilberry of the GSWR, following up a previous conversation with him on this subject:

> We are suffering from an entire change in the newspaper business under which the penny papers have almost taken the place in the country of the old established and dear papers. The profit derived from the newspaper business may be said to have disappeared as the public buy in the streets the papers which now take the place of those they obtained through the newspaper agent and at the bookstalls.

As the non-metropolitan market for newspapers picked up, the bookstalls gained a new market as part of a burgeoning news distribution system for local residents as well as for middle-class rail travellers.

The surviving data make it possible to form some fleeting estimate of the elusive question of newspaper circulation. The stamped circulation of the Dublin papers in 1857 suggests a figure of 2,000 for the *Dublin Daily Express*, 1,200 for *Saunders's News Letter*, and 600 for the *Freeman's Journal*.[7] These figures may seem small, but the scale was small in England too. In 1851 the House of Commons committee on newspaper stamps was informed by the first W.H. Smith, who was of course an interested party, that the circulation of London dailies 'scarcely exceeded 60,000'.[8] Smith's, the market leaders, transmitted about 9,000 of these to the provinces. At this stage all the Irish papers were printed on stamped paper, which meant that they could be sent through the mails without extra charge. As late as 1857 the prices of Dublin papers were still quoted on a subscription basis. The failure in the Irish market to issue an unstamped edition prior to 1858, though it had been a possibility since 1855, was in marked contrast to London, where publishers lost no time in bringing out unstamped editions. Dublin still lacked a large market and a retail trade which would make direct transmission of news to the public attractive. The belated appearance of the unstamped editions in Dublin is an interesting measure of the absence at that stage of casual newspaper sales in Dublin. In England, following the change in stamping requirements in 1855, the publication of unstamped editions at the greatly reduced price of one penny created a new market. At this time in England there were more unstamped editions of the papers, paying postage as an extra charge, being transmitted through the mails, than there were stamped editions. In 1859 in England, the total volume of unstamped newspapers equalled the volume of stamped editions, whereas in Ireland the unstamped editions accounted for only one-quarter of the deliveries of mailed newspapers.

A few figures survive for the early days of the penny paper era in Dublin. W.H. Smith's sales of the *Freeman's Journal* in a week in August 1860 averaged 1,236, and *The Irish Times'* monthly account in early 1862 would suggest sales of 1,862 copies per day through W.H. Smith's. As the newest of the Dublin papers, *The Irish Times* did very well. In 1860 and 1861, Smith was doubtful of its prospects, but Charles Eason was impressed by its circulation list, which came into his hands in December

7 *Thom's Directory*
8 Wilson *First with the News* p. 67

1862, and Smith himself soon reversed his opinion of the paper's prospects, writing in July 1863 that 'I have no doubt whatever that *The Irish Times* will increase — and that as long as Captain Knox controls it, any engagement he may make ... will be honourably observed'. His judgement, shrewd as always, was vindicated. There are no existing figures for circulation through W.H. Smith & Son for the 1860s, but a breakdown of returns by the Kingstown boys of unsold copies in 1863 probably reflects the relative importance of the papers. On that basis *The Irish Times* was already the leader, well ahead of *Saunders's News Letter* and the *Dublin Daily Express*, whose combined circulation cannot have much exceeded that of *The Irish Times*.

A further revolution took place in the Irish newspaper world over a period of some twenty years from 1859 to 1880. The Dublin conservative papers succeeded to a large extent in replacing English papers as the expansive element in circulation in the Dublin market. In turn, after a short time lag, the liberal press gained on the conservative press both in Dublin and outside it. The significance of the local press was also greatly enhanced. While Dublin papers circulated more widely than in the past, neither London nor Dublin papers remained as important in the provinces as they had been before the 1860s.

All these changes improved the status of the newspaper journalist. One of the Fenian leaders, John O'Leary, was a newspaperman, editor of the *Irish People* during the 1860s. The tone and the audience of his paper exemplify the emerging popularisation of the weekly press. Newspapermen and editors played a significant role in the Land League from 1879, and several of the Irish members of parliament were journalists by profession. James Daly, editor of the *Connaught Telegraph* at Castlebar in the 1870s, laid the basis for popular land agitation in Mayo, and for the upswell of unrest in Mayo in 1879, the year in which the Land League was founded with the support of Davitt and Parnell.[9] Newspapers helped to make their readers sensitive to political issues, although many other forces contributed to the same end. In turn, political excitement helped to sell the nationalist newspapers, though it caused the loss of some of the circulation of unionist papers. The land war and its innumerable public meetings were reported at length in the press, and there were journalists everywhere. Several left memoirs of their experiences.

9 J. Lee *The modernisation of Irish Society 1848-1918* (Dublin 1973), pp. 68-70. This is Smith's term; Knox's rank appears to have been major.

Although newspapers were cheap, and the rates agreed for carriage in the 1860s were low, the revolution in the newspaper market could not have achieved momentum without some increase in prosperity. Agricultural labourers in the 1850s earned as little as seven or eight shillings per week, and town labourers as little as twelve shillings. In such circumstances an expenditure of 6d per week on a penny daily was confined to those above the labouring classes, and in fact to those well above the ranks of the lower paid.

In the first instance, the increase in newspaper buying was triggered off because prices fell and not because money incomes rose. Many who could not purchase a newspaper at 3d or 4d were able to do so at 1d. Any increase in income tended to work towards establishing a news-buying habit, and so a gradual increase in circulations took place. But on nineteenth century incomes, though cheaper daily papers widened the habit, the market for daily newspapers soon reached temporary saturation. Much of the increased sales of the 1860s and 1870s was occasioned not by new readership for dailies but by a wider range of periodicals purchased by existing newspaper readers. After the 1870s, the increase derived exclusively from weeklies and periodicals, and not from dailies. A fall in prices combined with some rise in incomes helped to create a sustained rise in purchase of periodicals, right up to the 1890s. In 1859 the *Nation* was retailed at 4½d and the *Weekly Freeman* at 3d. In 1870 the *Nation* was only 2d, and in the course of the 1870s the cover price of the *Weekly Freeman* was reduced to 1½d. The rise in newspaper circulation was a long drawn out process, and final saturation in the sense of very widespread sale of daily papers was not attained until the 1920s. The sustained rise in the volume of news publications distributed depended on two distinct factors: a rise in the variety of weekly publications purchased by individuals already affluent enough to purchase daily or weekly newspapers, and more tardily the spread of weekly publications to classes who had had no previous tradition of purchasing newspapers.

News and periodical wholesaling, which catered for this rise, became increasingly the dominant feature of the firm. By 1860 a substantial wholesale newspaper business was already in the course of being established. In July of that year Smith cautioned Eason to 'be careful not to let the newsagents have too extensive credit'. Progress can be measured by the rise in the amount of credit: on October 1 1861, it was £610 as compared with £250 a year earlier. Smith reckoned the figure in 1861 to represent five weeks' sales. This suggests an annual turnover of approximately £6,300. Eason himself observed that 'this department is now doing a business of between £6,000 and £7,000 per annum'.

When the Retail side was still the staple of the business, the English papers loomed much larger than they were to in the last decades of the nineteenth century. Dublin dailies had only a small circulation, and English papers were in demand in clubs, and among the gentry and the military, so they accounted for a very high proportion of total newspaper sales. Smith reasured Charles Eason in July 1856 that he would endeavour to have the Dublin house named as 'Dublin agents to many of the London papers'. This fleeting comment suggests that at the time W.H. Smith & Son's hold on the Dublin market was far from complete. The large size of the London invoices to the Dublin house in 1861, amounting to £11,881, from which only the value of books for resale in the shop have to be taken, compared with an estimated total turnover of £13,000 at stalls and in wholesale news, indicated clearly the importance of the London newspapers. Dublin newspapers sold copies direct to subscribers of course, but the incomplete evidence suggests that London newspapers were a large proportion of total circulation. This was reflected also in the importance that the London papers held in the strategy at this time of Smith and Charles Eason.

The servicing of this demand for London news enjoyed a prominence in these early years which it was not to hold again until the invasion of Ireland by mass circulation papers in the early decades of the twentieth century. Special arrangements were made in 1860 for the transmission of newspapers for Ireland. W.H. Smith & Son in Dublin prepared special easily recognisable covers (wrappers), the addressed covers were dispatched from Dublin to the London house, and the papers were then forwarded to Dublin for delivery without delay to customers in central Dublin. As bookstalls came on the scene, requests were received for deliveries to subscribers living near them. An extra half penny was added to the price of four pence for *The Times* to meet 'the cost of delivery or of packing a single paper in a cover and forwarding it from the station'. The Dublin delivery was confined to the central districts, although in response to a request from readers, Charles Eason attempted without success to get agents to deliver the papers in the affluent and fast growing suburbs beyond the canals. In October 1862 he informed Smith that:

> I have often been applied to make a delivery of London newspapers in the district of Rathmines and Rathgar and have asked several shopkeepers to take up the matter without avail: about a month ago I determined to take it up from the 1st October and to make a delivery

> by a special car. I will try it for 6 months and if I can get 100 daily papers subscribed for it will pay.

The attraction of this service to the subscriber was that it should ensure delivery one and a half hours before the post.

CARRIAGE

The large and growing volume of newspaper and periodical material moving across the Irish Sea, some of it in turn to be distributed further afield in Ireland, made carriage rates a crucial feature both for the rise of the business and its continued growth. In the early years, when distribution of newspapers outside Dublin was limited, the cost of carriage payments from England to Ireland was the dominant element. Even as late as 1873, they accounted for a half of total carriage costs. By the mid-eighties the proportion was down to a third.

Carriage arrangements raised questions both of reliability and charges. Charges were one of the major issues that preoccupied Smith at the outset of the 1860s when he was seeking to establish the basis for the growth in his Irish business. In August 1860 he was anticipating the finalisation of a rate of carriage of ⅜d per lb or almost 4s per cwt, with a minimum annual payment of £500 on parcels from Euston to Dublin.

He planned to visit Dublin with a view to making arrangements with the City of Dublin Steam Packet Co. for carriage across the Irish Sea. Carriage rates were crucial, and the introduction of the library service in Ireland in the 1860s hinged in part on the negotiation of favourable rates for this traffic, which was not covered by existing understandings with the companies. There was also competition between two alternative companies — the LNWR carrying to Holyhead to meet the City of Dublin mail steamers for Kingstown, and the GNR connecting with the City of Dublin cargo steamers from Liverpool for Dublin Port (North Wall). In fact, in those days traffic seems to have been switched between the two railway companies from time to time, and occasionally with great rapidity, as events in late 1862 showed. In November 1862 there was a failure of service on the part of the LNWR and traffic was switched to the GNR. Charles Eason unwisely caused a letter of apology from the LNWR, promising 'never to be bad again', to be published in the *Morning Mail*. Smith's astuteness showed on this issue, and he immediately rebuked Eason: 'Come what may we shall never get another admission of irregularity to clear ourselves from blame in the eyes of the public. You should be very careful in matters of this kind. I never like to get into the papers'.

In fact the GNR gave cause for dissatisfaction quickly, with parcels being twice delayed. As a result, Charles Eason proposed a division of traffic between the two companies. In January 1863 Smith agreed to a somewhat modified version of Eason's proposal: all books were to be sent by the GNR, and periodicals and newspapers by the LNWR. This meant that some traffic would go at parcel rate — parcels delivered at the station in London on Wednesday would reach Dublin on a Friday morning by steamer, whereas the LNWR traffic would be the more lucrative traffic at mail rates i.e. delivery overnight to Dublin. At some stage, not apparent in Eason's records, the contract for goods traffic reverted to the LNWR. They redirected the traffic to Holyhead to steamers of their own bound for the North Wall. Thus, a division of traffic between two sea routes continued, via the North Wall at goods rates, and via Kingstown at mail or express rates. The proportions were roughly 2:1 in the 1890s when the volume had risen to 700 or 800 tons per year. In the 1870s, total payments at express rates exceeded those at goods rates, but in the 1880s a switch took place so that by 1884 goods exceeded express payments in the carriage accounts. This reflected the rise in sales of periodicals, which could be despatched well in advance of publication date, relative to a comparatively unchanging volume of newspapers, which even with express delivery reached the Irish market well after the hour of publication in London.

If the business was to become nationwide, it was equally important to secure agreement on rates with the Irish railway companies. One of the difficulties was in getting the agreement of the companies to a special rate per lb in place of a standard parcel rate, which, as Smith observed, would be prohibitive on small orders, and often nominal on others. Charles Eason commented on this: 'If the minimum of a parcel is set too low at say 2d it will foster the present system of class agencies in the towns, each section will have its particular representative and we should have to keep four accounts where one or two would suffice'. Smith complained in 1860 to Barker, Charles Eason's assistant, that 'The railway companies will do nothing to lessen the cost of carriage, which is a very heavy item. I do not think you can reckon it as less than 1d on the *Times* and ¼d on the other papers'.

After four years of negotiation the companies had still failed to come to any understanding on charges by 1860, and as late as July 1860 Smith cherished the hope that it might be possible to get the GSWR to accept the rate of a farthing per lb, the charge common in England, as the rate for inland carriage within Ireland, and that the other companies would then follow suit. At this stage, the charges by the railway companies worked out at a farthing per copy, which was more than the agency profit to Smith's, and the whole strategy of taking over the agency of the penny dailies, including the understanding which was on the verge of being reached with the *Morning Mail*, had to be held in abeyance until an agreement was reached with them. Charles Eason himself was on the point of reaching an agreement with Ilberry of the GSWR on a rate of a halfpenny per lb. He observed to Smith that

> To offer them only ¼d per lb in the aggregate would shatter their present fine revenue and leave only an uncertain expectation of future development of this business. I could scarce hope to get them to do this. Would you think ½d per lb anywhere too high? I think we can promise them that if they will adopt this they would not lose much of present revenue.

The GSWR held out for extra charges where parcels were to pass over the lines of other companies, but this claim was eventually dropped in favour of a single charge. Smith himself held out for some time for a lower charge of a farthing, at least for journeys of less than 120 miles, but Eason's proposal was a reasonable compromise between the lower charges in Britain, where the traffic was much heavier, and the unduly high charges of the Irish companies for what was at those rates a lucrative but small traffic. When W.H. Smith's went into wholesaling books in 1864, it proved possible to extend the halfpenny per lb rate to book parcels. The other companies followed the example of the GSWR, and new companies of the late 1860s and early 1870s also imposed these charges.

THE DUBLIN PAPERS

The key to the future growth of Smith's business, however, lay with the Dublin papers, in whose distribution they had a small share, rather than with the London papers, of which market they already held a significant share. The prospect of a Dublin penny daily, which was to be fulfilled in 1859, made this strategy urgent.

In June 1857 W.H. Smith's bookstall contract with the Dublin & Wicklow Railway entered into effect. At that time the *Dublin Daily Express* was sold at the stations by employees of the newspaper. In 1857 W.H. Smith opened a bookstall at Kingstown, creating direct competition for sales between themselves and the newspaper. But it was not a serious conflict, as the *Dublin Daily Express* 'servant' at Kingstown did not attend the trains and only occasionally came on to the platform. But the matter became more serious in 1858 as W.H. Smith's extended their sales along the railway line through the 'Kingstown boys' and as the *Dublin Daily Express* stepped up its efforts in order to hold its place in sales. Smith personally complained to Robinson, the manager of the *Dublin Daily Express*, that, 'during the present year you have had new persons employed and they have come fully into competition against us. They have frequently come on to the platform and have served the trains and by their doing this we have suffered considerable injury'.

The *Dublin Daily Express* had in fact succeeded in expanding its circulation between 1854 and 1857, and in so doing had become the largest Dublin daily. In selling copies directly at the stations, the paper was not only violating W.H. Smith's exclusive right under his contract with the railway company, but was also calling into question W.H. Smith's role as an agent for all newspapers. Robinson indicated his readiness to withdraw from the stations on condition that W.H. Smith's undertook to sell the *Dublin Daily Express* exclusively along the line. The conflict thus became of crucial importance. W.H. Smith & Son were faced with the competition of the largest Dublin daily on the platforms or, if the vendors were denied access to the platforms, along the approaches to the stations. If Robinson were to have his way, any agreement reached with him would be at the price of giving up W.H. Smith's role as a seller of other newspapers along the railway line. Such an agreement, even if it had been limited to the Dublin & Wicklow line, would have demolished W.H. Smith's credibility as a general newsagent, and would have invited similar tactics from the *Dublin Daily Express* elsewhere, or indeed from other papers.

The whole relationship with Dublin papers therefore depended on meeting this challenge. In September 1858 Smith wrote to Charles Eason:

> Whatever may be the pecuniary results, I could not permit of any other course of action than the resolute maintenance of our right. I look upon Mr. Robinson's expressed intention as a threat to do us and himself also grievous injury if we will not allow his undisturbed possession without payment of rent of our leasehold — simply because he has held possession of this valuable property for some time without payment of rent to the lawful owners. The whole affair is much more Irish than I believed Mr. Robinson to be.

As always in moments of consequence, Smith addressed himself to the issue in terms of moral rectitude, lecturing Charles Eason on the subject at some length in a letter of 18 December in the same year:

> I have thought over the fight which is impending, and I do not feel

> the least fear or even depression as to the result, and I tell you so that you may not suffer yourself to be overanxious. I believe that hitherto we have done no wrong, and it can scarcely be necessary for me to say that as you withal will be responsible for our future acts in reference to the struggle, we will not knowingly do that which our conscience disapproves, or that which will be directly wrong in the sight of God. I believe thoroughly that he direct (sic) all things aright — even our little business troubles and successes — if we earnestly desire that direction.

Smith's strategy at this stage was masterly, and the tone of his private letters to Charles Eason shows that no bluff was intended. At one level he held out to Robinson the prospect of arbitration to buy out any interest Robinson had in selling papers, while at another level he put out feelers about the publication of another Dublin daily conservative paper. His eyes fell on the languishing *Dublin Evening Mail*. If it were to appear as a daily, it would in Smith's estimate retain its existing subscribers and take about half those of Robinson's *Dublin Daily Express* in three months. Smith's inducement to anyone ready to bring out the *Dublin Evening Mail* as a daily paper was 'to take 500 copies for three months certain and lodge the trade cost to his credit at La Touche's at once'.

He contemplated offering the proposed daily *Mail* at half price for three months, adding that, 'It is an important point if we do fight to make our adversary thinner and poorer rather than the reverse by his own act.' Smith instructed Eason to leave Robinson in uncertainty as to the course of action they would take. At this stage Robinson intimated that W.H. Smith & Son would be refused the trade discount on copies of the *Daily Express* they bought direct; Smith in turn envisaged getting copies through the trade or, if that was refused, replacing the *Dublin Daily Express* with *Saunders's News Letter* in W.H. Smith & Son's sales. In fact, there was no Dublin paper strong enough to contemplate a struggle which might end up in the launching of a rival daily, and in December Robinson capitulated and accepted the arbitration which had been held out and refused at an earlier date. The terms of the arbitration, conducted by Copland, manager of the Royal Bank and La Touche, do not survive, but it is likely that they included the payment of £200, which was mentioned as a settlement price at one stage in the struggle. The moral of the tale was the power of W.H. Smith & Son, with their English resources behind them.

The first Irish penny dailies were the *Morning News*, which appeared as a daily for the first time in 1859, four years after the London *Daily Telegraph*, and the *Freeman's Journal* which had been a daily under the old higher prices. In July 1859 Charles Eason wrote to Smith informing him that 'they had four months of penny dailies in Dublin'. Stiff competition created a precarious situation for all the papers, but in spite of this the number of penny dailies rose to four, with a change in the price of the *Dublin Daily Express*, and with the appearance of a new daily, *The Irish Times*[10]

Charles Eason's view at the time was that they could not all survive, and indeed the competition was so intense that in the course of the struggle proprietors even seem to have purchased copies of their own newspapers in order to keep up circulation. In September 1861 Smith thought that some of them would give up the struggle altogether. The condition of *Saunders's News Letter*[11] was shaky, and Robinson's *Dublin Daily Express* was considered to be vulnerable as well. In the spring of 1862 *The Irish Times* was reduced to seeking an advance of the monthly account due to it. Smith agreed to an advance not exceeding £150 but advised Charles Eason not to proceed beyond the amount authorised 'or otherwise he may get you into a string and leave us one day with a heavy loss. Is it the beginning of the end with him?'. The financial condition of the papers greatly assisted Smith in negotiating terms with them which would enable W.H. Smith & Son to distribute to the retail trade. The *Dublin Daily Express* had accepted Smith's conditions at the end of December 1858, and the dailies, mindful of this struggle, were in no condition to impose their own terms in the early 1860s, all the more so since the competition amongst themselves was ruinous to their already precarious finances.

The conditions which Smith sought to impose on the Dublin penny dailies were terms of 1s 6d per quire of 27 copies, i.e. ⅔d per copy, which Smith in turn sold to newsagents at ¾d per copy. This left Smith with a margin of 2 ¼d per quire, or 11.11 per cent of his sales, which in his view in May 1860 'is a good business at that rate, but I very much doubt if it would pay us to keep accounts, give credit, provide carts to carry the papers from the offices and to the stations, with string, packing paper and staff, for less.'

He even envisaged terms of 1s 5d per 27. Terms arranged with *Saunders's News Letter* from an early date were on these lines, and in time these seem to have been the terms under which W.H. Smith & Son handled all the

10 Excluding evening papers which became pennies. There were two in 1860: The *Evening Freeman* and the *Evening News*.

11 *Saunders's News Letter* was the last of the morning dailies to become a penny daily.

Dublin papers, although at first there was a struggle with the hard-pressed dailies both as to rates and as to the practice in regard to returns. The papers were slow to take back unsold copies, and over the first three years there was considerable difficulty in getting an agreement on this. It involved a great amount of uncertain and tortuous negotiation, most of the detail of which does not survive. In fact, their reluctance on this point left a lever in Smith's hand, as by deliberately cutting down the number of copies to a minimum, he was able to being pressure to bear on them to agree to his terms. Thus in July 1861 Robinson, the proprietor of the *Dublin Daily Express,* while attempting to negotiate favourable terms with Smith, was at the same time begging him to keep an adequate stock of the paper at the bookstalls.

SEEKING AGENCIES

The successful termination of the struggle with the *Dublin Daily Express* left Smith free to develop the selling of Dublin papers. The crucial advance was not simply to sell the papers on agreed terms, but to act as agents for a large proportion if not all of the distribution. The strategy of the house at this stage was essentially one of seeking agency rates and conditions identical to those which had previously been worked out in England. Smith was able to negotiate agency rates from a position of strength. The first breakthrough of this issue occurred in 1860 in negotiations with Sullivan of the *Morning News* and *Evening News*. The proprietor, George Pigott, announced in a printed circular of 26 May 1860 the terms on which 'Messrs Smith & Son have contracted with the proprietor of the *News* to undertake the supply of all agencies'. They were the standard terms which Smith was seeking to impose on the Dublin trade. But Smith's hand could be seen also in the details. If parcels containing the *News* also contained the other Dublin newspapers in the total amount of four dozen, the carriage would be paid by W.H. Smith's. Piggott's circular exhorted the agents to 'lose no time in writing to Messrs Smith & Son offering to undertake the agency of all the Dublin papers, as this will be an advantage to you, and the proprietor of the *News* will give his support to your application.' In fact this arrangement fell through, apparently because of a change in proprietor. In December 1862 Sullivan indicated to W.H. Smith & Son that he would urge the arrangement upon the new proprietor of the *News*.

By 1861 Smith had still to make an effective agency arrangement with any Dublin paper. Somewhat in desperation, he even considered

Saunder's News Letter, which was one of the two weakest of the five morning papers, and one of the most amenable in meeting his terms, as a possible lever to achieve his object: '*Saunders* is a serious opponent to the *Irish Times* and if it is pushed vigorously as it ought to be, it will have a very large sale in and near Dublin'. By September 1861 he had still failed to come to an agency arrangement with the *Dublin Daily Express*.

The breakthrough was achieved finally in late 1862 with *The Irish Times*. By October of that year it seems that an understanding was reached that W.H. Smith & Son would distribute the unstamped issues to the Dublin trade. Charles Eason reported that:

> *The Irish Times* have recently closed with one who took 400 copies, Davis of Blackrock, and put the man in prison for the debt due to them, and they have an advertisement daily in their paper inviting the public to transfer their orders to our boys. I have taken advantage of this to compete strongly in all the districts worked by the boys and family of Davis. And I think they cannot keep on long. *The Irish Times* will permit returns while we are carrying on this experiment, and I think the present is a favourable opportunity to urge the general practice of returns.

In December an agreement was reached whereby W.H. Smith & Son took over the entire stamped distribution of *The Irish Times* to its regular subscribers. As *The Irish Times* bookkeeping had been careless, this new arrangement with W.H. Smith's was of immediate benefit to the paper. In 1863 Barker, the W.H. Smith's employee who handled business with the paper, was recruited by *The Irish Times* into their office. However the arrangement was also of great benefit to W.H. Smith's, for as Charles Eason observed 'the list of *The Irish Times* will certainly promote new business. Some of the names are really very good.' One of the attractions of the arrangement for W.H. Smith & Son was the prospect of developing a significant volume of sales outside the Dublin area. As far as the house was concerned country sales of Dublin dailies were probably still smaller than the business in London papers. It even seems possible that the total circulation of Dublin dailies to the provinces through all channels was less than that of the London papers. Because country customers were few and isolated, and provincial newsagents were very few, almost all country sales took the form of subscriptions serviced by post. As long as postal subscriptions remained in use, the service that W.H. Smith's offered was slight. In order to take over the market, the house had to ensure delivery before the post, as Smith himself reminded Charles Eason in September 1861: 'The mails must *never* beat us'.

The negotiation of carriage rates with the railway companies in 1862 was the first crucial step in establishing the country wholesale business. Agency understandings with the Dublin newspapers at the end of 1862 or in the following months carried the progression further, ensuring Smith's role as wholesaler to Dublin as well as to the country. Before the new arrangements were fully operative, the Retail side of the business exceeded the Wholesale. In 1864 and 1865, once they got under way, Wholesale receipts rose sharply, and the house had acquired the character and style which dominated its history for the next hundred years.

Postal subscriptions were still important as late as 1871 in the distribution of English papers. Despite circulation through bookstalls and agents, W.H. Smith's despatch office serviced 798 subscriptions to English dailies by post on 28 October 1871, compared with 377 unstamped subscriptions. Distribution of the unstamped editions of the Dublin penny dailies by the railways began within months of their first appearance as penny papers. In a private letter of May 1860 Charles Eason indicated that by contract between the company and the papers, something between 660 and 825 copies of *The Irish Times* and 400 copies of the *Freeman's Journal* were being carried daily on the GSWR system. When negotiations were re-opened with the railway companies on carriage rates in 1861, Smith represented that in England; 'By far the larger portion of the edition of each newspaper published circulated by means of the railway in its unstamped form ... while such traffic here is extremely limited and chiefly of recent growth'. The consequences of the growth of such a business in Ireland, of which Smith himself was the driving force through his role in negotiating carriage rates as well as agencies, was a two-fold one. Firstly, the circulation of the Dublin daily papers increased significantly. Secondly, in servicing enlarged outlets in Dublin and outside, the Dublin press gained on the English press in circulation outside Dublin.

There is little doubt that the bulk of W.H. Smith & Son's newspaper business in 1860 was in English papers. Even on a typical day in 1871, in the firm's retail office Irish dailies accounted for only 1,127 of 2,302 sales and subscriptions. By 1871/2 cash receipts for wholesale newspaper sales were somewhat less than £28,851, of which sales of the four Dublin dailies through W.H. Smith's amounted to £15,113. In other words, more than half the news turnover was accounted for by the Dublin papers. By 1885, however, the cash receipts of the three surviving Dublin dailies amounted to £33,231 out of wholesale news receipts of no less than £81,600. This was not because of the competition of English dailies, but because as the market grew, there was an increasing amount of periodical literature. Inevitably, then as now, in a small market, domestic periodical production was small in comparison to production in the larger market. As literacy and publication grew, the relative importance of daily newspapers in total periodicals sales, whether English or Irish, fell significantly. On the other hand, within the area of daily news, the Dublin press improved its position, and acquired a national rather than a local significance.

EXPANSION INTO NEW AREAS

Smith maintained a very close interest in the Irish business in the 1850s and the early 1860s. In this period his visits to Dublin were frequent, and Charles Eason acted under very precise instructions. The vital negotiations with the railway companies on various issues were frequently conducted by Smith in person or in correspondence. As time went by, his personal interest decreased, particularly as his involvement in public affairs developed and took up more and more time. In February 1868 he told Eason that 'I am personally averse to the purchase of any business as I find my responsibilities increase in spite of my efforts to lessen them'. At that time the reason was still said to be the scale of the business. But in the 1870s Smith's political interests had become explicit. In January 1873 he deferred a visit to Dublin because of parliamentary commitments, and so the negotiations with the Ulster Railway were left in Eason's hands.

At an even earlier date, when the Dublin business still commanded Smith's close attention, Charles Eason had already become an independent driving force in its expansion. In a letter written on 1 November 1861, Eason anticipated an 'adverse judgement' on the scale of the expansion, and in January 1862 Smith was to respond critically on the matter of office modifications: 'I am very sorry that you have made alterations in the office again as every farthing spent in that way that could be saved by any possibility is a loss. This and the last year's accounts, when they are made up, will not leave anything to spare for mere convenience.'

One of the first areas of development was into books. Books were a very important part of the early business of W.H. Smith & Son not only in England but also in Ireland. The fact that the railway stalls were called bookstalls is itself a reminder of this. While newspaper sales were limited, book sales loomed much larger than later in the business, and although little is known of the composition of bookstall sales in detail, a slow sale of books to tourists was one of the facts which, in Charles Eason's view, accounted for the low turnover in the summer of 1860. Because of the significance of books in the business it was important to be fully alive to the trends in the book trade. The success of Mudie's subscription library, which had been started in 1842, and the fact that Mudie had no agent in Dublin caused Smith to encourage Eason to extend W.H. Smiths' own proposed subscription library, which was finally launched in June 1860, to Ireland. Smith was keenly aware of the need 'not to play second fiddle to him ... the more I consider it must be done before Mudie gets too strong through the country, already his plans pervade every channel open....' Smith intimated to Eason in November 1859 that 'you may make a good thing of it, as I feel persuaded it must be successful ... the day of accumulating books is going out and while there is such rapid production it will tend in that direction.' On this occasion Smith was keen to take on a new commitment, which was unusual in his approach to the Irish business, even holding out to Charles Eason the prospect of a skilled assistant from the London house.

A fall-off in the sales of books was a factor in making involvement in a subscription library attractive. A minor additional appeal of the scheme was the fact that used subscription library stock could be sold at the bookstalls at a reduced price. Charles Eason set out detailed proposals in July for the operation of the subscription library in Ireland, drawing on the English stocks, and working to the catalogue of the English house. The same stocks would be held in Ireland, although a week's notice would be required 'for such as would appear unsuited to the demand here'. Eason also suggested that 'as the prominent feature in this library is its connection with railways, the word railway should stand before subscription.... I think that if some such reference is not put to Railways the prejudice excited here will be very strong indeed, and that this will go far to allay it.'

What Eason was anticipating was opposition from the railway companies. Both the GSWR and the Dublin & Drogheda put up a very strong resistance to the introduction of the scheme. Smith felt that it was arguable that the conduct of the library was covered by the existing contracts but was eager not to press the point. He sought an arrangement with the GSWR, the more obdurate company, for an additional payment to cover the conduct of the library. Given the impasse, he advised Charles Eason in November to

> show no annoyance and no ill feeling to any of the people who have brought this about, but go on working the Library steadily in those parts where it is appreciated and where no difficulties arise. I am

> quite sure individual interest and public feeling will influence the Board in an opposite direction before the contract expires.

Eason was instructed to intimate to the two senior officials of the GSWR that there was a free list, and that they could obtain any books they desired: 'the secretaries and managers of all our contract lines should have one or two library books free. It will be a convincing proof of the value of the scheme.' In fact, Smith's enthusiasm for the library business was somewhat misplaced. Quite apart from the special difficulties it created with the GSWR, it did not prove specially remunerative, and in May 1863 he wrote to Charles Eason 'of our sense of the unprofitability of library business under present circumstances.'

Smith's eagerness for the library scheme had been encouraged in part by the recession in book sales in 1860 which he had generalised into a more deep-seated change in the book trade. He was proved singularly wrong. Book publishing became even more competitive and price cutting reduced rather than enhanced the attractiveness of lending libraries, which Smith in 1860 had seen both as a cause of the difficulties in the sales area, and as a panacea for the problem. In May 1863 he had to admit to Eason:

> we may work the library at a profit — but at so small a profit under present conditions of novel publishing and competition as to be universally of consideration if we are asked to incur risk to obtain it. I believe it to be impossible for Mudie, Morrow or any other libraries to satisfy their subscribers and make a profit in the present condition of the trade and I wait patiently until they break up, when it may be possible perhaps to come to some understanding with the novel manufacturers.

Moreover, the book trade was changing. What Smith had described as 'first-class books' were relatively fewer, but cheaper and more ephemeral productions — the product of Smith's 'novel manufacturers' — were increasing rapidly. Smith himself had encouraged this trend by buying copyrights for Chapman and Hall to publish as 1s 'yellowbacks', mainly to be sold on his new network of railway bookstalls. Charles Lever was one of the first authors in this series. Other publishers such as Routledge, and the fiction specialist Bentley, also published 'Railway Library' collections. This development gave wholesaling a new significance in the book trade, as wholesalers were in a better position to establish a niche in cheaper wares for a mass market than in more expensive books.

Over the 1860s the scope of the business widened further. The decision to open a wholesale book business was made in 1864. In 1860 there had been several book wholesalers in Dublin. In that year, for instance, W.H. Smith's built up the stock of the Irish library by purchases from the house of McGlashan & Gill, and from William Robertson. The failure of Robertson in 1863 raised the question as to whether Smith's should expand into book wholesaling in the Irish market. Smith was apparently against the extension of business. It seems that it was the wish of Charles Eason, and his readiness to take on the business without the dispatch of a specialist bookseller from the London house which swung the decision. Smith not only expressed his reluctance but made it clear that in his opinion: 'I don't think it would be remunerative to us, to give you a head of department for either business of sufficient knowledge and responsibility to relieve you of the care and weight of the new business.' The growth of the wholesale book business was thus comparatively informal. While some activity in books can be dated from 1864, correspondence with Smith suggests that this section was fully launched only in 1867. Carriage rates were negotiated which extended to books the advantageous rates recently established for news. These were to prove vital, because the country book trade became much larger than the town business. Possibly because of Smith's attitude, the launching of the new service was only slowly formalised. As late as January 1867 Smith wrote to Eason: 'I hope you won't start up with too large amount of stock, or of too heavy a back-up of capital. You will always remember that books are like fish the worse for keeping.' W.H. Smith & Son in England were already dealing in this area of trade, and so it seems that Smith's reluctance to introduce wholesaling in books in Ireland stemmed in part from a desire not to overload Charles Eason with responsibilities.

The extension of the house into other activities seems usually to have been Eason's initative, and he even undertook lines of business which were not covered by W.H. Smith & Son in England. In 1866 Eason commenced publication of catholic prayerbooks. The later prayerbooks have both the imprint of the firm and carried the name of Charles Eason, since the bishops wanted to have a clear-cut agent to be responsible for their accuracy and acceptability.[12] In or perhaps before 1870 the stationery business was opened,[13] and this extended the trade of the house to many towns with which it had had no previous contact. A special

12 See p. 221.

13 There seems to be evidence of dealings as early as 1868 (p. 85) and some dealings may be even earlier (p. 32).

14 There seems to be evidence of dealings as early as 1868 (p. 85), and some dealings may be even earlier (p. 32).

warehouse was opened in 1882 in Gloucester Street, because of the growing scale of wholesaling in stationery. Some years previously the involvement had already been taken a stage further with the establishment of a 'stationery work room' for the manufacture of stationery, and in 1889 this work room was moved into new factory premises in Gloucester Street. In correspondence with Smith in later years, Charles Eason emphasised how the range of activities of the house in Dublin had no parallel in London. This was not simply his own view. In an obituary notice for Charles Eason in 1899 in the *Newsagent and Booksellers' Review* the paper wrote that: 'we hope in the near future to give an interesting account of this firm's work and methods, many of which are distinct from what is actually practised in England and Scotland'.

Chapter 5 ❧ The Business Established

A PERIOD OF REAL PROSPERITY in Ireland began after the early 1860s and continued through the 1870s. Agricultural prices remained high, and the linen industry in the north attained a boom in the cotton famine of the early 1860s. This boom faltered in 1866 but recovered quickly to last into the early 1870s. Confidence in the economy was quite evident. Irish investors bought out the English investors in railways and banks in Ireland. There was also a banking boom, with several new banks being launched in the early 1860s. While none of them proved to have a permanent existence, the business they created was taken over in time by other banks.

The best measure of the increase in wealth is the fact that per capita bank deposits doubled between 1861 and 1876. At the latter date they were a respectable £6.1 per head. They were to double again between 1890 and 1913, another period in which reading habits were to change profoundly. The 1860s and early 1870s were among the few periods in the nineteenth century in which the Irish economy experienced a boom whose benefits were widely diffused. This growth in prosperity was every bit as significant in its own way as the cheapened cost of papers, rising literacy and the railways in creating a national market for newsprint and a need for efficient channels of distribution. W.H. Smith & Son's Wholesale side turnover in Ireland rose every year from 1861 to 1878, a phenomenon which could be paralleled more or less in other areas of the business world during these two decades, but which was never to be repeated again in the history of Smith's or later of Eason & Son Ltd.

WHOLESALE TURNOVER

By 1863 the Wholesale side, which at that time consisted only of the station bookstalls, advertising and newspaper wholesaling, equalled the Retail in size. Cash receipts survive for the entire year 1863, and amount to

£35,429. If we take the amount of the London accounts in 1861 — £11,881 — and we assume that the wholesale news receipts estimated in 1861 at £6,000 to £7,000 consisted exclusively of Dublin newspapers, we arrive at a figure of some £18,000 to £19,000 for the total turnover in 1861. This estimate involves a good deal of double counting. The impression that the turnover at least doubled between 1861 and 1863 is therefore all the more valid. In 1864 Wholesale side business exceeded the Retail, and then began to draw away from it rapidly.

TABLE 4 *W.H. Smith's Dublin turnover, 1863-72*

	£ *Retail*	£ *Wholesale*
1863	18,567	16,862
1864	19,039	19,998
1865	19,064	28,775
1866	19,777	34,965
1867	20,065	37,095
1868	19,983	41,911
1869	20,228	46,538
1870	19,309	52,540
1871	19,907	59,101
1872	18,513	64,479

The scale of the Dublin business can be appreciated somewhat more fully if it is compared with that of Smith's Manchester wholesale branch, which seems to have been the largest of the English branches of Smith's outside London.[1] It is also the only one for which figures survive from before the beginning of the twentieth century. Its turnover in 1863 was £13,379, and in 1872 had risen to £45,546. It was growing more rapidly than the Dublin house in the 1860s, but its turnover was still not much more than half that of Dublin in 1872. In that year the Dublin house's total wholesale turnover was £64,479; of this the amount for books, wholesale stationery and railway advertising comes to £33,115, and

1 W.H. Smith & Son, London A 22.

wholesale news and bookstalls £31,364.[2] There is some double counting in these figures, because the bookstall figures include some books and stationery, and books were still a significant component of bookstall sales. Subject to this qualification, these figures provide a general outline of the character of the Irish business fifteen years after Charles Eason's arrival.

The wholesale character of the business was only partially established at this stage. In 1863, for instance, true wholesale sales were still short of retail sales. In 1861, at the height of the crisis of the early 1860s, wholesale news sales bore a ratio of 1:1 to bookstall receipts; by 1871/2 this figure had become a ratio of 3:2. In 1861 sales of penny papers were largely local to Dublin, by 1872 wholesale news sales were increasing countrywide. Distribution was via the railway network, and the symbiotic relationship of the business to the railways was gradually being enhanced. In January 1870 the GSWR train changed its timetable, and began to leave at 6 am. Eason's routine had to change too: 'the news office grumbles, but it must be done', Eason noted.

The railway contracts for bookstalls and advertising are of course the most concrete evidence of this close involvement, but one of the largest expenditures in the ledgers of the house were the payments for carriage to the various railway companies. In 1867 carriage payments to the railway companies were £2,198 and they rose to £3,140 by 1878. This was more than the payments which the house made to railway companies in rent for bookstalls and railway advertising. Railway carriage of news and book parcels is one of the classic instances of elastic returns. A reduction in rates led to a large turnover through W.H. Smith & Son, as well as constituting an important traffic to the railways.

The shift in emphasis to the Wholesale side activities was evident from the early 1860s. The Retail side had reached its peak for all practical purposes in 1863, and in 1911 was little different from the level of business of the 1860s. The Retail side's receipts often rose and fell in unexpected ways against the trends in wholesale trade or in the economy at large. In particular they remained at a low level during the 1880s and 1890s, in marked contrast to the underlying upward trend in Wholesale side receipts. Many years later this trend puzzled J.C.M. Eason (grandson of the first Charles Eason, and Managing Director 1926-1950) in one of his retrospective looks at the firm's business, and he was inclined to think

2 For details of the turnover for 1871/2 see p. 37. Detailed figures did exist although they no longer survive. An isolated profit and loss account for the wholesale news department for four weeks ending 27 October 1877 gives sales as £2,753, the equivalent of £35,887 on an annual basis.

that the variations were accounted for by the fluctuations in newspaper advertising which were included with Retail side receipts. But this was not the main reason. A decline in retail sales as such followed the growth of a wholesale news network and reflected a transfer of business from the passive retail department to new retailers around the city of Dublin. In fact since advertising agency receipts were buoyant, the relative decline in retail sales was sharper than appeared, particularly in view of a striking advance in the sale of periodical reading matter which took place during the 1880s and 1890s.

The circumstances for the growth of W.H. Smith's wholesaling were very favourable at the outset of the 1860s, even if depression at the outset of the decade held down the bookstall receipts. The wholesale business grew every year from 1864 to 1877/8. Wholesale receipts doubled in the period between 1863 and 1866, and had doubled again by 1873/4. They rose a further 24 per cent by 1877/8. The first year in which receipts fell was in 1878/9, when they dropped from £96,775 in the previous year to £90,397. Halfway through the accounting year Charles Eason had already noticed the slide, and wrote to Smith in January 1879:

> For the first time during the eighteen years, the wholesale cash receipts of the second half of the year show a decline reaching nearly £2,000 and unless some very serious and real change in the social and political horizon appears, we may expect that the first half of this year will show even a still larger decline.

W.H. Smith's business closely reflected the trends in the economy, as well as the social habits of the period. The years 1867 and 1872/3 were both times in which the Irish economy and rural society experienced difficulties. The railway advertising business was particularly sensitive to the state of business confidence. In March 1877 Charles Eason stressed to a railway manager that 'our railway business in Ireland has never been a steady growing one, but has shown frequent fluctuations from bad seasons and political disturbances.' There are many references in the files to falling proceeds from early 1876 from the northern railway companies, where receipts reflected difficulties in the linen trade from the mid-1870s.

The fall of £2,000 in turnover in the second half of 1878 was followed by a fall of a further £4,000 in the first half of 1879. The fall in 1878/9 preceded the disastrous harvest of 1879, because the economy had already begun to slide into sharp recession; the bad harvest was consequently all the more devastating in its effect. Other business data, such as the deposit figures of banks such as the Royal and the Provincial, which were closely attuned to the level of business activity and business confidence, provide evidence of trends elsewhere which were similar to those experienced by W.H. Smith's at that time: a downturn before 1879, and evident in the north ahead of the south.[3] Turnover remained depressed during the following two years, but staged a strong recovery in 1881/2 and 1882/3. Smith himself was somewhat startled by the recovery in the wholesale business, and he was prompted to write on 4 January 1883: 'What however is the explanation of the prosperity of Abbey Street during the past year? It is certain many people have suffered and we are told so by Irishmen on both sides. Is the country settling down or is strong Government by reason of the powers of the coercion Act giving a temporary security?'

The political scene was helping in a way to which Smith did not refer. The intense politicisation, the conduct of Land League affairs by a party with disproportionate journalistic representation, and the reporting of meetings at length in the press, meant that a mass public opinion was engaged, and the press, or at least the nationalistic press, gained from the events. However, it was the general recovery of the economy in these years, rather than politics, which accounted for the healthier state of W.H. Smith's business. There was no real momentum in the recovery. Turnover fell again in 1883/4, and although it recovered in 1884/5 the turnover of the following four years was unchanged.

The business grew during the 1890s but rather slowly. Wholesale turnover in Dublin rose from £107,890 in the year 1889/90 to £127,572 in the year 1898/9. This was the year of Charles Eason's death, and it marked the end of an era. He had guided the firm both through its rapid expansion, and through the subsequent period in which the prospects of expansion were more modest. While Eason & Son no longer had a formal association with W.H. Smith, it may be of interest to compare the Irish business with the provincial branches of W.H. Smith's in England. The turnover, wholesale and retail, of Eason & Son in 1898/9 was £161,196 (Dublin on its own was £144,310). Easily the two largest provincial branches of W.H. Smith's were Manchester and Liverpool, and the turnover for them was respectively £111,663 and £90,782 for the year ending September 1900, the first years for which audited figures survive.[4]

3 Allied Irish Banks, Dublin. Annual reports of Royal Bank of Ireland, and of the Provincial Bank of Ireland.

4 W.H. Smith and Son, audited accounts.

TABLE 5 *Components of Wholesale Turnover, 1865-99: Dublin and Belfast combined*

	News	*Bookstalls*[6]	*Total News*	*Railway*[7] *Advertising*	*Stationery*	*Books*	*Catholic*[8] *Prayer Books*	*Total Wholesale*
1865[1]	8,688	6,500	15,188	1,674 (2085)				16,862
1872[2]	18,441	12,923	31,364	1,267 (3780)	7,536	22,312	(2,000)	64,479
1878[3]	36,612	20,576	57,188	4,436	11,865	19,208	4,078	96,775
1888[4]	57,859	23,002	80,861	8,548	12,616	17,762	(3,500)	119,787
1899[5]	65,848	21,885	87,733	12,739	17,187	19,481	4,700	141,840

(1) year ended 31 December 1865.

(2) based on a year probably ended June in respect of gross receipts, stationery and books, and a year ended 31 December 1872 for bookstalls and railway advertising.

(3) based on a year ended June in respect of gross receipts, stationery and books, and a year ended December 1878 for bookstall receipts and advertising receipts.

(4) all figures relate to a year ended 31 March 1888, except for bookstall receipts and railway advertising receipts which are for a year ended 31 December 1887.

(5) all receipts relate to a year ended March 1899

(6) includes an undisclosed amount of stationery and books (which are also included in the column for books and stationery). In 1899 bookstall receipts, if books and stationery are included, amounted to £31,287.

(7) except for 1865 and 1871/2 the figures for railway advertising are for orders, which overstate actual receipts in the same year. Figures for orders in 1865 and 1871/2 are given in brackets.

(8) estimated figures for 1865 and 1888. The Catholic Prayer Book department was an independent legal entity in 1888 and is not included in the gross receipts of that year; the estimated turnover in the department is given in brackets, however, and is of course not included in the overall wholesale turnover of the firm for the year.

Before 1865 the only diversification was into the library, which had been prompted a few years earlier by the lack of growth of bookstall receipts, particulary in respect to sales of books. As the news department was still largely a Dublin-oriented business, Eason's desire to extend the business into book wholesaling, stationery and catholic prayerbooks may have been prompted by discouraging bookstall receipts, a fear of limited horizons, and the experience in previous years of stagnation and low profits from newspaper sales. Even in 1871/2, when bookstall receipts had begun to grow again, the non-news items accounted for more than half the turnover. Wholesale sales of books and stationery had both risen rapidly. Book sales were worth £22,312 in 1871/2, the earliest year for which complete figures survive. At that date they were far and away the largest single item in the company's turnover, a good deal larger than wholesale news sales, and almost twice as large as bookstall receipts — the next two largest items in the company's business.

The wholesale stationery business was only in the process of being built up. In the second year for which figures are available they already amounted to £4,516, and jumped to £7,536 in 1871/2, and subsequently climbed steadily, reaching a peak of £14,939 in 1876/7. During the 1860s and early 1870s books and stationery were the mainstay of the business, during a period when news was unprofitable. Thereafter wholesale news increased dramatically, while books lost buoyancy through the 1870s and 1880s and stationery after 1877. In contrast wholesale newspaper and periodical sales (net of sales at the bookstalls) doubled between 1871/2 and 1877/8, and the buoyancy of the news market helped to account for the sharp rise in receipts at the bookstalls. News distribution, whether wholesale or at the bookstalls, was now overwhelmingly the main activity of the firm. Between 1877/8 and 1887/8, periodicals and bookstall sales rose from 59 per cent of the Wholesale side turnover to 65 per cent, and was still at that level ten years later in 1899.

The revenue in bookstall sales and advertising earned under railway contracts was at its highest level in 1899, accounting for 29 per cent of total Wholesale side receipts. At no other time was the business of the firm so closely involved with railways. In 1898 Eason & Son published their own railway map of Ireland with the contract lines (i.e. the location of their bookstalls and advertising sites) clearly marked. The news distribution business, with its regular daily deliveries by rail, accentuated the railway dimension of Eason & Son even more. The news business of 1899 was nationwide, in contrast to the largely metropolitan market of 1865. As business grew in volume, parcels for provincial centres were dispatched direct from London on Eason & Son's account to Cork and Waterford in 1889, and to Limerick in 1892.

A separate branch was launched in Belfast in 1870, where there had been a warehouse since 1868. It remained a very small division of the Dublin house. No clear record of sales in the Belfast region is available, because some northern distribution continued to be included in the receipts of the Dublin house. Its turnover in the first full year 1870/71 was £5,650, rising to £10,476 in 1873/4, but its peak of £11,533 achieved in 1876/7 was not exceeded again until 1885/6. It continued to grow during the second half of the 1880s but during the following decade sales hardly increased. The Belfast turnover was almost invariably about 12 per cent of the total Wholesale side turnover of the house, though this proportion overstates its importance, as the Belfast figures include some retail business, which cannot be separated from the Wholesale figures in the earliest surviving records. Receipts consisted mainly of bookstall business and railway advertising orders in the Belfast area representing a passive segment of business conducted from the Dublin office. The proceeds from the stations on the Great Northern line, for instance, were divided between the two houses.

The role of the Belfast house even after 1870 was more as a warehouse than as an active branch. This did not matter much as long as no wholesale rival existed in Belfast. But in fact during the 1890s competition was experienced from rival wholesalers in the north — the first serious competition experienced by the firm since its establishment, north or south. Charles Olley's business, which had already acquired the contract on the Belfast & Co. Down Railway in 1891, was turned into a public limited liability company later in the same year.

In 1893 Olley's defeated Eason's in bidding for the Great Northern contract. Between 1892 and 1899 Eason's Wholesale side business in Belfast rose from £13,731 to £16,686. Olley's sales were £8,500 in 1892, and rose to an average of between £22,000 and £23,000 between 1897 and 1899. At that time, they significantly exceeded those of Eason's in Belfast, which stayed at about £16,000 over the four years 1896 to 1899. Another challenge — Porter's, after 1899 — was serious because it centred on wholesale news business, and not on railway contracts. The impact of Olley's had been reflected most directly in the bookstall receipts of the Belfast branch, which were almost halved in the mid 1890s. Moving into the twentieth century, Porter's wholesale business in the north, small at first, was on a comparable scale to Eason's from the 1920s.

As the market for news grew in depth, small wholesalers with greater flexibility in meeting local needs were to challenge Eason's in the major centres of population. This was a lesson whose implications were appreciated in the twentieth century. In the 1920s Belfast was converted into a subsidiary company with much more initiative and commanding much more attention from the Dublin house. The dramatic challenge in Belfast, with the loss of major railway contracts in the 1890s and again more broadly in the 1920s, had a counterpart on a more modest scale in Cork, where the firm of Henry Lawrence Tivy and two of his sons, later trading as News Brothers Ltd. built up a business from the 1880s. Correspondence in the 1920s suggests that while Eason's dominated Kerry and West Waterford, they had little foothold in Cork city itself and its environs. N. Harvey & Co. seem to have been in competition with W.H. Smith & Son in Waterford — at least in the distribution of the Christmas numbers of the *Graphic* and the *Illustrated London News* in 1885. However, Belfast and Cork were to remain the only centres where rival wholesalers succeeded in establishing themselves firmly and permanently in news, though a short-lived challenge in Dublin from Dawson's, the only challenger from outside Ireland, was experienced between 1911 and 1923.

RETAIL TURNOVER

The Dublin retail shop of the firm occupied part of the ground floor of the Lower O'Connell Street building, and was regarded as of minor importance. The retail division of Smith's in the Strand was in a similar position. The library and the advertising agency were included in the Retail receipts total. Not a great deal is known about this latter activity of the firm. It serviced not only advertising by institutions and firms but also by individuals. In July 1859 in one of the rare explicit comments which survive on the advertising business, Charles Eason noted the loss of 'the Cork Colleges', and that 'we are doing a little more of miscellaneous business.' For instance, an isolated surviving invoice of 1860 suggests that W.H. Smith & Son were handling all the statutory newspaper advertising for the Ulster Railway Company in connection with extensions to the company's line. The only surviving figures are for the years 1884 to 1888, which distinguish between the general orders and the government orders. The latter orders included constabulary notices, and a letter survives from the Secretary of the Dublin Metropolitan Police complaining about newspaper charges in 1873.

TABLE 6 *Advertising sales*

*Year**	*General Orders*	*Government*
1884	£1,396	£462
1885	£1,353	£284
1886	£1,121	£323
1887	£1,232	£383
1888	£1,295	£306

*Terminal date of year not specified in source.

A big proportion of the advertising seems to have been taken in the Dublin daily papers: in the calendar year 1892, *The Irish Times* accounted for £1,013, the *Freemans Journal* for £363 and the *Irish Daily Independent* for £268.

TABLE 7 *Library Receipts*

1872*	£1,387
1878*	£1,493
1888*	£1,421
1898/9	£2,297

*Calendar Year

The library business did not live up to the hopes with which Smith and Eason had started it. Library receipts and sales in the 1870s, the earliest available, were only between £1,000 and £1,500, a very small proportion of the turnover. They were not much higher subsequently, and passed £2,000 for the first time in the year ended March 1895, at which time of course they were even less significant as a proportion of turnover.

NEW PREMISES

As Smith's in Ireland expanded, capital investment grew steadily. Some of this rise involved increased stock in trade, but the most striking aspect was the expansion in fixed assets, especially premises. In 1856 the firm's premises were modest ones on Eden Quay. One of Charles Eason's early steps was to propose a move to premises on Sackville Street (now O'Connell Street). Sackville Street and the adjoining streets had formerly been residential, but were now rapidly becoming the commercial centre of Dublin, a fact recognised by the Royal Bank, which of all the Dublin banks was the one most closely associated with the city's traders, and which opened a branch in Sackville Street in 1869, 'a district which has latterly exhibited marked commercial improvement and activity.'[5] Charles Eason had correctly discerned the trend of events when he proposed to Smith to lease part of the ground floor of the Imperial Hotel at 21 Sackville Street. Smith signified his agreement in December 1856:

> We are willing that you should take it if it will fully answer the purposes required — of which you have of course satisfied yourself. My only doubt was whether or not there was sufficient room to admit of all the counting house work as well as the cover writing and packing being done within the space — in your sight. It might be very inconvenient on an occasion of great public interest. You have, however, authority to deal with these details as you may think fit.

The comparatively small scale of the business at the time of this change is illustrated in the fact that Smith could envisage virtually the entire range of operations being done within sight of the manager. A week later Smith agreed to having partitions erected between the public and the cover writers who addressed the special wrappers for newspaper subscribers. He emphasised that 'they would be within your sight constantly — even if it is needful to keep them out of sight of customers.' In 1857 Smith agreed to a further proposal from Charles Eason to take premises in Sackville Place, without a frontage on Sackville Street, but connected by a passage to the existing premises. The front premises were now exclusively a retail shop, and the rear premises served as the despatch department. Henry Digges, who was employed for many years in the firm and who retired as manager of the O'Connell Street shop, recalled his impression of the shop in the 1860s:

> No. 21 had not much appearance, there was not any window display, merely zinc (perforated) blinds, with the name of the firm, Newsagents, on one and Advertising Agents on the other, the door not being in the centre but at one side, and a long upholstered seat running the whole length of the windows (inside); the left flanking wall was completely covered with the Library shelves from floor to

5 Allied Irish Banks, Dublin. Annual reports of the Royal Bank of Ireland.

ceiling; the back wall was occupied by a large heating stove, standing well out into the room, and a double desk with brass rails on top and low shelves against the wall for account books with a partition about five feet high between it and the stove.

The arrangement of the 1850s had been altered in the early 1860s to accommodate the library. Charles Eason also changed the layout at this stage to give more privacy to himself and to separate the library from the sales counter, against the wishes of Smith, who did not see

> any difficulty in carrying on the library and attending to cash customers at the one counter as it stood when I was last in Dublin. The only really serious inconvenience was the want of room in your office, as it was difficult for a further man or two to sit down in it to talk over serious business which might bring them to you but it was better to put up with that in the then conditions of the business rather than incur expenses to alter it.

In 1863 the Imperial Hotel wished to reacquire the Sackville Place premises. Charles Eason bought the lease of 86 Abbey Street in 1864. The wholesale business was transferred to Abbey Street, while the retail business stayed in Sackville Street. Abbey Street now became the focus of expansion. In 1867 and 1868 it accounted for two-thirds of the firm's turnover. In 1867 the lease of 85 Abbey Street was purchased and at the end of some three years of building at a cost of £4,052, it was possible in 1869 to centralise the whole of the firm's operations in 85 and 86 Abbey Street, closing the separate premises in Sackville Street. The future development of the firm was to revolve around this part of Abbey Street site and the adjoining properties. The growth of the scale and complexity of the business necessitated further expansion in the 1870s. In 1873 the printing office and paper storage were temporarily accommodated in 82 Middle Abbey Street. The retail business and the library were at this stage conducted on the ground floor of no. 85, and the wholesale business in no. 86 and the upper floors on no. 85 'but even then we were much pressed for space and could scarcely handle the work properly.' The crucial purchase was that of 79 Middle Abbey Street in 1875, for £1,200. The lease of no. 80 was subsequently acquired. This investment made it possible for the wholesale side to take over a larger amount of the space in 85 and 86 Abbey Street. The plan in 1875 was that the purchase of no. 79, 'will give us full room when rebuilt for the printing offices, counting house, office for the railway advertising canvasser, and leave us the ground floor of No. 80 for the Library and Newspaper office and the ground floor of No. 79 to let as a shop if we do not at present care to take the whole space for our own purposes.' The costs of buildings and fixtures in Nos. 79 and 80 amounted to £5,323. Additional premises at 130-132 Gloucester Street[6] were erected for £1,338 in 1882. All these steps from 1873 onwards were undertaken without any visit or inspection by the London partners.

Between 1869, when the firm vacated 21 Sackville Street, and 1887, the firm was without premises in the city's premier thoroughfare. In the year 1887 40 Sackville Street was acquired, and the retail trade was transferred there from Abbey Street. As described by Digges, 'The ground floor had a long counter for newspapers, with a shorter one for books, and side staircase leading to upper part of house, the library at the rear up three steps and centre staircase leading to two galleries, all filled in Library books.'

The firm's stables had been erected at 129 Gloucester Street in 1859. The growth of the wholesale business meant a gradual increase in the importance of the stables. In 1862 there were four cars and four horses, by 1868 seven cars and six horses: for the latter year, even the names of the horses survive: Tommy, Kate, Lucy, Topsy, Ellen, Topsy No. 2. Later this area became the focal point of activities not immediately related to sales and despatch such as warehousing, manufacturing, and for some years prior to 1898 making of frames etc for railway advertising.[7] The building of the factory at Gloucester Street in 1889 and the transfer of advertising to Great Brunswick Street in 1898 completed a complex series of building works and internal reordering of the business which reflected the growth of the firm across the three decades.

THE DEVELOPING NEWSPAPER MARKET

The 1860s had started with five Dublin penny dailies. During that decade the original leader, the *Dublin Daily Express,* lost its position and first *The Irish Times* and then, in the 1870s, the *Freeman's Journal* took the lead: in 1871, the first of a series of years for which the annual accounts of W.H. Smith with the Dublin dailies survives, *The Irish Times* still had the largest account. The amount was £4,603 as compared with £2,918 for the *Freeman's Journal,* £2,069 for the *Dublin Daily Express* and a mere £489 for *Saunder's News Letter*. The *Morning News* had disappeared by that time. *Saunder's News Letter* had not been in a healthy position from the start

6 Now Sean McDermott Street
7 The present building in the street contains the wholesale book department.

of the newspaper war, despite protesting in June 1860 about Smith's trifling with 'its high position and respectability.' Its account fell inexorably through the 1870s and the paper ceased publication in the course of 1879. As Eason had foreseen in 1860, the Dublin market could not support three flourishing dailies. The *Dublin Daily Express*, which had lost its original position in the lead, did not increase sales significantly throughout this period, and the field was effectively shared between *The Irish Times* and the *Freeman's Journal*. Both papers had increased their sales during the 1860s and continued to expand their circulation steadily into the 1880s. The most striking feature of all is the speed with which the liberal *Freeman's Journal* expanded its circulation. In 1863 it had been well behind all three leading conservative penny papers. Its account with W.H. Smith's exceeded that of the previous market leader, *The Irish Times*, for the first time in 1875.

In 1885 the *Freeman's Journal* annual account amounted to £12,437 while that of *The Irish Times* amounted to £8,644. For the first time a liberal paper led the Dublin newspaper trade; its position was closely linked to the changing political character of the period, and to the emerging weight the literate nationalist opinion. In 1871 the total regular circulation of the dailies through W.H. Smith's was 10,317. By 1885 this had become 20,008. *The Irish Times'* circulation had less than doubled, from 4,705 copies to 7,360 copies, while the circulation of the *Freeman's Journal* had increased three-fold, from 2,964 to 10,904.[8]

As newspaper circulation grew, yearly or half-yearly postal subscriptions became less important and people purchased newspapers casually. This echoed a decline in direct sales by W.H. Smith's to the public, and increased sales through newsagents and vendors, who had been few in number in the 1860s but were now beginning to acquire a significant role in the trade. This is reflected very strikingly in the role of the 'Kingstown boys' employed by Eason in stations on the Kingstown line. Their sales were of major importance through the 1860s, but they fell off from the outset of the 1880s and ceased in 1884. Smith took over the bookstall at Westland Row station in 1876 most reluctantly and, as

8 The figures for 1871 and 1885 are not quite comparable as the latter include the weekly editions. The circulation for 1885 has therefore been calculated on the assumption of ¾d wholesale price and on the basis of seven issues a week. As the wholesale price of the *Weekly Freeman* was 1¼d, this somewhat overstates the circulation of the daily *Freeman*. The wholesale terms of the *Weekly Irish Times* were 9½d per dozen, i.e. very close to the daily terms. This overstates the rise in daily circulation, as the weekly edition increased disproportionately.

he put it to the railway company, only 'at the express wish of your board', representing to them in the early stages of the negotiations that, 'the opening of several shops in Brunswick and Nassau Street with other causes has lessened the business at Westland Row while the sale of newspapers in the hall below having been tolerated so long has given some vendors a sort of prescriptive right which will make it extremely difficult to remove them....' In fact Smith had misjudged the prospects at Westland Row. Though there may have been serious competition in dailies, the growth of periodical reading helped the bookstall to become as early as the 1880s the most lucrative on the railway system.

The position of the Dublin dailies changed again in the 1890s. While *The Irish Times* newspaper account ran at a figure of £700 per month, which was similar to that of the mid-1880s, the account of the *Freeman's Journal* for July 1892 was only £512, or about half the figure for the early 1880s. The appearance of the *Irish Daily Independent* (which was relaunched in 1905 as a ½d paper called the *Irish Independent*) made inroads on the *Freemans Journal*. Its monthly newspaper account ran at about £300. The combined figures for the *Irish Daily Independent* and the *Freeman's Journal* suggest a turnover with Eason's not much below the figure for the *Freeman's Journal* alone in the 1880s. The *Dublin Daily Express* had trailed off to half the turnover of the early 1880s. The *Freeman's Journal* account continued to fall in the 1890s to only £388 in July 1898. In other words, the figures suggest a quite static market for daily papers, although one in which the Irish dailies held their own. A few isolated figures for what appears to have been the weekly number of copies handled by the firm bear out both these features.

TABLE 8 *Sales of Daily Newspapers (copies per week)*

	Irish	*English*	*Total*
1878	99,558	16,033	115,591
1883	133,128	12,876	146,004
1888	148,998	13,338	162,336
1894	119,442	16,188	135,630

These figures demonstrate the domination of the market by the Irish papers during this period, even if some rise in English papers at the end of the period foreshadows the later growth of English competition. Equally striking is the relative stagnation in the circulation of dailies, which underlines the fact that a mass market for daily newspapers did not exist, and that there was no progressive development in that direction. The daily circulation in the 1880s was double that of 1871, but there had been no real growth since the end of the 1870s.

Eason's had 422 agents across the entire country in August 1887 and of these no less than 66 had accounts for less than five shillings worth of newspapers and periodicals per week. The only agents whose names and locations survive are those with less than 5s, but few even of these were outside towns and large villages. In other words, news distribution in 1887 still did not reach outside the town network, and even in the towns, one-sixth of the accounts would have totalled less than 15 sales per day, even if all the papers had been dailies. In fact, relatively few of the papers would have been dailies. At the beginning of the 1880s, weeklies accounted for half of all the news items sold in a week. The only daily which had a wide circulation outside the city of publication was the *Freeman's Journal*. In 1887 Eason's Belfast house held 14 standing orders for *The Irish Times* and a like number of the *Freeman's Journal;* through agents it supplied 17 copies of *The Irish Times* as against 150 copies of the *Freeman's*. A mere six copies of the *Dublin Daily Express* were distributed in the North. A newsagent in Newcastle West, Co. Limerick, regularly handled 50 *Freeman's Journals* (and a sole copy of the *Irish Times*); newsagents in Lismore, Co. Waterford, and Leighlinbridge, Carlow, around 20 copies, Limerick bookstall 116 copies (but only six copies of *The Irish Times*). Above all the absence of a record of shortfalls in the supply of other Dublin dailies illustrates their rarity in the provinces.[9]

The pattern in the delivery of papers from Bray bookstall in August 1878 gives some idea of the contrast in the Dublin region with the *Freeman's Journal* accounting for only one-third of deliveries (see Table 9).

TABLE 9 *Daily delivery of Irish Newspapers, Bray August 1878*

	No.	%
The Irish Times	174	36
Freeman's Journal	156	32
Dublin Daily Express	140	29
Saunders's Newsletter	12	2
	482	100

9 Some details of shortfalls are the only evidence of circulation to individual locations which survive.

W.H. Smith's own retail sales confirm the Dublin dominance of *The Irish Times*. An interesting dichotomy existed of dominance by a Unionist paper in Dublin, and by a nationalist paper outside the capital. In 1870 Charles Eason had advised a proprietor of another Dublin conservative paper, who was considering coming out as a daily to be 'a little less frantic in their writing if they want readers beyond the country gentlemen.' By the early 1890s the *Freeman's Journal* had lost out to the other papers, and it relied increasingly on country sales, in which the *Irish Daily Independent* was slow to match it, and on the sales of its weekly edition. *The Irish Times*, even though it was not enlarging its sales, had improved its relative position in Dublin. While Major Knox had built it up, its purchase by Sir John Arnott in 1873 for a reputed £20,000 may have helped to consolidate its position, with no other successful conservative paper remaining, as the undisputed voice of Dublin unionism.

Limited reading habits and low incomes in combination meant that the real thrust in growth lay in weekly papers. Even in the 1860s when a restricted market gave dailies a greater prominence than they held later, the importance of the periodicals was already evident in W.H. Smith's business. The circulation of weeklies, in contrast to that of dailies after the 1870s, continued to grow.

TABLE 10 *Sales of Weeklies (copies per week)*

	Irish	*English*	*Total*
1878	26,859	88,301	115,160
1883	42,864	108,978	151,842

The total stamped circulation of the Irish periodicals, the *Dublin Gazette, Weekly Freeman, Telegraph*, and the *Nation* in 1857 amounted to 28,581 copies. There is, superficially, no evidence of dynamic growth in the Irish element of the market. But since the *Telegraph* folded up shortly afterwards, the figures for 1878 and 1883 are more meaningful if they are compared with those of the *Freeman* (6,023 copies) and the *Nation* (3,246 copies) in 1857. Such a comparison implies both growth and a degree of diversification. If this was true of Irish weeklies, it was decidedly more so in the case of English weeklies.

The number of English weeklies grew quickly in the 1860s, as did their circulation. Even in 1862 the Dublin house was selling almost 4,000 copies a week of the *Budget* and 3,000 copies of the *Penny Illustrated Weekly*. The circulation of the weeklies can be measured somewhat crudely from the distribution of the Christmas numbers which were a feature of the 1880s. They were distributed to the trade in November and special arrangements were made for handling their distribution. The *Irish Retail Newsagents Gazette* in December 1947 recalled that

> Few now will remember those times ... these issues secured their sale because during the course of the year the public had little opportunity of seeing high quality printing and illustration.... The supplies would reach Dublin a fortnight in advance of the date of publication and a staff would be employed on overtime each evening for some days before, in packing the parcels for dispatch by passenger or goods train.

In 1885, 560 quires (of 27 copies each) of the *Graphic*, 452 quires of the *Illustrated News* and 192 quires of the *Penny Illustrated*, i.e. 1,204 quires in all, or 32,508 copies, were ordered. But the numbers of some other papers were also significant: 80 quires of *Yuletide*, 52 quires of *Truth*, 50 quires of *Father Christmas*, 33 quires of *Santa Claus*, 28 quires of *Work*, 80 quires of *Illustrated Sporting and Dramatic*, 63 quires of *Queen*, 37 quires of *Pictorial World*.[10] Some agents took large numbers of the *Graphic* and *Illustrated London News*. Gill's order was invariably the largest, amounting to 597 copies between the two publications in 1890, and four other Dublin newsagents had in excess of 130 copies, while ten country newsagents had orders in excess of 110 copies. In the case of those with the largest sales, engravings or plates were distributed with the Christmas editions. The plates came separately from London and were collated with the issue as the colour supplements are today. These papers were the cream of late nineteenth century circulation, and the number of such publications was large and growing. Regular lists made by Charles Eason of the year's new periodicals testify in the 1880s both to the wide range of publications and to the novel feature of journals emerging to cater for special interests.

Irish periodicals, with their small market, could not match this competition in any way. Only a few seem to have had Christmas editions, and their circulation was modest. Even the *Freeman's Journal* could only manage 2,350 copies for its Christmas number in 1890. In the same year 11,752 copies were received of the *Shamrock*, and the *Irish Fireside* in an earlier year reached 4,256 copies. In the 1890s between thirty and forty

10 *Answers* Ltd seem to have given 26 copies to the quire (see p. 179). 27 copies was a more general figure.

Irish titles were handled apart from the daily or evening newspapers. Only a few of them had significant circulations: *United Ireland*, which declined and died in the 1890s, *Shamrock, Irish Catholic, Emerald*, and *Irish Bits*. Much more modestly than in England, some specialist journals began to appear also, such as the *Irish Cyclist, Wheelman* (1892 only) and from 1894 the *Irish Wheel*. The effort to launch some of them can be traced. Eason's distributed 500 circulars to announce the *Irish Wheel* in March 1894, and 4,455 copies were sold in the same month. *Today's Woman* was launched from an address in Grafton Street in March 1895, but of the 6,310 copies distributed in March, 4,156 were returned, 960 were sold in June, and the journal was discontinued early in 1897. A large number of the journals which were launched were abortive. The first Irish language paper, *Fáinne an Lae*, made its appearance in Eason's records in 1898.

As circulations increased more popular magazines emerged to cater to wider markets. *Answers* Publications, promoted by Alfred Harmsworth, the future Lord Northcliffe, were the leaders in this field, with astonishing success in the decade after 1885. Their circulation through Eason's grew steadily during the 1890s, judging by their monthly account which grew from £174 in February 1893 to £454 in December 1897. A breakdown of the latter account furnishes an idea of their range.[11]

TABLE 11 *Answers Publications Monthly Account — December 1897*

	£	s	d
Answers a/c	112	16	5
Boys Friend	9	1	4
Chips	43	9	0
Comic Cuts	28	19	4
Forget-me-not	44	10	3
Home Chat	59	14	5
Home Companion	10	9	10
Home Sweet Home	30	5	6
Wonder a/c	27	9	8
Belfast a/c	87	10	8
	454	6	5

The account for all the *Answers* publications in 1897 amounted to a total of some £10,000 on a news turnover of around £90,000. *Answers*, or to give it its full title, *Answers to correspondents on every subject under the sun*

11 No circulation figures for the Irish market are extant.

— was first published in June 1888 with an initial capital of £1,750 in part provided by Alfred Harmsworth and in part by W.F.D. Carr, son of the rector of Whitechurch, Rathfarnham, out of a legacy. Returning to Dublin in 1892, Carr became the sole agent in Ireland for all Harmsworth publications. Harmsworth was a loyal personal friend of Carr's, and he ensured that the Harmsworth publications should be available one day earlier in Dublin than in London. This effectively gave Carr and his Dublin '*Answers* Office', which later became Carr & McKay, a monopoly of the Irish market. Eason's drew their requirements of Harmsworth publications and later of Amalgamated Press publications for the Dublin house from Carr. Harmsworth's wishes were respected beyond his own death in 1922, and it was only with the death of W.F.D. Carr's partner, McKay, in 1931 that this privilege of the Dublin office ceased. Eason's then began to order these publications directly from London.

Irish journals could compete even less effectively in this popular market and by the 1890s in a rising amount of weekly publications handled by the firm the proportion of Irish material was falling rapidly. As daily newspaper sales were generally static, and in the absence of any successful Irish ventures into the field of periodicals (outside local weeklies) the upsurge in periodical wholesaling between 1878 and 1888 signified a massive increase in the proportion of English publications handled. As far as can be judged, they were increasingly in the area of entertainment and light reading as opposed to news, and many were illustrated. These were both fields in which the economies of scale worked against the would-be publisher from a small market. A wide range of reading material is recorded in Joyce's account of 16 June 1904 in *Ulysses* which affords an interesting perspective of the news and periodical literature circulating in Bloom's milieu. The womanfolk in Joyce's novel seem to have been conversant with *Lloyd's Weekly News* and *Pearson's Weekly* as well as reading the *Lady's Pictorial* and the *Gentlewoman*. Bloom himself read an odd issue of *Titbits* on 16 June, and had a picture of a Nymph clipped from *Photo Bits* over his bed.[12]

BOOKS

Movements in book sales, which category included monthly and quarterly magazines, can only be surmised for the 1860s from the purchases from the house of Longman, which show a consistent pattern of growth from

12 I am indebted to Professor R.B. Kershner of the University of Florida, Guinesville, Florida, for details of news and periodicals in *Ulysses*.

1865 onwards. By 1872, the first year for which sales figures for the wholesale book department survive, the expansion had been such that the department had in that year by far the largest turnover in the Dublin house — however that turnover was not to be exceeded for the rest of the century.

The expansion of the book business can also be measured by its impact on the only other significant Dublin wholesaling house — McGlashan & Gill. The two sons of Henry Gill approached Eason in 1868 about the sale of the business to W.H. Smith's, because, as Eason reported to Smith in London 'as we are more active, much of the general business which used to come to them has been diverted to us, and though at present there is a profit, yet it is not adequate to the capital employed or the risks run.' If the outlook for Gill did not look promising, neither did the book business of W.H. Smith's prove expansive. It failed to hold the momentum that it had temporarily acquired in the late 1860s, despite a captive market in the expanded network of bookstalls. Relatively, the country trade if anything did even worse than the city trade. Sales in the country fell sharply in volume (from £16,794 in 1871/2 to a nadir of £10,191 in 1886/7) whereas the (smaller) Dublin sales were more buoyant. The wholesale book business suffered from competition from London publishers through the mails. This was described in a memorandum which had been prepared in the 1860s to support the case for low railway carriage rates for books, as a 'prime cause in the failure of booksellers throughout the country as well as in Dublin.'

> Gentlemen in ordering books for most of the country parts of Ireland can obtain them from London in 48 hours from the publishers, or from London booksellers; and these postal facilities for the supply of books are now largely used. It is within my knowledge that the London book and publishing houses constantly send to orders, books, reviews, magazines etc. to all parts of this country. . . .

The decline in country sales, moreover, took place despite the support that the firm's own commercial travellers offered in canvassing for business. If book sales through the bookstalls, running at £8,000 in retail prices in the 1890s, are excluded, the small scale of wholesale book sales, especially in the later years of thriving bookstall sales, is particularly evident. Travellers' journeys achieved only £2,000 in sales of books. Part of the problem of course lay in the fact that country booksellers were few. In Dublin itself, the comparatively low sales reflect the precarious state of bookselling in Dublin, because of the ease with which the Dublin reader could order books directly from London. When a booksellers' trade association was formed at the end of the century, one of the striking features was the comparatively small numbers of booksellers in relation to the size and wealth of the city. The disappointing fortunes of W.H. Smiths' Dublin business in books contrast quite strongly with those of the stationery trade, which expanded steadily over the years, and always displayed an impressive buoyancy when business conditions were good.

Detailed figures which survive from the years 1878 to 1892 throw a little further light on sales by the book department. These figures show separately cash sales and transfers to the Belfast house as well as wholesale trade, and also make it possible to distinguish from 1878 onwards between quarterly and monthly magazine sales and books. Wholesale book sales from the 'country day book' and 'town day book' figures show that the static overall turnover figures of the book department between 1878 and 1892 masked a continuing decline in book sales as opposed to magazine sales. In 1878 town and country magazine sales were only a half of sales recorded in country and town day books. By 1892 they amounted to two-thirds of the total figures in the day books. This reflected what was taking place in London. Fred Kingdon, head of W.H. Smith's book department in London, in commenting to Eason in 1893 on the increase in sales, noted it as 'a progressive one for four years, largely due I suppose to the popularity of the new magazines.'

In the 1870s and first half of the 1880s Murray's was the most significant publishing house for the book department followed by Routledge, with Chatto & Windus rising rapidly in importance. Sales of books from the Religious Tract Society rose steadily in importance and by 1883/4 were second to Murray's. Duffy was the only Irish house which featured in sales, with a figure of around £300 in the early 1870s. Sales numbers of Irish books at the time of Eason's purchase of the company in 1886 may be glimpsed in a note of sale in April 1886 of books by James Murphy of the *Irish Fireside*. His *Hugh Roach*, supplied by Duffys, sold 85 copies, his *Forge of Clohogue* 338 copies, and *House on the Rath* 507 copies.

WHOLESALE STATIONERY

Stationery provided ample opportunity for wholesaling. The wide range of items gave the wholesaler on the spot an advantage over the wholesaler at a distance, since he was able to display stock at his own showrooms, and to take samples to the country by means of commercial travellers. In consequence Smith's and later Eason's were not only able to build up a trade, but to do so quickly and to hold on to it successfully. They came to be the most prominent stationer in Ireland. Investment in commercial travelling and showrooms meant that the numerous local competitors did not represent a serious challenge, and the business grew steadily. On the other hand manufacturers of stationery, greeting cards and view cards, as well as of gifts and toys were always ready to supply the retail trade directly if the orders were of a reasonable size. In general they did not hesitate to compete with local Irish wholesalers either directly or through their Irish selling agents. Naturally this happened more often in Dublin and the larger towns than in the country.

1870 is the reputed first year of operation of the stationery business, and while the starting date can not be fixed precisely, the firm's commercial travelling, which before that date was small and exclusively in books, expanded rapidly thereafter.[13] Travel was usually by train and samples were carried in large cases or 'skips'. Mr Wilson, the first traveller, made three journeys during the year 1870 — spring, summer and winter — and the winter journey was later supplemented by canvassing by a second traveller. A journey consisted of a complete round of the salesman's territory. This usually entailed a return to Dublin each Saturday, but at times involved absences from home of two or three weeks at a time. In all, orders worth £2,329 were acquired in 1870. The 44 days of travelling in 1868 had brought in orders (for books) worth £1,421. In 1871 Wilson's orders amounted to £3,675, from 72 days of travelling. These orders included books and stationery. Total sales for stationery alone in the year were £4,516.

In 1872 travelling was increased to 123 days and stationery orders on their own amounted to £1,727 out of total sales of £7,536. By 1876 when stationery sales were at a peak of £14,664, travellers' orders amounted to £5,701. Journey orders thus contributed a very high proportion of business, and were indirectly responsible for a much higher proportion, as the contacts made by travellers and the samples they displayed frequently led to repeat orders in the intervals between visits. Charles Eason explained this to Smith in February 1872: 'The record only gives the actual orders given to the traveller. The country orders from places only once visited have increased greatly.'

Christmas cards were an important special item: they were the only product in the entire range of stationery to be itemised separately, and a detailed run of gross sales figures survives from 1878. The travellers'

13 Some dealings by Eason's in stationery may go back as far as 1865 (see p. 32). See also p. 63 for details of the departmental structure before 1870.

visits were of vital importance, as customers liked to base their orders on samples. Total sales of Christmas cards to all outlets usually amounted to around £2,000. Journey orders accounted for two-thirds. The autumn journeys were divided into the 'Christmas card journey' which took place in July-August, and the winter journey which took place in November.

Unlike any other department the stationery department's activities and success depended heavily on travelling. The 1870 journeys were limited, and the summary returns for both 1871 and 1872 list various towns visited for the first time. In February 1872 Charles Eason was able to report to Smith that 'the travelling particulars will show you the extent to which we are now covering the country. This last season we went to about 25 new towns to which if we had not had the stationery we could not have gone.' In the early years, book orders were larger than stationery orders; but for the travellers, and their sales of stationery the country sales of books would have been still more precarious.

Wilson continued to operate in the south and west until 1890. A second traveller, Connolly, was recruited in 1873; for the next five years the country was shared between the two. In the course of 1878 Connolly was replaced by two travellers, Allen and John Toms. Allen travelled the north and west of the country, Toms did the English journeys, mainly to sell the firm's catholic prayerbooks, and from 1891 to 1924 the south. A year's work meant three to four months on the road, usually divided into four journeys, travelling by train to towns on the railway and by side-car to other towns from the nearest railhead. In the bigger centres, the traveller spent two or more days canvassing orders on each visit. The English journeys were not important in the overall total, but two visits were made by a traveller to England each year. In 1881, for instance, Wilson visited five British centres, obtaining orders worth £1,057. Of this, the stationery orders were worth £34 and the remainder consisted of catholic prayerbooks. The work of the travellers was supplemented by sales through the showroom, and a division between town and country showroom in accounts for the 1890s suggests some emphasis on meeting the requirements of the country trade. Although the total turnover of stationery increased, the number of days on the road seems to have fallen in the course of the 1880s. As the stationery trade became more developed, the time of the travellers was directed less towards promoting sales and more towards taking orders in what was now a well-developed business. The importance of the firm's travellers is reflected in the fact that in the early years they were among the highest paid employees.

Stationery sales were very sensitive to the state of the economy. They doubled between 1871/2 and 1876/7 to reach £14,939. They fell in 1877/8 and fell more sharply still in 1878/9 and 1879/80. They then recovered to a high level in 1883/4 before dropping again. By the year 1891/2 they had reached a new record figure of £15,527, and rose to £17,187 by 1898/9. They contrasted sharply with the dullness in book sales, and indeed in the following year 1899/1900 they exceeded total book sales for the first time. Thereafter they were increasingly more important than book sales.

The first clear breakdown of the disposal of stationery stocks is from the year 1892/3. Internal use — consumption within the firm, or sales through their own retail department and bookstalls — was quite important; accounting for £2,076 of total sales of £16,073. Of the balance, town sales accounted for £2,930, country sales for £3,984, journey orders for £2,208, card sales for £1,982 (of which almost half were canvassed by journey), cash sales £2,076, and commission sales (apparently all to England) accounted for £817. There is little information on the details of the items sold. Total purchases amounted to £12,185, of which plain stationery accounted for £6,859, and fancy goods and Christmas cards combined to £5,326. The total for plain stationery was made up of purchased stationery amounting to £5,674, and house-made stationery valued crudely at the wages paid in the factory, at £1,185. This underestimates the house-made component of total supplies. None of the fancy goods were house-made, and the importance of the Christmas card trade is shown by the fact that it accounted for almost one quarter of fancy goods purchases. Christmas cards came from a wide variety of sources, of which Guy of Cork was the only Irish house mentioned. German names seem almost as numerous as English. John Dickinson & Co supplied envelopes, cards and coloured papers.

RAILWAY ADVERTISING AND BOOKSTALLS

After 1870 the wholesale news turnover was much more important than the bookstalls and railway advertising receipts. Yet these two departments continued to receive much closer attention. The reason for this was twofold: the contracts for these activities represented the closest formal link between the railway companies and the firm, and were of mutual advantage, providing a close business association which made it easier to achieve understanding on carriage rates and timetables. A close supervision of the railway business was also essential because of the high rents payable for the contracts, and because of the periodic renegotiation of them, usually at five or seven year intervals.

The bookstalls were never regarded as part of the Retail side of the firm although the bulk of sales at them were retail sales. They were always regarded as part of the railway business, since they were supplied by rail, as the country news agents were. They also received supplies for local newsagents, although this was incidental and was not central to the running of the wholesale function of W.H. Smith & Son. Within the firm the bookstalls were regarded as a department in their own right. Parcels for newsagents were sent out to both suburban and country bookstalls, and collected by the newsagents. This arrangement reduced carriage costs. Newspapers were sent in large parcels, and split up at the bookstalls. In fact when rates had been negotiated with the companies, a minimum parcel size of 4lb was provided for. This was highly advantageous and helped to create or protect the effective monopoly of W.H. Smith's, who were the only ones whose business necessitated such large parcels.

The railway bookstall and advertising site business is by far the best documented part of the company's activities. This is partly because it was operated on the basis of detailed contracts with railway companies, and partly because it required a close knowledge to obtain results. It was also the only aspect of the business in which in the nineteenth century there was more than local competition. A Mrs Buckle had the contract for advertising on the Ulster railway before 1873, and operated three bookstalls. The loss of the Great Northern Railway (GNR) and the Belfast and Co. Down Railway contracts to Olley's in the 1890s, when Eason's were well established, illustrated the existence of competition still more dramatically.

The railway business grew slowly after the first years. Advertising orders showed real buoyancy only from the end of the 1860s. After a sharp rise between 1863 and 1864 they showed no marked rise until 1869. Bookstall revenue likewise was slow to grow during the 1860s. It had been £6,243 in 1860. In 1869 the revenue from the sixteen bookstalls continuously open through the second half of the decade was only £8,965, and seven bookstalls opened more recently added only £700 in 1868, and £1,385 in 1869. In fact a few of the original bookstalls seem to have closed, and others to have operated discontinuously. The spirit of caution engendered by the depression of the early 1860s was reflected in the failure to open any new bookstalls between 1862 and 1866. Most striking of all, the opening of bookstalls at railway stations as important as Waterford and Derry seems to have been deferred until 1866. (Derry was not actually operative until after 1869 and Belfast not until 1868.) It was almost certainly this slowness to spread into the north that provided the opportunity for

Mrs Buckle to develop a business on the Ulster Railway. Outside Dublin-Kingstown-Bray and the three military barrack centres of Newbridge, the Curragh and Fermoy, the only successfully established bookstalls in 1866 were Mallow, Cork, Killarney, Limerick Junction, Cahir and Drogheda.

Railway advertising orders rose from £2,273 in 1869 to £4,538 in 1875, and bookstall revenue which was £10,349 in 1869 rose to £20,915 in 1877. This rise was a product both of the very prosperous economic conditions of these years and of W.H. Smith's vigorous response to them, in extending its contracts and exercising them to the full by the opening of additional bookstalls. No less than eighteen bookstalls were opened between 1873 and 1877. Most of them were on new or extended lines. The signing of new contracts occasioned the growth of business on the Northern Counties line in and after 1869. Ballymena and Portrush bookstalls were both open in that year. The Midland Great Western Railway (MGWR) was a victim of the depression of the 1860s. The contract dates only from 1870, and three bookstalls were opened during 1870 and 1871. The opportunities on the Ulster Railway were exploited vigorously after 1873, when the contract was taken over from Mrs Buckle, as was the Belfast, Holywood and Bangor railway in 1877. The construction of the Dublin, Wicklow and Wexford Railway (DWWR) line proceeded slowly, offering little opportunity apart from railway advertising and bookstalls on the Dublin to Kingstown section. The slow extension of this line meant that in the late 1860s newspapers and magazines still arrived in Wexford after the transfer of parcels from the rails to the public car at Enniscorthy. The Westland Row bookstall, which had been held by a small contractor, was taken over — reluctantly — only in 1876.

In the course of the 1870s a national network of bookstalls emerged and a large number of new bookstalls were erected on lines covered by existing contracts. By 1887 there were forty-two bookstalls in all. The 1880s were a period of marked depression. Virtually no bookstalls were added after 1877 and by 1887 there were few if any additions. The network was curiously incomplete. Though Tralee had been opened by 1887, there was still no bookstall in Sligo, Galway or Wexford, and the bookstalls at intermediate stations were few outside the lines in the north-east. With renewed growth of business in the late 1880s some new bookstalls were opened. Thurles, Greystones, Cahirciveen, Kilkenny and Sligo were open before 1895, but they were classified in that year as among the 'least profitable' bookstalls. The last stage in the extension of the bookstall network did not come until after 1900.

Railway advertising orders fell from 1876 and a significant recovery was not evident before 1884. Bookstall revenue passed the 1877 level again only in the year ended December 1885. Thus recovery from the severe depression was evident only from the mid-1880s. But it gradually gathered pace and by 1899 the business had reached new heights. Advertising orders, which were £5,540 in 1883, jumped to £9,640 in 1885, and reached £12,739 by 1898/9. Bookstall revenue rose from £19,900 in 1884 to £31,287 in 1898/9.

A remarkable feature of the progress of the railway business was the depth of the depression in the late 1870s and early 1880s. Depression was evident in the business district around Belfast as early as 1874, as the international business recession hit the linen trade. The rest of the country was relatively immune at that stage, but as a result of falling agricultural prices a few years later, and of the disastrous harvest of 1879, depression became general. The land war, which began in 1879, reflected a wider economic malaise, and the 1880s opened in a deep sense of gloom and foreboding in town and country alike. The depression was most marked in railway advertising, and more on the northern lines than in the rest of the country. Advertising had been negligible in the north-east in 1870 but with the rapid exploitation of the new contracts, it accounted for roughly a third of orders in 1875. All the northern railway accounts were lower in 1876, and the Belfast difficulties became a constant refrain in correspondence. Charles Eason wrote to the Belfast and Northern Counties Railway in February 1877 that 'The long continued depression in business occasioned by leading failures in Belfast has told upon the spirit of traders, and they tell us they have no heart to speculate on advertising.' Many orders were cancelled, and those retained were frequently at a reduced price. Bad debts mounted.

On the southern lines, however, business was stable and Charles Eason displayed a much more sanguine opinion about their prospects, remarking to the Great Southern and Western Railway (GSWR) in February 1878, that 'We think that the causes producing this change are temporary, and in that view we are hopeful of the future.' The rent was increased in the renewal of the contract in 1878.

In contrast, in the north W. H. Smith's were able to hold out successfully for a lengthened period for the contract with the Northern Counties (due to expire in December 1879) and with the Belfast and Co.Down (due to expire in December 1881). At the end of 1881 W. H. Smith's replaced the existing contract with what seemed in the depressed condition of the trade to be a more advantageous contract for them —

a contract modelled on those in force in England in which rent was based on 50 per cent of advertising orders, and 5 per cent of bookstall receipts.[14] As time went by, this form of contract gradually became more general over the entire Irish railway system.

Advertising orders often involved multiple copies of the same message. As many as two hundred bills might be required, and in some cases also advertising at up to fifty English stations. Advertisements for Irish firms at English stations, arranged through the London office, produced a mere £210 in 1881, but revenue expanded from then to £2,139 by 1893 after a reduction in rates. An order from Wm. Russell & Co. of 5 Lower Sackville Street for three years from 1 October 1877 may serve as as example of costs: it provided for 95 advertisements for a total of £60. The invoice included the costs of printing bills, making frames and providing battens for them at stations, and the costs of fixing them. The railway companies provided free carriage for the advertising materials, and passes for the firm's workmen and inspectors in the execution of advertising work. In fact, the advertising frames required a good deal of attention. Stations were visited for this purpose two or three times a year. The inspector of railway advertising and a workman travelled the system regularly to adjust and repair the boards. As Charles Eason put it to a railway manager who was reluctant to agree to free travel for them in 1873: 'It has been more than ever shown to us that the success of railway advertising is dependent upon the improved condition of the boards, exhibits, repair of damaged frames, cleaning and repairing them, and we incur an expense of some £300 p.a. in doing this over the whole Irish lines.'

It was therefore quite tempting to put the boards in waiting rooms, especially where there was a shortage of suitable locations elsewhere on the station platforms. Their removal had been requested by the GSWR in 1875, and W.H. Smith's had agreed. But the matter was still a live issue three years later. An extensive correspondence arose between the company and W.H. Smith's in 1878 as to whether advertisements within waiting rooms came within the terms of the contract or not. Bills had been put up in the waiting rooms at no less than twenty-three stations, ranging from one to two bills in some stations, to as many as thirty-two. In 1881 Westland Row station was enlarged with large walled panels which were rented to W.H. Smith's for half the advertising revenue of the panels, and the condition that 'No more than one advertising panel is to be in

14 Contracts also stipulated a minimum size of payment.

each wall panel.' W.H. Smith's maintained their own workshop for their railway work. In many cases however advertisers supplied their own advertisements. The advertising revenue as calculated for payments to the companies was on a net basis i.e. net of outlay on printing bills and making frames.

The nature of railway advertising revenue seems to have changed a good deal over the years. In the 1870s it was much more commercial and industrial than later. Until 1874 revenue from the GSWR was larger than the DWWR, and when orders were at their peak in 1875 the orders from the three northern companies which were shortly to be amalgamated into the GNR were larger than from either the GSWR or the DWWR. By 1881, however, advertising revenue from the DWWR line exceeded that of any other company, and it thereafter maintained that position. About this time there was a shift to more sophisticated advertising directed towards the comfortable middle classes, and frequently advertising proprietary brands. The two southern Dublin lines offered the only concentrated market for this advertising in Ireland. By 1883 to 1885, one of the rare periods for which an outline of the details survive, the importance of Dublin business houses was strikingly evident. Gilbey's, Bewley's, Elvery's, Arnott's Prescott's, McBirney's, Brooke Tyrrell, Hamilton Long & Co., Clery & Co., and Jacob's had become customers. Hotels were of course important in an age when travel for pleasure was increasing among the leisured middle classes. In 1884 some fifty advertisements for Cruise's hotel were provided in colour, and in August 1885 the photographer, William Lawrence, was paid £3 13s for photographing hotels in Wicklow and Rathdrum. By this time many of the advertisements were made in enamelled iron, durable as well as attractive. In fact advertising revenue which had grown in the second half of the 1880s was very buoyant in the 1890s. It actually rose in spite of the loss of the GNR and Belfast and Co. Down contracts in 1891/2. On the Belfast and Northern Counties, and the Waterford, Limerick and Western, it doubled between 1892/3 and 1898/9, and increased by a half on the GSWR, DWWR and MGWR in the same period.

Advertising revenue came largely from the two suburban lines of the DWWR as far as Bray. On the other hand, the GSWR always provided the largest bookstall income. Indeed between them, the GSWR and the DWWR provided fairly consistently half or more than half of total bookstall revenue. The GNR, which had the largest, and then the second largest advertising revenue, was only third in bookstall sales. The contrast reflects the relative importance of the reading public, resident or travelling, at the bookstalls in Dublin, whereas advertising revenue was less concentrated. While intended to cater for railway travellers, the bookstalls in fact depended to a large extent on suburban travellers and residents in their vicinity. In 1886/7 Westland Row, which catered largely for suburban traffic, had easily the largest receipts of any on the system, twice those of the next largest station which was Bray. Bray had a substantial local news delivery. In 1883 some four boys delivered almost 500 papers daily from the stall. These two stations along with Kingstown accounted for £5,486 of the total receipts of £5,559 on the DWWR.

The other two Dublin terminals (Broadstone, £1,046 and Kingsbridge, £1,204) accounted only for £2,250. Nevertheless, Broadstone contributed more than half the total receipts of the MGWR, while Kingsbridge on the more prosperous GSWR provided less than a quarter of the total on that line. Kingsbridge, Broadstone and Amiens Street, the Dublin termini of the three largest rail networks, sold £3,294 worth between them. The three Belfast termini turned over £2,668, and the Co. Down line, the most distinctively suburban of the three lines had the largest receipts in Belfast. The Dublin area stations of the DWWR together with the Dublin and Belfast terminals of other lines provided a receipt of £11,448 or almost 50 per cent of the total bookstall receipts.

The reading public was concentrated in the larger centres, and in Dublin, more than in Belfast. Bookstalls on the DWWR from Westland Row to Bray accounted for a quarter of the receipts in the entire country. Sales at provincial bookstalls, with the exception of the few really busy junctions and country railheads, were small. Low sales outside Dublin and Belfast account for instances of temporary or more prolonged closure, and for a marked reluctance throughout the 1880s to open new bookstalls. As late as 1895, when receipts were much more buoyant than eight years previously, there were fifteen bookstalls with annual receipts of less than £344. In 1887 there had been twenty-two in that category.

TOWARDS A NATIONWIDE MARKET

Despite the widespread network, the market which the firm supplied was still heavily concentrated on the Dublin area, and on the literate middle class, professional and clerical, in the metropolis. The business had of course changed significantly over the preceding forty years, and the firm was a nationwide business in a way that it had not been at the earlier date. But the nationwide market was still a thin one, a characteristic which led to the more rapid progression of weekly than of daily news business.

The relatively expensive — 4d or 5d a copy — illustrated periodicals provided the main thrust of growth in this market, which emphasises once again how restricted the market was, both socially and geographically, for news at this period. The concentration of the market around Dublin put an effective limit on the geographical penetration by Eason's, as W.H. Smith's had become in 1886. Caution was the keyword in the expansion of the firm even in the 1880s, and but for its sales of articles such as catholic prayerbooks and stationery, in which it had the key role in the country, the impact of the firm would have scarcely reached the smaller centres.

In the absence of a mass-market for newspapers and periodicals, the bookstalls and the advertising business were the pivot on which the business of the firm hinged, except in the rich, literate metropolitan district of Dublin and its suburbs. The railway contracts were also profitable, especially in advertising, in which overheads were low, and which became increasingly the main support of the firm's profitability. In fact, because of the extra overheads resulting from expansion, profits had proved remarkably static after the 1880s. Certainly the strong growth of profits in the 1870s was not to be repeated again despite a much larger volume of business. Net profits before interest payments grew steadily over the 1860s, reaching around £3,000 at the end of the decade. Between 1857 and 1873 they averaged £2,884. In the next ten years (1874 to 1883) they averaged £5,283. In 1876 they reached £5,253 and in 1882/3 they reached £6,870. Not only was this a very satisfactory return, but as some of the capital had been paid off, in the second period the return on capital actually rose from 26 per cent to 40 per cent.

In the 1880s the rising trend stopped and profits fell. In 1883/4 profits were down to £5,768 and in 1887/8 they were £6,166. This was however a still healthy 40 per cent return on capital. In 1902/3, on a much larger turnover, the profits were still only £7,500. Moreover, by 1906, the capital in the business, which was down to £17,000 in 1883 and £15,000 in 1886, was around £26,600, so that the rising return on capital of the 1860s and 1870s had been replaced by a falling return. This explains the interest later in the century in railway advertising, a relatively minor area in the 1870s, but which by 1900 contributed half of the net profits.

The facade of expansion and market penetration had concealed the rising overheads and, outside the railway advertising business in the 1890s, diminishing rates of profit. The problem for wholesale news distribution and for bookstalls was the low population density outside Dublin and Belfast. This meant that the effort to cater for expanding readership inevitably reduced overall profits. Every new customer cost relatively more to reach. In the depressed early 1880s profits held up well, whereas in the late 1880s as a proportion of turnover they fell as the wholesale distribution network and bookstall numbers began to grow again.

As the carriage accounts show, the country business up to the mid-1880s was very much concentrated on the GSWR, the Belfast district and the suburban reaches of the DWWR. It was only in the 1890s that the firm began to extend seriously to the less profitable regions. The firm then displayed the paradox of assured dominance of the market, while becoming distinctly less profitable. Some of the decline in return on investment was to be explained by changes in railway advertising after 1901, but changes in that department cannot be isolated from the fact that the expansion in the rest of the house was failing to generate a commensurate rate of return.

Chapter 6 Employer and Employees

SMITH'S ATTENTION TO THE IRISH BUSINESS remained close after Charles Eason's arrival, and he was subsequently to visit Dublin often.[1] For the next seven years, until mid-1863, he came to Ireland at least twice a year. These visits and correspondence with the Dublin house took a significant share of his time. In September 1861 Smith had written to his wife, that, while disliking these enforced absences from London, 'it is necessary that I should be over here at intervals not more than 3 or 4 months apart — and so we must make up our minds to it.' As far as can be judged there was only a single visit in each of the years 1863, 1864 and 1865. This reflected Smith's growing external interests, which led to a decline in his active management of the business at large. The first partnership deed between himself and William Lethbridge was signed in June 1864, and Smith's first, unsuccessful, attempt to enter Parliament took place in 1865.

SMITH AND EASON: AN ANGLO-IRISH RELATIONSHIP

At the beginning Charles Eason, though two years older than Smith, was much less experienced, and admitted this himself in relation to negotiations with the railway traffic managers as late as March 1861. Smith's view of Eason in a letter to his wife in November 1859 was that he was 'faithful and zealous as ever, and all that is necessary is a little direction which my presence here enables me to give.... I feel it my duty to him and to others that I should come here from time to time so long

1 Copies of letters to Smith, and originals and copies of letters from Smith survive in Dublin. In the Hambleden papers in W.H. Smith's, London, are the letters to W.H. Smith's wife (series A) and his sister Gussie (series B) and from Lady Crosbie as well as Smith's surviving letters to his partner Lethbridge. Fewer of Lethbridge's letters to Smith survive: those that do are in the series D.D.

as I am the head.' In those days relations between the two men were easy, and at times almost at the level of equals. Eason sometimes enlarged in his letters on religious matters, in one instance in 1861 concluding that 'I scarcely intended to write thus, but in the calm of the evening when all are gone to rest, I have been led on.' Smith, who had been married in April 1858, wrote to Eason in the same month that 'when I tell you I believe I have as good a wife as you have, you will know how happy I am.' Nor was this familiarity affected at this time.

More than three years later, in the course of a visit to Dublin in September 1861, Smith wrote to his wife that he had dined at the Easons, adding that it gave pleasure to both of the Easons. However, as time went by, Smith found these visits more tedious, and in November 1865 he complained to his wife that 'I have the "duty" visit to Mr. & Mrs. Eason to pay directly which I do not like quite so well. It is a bore to have to go out, but I must remember they think much of it.' And the unkind tone of his subsequent letter is ample confirmation that he had indeed found the occasion tedious.

Smith laid emphasis on delegation, and the emerging pattern in Dublin reflected to some extent his preparedness to leave management in other hands, as soon as he became confident both that the initial problems were overcome, and the local management was reliable. He had already hinted as much to Eason as early as April 1858: 'I do not care much that men in your position carry out every detail of my own schemes, in fact I had rather they had [ ] and a strong measure of individuality.' Moreover, despite the fact that after the late 1850s Smith, at least initially, expressed reluctance about every measure of expansion, apart from the library book lending scheme at the outset of the 1860s, in the last analysis he was always prepared to go along with Charles Eason's proposals.

There was a marked difference of personality and outlook between Smith and Eason which was bound to become accentuated as their paths diverged. Smith was relaxed towards the detail of business, leaving this to others, and concentrated in the grand manner on the large issues, rather than on the lesser problems. In February 1862 he upbraided Eason for his worrying disposition, observing in a lofty tone that 'if I permitted myself to give way when similar occurrences befell the staff on this side, what would be my condition, with many times the number of hands, and a proportionate number of casualties to provide for and guard against'. Charles Eason on the other hand was a tense, worrying man, concerned not only about business, but about his own health. The state of his health came up time and time again in his correspondence, and expressions of sympathy with him on health grounds are almost a refrain in the surviving correspondence. The first references to colds came twice in letters to his mother in 1855. He was ill again in 1861, and health became a constant topic in correspondence. He complained of a cold and swollen throat in February 1872, and most of his complaints came in winter months. In March 1892, his old friend William Fred Kingdon of W. H. Smith's book division in London noted 'with much regret how very trying you have found the winter of the last five months.' Other complaints sometimes took over: 'I hope your wrist is now quite strong', Lethbridge responded to a letter of 1882. From 1884 onwards gout seems to have been added to his complaints. Eason may indeed have had real health problems, but what is striking to the reader is how often the issue obtrudes in the correspondence, suggesting an anxious or hypochondriac temperament.

There undoubtedly was a pronounced element of anxiety in Charles Eason's personality. In February 1862, in response to a woeful list of staff problems in the Dublin house, Smith observed that 'I am sorry you have had such a long list of troubles to tell, I cannot however look upon them as cause of personal depression or overwhelming anxiety on your part...'. A year later he commented that 'you have from time to time shown that you felt the pressure of business severely as it is...'. In the same year he advised Eason to take a day off in the middle of the week on some occasions, or to add a Monday holiday to Sunday rest, 'repeated once or twice'. Eason's holiday in 1884 and visit to North America were undertaken with the strong encouragement of Lethbridge and Smith. His tension rings through the lines of his letter of 21 March 1864, which reports on Ferguson's absconding from the railway advertising department, opening with the cry of anguish that 'I scarcely know how to take my pen in hand to tell you...'. No doubt some of the anguish derived from the fact that Ferguson had gone to America with Eason's permisssion, ostensibly to visit his dying mother.[2]

Eason's personality was very different from that of his serene and self-assured employer. Given such a difference of temperament, even without taking into account Smith's wide interests outside the business, it is easy to see how Charles Eason could seem almost comical to his detached and cold employer. Through the correspondence and the regular visits to Dublin, Smith quickly became familiar with this anxious side of Eason's character. Others who worked with Eason as subordinates remembered

2 Wilson *First with the News* p. 145

how the burden of detail preyed on him, and left him permanently irritable. Smith, who was above him, and was not subject to such tensions, could only see these characteristics in a comic light. In December 1858 in the course of one of his visits, Smith wrote to his wife that 'I am very pleased with Eason, the head here. He is an odd little fellow, and you would laugh at him, I am afraid, if my eyes caught yours while he was in the room, but he is thoroughly honest, true and good.' It is quite clear that the estimation that Smith made of Eason's personality led him in later years to give insufficient consideration to Eason's views and hence to misunderstand some of the issues which came up between Eason and Smith in the 1880s. As time went on, their paths diverged increasingly. Politically and religiously they had less and less in common.

From the start, Smith had much wider interests than Eason. Like Eason, he had a dissenter background, but he was himself an Anglican, and had reluctantly given up the idea of taking Anglican orders only at the wish of his father. His Irish circle of acquaintances was wider than Eason's, and indeed wider than one would have expected of a single-minded businessman. His closest Irish friends were Sir William and Lady Crosbie, though it is not clear how he originally made their acquaintance. In the 1850s they were living in Bray. Even as early as 1850 or 1851 letters from Sir William Crosbie show a warm bantering familiarity and an expectation of visits at short notice, 'as we know that your movements are always sudden, to keep the good folks at Eden Quay on the *qui vive*' (February 1851). What little property remained to them was in chancery, and after her husband's death, Lady Crosbie was assisted financially by Smith on repeated occasions. On his Irish visits he almost invariably visited Bray. Although no lover of duty visits and a reluctant visitor to the Easons' home after the first years, he spent three hours with Lady Crosbie when he called unannounced in November 1865, and wrote to his wife that 'it does me good to hear of such trouble as she can tell of, and yet see so much happiness through it all.' The Crosbies seem to have had similar religious views to Smith, and this may have encouraged the friendship. Smith had spent holidays in Ireland with his mother and sisters in 1848 and 1849, and it is possible that he may have made the acquaintance of the Crosbies in Kerry at that time. Some undated letters, probably at the outset of the 1850s, from a friend of Smith's, William Silver, hint at acquaintances in the south-west, and at the prospect of a visit by Smith to County Cork, no doubt as an extension of a visit to Dublin.

The Crosbies were in too straitened circumstances themselves to provide an entree to influential circles. However, they had been friends of Lord Cloncurry, and Lady Crosbie was related to the Earl of Milltown. Through the Crosbies, Smith made the acquaintance of Dr Maunsell, one of the Dublin newspaper proprietors. The Crosbie friendship was a warm, lasting one, but its wider significance was that Smith's first introduction to Ireland was through a beleaguered unionist circle in the south-west and in the Crosbies' modest circumstances in Bray. William Silver had warmly exhorted Smith to visit the Rev. J.R. Cotter at the rectory in Donoghmore, near Coachford in Co. Cork, and the Cotters in turn were said to be 'most anxious to see you'.[3] Whether in fact Smith did visit them is not clear, but it is likely that his views of Ireland must have been coloured by this circle and its outlook. William Silver had told him that 'you will there see what is working to regenerate that priest-ridden people — the excellent schools and the famine-made orphan refuge.... I write my friend of this post, in case you can visit him in that hotbed of popery (to give you an idea, hand grenades are always ready for use, besides muskets etc.).'[4] Lady Crosbie's views were quite odd, even if the only coherent expression of them was at an advanced age in 1874: 'Ireland is in a bad state — but Popery is the sole cause. We have a fine climate, a fine soil, most of all that she requires for life but the Jesuits blight everything....'

Smith made no acquaintances at all in more liberal Irish circles. When he became a prominent Tory politician, the early impressions of Ireland he had acquired were reinforced by those of a wide circle of politically well-found Irish landowners who spent part of the year in London, and moved in the higher reaches of the Tory party. The King-Harmans, the Abercorns, Lord Waterford, and others were among those who formed his London social circle. But his Irish circle had begun to widen even before he became a politician. There is a fleeting reference in a letter in 1864 which would make no sense unless both Smith and his wife were already acquainted with the Guinnesses.

Smith's political interests corresponded to the widening circle he cultivated, and were evident from an early date. He prided himself apparently on the confidential character of his information. As early as 1853 William Crosbie thanked Smith 'for the explanation of the late fracas in the cabinet — I will of course keep this to myself.' Though he was not seriously interested in Irish issues, we find in 1861 that Smith had studied the Maynooth question, a topic of interest to any aspiring politician,

3 W. H. Smith, London, N 17. William Silver, no date.
4 ibid, N 16. William Silver, no date.

because its provision of public funds for denominational education made it relevant to the thorny question of church-state relations in education in England. The partnership in 1864 with his old school friend, William Lethbridge, who had been invited into the business in 1862, is a reflection of Smith's growing involvement outside the business. He was elected to Parliament at his second attempt in 1868, as Conservative member for the borough of Westminster. His involvement in the Irish business slipped into the background when he was appointed Secretary of the Treasury in the Disraeli administration of 1874. His visit to the Dublin house in 1873 was the last for a decade, unless he happened to visit the house (which is not clear) in the course of a short official visit in 1875. The perfunctory nature of his relationship with Charles Eason at this time is brought out in a short letter from Smith to Eason in August 1877, apologising for not being able to see him and a 'Mr Berks' — no doubt one of Eason's Birks relations — when they called at the House, as he was 'more than usually driven on that evening, and was therefore, totally unable to look after you.'

In his cruise off the Irish coast in 1881, Smith did not touch Dublin, and his visit in April 1882 was so politically oriented that it does not seem to have left time at all for visiting the Dublin house. Not until October 1883, when he dallied a morning in the Dublin house on his way back to England after spending ten days with the King-Harmans at Rockingham, did Smith appear again in Abbey Street. He does not appear to have visited it during his two-day visit in January 1884, to address a public meeting, at which he made his speech opposing the extension of the suffrage, which would in his view enfranchise the occupiers of 425,140 mud cabins 'so that if the mud cabins are enfranchised, the mud cabins will be the majority of the electorate of Ireland ... and not only so, but in many counties the majority of the electors will be of that class which are perfectly illiterate.' Unless he did visit the house in 1875, ten years had lapsed before his next visit. In other words, there had been no occasion since 1873 on which the business itself had drawn him to Dublin.

In the day to day running of the business and in his visits to London, Eason's regular contacts after 1868 were with Lethbridge. But Lethbridge also failed to visit the Dublin house from 1873 onwards. The conclusion is inescapable. It was not simply Smith's political commitments which account for the increasingly casual relationship between London and the Dublin house, but a view that the Irish business was peripheral to the central interests of the house. Smith's reluctance to assume new Irish commitments was evident even in the early 1860s, well before he had achieved a seat in Parliament, let alone political office. While there is no explicit evidence to support the view, one plausible explanation of the situation, which accords with Smith's consistency in behaviour and outlook, is that his interest in Ireland was simply to secure newspaper distribution. As long as that was at stake, the Irish business merited his closest attention. The emergence of other channels of newspaper distribution in Ireland, served by London rivals, would have impaired the dominant position within newspaper distribution which he was building up in the 1850s. Once that object was achieved Dublin had served its purpose.

During the 1850s Smith was still in the process of establishing himself as the largest news distributor in London, and the fact that Clayton's, a London rival, had a base in Dublin, gave the Dublin market a real significance, but only as far as news was concerned. While no pains had been too great, in terms of attention and visits, as long as the newspaper business was being established in Dublin, every other proposal which came up, even the wholesaling of books which was a standard feature of the business in Britain, was greeted with expressions of reluctance on his part. The evidence leaves no doubt that Smith was personally uninterested in the expansion of the Irish business in the 1860s. Even more positively, his attitude in the early 1860s was against further direct investment in the Dublin business, and he was seeking repayment of some of the existing capital in the Dublin house. This expectation of reduced investment is somewhat surprising as the Irish business was in the crucial phase of consolidation in these years, both because they were years of recovery from the depression of 1859-61, and because the railway network was still expanding. Even as early as April 1858 Smith had observed to Eason that 'some rest in acquisition is frequently necessary.' In May 1863 he was once again expressing a preference for 'natural and gradual growth ... rather than jumping into additional new business.' In other words, the rapid expansion of the Irish business over the 1860s and 1870s was neither envisaged by Smith, nor desired by him. Nor would Smith have been inconsistent in approaching the Irish business in this way. As early as 1856, he wrote to Charles Eason (on 20 October): 'Ireland ruins Englishmen by first luring them into a path a little off the old road for the sake of expediency, and although for a time the two paths seem to run side by side, and almost into one another, a short interval discloses how widely they have diverged, and the man is lost.'

Only the restored prosperity of the English business after the early 1860s, which ended the cash restraints that Smith had experienced at that time and eliminated the need for an early return on the Dublin investment, prevented Smith from translating policy into practice. The very high regard in which Smith held Charles Eason's business abilities, often reiterated in letters from Dublin to his wife, may also have induced him to refrain from active steps to halt the growth of the Dublin house. Although the business in Dublin continued to expand, it was with tacit and somewhat reluctant approval rather than with explicit encouragement. The expansion was never part of a grand view of Smith and Lethbridge for the business of W.H. Smith & Son as a whole. Consequently Smith and his Dublin manager had an entirely different concept of their relationship, and Eason's proposal of a partnership, which may have been raised as early as the 1860s, was wholly foreign to Smith's thinking.

The fact that Lethbridge, on whom the routine management of the business in Britain devolved after 1864, rarely visited Dublin is another instance of the peripheral character of the Dublin business. On his accession to full partnership, Lethbridge accompanied Smith to Dublin in November 1864, and Smith praised him in a letter to his wife: 'Lethbridge seems to like his work, for he really gives time and attention to it with more interest and acuteness than I can show.' Lethbridge visited Dublin again in 1873, but there is no evidence that he was there again until the general inspection which Eason forced on London in 1884. Dublin was of course only a small part of a growing empire: in 1857 the Irish house had 23 staff, the English 350, and by the mid 1880s the Dublin staff only amounted to some 175 compared with 4,000 in Britain.

The interests of the partners have to be seen in the perspective of the business of W.H. Smith's as a whole, and at the same time in the perspective of their trust in Eason's probity and dedication, which created an aura of confidence around the Dublin house. When problems arose in Liverpool and Manchester in 1872, John White, who was established in London as the powerful head of the News Department, was despatched to look after them. Nevertheless, it was a serious fault to permit the links between London and the branch in Dublin to become so tenuous, and much of the responsibility for the situation rested with Lethbridge. The fact that he accompanied Smith to Dublin in 1864 seems to indicate what was envisaged as future practice, but Lethbridge, who was a bachelor and something of an hypochondriac, seems to have displayed a marked lack of readiness to throw himself into the work without reserve or on the other hand to delegate. Little of his correspondence survives to provide detailed evidence. In 1886, at his own request, he ceased to be the managing partner, and Charles Awdry, the Winchester and New College sportsman who had been his assistant since 1870, took over. Lethbridge's deficiency would not have been so serious, had he been more willing to delegate: his concept of a highly paid private secretary to the partners exemplifies this unwillingness. He wanted, as he wrote in 1895, 'some one who can write short-hand and hold his tongue'.[5] His whole idea, in one of the most extensive businesses in Britain, was to confine all decision-making to two or three partners, and in 1888 he expressed himself against the concept of finding partners from among the staff.[6] When White was about to retire, Lethbridge wanted to reduce the powers of his successor, and to direct 'all powers other than routine' into the partners' hands. This was of course unrealistic, and also in marked contrast to Smith's much sounder outlook three decades earlier, when he personally managed a much smaller business.

The relationship between Smith and Eason, and the differing perceptions of the business in Dublin and in London, cannot be fully appreciated without examining the capital structure of the Dublin house and the financial relations between London and Dublin. In 1856, because of the mismanagement of the house under Barker, the Dublin working capital had been impossibly large. The balance was gradually reduced; the capital seems to have been then set at around £4,000, shortly afterwards raised to £6,000. In a letter to Eason in 1872, Smith noted that 'in reckoning the profits of the business prior to 1862 you deducted £200 as interest.' In 1862 the interest payment to London was raised from £200 to £325. In the years after 1862, after interest on the capital sum of £6,000 had been provided for, profits were retained in the Dublin house. They were not capitalised, so that the question of paying interest on additional funds left in the Dublin house did not arise. The total investment in the Dublin house amounted to £23,000 by 1873. When Smith expressed dissatisfaction at the situation in January 1873, Eason responded: 'May I not urge that to your advantage your investment of £6,000 as it was in 1860 (sic) had drawn interest.' In 1872 Smith proposed that London should draw the profits in future, and that the accumulated profits in the Dublin house should be capitalised gradually. Eason suggested in response that the entire sum should be capitalised at once, the course which was in the event followed. Between 1862 and 1873 some £3,000 of the capital had been repaid to Smith, reducing the original 1862 capital

5 W.H. Smith, London, Hambleden papers, 110/34. Lethbridge to Awdry, 23 February 1895.
6 ibid., Hambleden papers, DD22. Lethbridge to Smith, 1 April 1888.

of £6,000 to £3,000. To this capital of £3,000 should be added the accumulated profits in the balance sheet of £19,313, making a total of £22,313. Some further payments on capital account out of the accumulated profits to London reduced this figure to just below £18,000, and the balance was capitalised at £18,000 from 1 January 1874. £3,073 out of the profits was retained in 1874-76, thus adding to the capital of the house in these years which were years of major expansion in Dublin. £4,000 of the enlarged capital was paid off in 1879-81, reducing the outstanding capital of the house to £17,000. Smith had agreed to the expansion of the 1860s somewhat reluctantly, but by the 1870s he had achieved all his desires as far as Dublin was concerned. The business had been capitalised at a realistic figure, and profits were disbursed to the London partners regularly. Between 1874 and 1883 profits including interest had averaged £5,283 per annum, and the business, now benefiting from the large investment of the 1860s and 1870s, was one of assured and sustained profitability. Only in 1874-76 had any proportion of the profits been ploughed back into the business. The increase in the capital at that stage was more than compensated by a reduction of £4,000 in the capital in 1879-81.

In the early years Eason was paid a salary of £256, which was later raised to £600, plus a share from both Smith and Lethbridge of the profits of the general and government sales respectively.[7] He had not, he remarked, bettered himself in moving from Manchester, and the share in profits seems to have been introduced in response to his dissatisfaction on that score. The share, which was discretionary and described as a 'gift', was a third of the profit after interest had been deducted. Smith was helpful in additional ways. He advanced Eason the money to build his house, 30 Kenilworth Square, in 1861, and he advanced money to him again in 1872.

7 After Smith's election to Parliament in 1868, a memorandum was addded to the partnership deed with Lethbridge, divesting Smith of all profits and emoluments from sales to government offices. In the Irish business, the accounts returned to London distinguished between business on government and private account, and the gross totals under both headings were computed in the London house. From these figures, separate calculations were made of profits for both categories, the profits on government business going to Lethbridge. Charles Eason's share of the Irish profits was made up of two components, one on foot of the general trade, and one on foot of the government sales.

WORKING FOR SMITH'S 1856-86

The operation that Charles Eason took over in 1856 was still an intimate business, easily superintended physically or visually by a single man, as Smith's suggestion about avoiding too high a partition for Eason's office area indicated. The informality of the office in the early stages is reflected too in the fact that Eason's own salary only ceased to be recorded with that of the other employees in the course of 1859. There is also evidence of general staff outings. The names of sixteen members of staff — about half the employees — are recorded in one of the early wage book as 'went to Glendalough as follows' on 6 August 1860, and a week later nine are mentioned as 'went to Lough Dan and Devils Glen'. In those days cash seems to have been advanced in what were fairly large amounts with reference to salary levels. Details survive of advances to four members in November 1859, and six names are mentioned with loans outstanding in May 1860.

By December 1875 the total number of staff amounted to 136 and by December 1886 it amounted to 175. The later figure, however, concealed a real slowdown in the rise in the number employed, because if the workroom employees are excluded, the total was only 142. The earlier hectic growth reflected both the rate of expansion between 1864 and 1876, and the ambitious physical development of the premises in the first half of the 1870s.

A departmental structure first emerged in the 1862 wage books. This was a simple one, embracing a retail shop, a book department, and a Wholesale division. In addition, two men were employed in the stables, and one in the railway advertising workshop. By 1869 a more complex staff structure had emerged. The Wholesale department was now divided into two departments, one confined to the city business, and the other a country department, corresponding to the recent and rapid growth of business outside Dublin. The counting house had also come into existence. The accounting side had become well-defined and was no longer an appendage of general management. Railway advertising had become a department in its own right, and a 'stock' department also existed. This was the precursor of the stationery department, and shows that expansion into stationery was somewhat earlier than the date traditionally ascribed to it. The stables employed five persons by 1869, and a printing office was in being.

By 1875 the basic structures, in the form in which they were to define the business for the next eighty years, had come into existence. At first the wholesaling of books had been handled as an adjunct to wholesaling newspapers, but by 1875 the wholesale functions were divided into well-defined wholesale departments for news, books and stationery respectively, and the old distinction between country and town departments had been abandoned. Apart from changes of detail over the intervening years, such as the division of accounting into two offices, cashiers and accounts, this was to remain the basic structure of the house. Subsequently the only major change was the growth of the manufacturing end. This already existed in embryo in the printing office whose establishment seems to have predated the year traditionally suggested for it. However for a long time the printing office was to be a mere service department to the house at large, and as such the numbers employed remained small. It employed five in 1869 and eight in 1882. It was only at the very end of the century that the number of printers increased sharply, from seven in 1897 to twenty in 1901. At this stage the firm expanded its printing significantly beyond its own service requirements. It began first to print its own publications and then to undertake contract printing.

The printing department was geared originally to the large requirements of the house for internal stationery and for order sheets for the trade customers. But its printing capacity had also encouraged the company to enter into stationery manufacture, and stationery manufacture at this time overshadowed printing in importance. It is not perfectly clear at what point the stationery workroom began operation. The surviving data suggest that it was already in existence in 1877, the first year in which employment in the workroom is unambiguously identified, with a total staff of twelve. Wages costs attributed to stationery manufacture rose very rapidly in 1874/5 and 1876/7, so that it seems likely that the expansion took place in these years. By 1886 the number employed in the stationery section had risen to 33. In 1889 the factory was opened at Gloucester Place, and printing and stationery manufacture were centralised there. In 1881/2 wage costs in the workrooms were still less than in wholesale stationery sales (£291 as compared with £855). But total wages in manufacture rose steadily over the 1880s to £750 in 1888/9 and the factory wages component in stationery costs reached £1,147 by 1891/2. Factory wages in stationery were now almost as large as wholesale stationery wages. By 1895 the total factory employment, which included printers as well as the staff engaged in stationery manufacture, amounted to 69. A major investment of £2,000 in the factory at the turn of the century carried it to new heights. Its staff increased to 107 by 1901, and in 1915 at 112, it was only four persons or so below its peak. It was now the largest single division within the house in Dublin. Average wages in the factory were lower than those in other parts of the business, because the low wages of women in stationery manufacture depressed the general average.

In its early days the firm attracted men who were to rise quickly to prominent positions, and who contributed to its sustained growth in later decades. One of the most intriguing features of the early wage books is that a member of the Toms family was employed at least as early as June 1857. Next to Eason himself, he had the highest wage, and could thus be regarded as second in command. What his first name was we do not know, nor why he left in the course of 1859. There is an inkling of the reason in a letter of Charles Eason to Smith in July 1859 when he wrote, that 'I have not given Mr. Toms any intimation of my intention to part with him but shall do so before long'. The circumstances of parting must have been amicable enough, as the Toms family link with the business resumed in the 1860s. In 1863 a Toms (identified in one entry as C. Toms) had reappeared. As his salary in January 1864 was the same as that of the Toms who had left in 1859, the same man may have returned. His weekly salary was increased smartly to £2 10s within a year. As the firm made its first venture into printing in 1863, the printing expertise of the Toms family was the likely reason for his employment or reemployment. He can be first identified beyond all ambiguity as head of the printing office in 1869, and since the man whose name appears immediately below his in the wages book had also been below him in the 1864 wages book, the likelihood is that they were both printers.

Other members of the Toms family were attracted to the house managed by their successful relative. There was a John Toms in the retail department in 1871. He was paid 5s a week, a typical starting wage of the period. He was obviously a new and young recruit. His arrival is dated elsewhere as 1870. In 1875 a Toms was second in line in the stationery department at £1 a week. This may well be the young recruit of 1870. The senior Toms can no longer be traced in the printing office in the 1870s. A junior Toms earning 12s is there, and by the 1880s he had risen to the second position. We may infer that both he and the Toms in the stationery department were sons of the earlier Toms. Digges, who had entered the business in 1866, was able to recall among the early figures in the house, 'Mr. Toms, head of the printing office, and father of another of our jubilarians'. A profile of John Toms in *Eason's monthly bulletin* in 1925 gives us a little more information on the John Toms who had entered the firm in 1870. The report, while stating that he entered the firm in 1870, somewhat inaccurately states that he entered the wholesale town news department. The wage data suggest that he first worked in the retail shop. The profile seems broadly accurate in mentioning his transfer to stationery, and gives 1872 as the date for his entry into that department, 'which was then in its infancy'. In 1880 he was made manager of the prayerbook department. In February 1885 Smith made over the prayerbook publishing business to Charles Eason, and John Toms moved to the separate premises which Eason opened for it on Aston's Quay. After the incorporation of the prayerbook business into Eason & Son in 1889 John Toms relinquished its management to travel. From 1889 Toms travelled for the wholesale stationery department, first in England and then, from 1891 to 1924, in Ireland, where he became something of a legend. J.C.M. Eason recalled that in his early days in the business he accompanied John Toms on his journeys, and learned to play billiards from him, while waiting for customers in country hotels. He was an old man in 1924 — a jubilarian as Digges accurately described him — and had transferred back to the prayerbook department. Another member of the firm recalled in 1931 that Toms played cricket with the Abbey cricket team: 'his weight militated against his successful running between wickets. He was an enthusiastic if not a successful cricketer'.

William Slark, who was described with the epithet 'Inspector' in some of the books, had been recruited by January 1859, and was for many years to play a key role in the company in superintending the railway bookstalls. In 1861 he ranked with one other man as the second highest paid employees of the firm at that time, and within a couple of years he had become for a short period the highest paid employee of the firm, reflecting the immense importance of the bookstalls at that time. He was paid a weekly salary of £2 8s, which was a large sum. The railway advertising department then carried a prestige second only to the bookstalls. Fred Cherry seems to have joined in 1862, when this area was taking shape as a small but immensely profitable division and sixty-three years later Digges recalled Cherry, 'who made such a rapid success of the railway advertising department'. Certainly this was reflected in the rapidity of the rise in Cherry's remuneration. In October 1862 he was paid only £1 1s, but by January 1865 he was paid £2 which put him on a par with the highest paid employees with the exception of Toms and Slark.

An intriguing feature in the books at the end of January 1865 is the entry of a Mr Dewar at a far higher salary level than that of any other employee at the time. He was the only one dignified with the prefix 'Mr' which seems to confirm further the special responsibility envisaged for him. According to Digges' later recollection, he was '... chief of the wholesale department, a typical Scot, of commanding figure and unmistakeable accent'. Presumably, as the Wholesale department grew in scale and complexity it had been necessary to call on outside expertise to help to manage it, and Dewar, his Scottish background perhaps an additional recommendation in an age when the managerial repute of Scots was at its highest, was brought in for this purpose. His initial weekly salary was £3, increased to £4 by 1869 and to £5 by 1871. By 1875 he had ceased to be head of the Wholesale News division, and was included in a small category of 'miscellaneous' which included Slark, the two travellers, Wilson and Connolly, and from August 1875 young Charles Eason, who had entered the business at a salary of £3. This suggests that Dewar had been given more general managerial responsibilities. He was now earning £6 a week. He may also have recruited another Scot at a managerial level, as a McLeod was recruited in September 1875 at a salary of £4. If it was an attempt to import further Scottish expertise, it was a short-lived one, as McLeod had disappeared by 1877. After Dewar's own salary, McLeod's was among the highest in the firm, equalled only by Slark's.

In 1875 when Dewar's responsibilities were apparently extended, James Dignam (who had entered the firm in 1856) took over as head of Wholesale News, with Bligh, who had come into the business in 1862, as his assistant. Both were energetic men, up to the demands of the major division of the house, although there was a personality clash between them. Digges recalled later: 'Mr. James Dignam, of the wholesale Newspaper Department — In present day phraselogy he might be called a 'live wire', as was often realised by those who came in contact with him. Mr. Bligh, was another "live wire" in the same department, and not infrequently the atmosphere in the Department became tense and electric with two "live wires".' In fact, Dignam had an interesting life outside the firm. As John Rowland recalled in 1934:

> He wrote guides to all sorts of places he never saw. His guide to Spain was famous for the remarkable statements made therein. 'The river Garonne (sic) is the driest river in Europe'! Went to Rome once for a holiday and stated on his return that he had obtained an audience with the Pope, who said, on his being introduced into the Pope's presence, 'Is that you James?' Believe this or not, Mr. Dignam was convinced of it and was very proud that his fame had spread to St. Peter's.

His early literary bent is reflected in an interesting diary he kept for 1864, the year of his marriage to a lady named Jane. The diary seems to have been prompted by her father's opposition to the match. We do not know whether Jane's illness in 1865 was to cast a shadow over their lives or not. Dignam was pensioned in 1893 and Bligh, who remained on in the department, died in 1904.

In nineteenth century terms it was inevitable that protestants should predominate among the early staff, and that they should also tend to dominate managerial posts. The character of the firm dictated this. Staff were recruited from the immediate circle of the principal, and since many recruits were accepted on the recommendation of the senior people in the firm, continued recruitment tended to be slanted in that direction. The pattern of early recruitment is amply borne out in Henry Digges' 1925 recollections of his own entry in 1866:

> My first experience of no. 21 was when I called there on September 28th 1866, in response to an advt. for a boy-clerk. My parents had some acquaintance with Mr. Richard Kershaw, who was then the manager of the Retail Dept., and he engaged me at once to begin duty at 8:30 a.m. on October 1st 1866, in succession to a lad named Hunt, three or four years my senior, who was leaving to join his uncle (Hunt) who had a Gents. Outfitting shop in Westmoreland Street.

Recommendations from members of the firm were reflected in the presence of several members bearing the same name in the firm: brothers, sisters or sons. Thus in 1882 Sarah Toms became one of the first two ladies recruited to the firm. Education and business experience in the nineteenth century at least also tended to favour protestants, and at senior level the firm was much slower to lose its protestant character than among the rank and file. This did not imply discrimination against catholics. The recruitment of Scots to a number of senior positions implied discrimination against Irish Anglicans as much as against catholics, and represented simply an effort to get the best experience then available.

To what extent Charles Eason had a free hand in recruitment is not clear. The comparative absence of references to recruitment in the surviving correspondence would suggest that he may have had a large measure of discretion. Given the lack of prejudice against catholics, recruitment tended to become more even over a period of time, and a large catholic base was inevitably reflected later in the promotion of catholics as well. After Dignam the first catholic to rise to prominence was Philip Brown, who was recruited in 1909 and became head of the wholesale news department in 1933. His promotion would appear to reflect the consequences of the subtle transformation which had taken place within the firm. According to *Eason's monthly bulletin* in March/April 1956:

> Outside his work Mr. Brown had many interests, and these too characteristically were concerned with people's problems. He was an active member of the St. Vincent de Paul Society and of the Irish Red Cross. He took a keen interest in anything connected with his local Parish Church, and in his earlier years, in many social and athletic activities in Eason's.

Digges, who had entered the firm in 1866, survived to become the doyen of all the employees. In 1925, as the longest serving employee, he made the presentation on behalf of the staff to Charles Eason junior, on the latter's passing fifty years in the firm. Eleven years later, as a pensioner, he was present at the jubilee of Eason & Son's emergence as an independent business. Digges' progression is an interesting illustration of the advancement of a young man who was personable and well recommended. In January 1867 his salary was increased from 6s to 8s a week. It rose to 10s in 1868, and to 14s in 1869, and from that to £1 in 1870, £1 4s in 1871 and £1 8s in 1872. By January 1875 he had advanced to £1 16s and to £2 in the July of the same year. In 1877 at a salary of £2 10s, only 2s less than his boss, William Porter, he was second in command of the Retail department. Porter, as Digges later recalled, had been in control of newspaper advertising for many years, which suggests that in practice Digges looked after the other activities in the Retail section. When Porter left in 1881 to become secretary of the Hibernian Bible Society, Digges succeeded him as head. His salary in the mid-1880s was £3 15s and it gradually rose to £5 10s in 1900.

Other figures who were to make a large contribution to the firm over many years had entered the business in the same period. James Butler, who was to become chief cashier, had entered in 1864, and E.W. Hallett, who was to become accountant, entered in 1870. In this case the normal progression from father to son seems to have been reversed, because Hallett senior entered in 1878 and at a lower salary. Both served in the same department. Butler is dealt with somewhat unsympathetically in the account in Sean O'Casey's *Pictures in the Hallway*. In fact by all accounts he was one of the most agreeable men in the firm. In Digges' view: 'what shall I say? Beloved by everyone from the smallest boy to the heads of the departments, from the youngest girl to the stateliest. When he retired we all felt that we had lost our dearest friend.' John Rowland's recollection is no different: 'was everybody's friend and adviser. A most charming and lovable man and tremendously popular with the customers'.

Hallett, the accountant, was second in the department, only a few shillings less in salary than Butler, but his impact does not seem to have been recorded by anyone recalling the past of the firm. To the student of the firm, his work over many years becomes very familiar. The original ledgers have all disappeared, but the summaries and abstracts he made survive in large numbers, set out in his ordered and methodical hand. In 1883 Hallett was required to detail his work for Lethbridge, who was at that time looking into the state of the Dublin house as a result of Charles Eason's urging the partnership question, and he listed in the recital of his duties: 'then in the preparation of the various abstracts and summaries which it is the habit of Mr. Eason to require, exhibiting the processes and results of the business in its multiform development, I am brought into contact with the details of the work in every direction.'

The wholesale book department was to be run for a long time by James Stephen. He had entered the firm in 1872. He was already head of it in 1875 at a salary of £2 16s, which was increased to £3 in July 1876, and he remained with the firm until he retired on pension in 1908. John Rowland's recollections note: 'the Caledonian Society claimed him as a staunch supporter for many years. He was a constant source of worry to the packing department owing to his unremitting protests against the hammering of the packers. He was a supporter of the "tall hat" brigade and was quite a noise amongst the Scottish brigade in Dublin.' He emerges as another proof of the importance of Scotsmen in the house in its early decades. The same was true of course of banking at a slightly earlier date, especially in the Provincial Bank whose early development relied heavily on the recruitment of Scotsmen.

The stationery department produced no figure who made a large impact in the early years, but by 1877 Scott had emerged as its main salaried figure. The department was somewhat more complex in its structure than others, reflecting the fact that it had larger overheads than any other division of the house. In 1877 it was divided into the Shop, which included John Toms as its number two, the Showroom in which Scott was head, the Stockroom and the Buyers Room, which in 1877 was headed by Coghill, who had entered the firm in 1877. In 1884 Scott and Coghill had been put on an equal salary at £3 10s and in 1885 Coghill succeeded him as head of the department. After 1889 Coghill's responsibilities for stationery also included the factory, and his salary rose sharply in the late 1880s and 1890s, reflecting the rapid advance of this side of the business. It rose from £5 to £9 between 1887 and 1895, and reached its maximum of £10 by 1906.

Ruthven's rise was due in large measure to the profitability of railway advertising and to the importance that this gave the activity in the house. As time went by, Cherry relinquished the routine outdoor work in the department to Stephen Stokes. Cherry was still in charge of the department in 1877, but by 1884 the work had become so important that Cherry became one of the general managers in his own right, and routine management was relinquished to Stephen Stokes, on a salary of £1 15s, as against Cherry's £2. Cherry's salary at this stage understates his earnings, as it takes no account of commission. From 1884 Cherry was on the managerial side, and this change allied to the sharp rise in his remuneration in subsequent years, and the bringing in of Ruthven seems to reflect the growing importance of the railway advertising. Cherry was now the highest paid employee of the firm, his salary reflecting the importance of the railway contracts and the delicate negotiations which surrounded them. Stokes' salary remained a more modest one. In 1886 it was only £2 and it did not reach £4 until 1899. Stokes' value derived from the fact that he had previously worked in a railway company. In 1934 John Rowland recalled that Stokes had been

> ... originally chief clerk to Mr Payne, general manager of the Dublin South Eastern Railway. Succeeded Mr Cherry as outside man for the Railway Advertising Department and was very popular with the customers. Was very fond of yachting, sailed with Mr Cherry and Mr Baker of Dalkey for many years. Knew all about painting and decorating having served his time with firm of Panter & Son, which was very well known in Dublin at one time.

Ruthven seems to have been a Scot as well, and to have returned to Scotland for his retirement. He was an engineer by profession and did much architectural work on behalf of the firm, quite apart from his managerial duties. He planned the layout of 40 and 41 O'Connell Street in 1905, including a stack of strong rooms on three floors which survived the fire in 1916. He also designed the new buildings which replaced the destroyed premises. The importance of railway advertising is reflected in the recruitment of Ruthven into that department, and to the fact that in the early 1890s it had two high-salaried employees, Cherry and Ruthven. Ruthven had already attained £6 a week in 1890. In August 1893, no doubt when he succeeded Cherry, he was advanced to £8, and reached £9 in 1895. He was advanced to £50 a month in October 1902, a fact which signals more than any other his rise to prominence in the firm. His salary was slightly reduced by 1916/17. This may indicate the tarnished glories of railway advertising, but as the rebuilding began to take up much of his time, his salary gradually climbed back to its former level. His strength was obviously giving out as he was on a reduced salary in 1922/3, and he retired at the very beginning of the next financial year.

The introduction of the stationery business had changed the all-male character of the firm. Women were employed in both sales and manufacture. Those in sales were better paid and from a higher social and educational level than those in the stationery workroom. In December 1877 ten of the twelve employees in the stationery workroom were ladies, including the forewoman, whose wages at 18s were a good deal higher than the ten women employed in sewing and covering, stamping, carding, folding notepaper and bordering. As usual, recruitment tended to be drawn from people with contact with the existing staff. The first female employee outside the workroom seems to have been a Miss Ruthven in 1881, no doubt related to Ruthven who entered the firm at around this time. The second was a Sarah Toms in 1882. The employment of a Miss Thomson can be traced between 1883 and 1886 in retail, the first female employee outside stationery. Her starting salary at 10s suggests that she was out of the ordinary in some way. In 1886 the number of females in the stationery department had risen to eight, and it included one of Charles Eason's own daughters, Frances Eason, who later married Albert Brunton. Her wages at £1 were the same as Miss Ruthven's. A female had reappeared in the retail department's list by December 1888. The first female employee in wholesale books can be traced by the beginning of 1890, in prayer books by January 1895, and the citadel of accounts had been entered by January 1899.

Clerical salaries were in quite a different category from other salaries. On recruitment, they were often no higher than those of messengers, porters, printers, who entered at low levels but quickly progressed to their top rates. Porters and messengers were also frequently recruited well above the minimum rates of entry. Clerical employment on the other hand was regarded as requiring a formal apprenticeship, which other jobs did not require. As one would expect, the printers received higher wages than other manual earners: the highest wage in January 1889 was £2 for one man; four others earned £1 10s, one earned £1 8s and one was at £1, while three were at lower wages. The stables, apart from the man in charge at £1 14s, offered wages between 17s and 19s. These wages would be akin to those of porters. Many of them were recruited at 14s and probably did not rise much above that figure. In a general sense it can be said that clerical staff commanded earnings about twice the level of manual staff. The higher-paid earnings — those over £2 a week — put their recipients on a par with professional and business people, whose residence was often in the best districts, and where the way of life and hobbies were upper-class ones. Cherry, as head of advertising, was earning commission as well as salary, and his salary in the early 1890s when he no longer received commission was £10 a week. Rowland was able to recall him in 1934: 'had been out in the East and fought under General Gordon with the Chinese troops. He showed me a number of photos of soldiers and civilians being executed by beheading. He was an enthusiastic yachtsman and had a ten tonner in Kingstown harbour for many years.[8] Stephen Stokes of Railway Advertising was one of his crew. Mr Cherry invariably wore a tall hat.'

The large turnover in staff also contributed to the low average earnings, since a high proportion of staff were new recruits or apprentices at the bottom level in wages. The total number leaving the firm for every cause including death between 1872 and 1886 was 327. This is an average of just above 23 per year on a total wage force which rose from a figure somewhat over 80 in 1872, to 175 in 1886. Excluding deaths, internal transfers and changes for which no reason was entered, reasons survive for the departures of 269 of the personnel listed; 177 were discharged, for one reason or another, 96 left voluntarily or for other jobs (the latter figure includes a double counting of 4, who were discharged, but who are noted as have gone to other jobs). While the figure of 177 is very large, it includes 45 who were discharged because of want of work, or reduced activity, and 26 who were sick or too delicate, including one who was too young. Thus, dismissals for reasons other than health or the availability of work amount to 106. The range varies from a mere statement of discharge, and from trivial grounds, by today's standards, to serious ones. Almost as many went voluntarily and in many cases for personal advancement. Apart from 9 who left without notice, and 6 who left to get married, 45 left to take up other employment, 8 to emigrate, and 27 others left at their own wish. Of these latter, one left because the wages were too low, another was withdrawn by his father, and yet another went on to study medicine. Leaving aside the special cases of lack of activity or sickness, the large turnover represents a fairly even division between cases in which the firm parted company with employees, and cases in which employees chose to part company with it.

Given a pattern of recruitement at relatively low wages and a long

8 His boat *Flirt* was one of six to start in the first race organised by the Dublin Bay Sailing Club in 1884.

period in rising to full earnings, there was bound to be a large turnover. The dismissal of long-serving employees was unusual, and the noting of the length of service against such dismissals in the wage books is in itself an illustration of the fact that they were unusual, and not embarked upon lightly. Charles Eason was correct in 1918 when he noted that 'security of employment' was one of the benefits of the firm. Even in the case of drink, a defect severely regarded, discharge only took place in the case of recent recruits. On the other hand, during the first year or two of service, the reasons for dismissal would be considered trivial or harsh by modern standards.

Wage books show that discipline was strict and that dismissal was often peremptory in the case of recent recruits. But the first Charles could be lenient. Even drinking, which could lead to summary dismissal, could be followed by a reprieve for longer serving employees. On one occasion in 1878 his wages book 1878-85 read: 'Bligh — worse for liquor Tuesday, took pledge on Wednesday.' This is probably not the Bligh who was assistant to Dignam as head of wholesale news, though, in the way of the firm, quite possibly a close relative. At the end of the same year for unstated reasons a Flanagan was 'allowed another chance — deposited 1s as security for good behaviour.' In fact Bligh was again reprimanded for drinking and fighting in 1887, and the other two with him were also reprimanded, which suggests that in the area where severity was most evident, justice was tempered with mercy. The flavour of discipline is perhaps well illustrated in the following note written in Charles Eason's hand on April 17 1887: 'Norton got week's notice. Dignam says he is constantly muddled but I did not see any signs of incapacity from drink. He was careless in reference to a price for Swallow and spoke offensively to Mrs. Swallow this morning at our counter. He had no right to speak to her at all.'

Charles Eason junior, who had taken over from 1895 was no different from his father, but dismissals did not leave an employer happy. He wrote to his younger brother Benjamin in April 1897: 'I have had to part with some of the staff rather summarily, one for clear dishonesty, two for conduct rendering them open to suspicion, two for drink, and today I have given Walsh of the Library notice. He is not trustworthy (I don't mean pecuniarly) but as to general character, truthfulness, and strict sobriety. So many changes are unusual and disappointing.'

For those with more than one or two years' service, there was considerable security. This is evident even in the case of porters, many of whom came into the firm from other employments on good discharges.

In the mid 1880s there were quite a number of such cases, who had worked with other employers, and who were taken on at 14s. These were not high wages, but the wage books show that porters with long service commanded higher wages — by the end of the century up to 17s and even 21s. Security, plus the possibility of this type of advancement, made working for Eason's a desirable employment. Of course it still remained true that men were trying to bring up a family on 14s a week, like the vanman quoted in O'Casey's *Pictures in the Hallway*, but this was less common in the case of clerical and shop assistants, because the normal pattern was for individuals to enter at a young age, usually at a salary of 5s or 6s a week, and to progress over time to significantly larger salaries.

In 1886/7 clerical workers taken on at the starting salary of 5s or 6s a week included one whose father was a commission agent on Rathgar Road, and another whose father was an officer in the MGWR, another whose father had worked with a firm in the flour trade, another whose father was a detective, and yet another whose deceased father was a policeman, and had been educated at Synge St. Another clerical assistant who was taken on at 8s had been a monitor in a national school. Charles Copland from 53 Sandymount Road who was taken into the Stationery Department in 1886 at 6s, was probably a son of the late Managing Director of the Royal Bank. While he does not appear to have remained on in the firm, the fact that recruitment from this milieu existed at all, suggests that a career in the company was well regarded. Clerical staff recruited at higher wage levels included one at 15s who came from a druggist, and another at 18s who had worked with Gill & Son. In 1881 a clerk was taken on at 16s who had worked for two years with a grocer, and another was taken on at 15s who had worked both with the GSR, and with a Mr Hennebry in High Street, as well as having had five months as a goods checker at 10s with the GNR — all giving good discharges. Another clerical assistant had been a clerk with the *Freeman's Journal* at 10s, and another young man was recruited to the cash desk at 6s whose father was a carpenter and who was known to Dignam.

The large number discharged because of sickness or delicate condition should be noted. This is not quite as harsh as it sounds because in many cases such discharges took place within a short time after recruitment. Poor health, along with bad time keeping, and absence without notice, was obviously dealt with strictly. There are also some cases of people losing their jobs through sickness at a much later stage of employment, and a few cases where the reasons given seem severe. A clerk in the book department in March 1880, earning 8s, who had entered the firm in

October 1878, and who 'got sprained hand', was dismissed, as was a clerk in stationery, more reasonably, in his third month of employment in 1882 — 'unfit for our work, very deaf' is recorded as the grounds. In nineteenth-century conditions, one could not expect an employer to carry a sick employee indefinitely. Policy with regard to health seems to have been very strict in the early stages of employment. A note in the Belfast house stated that: 'A deduction will always be made in payment of wages for time lost by absence through sickness. In special cases an appeal to waive this right may be made to the Principal Manager.'

A provision for sick payment did develop from an early date, and a pencilled contemporary note in one of the nineteenth century wage books noted: 'In sickness no clerk is entitled to wages when absent till after he has been two years in the employ of the firm.' By the early twentieth century sickness pay was accounted for separately in the accounts. In 1916-17 it amounted to £63, and in 1917-18 to £77. In some respects the firm was very progressive. A Saturday half-holiday was introduced in 1865. A memorandum from Charles Eason in June of that year provided for it on the following terms:

> Mr. Dewar will ascertain that all the work properly belonging to the Saturday must be completed before the Staff can be free for the Saturday afternoon
>
> 1. The counting house
> 2. Bookselling department
> 3. Periodical and News departments
>
> The clerks belonging to each of the above must not go until all is complete, and must assist in each department so as to finish up any arrears in hand.
>
> In connection with the above greater punctuality must be observed in coming to Office in the morning and in returning from dinner, on pain of suspension of this privilege.

Even more unusual was the granting of annual holidays. The earliest record of this is the granting of a week's holidays in 1864 to fourteen named persons. The practice of making advances to employees, evident in the early days, continued. In the later wage books there is some reference to requests for advances in a manner which would suggest that it was not unusual. Work conditions in the firm were exacting, especially in the wholesale news department. Work began early in the day. After the early years of the house a starting time of 6 a.m. was introduced. By 1864 the office was opening an hour earlier still, at 5:15 a.m., and by 1872 the time was even earlier, 5 a.m.

The morning work was extremely hectic. A great variety of papers had to be sorted quickly to catch the early trains. The pace and discipline of work had to be maintained to ensure that the work was done speedily, and that the bundles for dispatch to newsagents all over the country were made up accurately in accordance with their weekly requirements, which were communicated on the firm's order sheets in advance. Even with the greatest care, a fairly large number of complaints came in from newsagents who were left short, and who resented thus being put at a disadvantage to their competitors. This led frequently to recrimination by newsagents, and in the 1930s an action was even taken against Eason's by a frustrated newsagent in Castlecomer. A very close eye was kept on newsagents' complaints, and the work in the wholesale news department was carried out under some strain and with a discipline geared to fast and accurate work. The whole success of the firm and its ability to keep its leading place in the trade depended on its success in handling its crucial sorting and dispatch work effectively. This helps to explain the somewhat severe tone in regard to staff. One note from 1886-87 reads: 'F. Ennis dismissed — a tricky boy — not attentive — very talkative. Bligh [the second in command in wholesale news] found him very troublesome.'

The loads of papers to be moved into the wholesale department and then out of it to be dispatched were quite heavy. At one level this meant trying to ensure that the loads were manageable. A note written in July 1879 reads: 'Speak to Fitz about looking after bags — query are post bags too heavy in the evening'. At another level it meant that porters had to be strong enough to handle weights readily, hence the dismissals because men or boys were not strong enough, or even tall enough. O'Casey's account is the most graphic description of the business:

> A van drove up with a cargo of *Irish Times* followed by others filled with *Irish Independents* and *Freeman's Journals*, men and boys hurrying out, and coming back staggering under loads of papers on the shoulders, and dumping them on the various benches. Here other men, holding invoices in their hands, called out rapidly the papers required by country agents: others counted out the papers with great speed from the heaps on the benches, throwing them on brown paper wrappings to be snatched up by others, and parcelled up for the vans to take them to the several railway stations. It was hurry here and hurry there, carrying, dumping down, calling out, selecting, wrapping up, tying, pasting of labels, and flinging the finished parcels into their different bins; and in the midst of the stress waddles Show-a-leg [Bligh] and his son, both of them looking like what you'd

> surely sometimes see prowling about in the dim time of life, among the swishy reeds, the tangled ferns and the seamy shade of slimy mosses.... So midst the voices calling out ten *Independents*, twenty *Freemen*, five *Irish Times*, five *Freemen*, twenty *Independents*, ten *Times*, twenty *Times*, five *Independents*, ten *Freemen*; the crackling of brown paper as the papers were wrapped up in them; the swish of the brushes as the labels were pasted on; the scratching of tired feet over the rough boards; the thud of horses' hooves, timid of the frost under them; the inspiring hiss-hiss of Show-a-leg as if he were currying a horse in a stable — Johnny joined the bunch of men and boys following each other, bearing burdens of newspapers on their shoulders, like blacks in a jungle so that the whole of distant Ireland might know the newest news.

Having accompanied a van load of parcels to Kingsbridge, O'Casey on his return had to take a handcart full of parcels to Amiens Street Station for carriage to Belfast and intermediate places. All this before breakfast: early morning workers were paid an allowance for breakfast. After breakfast he was back to work, now dealing with news a little less urgent than the morning papers recalling 'the owner of the voice so musically calling out the sordid names of *Ally Sloper*, *Answers*, *Tit-Bits*, *Pearson's Weekly*, *Sunday Companion*, *Scraps*, *Weekly Budget* and *Forget-me-not*.' The morning rush with the dailies was of course the most hectic part of the day, and the staff for this work were augmented with what were called morning men, holding other jobs, and hired as part-time workers to work from 5 a.m.

On his own account, O'Casey can only have worked a week in the firm. He refused to take off his cap when collecting his wage packet, and the affronted cashier sent for Charles Eason....

> ... through the little window, Johnny saw the long face, pale eyes, greying golden beard, and bent shoulders of Mr. Charles coming into the cashier's office with short mincing steps, on his toes, like a creaking and cracked-up ballet dancer, to stare with wonder at the cashier and Johnny's head thrust through the little window.... Give it to him, hand it to him, let him have it, let him have it, and go! ordered Jason [Charles Eason], God bless us, how did such a person ever come to be employed here.

THE PARTNERSHIP QUESTION

Despite its immense size, with over 4,000 employees in 1886, W.H. Smith's remained technically a partnership until 1929, and only became a public company in 1949. Many day-to-day decisions were in the hands of Smith and his partners, who were selected by Smith himself. Although Smith prided himself on the fact that most of his heads of department had risen from the bottom, the rising stopped at the partners door. 'Liberal and patrician' outsiders were given a few years induction in the business before being elevated to full partnership. Lethbridge, the first partner, had been at school with Smith; Charles Awdry, promoted to partnership in 1881, came from a Wiltshire landed family. Alfred Acland, brother of the Regius Professor of Medicine at Oxford, was brought in from an engineering career in 1886 as a further partner. He had already married Smith's third daughter. Lethbridge was firmly opposed to making members of the staff partners, and Acland, the youngest of the partners was not only on bad terms with Awdry, but also wished to assert the partners' position vis-a-vis White, the capable and all-powerful head of the wholesale news department.[9]

The question of creating partners from among the staff in London had been raised in 1867, three years after Lethbridge had been made a partner, and Eason was alive to the implications for his own position. An unfinished draft letter survives from that year, but it is not clear whether in fact it was actually sent to Smith. The draft represents Eason's state of mind quite clearly:

> I know that in the judgment of my fellow business men of this city the House is well spoken of, and it has been a matter of surprise to some that my standing still is only that of a servant, albeit a confidential and trusted one. To aspire to a position of partnership of the Dublin house is not I trust a thing to gratify vanity or in order to [?] the world's esteem. It seems just and right for if the common experience of men is not fulfilled in my person, the world's inference will be that causes are operating against me which arise from facts unknown to them and which are to my hurt.
>
> Again and again have I been made to feel this, more especially since the wholesale bookselling has been entered on.

This view scarcely appreciated what was Smith's underlying assessment of the business. Smith could have pointed to his own reluctance to expand

9 Wilson, op. cit. pp. 185, 187-8

the Dublin business. On the other hand he acquiesced both in the diversification of the Dublin house and in the ploughing back of the profits. In the 1860s at any rate the question of partnership was not really a serious one. The fact that Eason may not have proceeded with his draft is one proof of this, as is the fact that his argument was largely couched in terms of the advantage of having a principal in the firm in Dublin. His views may have been simply prompted by the general thinking in the London house in that year.

The question of a partnership in the Dublin house was formally raised by Eason when he was in London in 1872. He was by now 49 years of age. Smith was opposed to the idea, and in September 1873 he was able to write to his wife stating that Eason had been very reasonable, and had quite abandoned the idea of demanding a partnership. Smith characteristically deferred personal questions affecting others, and had done so on this occasion. When he and Lethbridge were in Dublin in September 1873 he offered to deal with a subject of concern on Eason's part, which had featured six years earlier in the draft letter of 1867, namely, the necessity of providing for his family in the case of his death. Smith met Eason's concern on this point, in the absence of a partnership, which would have given Eason a permanent stake in the firm, by entering into a bond payable to the Eason family in the event of their father's death for £5,000, reducing to zero over ten years. At this stage, Eason's concern was still dictated by general considerations more than by a sense of what was due to him. The emphasis changed in subsequent years, as the supervision of the Dublin house became more perfunctory, and neither of the partners ever came across to Dublin. The concern was all the more pressing because, in contrast to the past, the house was now fully capitalised, and interest and profits were both being remitted to London.

Eason's eldest son, George, had entered the business in 1868, and his second son Charles in 1875. Smith had been dismissive of the idea of one of Eason's sons succeeding him in the business when this had been raised in 1872/3, suggesting that it would be best if he first obtained experience in other houses before any promises could be held out at that score. At a later stage, apparently in the second half of 1878, the prospect was held out that one of his sons should succeed him, if he were satisfactory. However, by that time, Eason was seeking senior places in the house for two sons, one to succeed him as manager, the other to look after some of the departments on the grounds that: 'the risk will be extreme to leave any member of my family to succeed me unless means are also provided to secure competent support to him in administering the varied details of this business.' In writing to Lethbridge, Smith's reaction to Eason's somewhat tortuous letter was quite tart: 'he has come to the remarkable conclusion that he himself is a very remarkable man and that it will take two sons to be equal to one Father. He forgets the fact that if two ride on one horse, one must ride behind and he does not give us any assurances.... Poor fellow, I am sorry for him.'

Smith's dismissive attitude to the concerns of others, and his amused view of Eason, both came into play in this reaction. He seems to have postponed passing this correspondence on to Lethbridge until January, 1879, when he wrote saying that 'the poor fellow is evidently very much in earnest', an admission that, in the preceding months, Eason had not been taken very seriously. There was no follow-up to this, but inevitably the matter came up again later.

In 1879 the issue still did not hinge on the adequacy of material remuneration. Eason had conceded in his letter of January 1879 that 'the money reward may seem sufficient ...' even if his business status was less exalted than he would wish. However by 1883, when he reviewed his situation over the years for Smith's benefit, it was clear that his rewards had not risen in a way that was commensurate with the increased scale of the business, and the growth in his responsibility. From 1868 to 1873 Eason's share of the profits had averaged £1,165. In the nine years up to 1882 the figure had only increased to £1,231. Eason attributed the disadvantageous outcome to the way in which buildings had been financed out of current revenue. They were included in a separate account, and written off against 'rent' payments financed out of current revenue. In consequence the profits were lower than they would otherwise have been, and Eason himself was the loser. Therefore he had two subjects of concern: the inadequacy of his remuneration, and his wish to provide for his son Charles to succeed him. Even if his son were not to succeed him, it would in any event be necessary to identify an heir apparent for training to take over responsibility, since he was now approaching sixty. The question of partnership lay behind the issue, and all the more insistently because of the disappointing material outlook for Eason. In an undated letter to Lethbridge he wrote:

> Hence the great importance to you that the person who will follow me should now obtain as large an experience as possible under me, in order that the business may not suffer by my death, or by my leaving it. It cannot and ought not to be indifferent to me whether my work is to continue after me or not, and is there not a strong

> possibility of disaster if a stranger shall come to administer this business after me?

The bond which had been given to Charles Eason was due to expire at the end of 1883. Eason had raised the matter of the valuation as early as July 1883, but it dragged on interminably with perfunctory attention to the issue from the partners. Even though Smith happened to be in Dublin twice in the intervening period, his first visits to Dublin for a decade apart from one in 1875, there had been only a brief conversation on the first visit in October 1883, and even before the second visit it was envisaged explicitly that he would not have time to see Eason at all, the object of his visit being to deliver an important political address in Dublin. In August 1883 in a letter to Lethbridge, Smith was complacent in viewing the matter: 'Eason is getting old, and his family have been, I have no doubt, expensive to him and a little liberality or generosity may be well employed.' A letter from Charles Eason on 8 January 1884 set out the position quite briskly, but pressed for a decision, and added that 'very soon Parliament will meet and in the absorbing interest of public affairs you can have little leisure for consideration of your business.' Smith's reaction to it in a letter to Lethbridge four days later was as follows: 'Eason has sent me a very curious letter which shows I think that Father and Son have got into a very morbid condition.... They are very good in their work without doubt, but very foolish all the same: and it will be necessary now to settle the question'.

The question of partnership is crucial to an understanding of the problems of W.H. Smith and Son in the 1880s. Eason had made an explicit demand for a partnership, and an implicit demand existed among the managers in London, to which, as his later comments suggest, Smith was opposed. These demands were not caused simply by the personal ambition of the managers, but reflected a response to a rigid organisation, within which the managers of the day-to-day business were unable to take decisions, in spite of its enormous scale. White, who as head of the Counting House and head of wholesale news was one of the principal staff members in London, commented on the delays is making decisions, and the consequent problems for members of the firm, in a letter which he wrote to Charles Eason on 29 October 1883:

> You have but given expression in your letter to considerations which have long occupied the thoughts of some of us here — the opportunity has however failed us for bringing them under the notice of the house, and we have been content to work on loyally at each

day's duty waiting for the Providential opening, which by your act, I hope has now occurred....

In a lesser degree, we here, have a like solicitude for the future, and though we do not say it, we feel with alarm that a business can hardly be exposed to a greater peril than for its Principals to be constantly disowning responsibility when some important decision with respect to its future has to be made.

You know, as I know, that when a man's work is not felt to be indispensable the motive power for vigorous and successful prosecution of it has gone, and if this feeling should get possession of the men responsible for the conduct of this business, it will rapidly become depleted and broken up. I hope it may be given to you to do something to arrest this danger, not so much for our sakes as for the sake of work into which the best of our lives have been put and which humanly speaking, has a much longer life than any man in it.

Charles Eason visited London regularly, and was on terms of some intimacy with many members of the firm. The feelings of the staff could be expressed freely to him, as in White's letter, and their outlook can only have reinforced his own feelings. Underneath the surface, there was some resentment at Smith's offhand and procrastinating attitude, which had been evident for instance in the lack of immediate response to the issues raised by Eason in 1883. Although the matter had been first raised in a letter of 30 June 1883, it was not until the following 12 January that it is evident that Smith had resolved to take it seriously. White was sent to Dublin to view the books, and Lethbridge himself visited Dublin in April 1884. Even in 1872, the proposal to capitalise the balances and to regularise the relationship between the houses had emerged only when Eason himself had raised the issue of partnership, and the relationship of the Dublin house to London had been reviewed as a result.

When Charles Eason visited London in 1884, Smith proposed that he should take a three month holiday. Eason responded to this that 'it is quite obvious that a clear settlement of all these matters must precede my going.' Eason suggested arrangements under which the amount written off against working expenses should be reduced. He sought £600 as a settlement for excessive writing off in the past, and that these matters should be dealt with in the future on the same principles as applied in the past in the London house. He asked for £250 to compensate him for his work on the catholic prayerbooks division, and £50 per annum for his work there for the future, and suggested that his proportion of the profits should be raised to a half. In fact, the issue was avoided. Smith proposed on 7 April 1884 to make Eason a present of the stock of prayerbooks, which was estimated at £3,000, on the understanding that his imprint would be substituted for Smith's. The premises could be used for carrying on publication for five years and the profits would be Eason's absolutely. All this was to be 'in substitution of any other alteration in existing arrangement.' This was not quite as generous as it may seem. The prayerbooks had provided an occasion for embarrassing Smith in the House of Commons in February 1884, when T.M. Healy, an Irish member, had pointed to the imprint of the house and to the fact that Smith had profited from selling prayer books to a people whom he apparently despised.[10] At one and the same time Smith's offer to Eason disembarrassed himself of a problem, and avoided facing up to any of the underlying general issues that Eason had raised. The upshot of it all was that he had not treated Eason seriously. He had neither given due weight to Eason's argument about the value of his contribution to the Irish house, nor had he attached any importance to Eason's view that the political sensitivities of the Irish business had required particularly careful handling, and that consideration should be given to this in settling both his level of remuneration and his status within the firm.

Ultimately, there was a coldness, bordering on callousness, in Smith's attitudes to those who worked under him. The letter from Charles Eason to Smith on 22 October 1883 has been quoted as an instance of the affection in which Smith was held by his employees.[11] Taken in the context of the issues to which it referred, it is quite the reverse. In the light of the sentiment expressed by White to Eason on 29 October 1883, only seven days later, it is likely that Eason was voicing an opinion on behalf of senior members of the London staff as well as himself. Indeed, at one point in his letter, Eason stated specifically: 'if I might be prepared to speak for my fellows. . . .' The matter is so important for understanding both Smith's and Eason's character, and the situation affecting the Dublin house, that it bears quoting at some length:

> But the relation in which the trusted servants of your firm stand to you goes beyond any technical form of service. So much time and thought given by us to you, so much reward as gifts or wages paid by you to us.
>
> The dry hard facts of which Mr. Lethbridge spoke are all contained in the above, but we have a relation beyond all this, which this cannot

10 Hansard, vol. 284, 20 February 1884

11 Chilston *Life of W.H. Smith* p. 179

> describe, and which has existed all along towards yourself personally. That relation has a more human side. If I might be permitted to speak for my fellows, it began to be a force when we felt the influence of your character in our work and we have been willing to spend our lives in your service, not alone for the material coins you have paid us but for the love and honour in which you have personally been held by us.
>
> Are things to be changed? You have said that we might not expect you in the future to take an active part in the details of your business, and we can understand that in the weightier obligations of political life you might hardly have time to know us and our work as in former years. But is *your* place in your firm? It is no untruth to say that in a certain sense there is a void which Mr. Lethbridge cannot fill.... But Mr. Lethbridge tells us that before long he too may give up the direct part he has taken in the guidance of affairs, at most only be — to use his own words — consulting physician in your establishment. To whom then may we look?
>
> The older servants of your firm have entered the sixty period of their lives or are close to it.... But can this influence of the past prevail to energize your present staff and thus to give you your successors. I fear not.

After Smith's death and the publication of his will, valued at £1.78 million, William Fred Kingdon, head of the book department in London commented drily to Charles Eason, that 'so little of accumulated (sic) wealth had been distributed excited many comments'. Six months later the account of Smith in the *Illustrated Magazine* prompted Kingdon to observe:

> No doubt Mr. Smith was a religious man — one of the class that unites his deep religious principles with equally deep selfishness — probably taking his remarkable acquirement of wealth as special indication of divine favour. The world is not greatly benefitted by them.[12]

In fact, there was a deep sense of alienation within the firm at this stage, and it extended to the new man brought in as a future partner, C.H. St. John Hornby. Kingdon commented in a letter to Charles Eason on this in January 1893: 'have you heard that the partners' room has a new occupant? Mr. Smith has introduced an old school chum to assist in their clerical work. A Mr. Hornby, and he was introduced on Monday as "one of *us*", quite on the father's lines don't you think?'

12 Some personal letters from Kingdon to Charles Eason survive in Eason's.

The sourness in London sprang from the lack of central direction in the 1880s and from the failure to devolve responsibility on to the senior managers. A new partner brought in, in the old manner, seemed to presage a continuation of the old style of doing business. However, whatever the circumstances of his introduction, Hornby was in fact to assure the future of the business, and to rescue it from the perilous situation into which it had drifted in the 1880s. The exclusive attitude of the partners, Awdry and Lethbridge, at least to Kingdon's way of thinking in 1892, was held against them even in the matter of the obituary notice for Smith in the *Illustrated Magazine*. Kingdon pointed out that the writer was said to be 'inspired' by the active partners without the help of White in composing it: 'Mr. White could have helped him to make it far more interesting and I wish he would not so persistently coldshoulder everyone who wished for enlightenment in this direction.'

For Eason, at least, these matters had already been resolved. As Smith became increasingly prominent in the Conservative party, and the 'Irish question' remained a key political issue, it was inevitable that the future of the business in Ireland should sooner or later come under scrutiny. The catalyst for change, however, was Smith's appointment in January 1886 as Secretary for Ireland in Salisbury's government.

Chapter 7 Home Rule — The Transfer to the Easons

W.H. SMITH NEVER REALLY LIKED IRELAND or the Irish. This came across quite clearly in his letters. In 1856 he wrote to his sister Gussie from Dublin: 'I am well and very cross for the Irish are fast exciting all the dormant decision and anger in my character. I verily believe if I stay here much longer I shall be thought a fiend at least for I do insist upon their doing that which is right in my own eyes this instant. . . .' Writing from California in 1872 he stated that 'people there say they would gladly give us back all the Irish who have invaded the country in numbers, and substitute Chinamen for them. . . .' This dislike, muted in the earlier years, was to become more evident in the 1880s.

Smith's first visit to Ireland since 1875 took place in September 1881, when his yacht cruised off the south coast. He visited Cork, Blarney, Killarney and Glengarriff, where he assisted at a Sunday service and commented that 'the sensation was like being in a foreign country'. He experienced a warm welcome from conservatives, and more invitations flooded in than he could cope with. He was now becoming politically involved with Ireland for the first time. The choice of Ireland for the cruise can hardly have been unintentional, and his Irish correspondents at this point began to become numerous.

His views on Ireland were also being coloured by his new private secretary John Luard Pattison, who had been a land agent in Ireland. Smith had first met him in Canada in 1872, when Pattison had been secretary to Lord Dufferin of Clandeboye who at the time was Governor of Canada. In 1874 Pattison had been employed in the estate office in Clandeboye, and he became agent-in-chief of the Clandeboye estates in 1877. Because of his wife's ill health, which necessitated a change, Lord Dufferin secured employment for him from 1 May 1880 as Smith's agent-in-chief and general private secretary. He can only have reinforced Smith's jaundiced view of Irishmen and of Ireland. Writing of the expectations of an Irish sub-tenant on Smith's English estates in December 1880,

Pattison asserted that 'if one was not accustomed to Irishmen, it would be difficult to deal with such an application.'[1]

Even before he was appointed, Pattison was offering observations on the Irish land system and how land purchase worked. He may have been encouraged to give these views, but as the year progressed his own outlook cannot but have coloured his employer's thinking. He assured Smith that 'the thinking Irish' considered that the 1870 Act covered all cases of injustice. More seriously, he represented to Smith the view that civil war could develop in Ireland. In October 1880 for instance he told Smith that 'the Orangemen in the North are beginning to organise meetings as against the agitation in the south, saying that if the government will not deal with the Home rulers [i.e. Roman Catholics] they will take some other steps themselves, which in other words is the civil war Mr. Gladstone was looking out for.' His views were alarmist. He dwelt on 'such a revolution as practically exists', spoke of fears of disaffection among Irish soldiers in the regiments in Ireland, and asserted the need for coercion. In December Pattison told Smith: 'It is almost to be desired that you should have had an opportunity of making a public speech before the house met, as there is a great need of a calm and temperate review of the question at this moment.' By the end of 1880 Smith believed that arms were being imported wholesale to Ireland.

Smith's dislike of the Irish members of Parliament was transparent and persistent. He wrote in July 1881 that 'those dreadful men had broken out again.' This dislike became more marked in later years. As Leader of the House under a later Conservative government, the Irish question and the nationalists created many of the stresses and strains of his political life. Writing to the Queen informing her of one stormy debate, he remarked that 'the ordinary Irish members succeeded each other in dreary succession'. He wrote in similar vein to his wife in May 1887: 'here I am again droning on while the Irish and their allies spit and splutter and obstruct....' and again in September 1887: 'We had a bad night and excessive annoyance from the Irish and their allies.... It is very galling to have to endure insult and provocation from these men and to be unable to cast it back again, except at the cost of prolonging our suffering.' Later, like many conservatives, Smith slipped into the habit of regarding the Parnellite Special Commission of 1888-90 as a state trial. By an odd coincidence his burial took place on the same day as Parnell, and there was no Irish politician at his graveside.

1 Pattison's letters are in the Hambleden papers, series KK.

From time to time Smith had shown some interest in Ireland quite independently of the issues which were beginning to press in upon politicians. Years before, Smith, who had already built up a large English estate, seriously considered the purchase of the Connemara estate of the Martins of Ross.[2] The active interest he took in the East End emigration club in London may have extended to Ireland. A list of 297 emigrants assisted by Smith in 1869 bore mainly Irish names.[3] The possibility that assisted emigration might be a means of reducing the dimensions of the Irish problem was a live issue in his mind as late as 1882. At the end of 1883 he was seriously considering purchasing the Belleek china works. Charles Eason was instructed to appraise its prospects, and he advised Smith against it: 'A weak effort of philanthropy may go on alongside of it but if any real good is to come of it, the concern must pay its way, and give simple interest to the promoters.' Parnell's approach to Smith to join the Board of Directors of Parnell's scheme to finance internal migration was not as far fetched as it sounds, given Smith's interests at this stage, and his past involvement in emigration.[4]

Among senior English conservative politicians he was in fact the only one who had any first hand acquaintance with Ireland. His recent knowledge was largely a result of the visit which he made in April 1882, to study the feasibility of land purchase as a solution to the Irish land question.[5] In the course of a week he saw a large number of people, almost all officials or conservatives, and he dined among others with Lord and Lady Ardilaun, and on another occasion with Edward Guinness, 'people being asked to meet me who could give information'. King-Harman was another of the people he met. He travelled on 11 April by special train, accompanied by the Chairman of the Midland Great Western Railway, on a one-day visit to 'the worst parts of Ireland', Mayo, Roscommon and Leitrim: 'I fear that as long as there is "representation" for such places in Parliament and consequent agitation is a profitable trade, the condition of this people would not be improved — but it is a great danger to the State'. This letter accurately expresses the pessimism that

2 H. Maxwell *Life and Times of the right honourable William Henry Smith, M.P.* (Edinburgh & London, 1893) vol. ii, 68.

3 Hambleden papers QQ 25.

4 F.S.L. Lyons *Charles Stewart Parnell* (London, 1978) p. 263; Parnell's letters are in the Hambleden papers, P.58/83-87.

5 Chilston is wrong in suggesting that this visit took the form of a cruise around the Irish coast, a confusion caused by the fact that Smith spent a good deal of his time in the Royal St George Yacht Club, a conservative bastion, and addressed his letters to his wife from the club.

NEWSPAPER AND ADVERTISING

Agency Office,

ESTABLISHED JUNE, 1819, FOR RECEIVING

ADVERTISEMENTS AND SUBSCRIPTIONS,

FOR EVERY NEWSPAPER IN THE BRITISH EMPIRE,

BY JOHNSTON AND CO.

No. 1, EDEN-QUAY, SACKVILLE-STREET, DUBLIN,

To whose Office, Files of the Papers are transmitted for the inspection of Advertisers.

NEWSPAPERS.

JOHNSTON AND CO. respectfully inform the Irish Nobility and Gentry, Proprietors of News Rooms, Reading Rooms, Public Institutions, Libraries, &c. that they supply the LONDON, DUBLIN, and *every other* Newspaper in the United Kingdom by the *earliest dispatch*, with the *strictest punctuality*, and on the *most moderate terms*, (for any period required;) and when wished, exchanged at pleasure, or the address altered, during the period of Subscription, without any extra charge. J. AND CO's. Papers being made up in, and sent from London DIRECT, (and on all occasions when Second Editions are published in time for the Post, they are invariably sent,) *no possible advantage is, or can be had over them* in the supplying of Newspapers—and from the facilities of their Office, they hope for an extension of that patronage the Public have so liberally favoured them with, whos approbation *it is*, and *ever will be*, their study to merit

SUBSCRIPTIONS TO BE PAID IN ADVANCE.

ADVERTISEMENTS,

Inserted in all the LONDON, DUBLIN, EDINBURGH, English, Irish and Scotch Provincial Newspapers.

Patronized by ALL the GOVERNMENT OFFICES, JOHNSTON AND CO. solicit the orders of Professional Gentlemen, Surveyors, Land Agents, Booksellers, and every other Class of Advertisers, who will find great facilities in their Office; for by ONE order to them an Advertisement may be conveyed to *every* Newspaper in the Empire, and settled for in *one account*, (*without any Commission to the Advertiser*,) instead of having to pay each Individual Newspaper; and Papers containing the Insertions are reserved when desired.

☞ Files of most of the Papers in the United Kingdom for the last TWELVE YEARS, are preserved for general reference, and will be regularly kept for the inspection of Advertisers.

LONDON AND DUBLIN NEWSPAPERS,

Sent to every part of the United Kingdom, Postage Free.

Daily Morning.

Morning Advertiser, Morning Chronicle, Morning Herald, Morning Post, Public Ledger, Times

Daily Evening.

Albion, British Traveller, Courier, Globe and Traveller, Standard, Sun

— £9. 15s. per Annum, or £2. 10s. per Quarter.

Monday, Wednesday, and Friday.

Evening Mail, London Packet

Tuesday, Thursday, and Saturday.

English Chronicle, St. James's Chronicle

— £4. 17s. 6d. per An. or £1. 5s. per Quar.

Monday and Thursday.

	Per Annum.
Record	£3 10 0
Weekly.	
Age	1 16 0
Atlas	2 16 0
Bell's Life in London	1 16 0
Bell's Messenger	2 2 0
Cobbett's Register	3 10 0
Court Journal	2 16 0
Dispatch	2 2 0
Englishman	1 16 0
Examiner	1 16 0
Farmer's Journal	2 8 0
Intelligence	1 16 0
John Bull	1 16 0
Literary Gazette,	2 16 0
News	2 2 0
Observer	1 16 0
Spectator	2 16 0
Sunday Times	1 16 0
World	2 8 0

DUBLIN PAPERS.

Daily.

	Per Annum.
Morning Register, Freeman's Journal, Morning Post, Times,	£6 0 0
Saunders' Newsletter,	5 4 0

Monday, Wednesday and Friday.

Evening Mail	3 10 0
Pilot	3 3 0

Tuesday, Thursday and Saturday.

	Per Annum.
Evening Post	£4 0 0
Evening Packet	3 5 0
Evening Freeman	3 3 0
Weekly.	
Comet	1 6 0
Warder, Weekly Freeman, Weekly Register, Mercantile Advertiser,	£1 10 0

☞ SUBSCRIPTIONS TO BE PAID IN ADVANCE.

The utmost attention and punctuality observed in the execution of all commands, and in the transmission of Papers ordered from JOHNSTON AND Co. whose Customers are requested to be particular in addressing their Orders as under—

To
JOHNSTON and CO.
Newspaper Agents,
Eden-Quay,
DUBLIN.

As the most certain mode of their being promptly and expeditiously executed.

d 3

J. K. Johnston set up as a newspaper and advertising agent in 1819. *Post Office Directory* 1832

Top left and right: George Eason (1782-1828) and his wife Rebecca (1795-1856). *Left:* Charles Eason I (1823-1899).

NORTHERN CIRCULATING LIBRARY,

Castle-Place, Belfast,

Book Societies and School Libraries supplied on Very Advantageous Terms.

Library Books forwarded to all parts of the Kingdom.

JOHN HENDERSON, PROPRIETOR.

THOSE who have not yet favoured this Establishment with a visit, are respectfully informed, that its distinguishing features are

LOW PRICES, GOOD ARTICLES, & PUNCTUALITY.

Henderson's of Belfast, a newsagent/bookseller of the 1840s.

The proposed elevation of 79/80 Middle Abbey Street. *The Irish Builder,* June 1875.

The Retail — the front of the O'Connell Street premises circa 1900.

Charles Eason II and his family. *From left:* Keith, Charles, Mrs Eason, Alec, Edith and Jack.

Above: The elegant interior staircase to the lending library in the early 1900s. The figure on the right is Digges, head of Retail. *Below:* The wholesale and card department — postcards of actresses were a popular line.

Above: The first two vans employed by Eason's parked in Middle Abbey Street. *Below:* Hand composing and page make-up for printing in the factory in the early 1900s.

underlay Smith's outlook and that of even the moderate or less wild conservatives. Reform was intended as an effort to stave off revolution. He was also prompted by Edward Gibson, Conservative MP for Trinity College, Dublin, who had accompanied him to Ireland, to make a journey from Dublin to visit Smyth, a landlord in Westmeath, whose sister-in-law had been killed in an attempt on his own life: 'It is hardly possible to imagine a more indulgent landlord or a more religious man, but he is deeply moved by the ingratitude of his tenants, almost all of whom have shown either indifference to the wicked murder or to the fact that it was intended to kill him.' His Irish sojourn left Smith profoundly pessimistic, and subsequent correspondence with his new contacts can only have added to it. His only acquaintances in Ireland were landowners, hardly a source of balanced comment in the conditions of the 1880s, and his views were drawn from this selective and deeply reactionary milieu. One of his closest associates in the Conservative party was Sir Stafford Northcote, at the time leader of the party in the Commons who had paid a political visit to Ulster in October 1883, and who had met on that occasion many of the Irish Unionists, including King-Harman, Lord Waterford and the Abercorns.

R.M.A. Holmes of the Crown and Hanaper's office, Dublin Castle, assured him soon after the Phoenix Park murders of May 1882, that 'you are quite right in doubting the sincerity of Ireland's lamentation over those foul deeds of Saturday last.'[6] A. J. Hamilton Smythe of Athlone, who had given him a memorandum in April, wrote to him: 'I know as a matter of fact that the Roman Catholic servants of my father-in-law's home where I am staying, laughed when they first heard of the murders saying that it served them right, and it was not until they knew that the priests had denounced the crime that they drew in their horns.'[7] In October 1883 Smith spent some time with the King-Harmans at Rockingham, and during his two-day visit in January 1884 he was a guest of Edward Guinness in his house in St Stephen's Green. In January 1883 Smith seemed to think that coercion was responsible for the recovery reflected in the Irish firm's accounts, thinking that the Act had given a 'temporary security'. When business, which had slipped again in the interval, recovered in 1885, Lethbridge made the banal comment that 'it seems inconsistent with the ideas one ordinarily has with reference to the state of Ireland.' Smith's interest in land purchase has led one of his

6 Hambleden papers, P 58/37, 12 May 1882
7 ibid., P 58/38, 12 May. 1882.

biographers to see in him one of the progenitors of the Ashbourne Act of 1885.[8] In fact, Gibson, who was to become Lord Ashbourne in 1885, sponsor of the celebrated land purchase act of that year, had accompanied him on the April 1882 visit to Ireland. It is clear that Smith, Gibson and Northcote were in close consultation over the land issue. When Smith was appointed Chief Secretary in January 1886, Lord Waterford assured him, that 'there is no appointment that will give more pleasure to the loyal Irishmen generally'.

The genesis of the land purchase policy may even have lain in dismay among Irish landlords and Conservatives at the scale of the reduction in rents by the Sub-Commissioners under the 1881 Act. Northcote had written to Smith as early as December 1881 of the 'sweeping action' of the Sub-Commissioners 'who are going on the lines of the unjust steward, "Take thy bill and write four score".'[9] The pessimistic purpose which underlay the conservative support for land purchase was simply an effort to preserve the financial interest of the Irish landlords. The purpose did not spring from any far-sighted plan framed from a broad perspective of Irish conditions, nor from any deep appraisal of Irish problems. Smith was bitterly opposed to the scheme of land purchase on the grand scale which Gladstone had intended to couple with home rule. His sole object was to secure the best possible financial deal for Irish proprietors in the conditions in which the long-term outlook was assessed with deep pessimism.

In fact, Smith's continued interest in land purchase was sustained by his fears about the evil consequences of a wider franchise, and by the prospect of home rule. This fear was already on his mind as early as 1882, but it acquired a new significance from 1886. It was then a question of getting the British parliament interested, and avoiding the consequences for landowners of what would happen if land purchase fell through. As he put it to Fitzgerald on 22 September 1888: 'The question would arise how is the British elector to be induced to rise to the full measure of his responsibilities towards Ireland and the Irish landlord and if the effort is made and it fails, what will be the probable results to the landowner.'[10]

8 Chilston pp 171-2.
9 Hambleden papers PS 7/98, 11 December, 1881. For Northcote's Irish visit, see A. B. Cooke, 'A Conservative party leader in Ulster: Sir Stafford Northcote's diary of a visit to the province, October 1883', *Proceedings of the Royal Irish Academy*, vol. 75, section c, no. 4 (1975).
10 ibid., PS 14/78

With the aid of information supplied by Pattison, he followed the evolution of land purchase under the Ashbourne Act. He believed that land purchase legislation would scotch any expectations of compulsory purchase by tenants — an expectation which had led tenants to withhold higher offers for land. He had little optimism that the opposition to landowners could be worn down, as some hopefully thought, and the failure of the home rule bill meant that extensive land purchase could be proceeded with under the supervision of the imperial parliament. What was not acceptable, when coupled with home rule, was not only acceptable but desirable, in the circumstances of the late 1880s. The fact that a home rule bill materialised in 1886 had seemed to him to provide a concrete basis for his fears whose expression at this stage became wilder. In 1887 he wrote that 'it must be assumed that every priest in Ireland is hostile to any English government either from prejudice or self-interest and that nothing but a conviction that rebellion must fail will bring them round'. His reaction the preceding year to the home rule bill, and to the land purchase bill, as his biographer has observed, was 'quite startling for one usually so calm and philosophical': 'I have been studying the new Home Rule and Land Purchase Bill in the quiet which is afforded by the Lake of Como, and if these bills pass I am very much inclined to clear out of the old country altogether....'[11] Home rule to him implied independence, and civil strife. A long speech at Doncaster on 5 December 1887 set out his views on the Irish question. To Davitt, who took him to task for misrepresenting his views he stated that 'I have not disguised my belief that if Mr. Gladstone's proposals are adopted, complete separation or civil war are inevitable'.[12] This prospect gave a new urgency to the necessity for land legislation. He did not share the optimism of some Tories who saw the prospect of better conditions for themselves or for land sales. In September 1889 he wrote to a politician that 'I can only express my opinion, but if I was a trustee for an Irish property, I should like to put my home in order and make terms with the enemy while I had the chance....'[13]

His views on Ireland were deeply gloomy from the outset of the 1880s. He was, however, a realist, which helped to sway the balance in a party which was not seriously interested in a solution to Irish problems. Superficial though his contacts were with Ireland, he was the first English

11 Chilston p. 207

12 Hambleden papers, PS 12/118, 10 December 1887. See various correspondence in series PS 12 around that date, also PS 13/1, letter of 5 January 1888 to Davitt.

13 See letters in ibid., PS 14.

Tory politician who had tried to understand social problems, by visiting, however briefly, the stricken areas in Ireland, and by taking the advice of people on the spot. The idea of land purchase was planted by some of the wiser Irish conservatives who anticipated accurately the drift of events. Smith perceptively saw their point of view, and threw the weight of thinking Tories behind their ideas. It was this debate on the pros and cons of Irish policy that Smith had in mind when he wrote in July 1885 to his friend Colonel King-Harman, who was not likely to have adopted the moderate Tory view, that 'there are always two sides to a question even when it concerns Ireland.'[14]

The pattern of visiting problem areas in Ireland was to be followed by Arthur Balfour as Chief Secretary, when he spent a week at the end of October 1890 on a remarkable and hectic tour of Mayo and Connemara: this was a prelude to his Congested Districts Act of the following year.[15] Smith had preceded Balfour in his interest in Irish questions, and when Balfour became Chief Secretary he had had close contacts with Smith, though through conversations rather than correspondence. Parnell's addressing Smith as 'one of those who are known to be most liberally and favourably disposed towards any scheme of ameliorating the condition of the people of Ireland' implies also Smith's prominent profile in the formulation of Tory policy on Ireland.[16] In 1889 Balfour was drafting another land purchase bill, which became law in 1891. This was the broadest measure so far achieved, and Balfour wrote to Smith that he thought Smith would find his ideas 'not out of harmony with yours.'[17] The draft was shared with both Salisbury and Smith before any other eyes were set upon it.[18] Smith remained in touch with conservatives who proposed ameliorative measures for Ireland. In 1887 he was in communication with Lady Burdett-Coutts about the fisheries in Baltimore, Co Cork,[19] and he was, we can be sure, a supporter of the practical policies envisaged for the Congested Districts Board. His visits to the west of Ireland, and his prolonged inspection of the south-west coasts by yacht in 1881 had given him an acquaintance with Ireland, which, however limited, was unique among conservative politicians.

14 ibid, PS 9/55, 28 July 1885.

15 Public Record Office of Northern Ireland, Belfast. T 3221/1/134-144, 21 Oct.-31 Oct. 1890. George Wyndham to his wife. Wyndham, a later chief secretary, progenitor of the Wyndham Act of 1903, was Balfour's private secretary in 1890.

16 Hambleden papers, PS 8/83, 26 August 1883

17 Chilston p. 310

18 See in particular Hambleden papers, PS 14/93, Arthur Balfour to Smith, 11 October 1889

19 Hambleden papers, PS 12

The journalist Stead in July 1886 told Smith that 'I believe you are the only member of the new cabinet who has any clearly defined idea as to what should be done in Ireland'.[20] Nevertheless the perspective in which Smith's views were shaped was appallingly narrow. In no respect was this more evident than in his views of the franchise. His notorious speech on the extension of the franchise in Dublin in January 1884 was doubly unfortunate. The form in which his views were expressed was unpalatable, and Dublin was the last place where such a speech should have been delivered. The bad judgement displayed on this occasion is all the more disturbing as it seems that the speech was prompted solely by the narrow interests of achieving party unity in England. In an undated letter just before this, Bagenal had suggested the need for four or five speeches in January 1884 from leading members of the party 'who would *compel* attention to the subject of Ireland. It is evident that the extension of the franchise to Ireland will split up the cabinet.'[21]

Smith's high political profile and his lack of sympathy with Ireland gave concern to Charles Eason from the end of the 1870s. The sensitivity of the Irish business to the political situation was repeatedly mentioned from 1879 onwards in Eason's letters. The first occasion was at the very outset of 1879 when he noted that work in Ireland called 'for very special gifts in dealing with the people of this country so as to keep down prejudices both as regards the customers of the house and the staff who are employed in it.' In October 1883 Charles Eason noted, that 'during the past three years in a time of intense national disturbance I have kept your business throughout free of any complication with either of the disturbing parties'. He came back to the same theme in a letter of January 1884, observing that 'during these years I have never been free from haunting care, lest some sudden prejudice should attach to the firm and all my labour should be lost'. Smith's speech in Dublin three weeks later, considered in a purely Irish context, was utterly reckless, and demonstrated clearly to Eason, if he wanted further proof, both Smith's lack of interest in the Irish dimension of his firm, and the danger his political views presented to the local business. Smith repeated his views in February in the House of Commons.

At the end of 1885, when the Tory cabinet was undecided as to what its Irish policy should be, Smith sought Eason's advice for the first and only time as to what was the political condition of Ireland in the

20 ibid., PS 9/159, July 1886.
21 ibid., PS 8/135. Undated, 1884 added in pencil.

knowledge that 'a crisis is at hand'. In a letter of December 1885 Eason poured out his views.[22] This letter must have reflected all his frustrations, not only those on the business front, but his wider ones, as well. The letter flatly contradicted Smith's political views on Ireland; something which he anticipated, as he remarked: 'I fear this letter will appear long and be disappointing....'

> I know only a few of the personnel of the National party, and my views are formed by the acts and speeches of the leaders, and the general effect upon me has been to make me heart and soul with them in their objects.... I have at different times travelled all over the country and gradually as facts came to me I learned to have a deep sympathy with the Irish people under their wrongs, while my contact in business with the ruling classes, the Nobility, Gentry, Professionals etc. impressed me very unfavourably as to their justice and honour, and I felt and saw so much of their arbitrary over-ruling and tyranical conduct that I ceased to wonder at that intense class hatred generated against them, in their tenants and dependants. Nor does their example at all qualify this verdict, for the waste and extravagance not to say their immoralities, has left no counterpoise in conduct against the general verdict against them.
>
> I have an Englishman's love of law and order and the Irish outrages and violence as well as the darker murders of the Irish Invincibles have always been intensely abhorrent to me, likewise the persistent tyranny of the landlords and propertied class has been so great as to bring back feelings towards the people after several temporary alienations.
>
> And all along my judgement has been that the people of Great Britain and the ruling classes especially are accountable for the [?] mis-government under which rack-renting evictions and the clearing away of tenants has been possible.
>
> Then in the matter of religion the contempt — [?] shown by Protestants towards Catholics has come to be a matter of importance in the present crisis. There has been amongst the ruling Protestants a narrow proselytising spirit and efforts are constantly made to buy or compel people to change their religion or otherwise place them at a disadvantage because of it. This has produced a bitter feeling among the [?] and people generally.

22 The letter survives only in a copy in the Dublin house. There are a number of indecipherable words.

> The remarkable feature of the recent vote in Ireland was that of Conservative Catholics — voting for Parnellite members. This is a very general fact in Dublin and I do not doubt that it prevailed in the country too.
>
> I do not suppose any English Party Government can arrange a safe theme for the future Government of Ireland. Man proposes, and God disposes. I try to look away from man to a higher Governor and putting my trust there I can feel that although cabinets may be feeble and popular instincts may be very weak, yet God is over all and his handwriting is on the wall telling us that the present fabric has been weighed in the balance and found wanting.

All this implies in effect that Eason in December 1885 favoured home rule. If this interpretation is correct, it means that in the circumstances of late 1885 there was not only a conflict of interest between Eason and Smith as to the effect of Smith's political role on his Irish business, but a wide divergence of view between the two men on the Irish question. Rather ironically — because Eason was in essence apolitical while his employer was not seriously interested in Ireland at all — the Dublin house was to find itself for some days in January 1886 critically affected by a crisis in the Tory party and in Anglo-Irish relations.

At the end of 1885, the Tory cabinet was divided on the Irish question: the Lord Lieutenant, Lord Carnarvon, who favoured home rule, was on the point of resigning over the difference of opinion in the Cabinet. His resignation took place on 16 January, and the following day, Salisbury, the Prime Minister, wrote offering the post of Chief Secretary, under a new viceroy, to Smith, the only senior member of the Conservative party with any knowledge of Irish conditions. A description of him in 1887 by a shrewd outside observer such as Archbishop Walsh in Dublin as 'practical-minded, kind, sound of judgement and completely to be trusted'.[23] conveys something of the impression that Smith must have made in direct dealing with individuals, and the high esteem that he enjoyed among his political associates. But while this judgement was true enough in terms of his human qualities, he had serious deficiencies especially of temperament for an Irish post. His views had been formed by the upper echelons of the Irish landed class. Ultimately he was not well briefed on Irish issues, nor really interested in them. Some of his private comments suggest that his customary calm and reason at times abandoned him on Irish questions.

23 Chilston p. 267

Smith arrived in Ireland as Chief Secretary on 23 January 1886. The appointment greatly increased Eason's alarm. He was already concerned over the way the business was sliding into indecision, and he had also failed to secure a more permanent interest for his family. Now the political opprobium which Smith would be likely to attract threatened the Dublin house. He had long striven to keep the firm free of the hostile attentions of both parties in Irish life, a point whose consequence he had stressed on several occasions in correspondence with Smith from as early as 1879. Now, his worst fears were about to be fulfilled. As he wrote to Awdry (who was about to succeed Lethbridge as the managing partner of the London house) on 22 January:

> We are open to attack from every traveller who visits the country and our trade rivals through their servants will invent, distort and exaggerate facts in a way we cannot reply to while the party politicians will seize the present opportunity to do us an injury. It will be a miracle if we will escape.
>
> And our business is open to this attack, the bookselling and stationery can be done as well by other persons as by us; and though the news and periodicals can be best done by us because of our organisation, yet given an adequate motive and some new machinery, can make us unneccessary, thus any cause fancied or real may irritate the Nationalists who will take their revenge upon us, however innocent we may be.

While in Dublin Smith, taken up with the details of a coercion bill, was unable to visit the Dublin house. So Eason wrote on 25 January proposing that the Irish business be transferred to him. The proposal was acknowledged the same day. Smith was due to return to London on 26 January in order to move the coercion bill in the House of Commons. He had not time to deal with Eason's proposal, referring it to the London house in a letter of 26 January: 'I have not a moment and I must be very careful to keep my head clear of all distracting subjects. My work is very serious.' But by the time he arrived in London the government had already fallen (27 January). With the danger receding for the time being, Eason now made a modified proposal (28 January): that the business be carried on in his name and that he put up half the capital. Smith's mind was now being made up with remarkable rapidity. Awdry had acknowledged Eason's letter of 25 January on 30 January stating that 'the great question there dealt with of course cannot be settled in a moment....' The modified proposal of 28 January was referred to Smith by Lethbridge on 31 January with the observation that 'if it is desirable to transfer the business it must be done absolutely. . . .' Smith made his final decision quickly, and it remained only to work out the details.

Decisions had been taken so rapidly that both the course of events and the motivations have never been clearly understood even within the recollection of the immediate members of the Eason family. What moved Smith seems fairly clear. His remoteness from the realities of Ireland, and his somewhat inflamed imagination where Irish matters was concerned, meant that his pessimism on Irish issues ran deeper than ever, and the danger of civil strife was a real one in his mind. Indeed he even misunderstood what Eason said in his letter of 25 January where it was stated that 'each day the gravity of the position increases and you will be surprised to learn the business is considered by outsiders to be in imminent danger.' Smith's reply the same day suggests that he took this to mean physical attack on the business, as he said that 'I do not myself think the danger to yourself and your family imminent as you appear to do. . . .' This interpretation was no doubt facilitated by his knowledge of Eason's chronic anxiety state, but in fact Smith himself was less calm than he had professed to Eason, writing the following day to Ford, his solicitor, in London that 'I am not quite as much alarmed as he is but there is enough in what he says to make me anxious to move in the direction he desires.' That what Eason had said had been misinterpreted and that Smith read fears of his own into the letter are evident from Eason's letter of 30 January to Smith which went to considerable pains to state that:

> I have no fear of personal injury either for myself or any persons employed. But the anxiety and care thrown upon me is very great, and all of this I have suffered for many years past during our distressed periods. I have had to fear that some political act of yours might create prejudice against this business, and so people would take their revenge upon us. In building up this business I have tried to secure the goodwill of all parties and creeds, but that goodwill can be lost, and it will be lost by any measure of coercion imposed by Parliament upon this country *with which your name as Head of this business can be identified*.

Eason's son Charles later sought to set out the correct position in a letter to the W.H. Smith's house journal *The News-basket* (11 February 1933), but in fact perpetuated the old version by stating that 'my father was apprehensive that in the excited state of feeling the business might be attacked.' He referred to an interview which he (Charles junior) had had with Edmund Dwyer Gray, the proprietor of the *Freemans' Journal* in which

Charles was warned that this might happen. Eason did refer in his letter of 25 January to having talked over the matter of a transfer with his son, but at no point in the correspondence is the fear of physical attack mentioned by him, and it seems to be rebutted in the letter of 30 January. In fact, what was on Eason's mind appears to have been the wider question of political unpopularity adversely affecting the business, and he had added in his letter of 25 January that 'already our position is the subject of discussion in the higher business circles of the city. I called upon our bankers and saw Mr Niven, the managing director of the Royal Bank, who told me this in confidence.' Rumours of a physical attack, if they were in the hands of a newspaper proprietor, were of course just as likely to be known in the circle around the Chief Secretary, and they could have been as likely as any other factors to have influenced Smith's thinking.

Moreover, the general view in the London house was already that the Dublin business was likely to be adversely affected by Smith's political associations. Awdry, in a letter of 21 January to Eason stated that 'the announcement contained in today's papers adds largely to the risk'. Awdry speculated about the behaviour of 'the disloyal public' and took heart from the fact that in recession they had less to withdraw from the house.

In a sense the outcome of events represented an exceptional coming together of two minds which were normally poles apart and which had become increasingly alienated over the years: the tense, worrying disposition of Eason who saw utter business ruin in prospect for himself and his family, and the usually calm mind of his employer who on Irish questions was not always rational and who in consequence was for once likely to reach conclusions as pessimistic as those of his chronically anxious Irish manager, if not more so. For Smith the Irish business had become a political embarrassment. Two years previously Tim Healy had launched a vicious attack on Smith in the House of Commons, while holding one of the firm's prayer-books in his hand:

> What would the Orangemen of the North of Ireland think if they knew that the leading light who addressed their heroes made a profit out of darkening the souls of the unfortunate papists? Curiously enough, the Right Hon. gentleman is himself ashamed of the transaction, because he published the books through his manager Mr Charles Eason, manager to Messrs. Smith and Sons, and he leaves out the number in Abbey Street where the great firm enlightens the country. His manager who publishes the Catholic prayer books is

> himself a Freemason. The Freemason manager of an Orange proprietor who issues *A Manual of Catholic Devotion for private use and for the service of the Catholic Church* with the *nihil obstat* of the new coadjutor bishop of Dublin, and the *imprimatur* of the late Cardinal Cullen – these are the gentlemen who profit on the one hand by the circulation of this literature among the benighted Roman Catholics and on the other hand have the face to come over to Dublin and stir up passion in order that these Catholics may be slaughtered.[24]

Soon afterwards, Smith made over the prayerbook business to Eason. If the Irish business generally was to have the same embarrassing effect, transfer was the logical step. Even on 26 January, before he had time to make up his mind on the issue, he observed that 'a time must come when the branch will drop off of itself.' His interest in the Irish business had stemmed originally from the desire to pre-empt the growth of rival businesses in news distribution. But a successful independent Dublin business with a virtual monopoly in Ireland and continuing close connections with W.H. Smith in England posed none of the problems that a disorganised Irish market might have in the 1880s and certainly would have had in the 1850s when it might have provided one of the supports for Smith's London rivals. The fact that the Dublin house was not only a separate branch but one which had virtually become independent, underlines how after the 1850s and early 1860s Dublin had drifted apart from the main stream of preoccupation in London. This was a point which Eason made somewhat casually in 1884 but more explicitly in January 1886:

> If the Irish and English businesses were necessarily bound up together, each an integral part of the other, we might have to suffer without avail, but it is not so, and the very separatedness of this business, and its having been so long guided by me would make the transfer to my name natural and easy.

The transfer of government accounts to Lethbridge's name at the time when Smith had become an MP – several years before he assumed any government office – illustrates the process at an even earlier date of ensuring that business concerns did not obtrude on public life. His growing seniority within the Conservative party and the certainty that the shortlived Chief Secretaryship would be followed by other high office made it inevitable that an Irish association would have embarrassed the

24 Hansard, vol. 284, col. 1496. Many years later, when T.M. Healy was Governor General, a friendly correspondence took place between himself and Charles Eason, junior, about the matter.

Conservatives as much as, if not more than, the business itself. Tim Healy and the prayerbooks two years previously were as influential a factor as the events of January 1886, but fundamentally the step was simply a logical progression of Smith's general attitude to public life and an expression of his pragmatic outlook.

For many reasons, therefore, once broached and faced, the proposal by Eason proceeded rapidly. Smith's decisiveness, characteristic of his whole life when major decisions were finally to be taken, came into play immediately. Back in London, after the fall of the government, with the hectic events of the preceeding ten days now behind him, he wrote to Eason on 29 January that he hoped that 'the events of the last 48 hours have relieved you from all pressing anxiety about the future', but he also made it clear that he was willing to proceed. He suggested a meeting between Eason and one of the partners either in Dublin or London. Eason's response suggested an immediate meeting in London, and father and son quickly crossed to London to open the negotiations for the transfer. Smith's attitude is reflected in an undated letter to Lethbridge from his private secretary in which it was stated that 'Mr Smith himself wishes to do nothing in a grudging spirit.' The one significant proviso added by Smith was that not only should the business be transferred but that the house property should be transferred also. This enlarged the scale of the purchase somewhat.

On 28 January a payment on capital account from Dublin had already reduced the capital outstanding to £13,000. On 8 February Eason, back in Dublin, proposed that the transfer of the business should be paid for in a cash payment of £6,000 followed by seven bills of £1000 to be paid in successive years. The house property was valued at £9,000. This he proposed to purchase for a cash payment of £4,000 and bills of £1,000 each paid over five successive years. Eason indicated that he hoped to raise £4,000 for the premises from the Bank. He hoped to realise the prayerbook business to help pay off maturing bills, and envisaged help from other sources to accelerate the discharge of the balance of the debt. White, who was head of the counting house as well as head of news distribution, wrote in reply on 11 February that in the prevailing business conditions Eason was proposing too onerous a commitment in regard to the purchase of the premises. 'Your proposal as to the immediate cash payment on the property is too much by one half, and you ought also not be committed to any earlier clearance of the acceptance by a forced realization of the Prayer Book business. Your risk is great enough without this....' In fact in the outcome the property was leased to Eason with a proviso in the agreement under which he would be required to purchase on request. In the event, the payments were greatly accelerated, the last three acceptances for the business (as opposed to the property) being paid off in July 1888. Smith wrote to White that 'I am very glad, indeed, the arrangement has turned out so well for him.' With the business paid for in an accelerated fashion, the purchase of the premises followed in July 1889, Eason paying £4,000 on the spot, and the balance was paid off in instalments by January 1891. At the time the Easons felt that they were dealt with handsomely by Smith, and the record bears it out. The amicable termination meant that a close bond remained between the two houses. Eason himself, from the surviving correspondence, was on terms of warm intimacy with figures such as White and Kingdon, and the relationship was cordial with Awdry, the newest of the partners. The transfer was handled with the goodwill of the members of the house, and with a ready and ungrudging spirit on the part of Smith himself.

Chapter 8 ❧ Charles Eason 1: Man and Family

THE RELATIONS BETWEEN THE HOUSES in London and Dublin had for thirty years been governed by the differing attitudes of Charles Eason and of his employer. Eason was anxiously determined to make a suitable living for himself and his family. From Smith's point of view, the Irish business was always on the periphery, and became ever more so as politics became his major preoccupation. The relationship between the two men was also coloured by their religious outlook. It seemed at first to have drawn them together, but in fact it was a divide. Smith was an Anglican, and increasingly identified himself with the ruling establishment. Eason remained a dissenter, independent, not to say idiosyncratic, and always divided, as in his youth at Yeovil and Chard, from the religious and political establishment around him.

In the last analysis there was an added source of alienation between the two men. Eason remained a dissenter of strong views, whereas Smith's identification with the establishment became more complete. Smith's own father, admittedly a difficult man, had charged his son that 'your greatest error is being too fond of Public honour and pursuits'[1] The tension between Smith and Eason in the 1880s reflected an underlying current of political feeling, which became evident as the political crisis in Ireland became more acute. This accounts for the remarkably outspoken tone of Charles Eason's letter of 20 December 1885. It was the only occasion on which Smith ever formally sought Eason's views on any subject, business or political, and Eason, who had always respected the subordinate role of a servant in the firm, took the chance to write with outspoken conviction. As a dissenter, Eason's instincts were opposed to paternalism. One of the entries in his commonplace book is an aphorism attributed to Sir J. Lubbock in 1872 that, 'It is impossible to have in any country what is called a paternal government without having a childish

1 C. Wilson *First with the News* p. 154

people'. In Somerset as a young man he had felt alienated from the established church circle, and in the politically charged atmosphere of Ireland in the 1880s, which even implied a direct threat to the business, this feeling came to the surface again. Some of his friends seem to have had strong feelings about establishment politicians. His son, Charles, recalled years later that he had heard much talk from R.G. Norman, a Grafton Street jeweller who knew his father intimately, '... of the Dublin election of 1868, when money flowed too freely. Sir Arthur Guinness was elected but was unseated on petition (quite rightly)'.[2] The Guinnesses were among the Irish acquaintances of Smith.

The thorough-going nature of Eason's radicalism is reflected also in his views on the place of women, shared with his wife, which were advanced for the time:

> Some say women will be influenced by their clergy — I trust they will and the clergy in turn will be influenced by women, by the story of their wants. The message of the Gospel must be a meeting of wants. I would say that all fathers should teach their sons that the day is come when 'Woman's questions' will be test questions with a suitor and that they must study for themselves the wrong doings of Parliament and sustain them if they think them right or seek earnestly to amend them if they think them wrong. I would also say, let parents encourage their daughters in acquiring a knowledge under which they, as women, labour and settle for themselves if they think existing laws should be maintained.

All this was embedded in some observations on politics, which underlines the political as well as the moral dimensions of his feminist views. In general however, Charles Eason's interests were restricted. Business took up most of his time, particularly the prayerbook branch, which devolved on him personally a mass of petty editorial detail. He had little leisure, and it would be true to say that outside business his only wide ranging interest was religion. He was an earnest Christian throughout his life. The books he read were largely, though not exclusively, on religion. Religious observations and extracts dominate the commonplace book.

When his house at Kenilworth Square was built, he joined the Baptist Chapel in Rathmines, and was one of the two trustees for a new Baptist

2 Memorandum by Charles Eason Jnr. about the family and his own early years. He is incorrect in referring to Arthur Guinness in this context; the candidate was Benjamin Lee Guinness.

Chapel on Grosvenor Road. When this chapel failed, he and his fellow trustee, Orlando Beater, had to pay off the balance of the debt, and a payment to Beater of £300 in 1873 may have been on this account. In 1863 or thereabout, as his son recalled, he took six Baptist missionaries for a week in Killarney where they stayed at the Railway Hotel. In his son's recollection, the Plymouth Brethren were really responsible for undermining the Baptist Church, and the opening of Merrion Hall in particular drew off many members. But though the Baptist Church in fact survived in Dublin, Eason joined the Presbyterian congregation at Christ Church, Rathgar in 1865, under Dr William Fleming Stevenson, who became a Moderator of the General Assembly in 1881. He was very much attracted by the personality of Stevenson, who had become the first minister in 1860 of what was then an 'infant congregation' at Christ Church, Rathgar, and in 1886 the company published a new edition of *Praying and Working* by Stevenson, who was then deceased.

The independent quality of his adhesion was reflected on several other occasions in his religious life. His son Charles was in fact baptised a Baptist (in 1867) and though the family continued to attend Dr Stevenson's church, Eason later left it to attend the Church of Ireland at Harold's Cross. It was while he was attending this church that he heard the course of lectures by Patterson Smyth on the bible which profoundly impressed him, and which he published also in 1886. In the last years of his life he resumed attendance at the Presbyterian Church under a Dr Stewart. The keen interest in church matters reflected his family background, but the changes from Baptist to Presbyterian to Anglican and then back to Presbyterian attendance denoted a strong individualism. He did not take any active role in church administration or in ecclesiastical politics, which then consumed the time of many committed Christians. It was the fringes of religious life, its social concerns, more than church matters which absorbed him: temperance, missionary activity, the needs of the poor, and the Young Men's Christian Clubs. He took a great interest in the clubs at the Presbyterian Church, and later at Harold's Cross. His son Charles seems to have frequented a number of Young Men's Christian Societies.

Eason's views were complemented by those of his wife, Caroline Birks. She had come from a variegated background, which even included a brother who had become a Roman Catholic priest. Unlike Eason she seems to have been a consistent attender of the Presbyterian church. She shared her husband's radical views, and possibly influenced some of them quite substantially. She is said to have given substantial support to the movement to open medical schools to women students. According to the obituary notice in the *Irish Temperance League Journal* in 1906 'She organised effective help for residents of poorer districts of the city in which she lived — information on hygiene, cookery, window gardening and above all, total abstinence'. She was president of the Irish Women's Temperance Union in 1901. In the latter point she shared the strong feeling of her husband.

It is clear from the surviving wage books how strongly Charles Eason felt about drink. Eason's views on moral literature were equally strong. In the nature of his business, there was opportunity of applying them. In 1861 he had written to Smith:

> Will you permit me to say that much that is very pernicious finds a place on your English stalls; there is a fungus in the literature of libraries.... I allude especially to the *Detective Note Book* and others forming the literature of crime. The tendency of these is positively to poison the minds that indulge in them. It seems to me that you have a noble opportunity of working indirectly for the welfare of Society. To purvey pure literature, to assist by giving prominence to works directly Christian in their tendency....

From time to time he seems to have taken up lapses in the moral tone of books with the London house, and the obituary in the *Belfast Echo* noted that 'Many years ago he determined that no literature of a pernicious kind should be offered for sale at any of his bookstalls, and to this day the firm, so successfully pioneered by him, has always refused to do so'.

He was obviously well-known in the London house for his strong views on this subject, and Kingdon, head of the book section there, who used to write him long, friendly, bantering letters, wrote to him in June 1894 that 'when you are needing rest for an hour I commend to your attention *The art of taking a wife* 5/- ... as containing passages you will not care to have circulating in the Library'.

Eason's circle of acquaintances was wide, but friends were few outside family, church and business. His style was very different from Smith's, as it embraced neither politicians nor public life. He did serve for a time on Rathmines Town Commissioners, but this activity does not seem to have loomed large in his life, quite apart even from the fact that he had no political affiliations. As he explained to Smith in his letter of 20 December 1885, he had resolved, on coming to Ireland, to take no part in political matters; and he had never attended a political meeting apart from one addressed by A.M. Sullivan in 1877 or 1878. He also avoided any prominent association with organised business life in Ireland, once liberal, but now increasingly characterised by unionist views. He did not play an active part in the Chamber of Commerce, nor in other bodies representing Dublin businessmen. The impression that we form is one of a guarded outlook, avoiding social entanglements or political associations. The only close associate that can be identified was R.G. Norman, in whose jewelry shop his son Charles spent a few months before going on to college. Norman was master of a Freemason lodge (no.125) and through him Eason was admitted in May 1876. Between 1869 and 1872 Eason advanced Norman £600. From January 1874 this was paid off in quarterly instalments.

Eason's marked lack of identification with political and social circles was reflected in the fact that obituaries in all newspapers spoke well of him, a tribute only attainable in Ireland through non-involvement in political activities of any sort. The tributes from catholic publications, brief or long, to his goodwill were remarkable, and they were paralleled by private letters. He took catholics readily on to the staff, and the wage books bear witness to the readiness to act on recommendations from parish priests and to his high estimate of an education from the Christian Brothers. The senior ranks were at first exclusively protestant, but this can be explained in part by the family background of the business, in part by the recruitment in the early decades of Scotsmen as the recognised best practitioners of office management in these islands. At the lower and middle levels, the recruitment policy of the house seems to have been deliberately non-partisan.

Eason's philanthrophy and interest in social welfare were testified to in many of the obituary tributes to him. Although he was a very strict disciplinarian in his employment, the working conditions were good by the standard of the day, and as the obituaries justify, in advance of those prevailing. The *Freeman's Journal* obituary spoke of 'his great idea' of creating employment in establishing the factory, and also stated that he was one of the first to give annual holidays. The administrator of the Pro-Cathedral parish, Daniel Downing, in a letter of sympathy, wrote that:

> He was always a big hearted benefactor of every good work in this city, and we here in this Pro-Cathedral parish have reason to be grateful to him, as we are to you for his unfailing support of any work for the general good such as poor schools and the rest, to which without any sacrifices of any view of his own, he could give a helping hand. Bear with a 'papist' who says, 'God give him eternal rest'.

It is always easier to identify old friendships than new ones. The links with the Toms and the Bagsters were enduring. As we have already seen, there was some small continuing link with the Bagsters. Several of the Toms worked in the firm, and the younger generations of Toms and Easons mingled a good deal. Ties remained with the Andersons, who were acquaintances from his Manchester days, and perhaps also from his wife's background. They sometimes visited Dublin, and as in the case of the Toms, visits continued as the children grew up. The Andersons were stationers in Manchester. Eason's son, Charles, recalled his mother commenting that 'Mrs Anderson's ambition was to make her sons Manchester Merchants. However, they none of them made any special mark'. The close family links with England explain why some of the Easons continued to be sent to school there. Charles' son, Charles, was sent for some two years to a school in Lowestoft, and he in his turn sent some of his children to England.

Eason's basic good qualities are testified to in Smith's private views, especially in the intimacy of Smith's letters to his wife. More relevant as a proof of an ability to get on well with people and to command respect, is the good relationship which existed between Eason and the departmental heads in the London house. The surviving correspondence with White, head of the Counting House and wholesale newspaper division in London, furnishes evidence of both warmth and friendship, and a similar but more intimate relationship seems to have existed with Kingdon, head of the books division.[3] Both these men knew Eason well from his London visits, and it is quite clear that they shared common views on many aspects of the business, and of the conduct of W.H. Smith's.

While Eason avoided any expression of political views, it is clear from his long letter to Smith in 1885 that he had a good deal of sympathy with the nationalists, and that this feeling contained an element of the dissenter's dislike of the political and landed establishment. He seemed to have had some interest in Irish history. The commonplace book includes a 'Precis of Irish history', the precise object of which is not clear. It may well have referred to an intended book, as it is a sketch of chapter topics. Eason himself had no literary bent, or at least no time for one — he was a good letter writer — and it is conceivable that he may have been either interested in commissioning a book on Irish history, or encouraging the preparation of one. Certainly, a distinct interest in Ireland is reflected in the publication of *Eason's Almanac* regularly from December 1873 onwards. He knew Dr Neilson Hancock, who wrote a large number of

3 Letters in Eason's, Dublin.

papers for the Statistical and Social Inquiry Society of Ireland, and it is even possible that the *Almanac* may have been prompted by Hancock, since the original assistant to Eason for the statistical content seems to have been a clergyman introduced to Eason by Hancock. When the clergyman left, Charles Eason junior assisted his father. From 1875 the statistics were prepared by Charles junior, who was responsible for the inclusion of a large amount of English material. Looking back on the *Almanac*, he thought that he had made a mistake in introducing so much English material into it, and that his father's plan of creating 'an Irish Almanac' had been the right one.

Eason's drive and shrewdness as a business man is not in doubt. A letter from him in 1879 to an unnamed businessman in printing and bagmaking gives us a good idea of Eason's business ideas. There is a heavy emphasis on the necessity of adequate costing, and on the common mistake in business of overlooking costs incurred incidentally in the course of operations; his advice from his own experience was that this was something to which special attention must be given. More specifically, Eason suggested that 'the scales of charges for classes of work should discriminate the incidents so that the charge should be in favour of the establishment in any doubtful case.' Eason followed modern trends in his opposition to bills of exchange, which were then the common currency of business, but which were beginning to go out of favour with Irish businessmen from the late 1870s. He was clearly sensitive to changing business practice, and laid down in a letter of 1879 that 'I discourage bills as much as possible, but they are often useful as closing the door upon disputes in accounts or when you do not propose to extend your dealings with a trader.'

A long paper on commercial morality from the commonplace book, perhaps written for delivery to an audience associated with a church, judging from the high moral tone of the piece, illustrates Eason's business and moral principles. He was opposed to excessive price competition, asking 'How many other honest men were ruined before the uniform low level price obtained?':

> Certain limits of competition seem to us right and proper: superior choice of stocks and improved knowledge of the goods dealt in, a prompter attention to the wants of customers, suavity of address, and disposition of some men before others, secures them a preference from customers. I scarcely know any trade going in which these qualities will not allow of a preference of some houses before others. The case is not only of competition because a tolerably uniform price

> may prevail in reference to any article. There may be the most genuine competition of character and attention. Competition merely of price seems to be an unmixed evil, and for this the public are to blame.

He noted that buyers and sellers both hoped to make a gain, and that buyers sought to understate the worth of an article. Something was wrong if a seller was selling his general run of wares at a price below what would earn him a living. He felt that the seller did not have the right to take advantage of the buyer's confidence, and in turn that 'he has no right to bring me into a position of competition so as to lessen the reward of my labour'. He was very much against speculation, which he saw as one party using prior knowledge to take advantage of another. For this reason he seems to have generally avoided dealing in stocks and shares. He purchased some shares in the Royal Bank in 1881, but these were sold shortly afterwards. Although he had a good deal of wealth, the only other shares which he purchased were in the McDonnell paper mills at Saggart. He may have been one of the parties behind the effort to get the mills going, at a time when Irish paper mills were closing down. It may have been prompted by an urge to support Irish industry and the mill was of course closely related to Eason's range of sales. He seems to have borrowed money from Smith's for the purchase of shares in the venture. Although against investment in joint-stock companies, Lethbridge was willing to make an exception in this instance. Eason became the owner of five shares in the mills, each with a face value of £100. Within the decade he doubled his holding.

Eason favoured mitigated competition, on the premise repeated very frequently in the paper, 'Do as ye would be done by'. His views on commercial morality were well-known in the London house. William Fred Kingdon writing to Eason in 1892, was obviously aware not only of Eason's views, but probably of the paper itself, saying, 'What world of good could have been done through this business if the principles you suggest for the merchant's guidance had prevailed here. . . .' This criterion is no doubt the one later described within the family as Charles Eason's 'golden rule'.

While narrow, Eason's interests were not in fact introspective. He seems to have gone on occasion to the theatre, and while his main reading was certainly religious, he read other books as well. In March 1890 he observed that: 'I have often read through a new book, to master its content to find its place in the world of thought, and so have sold 25 or 50 copies to persons to whom I have introduced it.' He read aloud to the family on Sunday afternoons. He had a keen interest in poetry — some verses in the commonplace book are probably his own — and he took to Tennyson. When *Middlemarch* appeared, it was brought home immediately. His son's wide and intellectual reading was almost certainly derived from enouragement from his father, and from the reading pattern in the home.

Though Eason's circle contained few intimate friends, it did provide for some contacts outside business and church. The acquaintance with Hancock for instance suggests some connections with the intellectual and largely non-business group (though including his fellow printer, Thom) which revolved around the Statistical and Social Inquiry Society, with which his son and grandson were to be much more closely associated. The essay on business morality seems for instance to have been written for a wider audience, and it assumed both Christian commitment and a business knowledge on the part of listeners. He may have participated at serious lectures in other subjects as well. A warm obituary in the *Irish Naturalist* stated that

> We believe that it would not be his wish that the part which he took in founding this journal would even now be made known; but at least we may say that the *Irish Naturalist* would probably never have been carried on without the help which he heartily and cheerfully gave us during its earlier years.... Though not a naturalist his mind was ever open to the teachings of science, and the bearing of modern biological thought on the great problems of existence was always a fascinating subject to him. His presence eleven years ago at a certain youthful essay on the life of Darwin was the beginning of a friendship which led him afterwards to freely place the technical knowledge and resources of his great establishment at the disposal of the editors and supporters of the *Irish Naturalist*.

This obituary was probably written by the zoologist George Herbert Carpenter, his son-in-law and editor of the journal from 1892. The meeting in 1888 may well have been the occasion not only of Eason's association with the journal, but also of the beginning of a friendship between Carpenter and Eason's daughter Emma which ripened into marriage in 1891. This tribute fairly aptly summarises the intellectual disposition of Charles Eason — contact with a wider milieu, but its intellectual basis fairly firmly rooted either in Christian thinking or in issues which either fascinated or troubled Christians, such as Darwin's theories, in the second half of the nineteenth century.

Eason's financial circumstances and standard of living are relatively easy to trace. Meticulous in his attention to family as to business detail, his ordered summaries of business finances and of the work force are paralleled by a series of personal accounts, which, though intended for purely personal scrutiny, can be followed more easily than is usual in such personal documents. He had the greatest grasp of detail of all of the Easons, and it is clear that it was the unremitting attention to detail at home, at work and in the editorial chores of the prayerbooks that caused much of the tension reflected in his correspondence, and in his irritability in the office. Only once, in 1884, were his accounts not set out, and he noted in a memorandum in April 1885 that 'my long illness led to my accounts getting astray, and the sundry effects account is increased by an amount of which I have no detail'.

Shortly after he arrived in Dublin, his salary was raised, in response to dissatisfaction expressed, but still only amounted to £256, a relatively low figure for a managerial role, no doubt reflecting Smith's severely circumscribed ambitions for the Dublin house. It was of course supplemented by a share of profits, which we can assume to be part of the deal that was worked out with Smith in the months following his arrival in Dublin. This 'gift' was already £600 in 1863, and rose to £1,300 by 1873. The salary itself was still £256 in 1873, but because of the sustained rise in profits in the 1860s, his total earnings by 1873 had reached the handsome figure of £1,556. This was on a par with many higher professional incomes and with those of second-line merchants in the city. He had moved into Kenilworth Square from Upper Rutland St in 1858, and in 1861 built a house in Kenilworth Square with the help of a loan from Smith. The expectations of profits were now firm ones, reflecting the arrangement made with Smith, and the house and location must have corresponded to what he himself regarded as his prospects at that date. When Eason first went to live there in 1858, the incomplete square was occupied by two MDs, and the remaining eighteen occupants were 'esquires'. It was already the most highly rated district in the burgeoning suburb of Rathgar.

In the year 1873/4 Eason's salary was increased from £256 to £600, no doubt in part in response to the expression of his own dissatisfaction with his position in 1872. The salary remained at that figure until the termination of the link with W.H. Smith's. His share of profits thereafter did not rise, reflecting unchanging profits in the house at large, so that in effect from the early 1870s, Eason enjoyed a steady annual income of around £2,000. From 1882/3 onwards, if the profits from prayer books are included, his income in the mid-1880s seems to have risen to the region of £2,500.

Eason's family expenditure was fairly modest and inelastic.

Housekeeping expenses, which were £520 in 1872 and only reached £600 for the first time in 1885, fell over the period from almost a third to about a quarter of income. The one obvious luxury, although it was not out of keeping with his own position, or with Kenilworth Square, was the maintenance of a coach. What were described as stabling charges could take up to £100 or more. Holiday expenses were modest. Categories called 'travelling, concerts, etc', 'travelling and seaside', or 'travelling', represented holiday and travel for pleasure, and rarely exceeded £100 before 1887. Seaside holidays were taken sometimes at Dalkey, though visits to English watering places started in the 1880s. The only foreign travel by Eason, apart from his regular visits to London, was accounted for elsewhere in the records, and related to visits to Europe in 1875, and to North America in 1880 and 1884. Schooling, at its peak in the 1870s, was also substantial, at about £150. The sums recorded variously as 'gifts' or 'charity' fluctuated a good deal, but from 1883 ran at £150 and upwards. Family expenditure was modest, devoid of great extravagance, and left a substantial margin for other uses. The basically frugal nature of the Easons is reflected in the fact that there was a large amount of income available for what might be regarded as items on capital account. There was little investment in the strict sense, apart from the shares in the McDonnell paper mill at Saggart. Regular expenditure on insurance exceeded £100 in the 1870s, although the combined item of rent and insurance in the 1880s can have included little additional insurance. The value of his insurance policies amounted to £3,814 by 1881 and increased little thereafter. Some of the surplus cash was absorbed by expenditure on the house or in 1884/5 in fitting up Aston's Quay for the prayerbook business. Another item was the repayment of loans: £1,500 was repaid to Smith between 1872 and 1880, and £647 in 1882.

What remained was largely employed in two directions. One was in loans: substantial amounts were lent to acquaintances in several years in the 1870s and again in the early 1880s. In the intervening years, a large amount of income was disposed of to the immediate family, either in helping them in their careers, or by grants and loans. In 1875/6 no less than £972 was spent on four sons, mainly on the travels abroad of Charles junior in 1875, and on George, in connection with his defalcation from the business and banishment to Australia. In 1879/80 there was substantial expense in connection with setting up two sons, George and Alfred, in Canada, including the expenses of a visit by Charles Eason senior to North America — £1,150 in all. Another £1,510 was spent in Canada in 1882/3, and £410 in 1885, largely in the purchase of land with Alfred's interests in mind. William Waugh Eason had also to be provided for. In 1879 £750 was spent in purchasing a place for him in Pim's, and in 1883 £900 was lent to him as capital 'for his partnership'. Much of the capital and all the interest charges were remitted in later years.

It was thus possible for Eason to make a substantial outlay on non-current purposes within the family and elsewhere. In fact in the peak years, expenditure exceeded income. In 1878, expenditure rose to £2,968, in 1879 to £3,316, in 1881 to £3,547 and in 1883 to £4,074. The exceptional expenditure was financed in several ways. In 1878 Norman the jeweller repaid the £600 he owed Eason, and £600 was also raised on the security of insurance policies from the Royal Bank. This was paid off in 1885. In 1881, £1,000 was borrowed from Smith. Part of this was paid off in 1882. Some more was raised from Smith in 1883, and it would seem that the balance was paid off in 1884.

Another feature of Eason's finance was reliance on deposits from relatives. His sister deposited £300 at interest with him in 1875, a figure raised to £600 in 1880. By 1882 there were five such deposits usually from members of the family, and the amounts increased sizeably in 1884. In 1887, when the purchasing of the Dublin business from W.H. Smith's had strained his resources, £1,000 was also raised from the Royal Bank on the security of the house in Kenilworth Square. When the Smith interest in the house property was purchased in 1889, £2,000 of the initial cash payment of £4,000 was borrowed in September 1889 from relatives, at least two of the three being Thomson relatives of Charles Eason junior's wife. Of the balance of £5,000 outstanding, £1,000 was paid off in November by raising £1,000 from Benjamin MacFarlane Eason and Mrs Anne Eason. Another £1,000 was paid off in June 1890 with the aid of £1,000 raised from the daughters, Caroline Vause, Emma and Fanny, and from Mrs Isabella Thomson, Georgina Thomson and Jessie Thomson, and Mrs Anna Eason. In October 1890, £1,000 from Charles Eason junior was raised, and the final balance of £2,000 was paid off in January 1891 with the help of £1,200 raised from Mrs Mary Eason. The success of this operation depended on the readiness of relatives to extend the duration of their debentures. The first debentures issued in 1888 for six years were extended for another six years by a Board decision of June 18 1894. They were replaced by new debentures in 1905, which were to be paid off in 1915, and an additional £1,200 was also raised by further debentures.

One of Eason's prime concerns — it was a central feature of his proposal for a partnership with Smith — was making provision for his own family. The eldest son, George, entered the business in 1868. As he was only sixteen, it can be concluded that his short education — at least for an Eason — must have reflected some unsuitability. This seems to have been confirmed by his defalcation from the firm in 1875, presumably from the Retail department where he was still employed, seven years after he had entered the firm. The sum involved seems to have been £236. George was shipped out to Australia to his Birks relatives. Whatever the reason, his stay in Australia was short, and in 1879 his passage was paid by his father to Canada. His death was to follow quickly in 1882. The next son, Charles junior, had already entered the business in 1875 on the completion of his education, and having spent some time that year travelling on the continent. He started in the fancy goods department. In November, when George left, he quickly moved to the wholesale department, the centre of the firm, where he started by opening the correspondence and entering the cash. One other son, Frederick Tucker Eason, entered the business.

Apart from Charles junior and Frederick Tucker, the sons had to make their way outside the business. One was William Waugh Tucker Eason, who was first apprenticed in an unidentified business, and then became, with the help of his father, an ink manufacturer at Oxton. Another son, Benjamin MacFarlane Eason, became a clergyman. Alfred, the second youngest son, went to Canada in the spring of 1879. It seems certain that George's going to Canada in the summer of the same year was intended to give him yet another new start in the company of his more stable younger brother Alfred. Alfred had left Moville in April 1879, arriving in the new world in May. He was a regular correspondent, writing home lively and interesting letters,[4] and displaying from the outset a typical Eason outlook. He wrote from Winnipeg in July 1879, that 'I have formed no high opinion of the Manitoba farmers in general. I have been in some houses where whiskey was taken regularly as an appetizer before every meal. . . .' He had letters of introduction from Dr Stevenson, the minister of Christ Church, Rathgar. His plan was to get experience working for a farmer, and then to take land, stocking it with cattle in the autumn when George arrived.

What happened in 1879 is not quite clear. Certainly land was purchased over the next four years both in Alfred's name, and in his father's, and the importance of the matter is reflected in the fact that Charles Eason senior made a visit to Canada and the United States in April and May 1880. Whatever the initial intention of George and Alfred making a go of it together, Alfred's marriage in December 1880 signified a parting of the ways. George died in 1882 leaving his father and Alfred to clear his

4 Letters in the Eason family.

debts. In 1882 Alfred had extended beyond farming to conduct a livery business and boarding house at St Leon in Manitoba as well. In the evenings he did some book-keeping for a merchant, and also did some conveyancing and sold machinery on commission: 'I have never let pass an opportunity for making a dollar.... Every dollar always adds to our comfort, only the other day I was offered a bargain and a good sewing machine and I bought it as a Christmas box for my wife.' Alfred's ambitions to get on overextended him, and he made the mistake of relying too much on credit. The extension into a livery stables and boarding house on town lots led him to mortgage the property. He also farmed in conjunction with his in-laws and helped his brother-in-law to stock a farm by putting his own name to bills. The long visit of Charles Eason senior to Canada in 1884 was to sort out Alfred's affairs. The upshot of it was that his father, who felt that Alfred had obtained credit too easily, maintained Alfred on a farm in his own ownership, but which was ultimately to go to Alfred.

Charles Eason provided for all his sons either by places in the business, or by a generous advance of his intended provision for them out of his patrimony. Of the daughters, Caroline Vause Eason, the eldest, remained a spinster. She was well educated, and throughout her working life she was a school teacher at Alexandra College. She was active in the choir and Sunday school of Christ Church, Rathgar, and helped to found the Band of Hope in 1884. A memorial card after her death recalled that 'she loved the Church both local and universal, and was never happier than when with open house she welcomed missionaries from any part of the field'. Emma married a zoologist, George Herbert Carpenter, who had graduated in the College of Science, and who later held a position in the National Museum, and became a professor in the College of Science. Fanny, the youngest of the three daughters, married Albert Brunton, at the time the most promising of the young men in the business.

All the children held shares in the limited company which was formed in 1888. The 'A' shares were confined to those who worked in the company, with the exception of William Waugh Eason, and the directors were drawn from this group. Frederick Tucker Eason was appointed first secretary. Albert Brunton, married to Fanny, was the first non-member of the family to receive shares in 1902. In 1904 he became a director. William Waugh Eason seems to have withdrawn from his English business in the early 1890s[5] and in July 1904 he was appointed a 'managing

5 In his 1936 address to the staff on the occasion of the fiftieth anniversary of Eason's as an independent firm, Charles Eason gave the date as 1891.

director'. His death in January 1908, at the relatively young age of 52, was recorded in the minutes as that of 'a late managing director of the company'. With the exception of George, all the others were characterised by the Eason trait of longevity — an average of 85 years for the surviving seven members of the family — the last one, Frederick Tucker Eason, dying as recently as 1964.

In the years that followed 1886 Charles Eason created the pattern of the independent business. Not only did he guide its day-to-day running, but he also laid down the new legal framework within which the family interests were determined by him. But he was getting on in years, and his health problems were now real ones. His attendance at company meetings became irregular in the course of 1895, and the last occasion on which he chaired a meeting was 7 April 1896. An accident in 1899 accelerated his decline, and he died on 5 November of that year.

Chapter 9 ❧ The Ascendancy of News Wholesaling 1899-1926

THE BUSINESS GREW SLOWLY FROM the 1880s to the end of the nineteenth century. The 1890s were in fact a decade of crisis for the firm. It lost two of its railway contracts, including the prestigious Great Northern Railway, and in the Belfast area it faced real competition in advertising and, at the end of the decade, in newspaper wholesaling. It fell to Charles Eason junior to consolidate the position of the house in the Irish market. For years he had had a major role in running the company; in 1884, for instance, he had been responsible for submitting the annual accounts to Smith's in London, while his father was in Canada. He had actively participated in the negotiations leading to the transfer in 1886. By the time he succeeded to the leadership of the company, on his father's death in 1899, he was forty-six.

The Wholesale side of the business, which by convention included the railway bookstalls and poster sites as well as the wholesaling of stationery and books, grew rapidly during the period 1900-1910. Cash receipts jumped 30 per cent, from £127,572 in 1899 to £165,420 in 1910. The recovery began in the mid-1890s, and Charles Eason junior wrote in April 1897 that 'business has been fair. Not as much growth as we would like but no going back.'[1] The first decade of the new century was crucial both in turnover and in margins.

Newspaper wholesaling in volume required a closely integrated distribution system involving the organisation of manual skills in the receipt and checking of large numbers of newspapers and periodicals each day, followed by packing, invoicing and despatch in daily parcels to a large number of relatively small retailers. It also entailed the retention and updating of standing orders for each publication for every newsagent supplied, and the receipt, checking and crediting of unsold copies of those publications (by no means all) which were returnable to the publishers,

1 Letter to his brother the Revd. Benjamin Macfarlane Eason, among letters in the possession of the late Caroline Vause Eason of Sheffield.

and claiming for credit from the publisher for the unsold copies. The amount claimed by Eason's from the publisher was usually not the same as the amount credited to newsagents because each publisher had his own formula limiting the proportion of unsold copies which he was prepared to credit, ranging from some which were fully credited to others who imposed sharp restrictions.

The practical restrictions to entry into the newspaper wholesale trade meant that the business in the British Isles tended to be in the hands of a small number of firms, although in England the services of the principal wholesalers were supplemented by a larger number of sub-wholesalers who usually obtained their supplies in bulk from one of the main wholesalers and not directly from the publishers. Obviously Ireland was too small and its population too widely scattered to make a sub-wholesaling system either necessary or effective. The essence of this wholesaling system was that the wholesaler worked on a narrow margin, but did not have to fund stocks and worked on relatively short credit.

The receipts on the Wholesale side (whose constituents are detailed in Table 12) rose sharply between 1899 and 1913, and more rapidly in Belfast than in Dublin. Unlike the upsurge in the 1860s and 1870s, which had been a result of the increase in railway bookstall sales, the significant increase in this decade was in the wholesale sales of newspapers and periodicals (through the 'News Department'). Wholesale stationery sales also increased. Bookings of advertising on the railway poster sites had already reached its peak by 1899, but the firm continued to dominate the Irish market in stationery and newspapers. Even in the Belfast wholesale trade, where it faced competition, Eason's held its own in the first two decades of the twentieth century. This period of rapid growth in sales of newspapers and periodicals was marked by a structural change in which the relative importance of the News Department increased significantly. Between 1899 and 1913 wholesale newspaper sales as a percentage of total turnover rose from 54 per cent to 63. Inflation in the later stages of the war sent the prices of books and stationery upwards more sharply than prices of newspapers and periodicals and so reduced the importance of news sales somewhat, but they still stood at 64 per cent of wholesale turnover in 1917 and 1918, or 61 per cent of total turnover.

As the volume of business grew, Eason's decided to establish direct accounts with publishers rather than rely on supplies through W.H. Smith's in London. A main advantage of this was the benefit of carriage-paid supplies, with the consequent improvement in gross margins. In

TABLE 12 *Cash receipts: Dublin and Belfast*

	Dublin			*Belfast*	
March	*Wholesale*	*Retail*	*Wholesale*	*Retail*	*Wholesale and retail combined*
	£	£	£	£	£
1899	127,572*	16,738	14,272	2,414	
1900	132,906*	18,040	14,850	2,362	
1901	138,019*	17,197	18,603	2,266	
1902	139,059*	17,342	20,317	2,256	
1903	147,097*	19,987	24,226	2,490	
1904	149,367*	19,660	24,824	2,384	
1905	143,773*	16,923	24,659	2,316	
1906	147,431*	17,914	27,608	2,334	
1907	145,058*	17,491	29,697	2,803	
1908	158,573	18,750			37,073
1909	159,657	17,535			37,889
1910	165,420	18,559			41,475
1911	172,812	20,163			47,200
1912	167,137	21,196			49,611
1913	170,198	22,385			50,606
1914	172,319	23,256			53,675
1915	194,693	23,476			56,241
1916	191,589*	27,059	51,548	3,171	
1917	188,250*	19,450	54,137	3,183	
1918	214,721*	22,226	62,156	3,407	

*'drawings' from Belfast (i.e. payments for goods and services and profits remitted) deducted.

1905 E.C. Scott of Smith's visited Eason's in connection with the loss of business, and this visit seems to have coincided with the decisive switch by Eason's to direct purchase. According to J.C.M. Eason's later recollection it was McDowell and Brunton who took up the policy of seeking direct accounts with publishers, and the advantages in terms were great.

Smith's themselves were about to undergo a great upheaval. At the end of 1905 two major railway lines refused to renew Smith's contract, and 250 bookstalls were lost. In a great effort between October 1905 and January 1906 the company opened 144 new 'High Street' shops to replace them. This move was not of course popular with Smith's newsagent customers.[2] The fact that Eason's did not develop any such outlets reflects the much smaller turnover per retail outlet in Ireland, even in the major centres of population. This in turn reflected the small size of the commuter population into city centre areas. Much of the middle-class commuter population was served by the bookstalls on the Westland Row to Bray line, which, against expectations as late as the 1870s, really flourished in later decades. Other districts of Dublin had too little regular morning and evening movement of passengers, and hence unlike Smith's, Eason's were not tempted into the High Street, even when newspaper buying habits spread widely. Turnover at the Sackville Street shop remained static throughout this period. In the absence of a commuter population from the northern and western suburbs of Dublin, turnover at the Amiens Street and Kingsbridge station bookstalls was relatively low, being sustained largely by long-distance passenger traffic.

In the nineteenth century, London newspaper publishers only supplied papers on wholesale terms to wholesalers on their doorstep. Wholesalers in provincial England as well as in Dublin had to order through London wholesalers. Increased competition among publishers, however, meant that to expand their sales, publishers began to woo provincial wholesalers with direct sales. Cutting out the London wholesalers in this way significantly improved the provincial wholesalers' margins. Indeed, the publishers were now beginning to provide supplies direct to local representatives other than established wholesalers. In October 1905 Eason's, with W.H. Smith's and forty-two other wholesalers, drew up a memorial asking publishers that 'they should not open retail accounts direct, that is to say, by appointing special agents in various towns.' The new margins were particularly attractive because the publishers provided carriage-paid terms to Dublin and Belfast, whereas previously Eason's were responsible for carriage charges. Direct supply also tended to make for earlier delivery of news.

But for the stray survival of details taken from a week's invoices in the Belfast house in June 1904, there would be little precise knowledge of Irish circulations in the first decade of the new century. The total Monday circulation through Eason's of the three Belfast papers, who generally managed their own distribution, was a mere 57 copies. The Belfast circulation of *The Irish Times* was likewise small — a mere 24 copies — and the *Freeman's Journal* with 83 copies accounted for almost half the total circulation of Irish dailies, which amounted to 178 copies. The

2 Wilson, *First with the news*, p. 242

circulation of English dailies already exceeded that of all Irish dailies through the Belfast house: 230 of the total of 408 copies of dailies. The *Daily Mail* was the best selling paper, its circulation of 89 copies just exceeding that of the *Freeman's Journal*. Albert Brunton in Belfast in July 1905 was sceptical about the demand for English dailies: 'I do not think an English illustrated daily is any use here even on the morning of issue. *Daily Graphic* never took in Ireland as far as I can see.' But when, from 1905, the *Daily Mail* became available in Ireland on the morning of issue, it led the way in creating a mass market for English dailies in Ireland. Extensive circulation of English dailies was very much a post-1904 phenomenon, something to be dated from the concerted Irish sales campaign by the *Daily Mail* in 1905.

In fact, because local dailies did not rely on wholesalers, daily newspapers were not as important in the overall business of the Belfast Branch as in Dublin. There the Dublin dailies relied on the wholesaler for much of their distribution. Even in later decades, with mass circulation of dailies, J.C.M. Eason reckoned that dailies accounted for only one-third of news and periodicals sales in Belfast, compared with two-thirds in Dublin. The total circulation of weeklies in Belfast in 1904 amounted to 88,506 copies. The big sellers of 1904 were mainly light or popular reading, often at 1d. a copy, frequently from the Harmsworth stable.

TABLE 13 *Circulation of weeklies through Belfast in June 1904 (No. of copies)*

Light or special weeklies		*News weeklies*	
Christian Herald	5090	Pearson's Weekly	2470
Answers	4069	Thomson's Weekly News	1976
Budget	2834	Reynold's News	1664
Forget-me-not	2392	Glasgow Weekly Mail	1050
Tit-bits	2197	Liverpool Weekly Post	319
Ireland's Own	1660	Lloyd's News	248
Sunday Companion	1559	Weekly Telegraph	200
People's Friend	1370	News of the World	166
T.P. Weekly	1370	Glasgow Weekly Herald	124
Home Chat	1339	Glasgow Weekly Observer	90
Sunday Stories	1235	Weekly Despatch	51
Chips	1066	Sunday Chronicle	26
M.A.P.	1053		
Horner's Stories	1001		

Circulation of 'news' weeklies, though still exceeded by the biggest selling of the light weeklies, was beginning to rise. They combined both news in a weekly format and the familiar light reading. The formula was a winning one. These weeklies were to spearhead the rise in circulations until the mass distribution of dailies in the 1920s. Their circulation exceeded that of English dailies through the house by a large margin. Three of them, *Pearson's Weekly*, *Thomson's Weekly News* and *Reynolds News*, already had substantial circulations which were chasing those of weeklies such as *Answers*, *Budget* and *Forget-me-not*. The *News of the World*, which was to pioneer the real push for mass weekly circulation, was on the eve of expanding its Irish circulation dramatically, and in 1911 was probably already the market leader.

The sales mix of the News Department was still curiously old-fashioned in 1904: a small circulation of dailies, a large circulation of light weeklies, and only an emerging sale of news weeklies. But the shape of things to come over the next decade could already be seen. In 1904 the news weeklies were still being distributed in editions containing no news later than Friday. However, as they emerged in the following years, the so-called 'Sundays' greatly increased their appeal over the weekly editions by giving the Saturday racing and sports results. The distribution between weekly and Sunday editions on the Irish market in 1910 is not perfectly clear, and the transition from the weekly to the Sunday edition seems to have occurred over the second decade. Up to then newspaper distribution had been a six-day business. The business generated by the new Sundays, which the conservative character of Eason's did not allow them to respond to, enabled a new breed of wholesale representatives to rise, particularly in the 1910s. In default of shops, they resorted to the use of street vendors. This example was not lost on the dailies, as they saw the Sundays amass enormous circulations by these means.

In the period 1899-1907 newspaper and periodical sales through the railway bookstalls rose more rapidly than sales in any other department, and much more so than bookstall sales of books and other goods. Between 1899 and 1907 sales of news items on the bookstalls rose from 25 per cent to 43 per cent of total News turnover. In the latter year bookstall turnover was a quarter of the total company receipts. In fact the figures overstate the importance of the bookstalls somewhat. Sales at the bookstalls are expressed in retail prices, whereas wholesale turnover proper was expressed in wholesale prices. But the relative rise in the importance of the bookstalls is real, and during those years the number of bookstalls, which had not grown significantly since the 1870s, expanded dramatically.

A nationwide network of bookstalls was developed which came to handle a very high proportion of national newspaper sales. It was the developments in these years that really gave the bookstalls the significance and prestige they enjoyed both in the traditions of the house, and in the eyes of the public. William Bulfin, for instance, in a description of a cycling tour in Ireland during 1903, mentioned as a matter of course that when he reached Mullingar he went to the bookstall at the station for his newspapers.[3]

So rapid was this growth that between 1899 and 1907 Eason's own retail distribution network (i.e. the bookstalls) expanded more rapidly than the number of independent retail newsagents. Such a development was necessarily short-lived. Bookstall receipts for 1913 were a little above the level for 1907, while sales to newsagents doubled between 1907 and 1913. One illustration of this trend is the story of the railway bookstall at Cookstown. When it was opened some local agents closed their direct accounts with Eason's. Later on in 1908 when the bookstall itself ceased operation, its closure no doubt implied that wholesale business, run from Belfast, had regained lost ground.

As the basis for mass readership began to emerge in the period between 1895 and 1913 the effect was seen at first in soaring sales at the railway bookstalls. But after 1907, the dynamic passed decisively from Eason's bookstalls to the wholesaling of newspapers and periodicals to independent retailers. One of the reasons — though by no means the sole one — for the change lay within the trade margins themselves. When Eason's own margins improved after 1905, as a result of switching to direct purchase from the publishers rather than going through Smith's, more attractive margins for retailers offered by Eason's in turn gave a stimulus to retail trade. The creation of a wholesale structure in depth to handle distribution of newspapers and periodicals was a post-1907 feature of the firm. Mass readership, even as late as 1910, was confined to the new category of weeklies, dispatched from London on Friday or Saturday and distributed throughout Ireland on Saturday or Sunday respectively. Sales of dailies, which hardly rose for three decades after the 1870s, expanded also in this period, though mass readership for dailies only developed in the 1910s and 1920s, well after the boom in weeklies. Despite the shift in the weekly publication market from Friday to Sunday editions, a sharp rise in circulation of Irish and cross-channel dailies had more than maintained Eason's news turnover. The relative improvement of cross-

3 W. Bulfin, *Rambles in Erin* (Dublin, 1907), p. 174.

channel dailies, which were immune to the tendency of Irish dailies to supply nearby outlets directly, contributed to this result.

TRADE RELATIONS

The growth in sales tempted a second wholesaler, Dawson's from England, to set up in Dublin, which they did on 27 March 1911. In fact the immediate reason for Dawson's coming was an invitation from a small group of Dublin retailers in 1910 who maintained that Eason's gave preference to their own retail shop in Sackville Street. The rival newsagents resented the fact that newspapers were on sale in Sackville Street long before they were on sale even in nearby newsagencies. This was because horse-drawn deliveries of cross-channel papers, which arrived at the North Wall at 8 a.m., took several hours to process, and the horses had to be rested. The increased competition, and resentment over delays in delivery, prompted Eason's to introduce motor vans. After a visit to London in March 1911 J.C.M. Eason put two Peugeot vans on the road, and by 1923 motor transport had completely replaced horses. The immediate advantage of the vans was that the crucial morning deliveries could commence without delay after the arrival of cross-channel news at 8 a.m.

The competition between the two wholesalers was keen. One factor which had brought Dawson's into the Irish market was almost certainly the change made in 1905, when Eason's by-passed Smith's to order directly from the English publishers. Some English dailies could now be offered at thirteen to the dozen, English weeklies retailing at 1d and ½d were charged at 9d and 4½d respectively for 12 copies less 2½ per cent and in May 1d papers, charged at 9d less 2½ per cent were further reduced to 8¾d. Carriage charges were eliminated, returns were accepted on more favourable terms, and magazines also were being sent carriage paid for the first time. By the start of the 1920s readership of dailies was widespread in the provinces as well as in Dublin. During the decade, a recognisable modern pattern of mass readership was established.

From 1917/8 the auditor's figures provide a clearer picture of turnover than the somewhat less satisfactory cash receipts.[4] Henceforth each

4 More importantly the audited accounts eliminate the double-counting which can be reduced but not entirely eliminated from the cash receipts figures. Wholesale news data, no longer surviving in the general accounts as a mere residue, were now separately available. Double counting was eliminated by attributing sales to other divisions to the original division. In the cash receipts figures, there was always a risk that the same book be counted as a full value sale for both departments.

division was charged with 'purchases' from other divisions. In the case of bookstalls, such transfers were valued in the department of origin at 75 per cent of the retail price, and only the remaining 25 per cent of the retail price was attributed to the bookstalls.

TABLE 14 *Growth of Wholesale Sales, Dublin house, 1918-1927**

	1918 £	1919 £	1920 £	1921 £	1922 £
Wholesale news	131,638	158,655	186,349	251,191	269,464
Bookstalls commission	12,726	16,389	17,099	18,503	18,342
Other Wholesale**	113,557	146,532	151,528	168,279	158,794
Total	257,921	321,576	354,976	437,973	446,600
	1923 £	**1924 £**	**1925 £**	**1926 £**	**1927 £**
Wholesale news	246,261	249,456	248,792	252,591	232,584
Bookstalls commission	14,768	15,933	15,312	15,045	13,882
Other wholesale**	148,641	150,885	137,402	135,781	132,094
Total	409,670	416,274	401,506	403,417	378,560

* Turnover figures derived from the audited accounts. These differ from the old-fashioned cash receipts which were also minutely documented even after 1917. Cash receipts record sales on credit only when cash payment had been received within the accounting year. The audited accounts included both cash and credit sales, and thus, despite eliminating some double counting that creeps into the old style figures, turnover as measured by the audited figures exceeds turnover estimated purely by cash receipts.
** eg Stationery, prayerbooks etc.

The new figures are not wholly comparable with those formerly used, but they give a clear picture.[5] In the case of the turnover of the Dublin

5 Within the Retail department, sales of newspapers and periodicals fell sharply after 1921/2, while non-news-related items soared. In Belfast, news accounted for a higher proportion of the small turnover. In 1924/5 for instance it accounted for £82,559 out of a wholesale turnover of £125,459. Combining Belfast and Dublin, wholesale sales of newspapers and periodicals accounted for 63 per cent of turnover. If turnover were to be calculated on the old basis (i.e. involving some double-counting because non-news sales could not be isolated from news sales, approximately 4 per cent should be added to the proportion of wholesale news. This gives a figure of 67 per cent, close to the pre-war figure of 70 per cent.) The wholesale news division was thus more than ever the kernel of the business.

house, they show the importance of wholesale news sales which of course were to the bookstalls as well as to independent newsagents. The importance of wholesale news sales (i.e. excluding the retail margin added by the bookstalls) grew over the period.[6] In 1918 newspapers and periodicals, less sensitive than books or stationery to rising prices, accounted for 51 per cent of wholesale turnover; in 1926/7, under more stable prices, for 62 percent. Wholesale sales to newsagents contrasted with the lack of buoyancy in bookstall turnover. In the 1920s bookstalls not only failed to maintain their previous momentum but began to decline. The Retail department sank to 4 per cent of cash receipts in 1918, but was back to 10 per cent of total cash receipts in 1927. Newspapers and periodicals accounted for a significant proportion of Retail business — over half in 1919.

In the 1910s, daily newspapers were being purchased far down the social scale, so newspaper selling spread to a growing number of shops. Shopkeepers who were not newsagents were becoming keen to sell papers, as customers coming to the shop to buy papers were likely to make other purchases as well. This development obviously did not please the more established newsagents, who faced increased competition, nor was it very satisfactory for the wholesalers, because it entailed an increased number of accounts to handle, and deliveries to arrange, without a corresponding increase in total sales. An abortive attempt to establish a retail newsagents organisation took place in 1910.[7] The prime movers were Tom Clarke — later a signatory of the 1916 Proclamation — Parsons of Baggot St Bridge and Lorcan O'Toole. A new Association, launched in 1916, was more successful. Eason's joined the Association in their capacity as retailers in July 1916, as did the second wholesaler in Dublin, Dawson's, a few days later. Some local newsagents' societies existed outside Dublin. In Tralee, for instance, an association was in correspondence with Eason's from 1919. The common interest of wholesalers and retailers quickly ensured that an agreement was established that the Association would be consulted by Eason's on applications for a supply of news. Hart, the secretary of the Association in 1922 commented that:

6 No summaries or break-downs of pre-1918 wholesale accounts survive. They must have existed, however, if only for the good management of the wholesale division, and a few isolated figures survive on a single sheet (see p. 37). What their absence suggests is the independence and secrecy that surrounded the wholesale division, and the transfer from it into the general accounting of the house only of very broad aggregates.

7 J. J. Hart, 'Early history of the Irish Retail Newsagents' Association', part 1, *The Irish retail newsagents' gazette*, Oct. 1943

> The state of the trade in Dublin previous to 1916 was very bad indeed, as almost every small shop stocked a few papers.... This agreement during the past six years has worked splendidly and has resulted in stabilising trade into a proper business way, thus enabling the newsagents to build up a fair trade in each district and consequently doing away with the useless practice of multiplying the newsagency shops, which really meant the dividing up into small pieces the trade in every district (without increasing trade).

The agreement could work on occasion towards restricting competition. The retailers succeeded in persuading the wholesalers within months to operate a "Distance Limit" policy i.e. a policy of not providing a news supply to a second retailer in proximity to an established retailer. In 1920, for instance, the Associations of Newsagents in Belfast and Dublin supported the case of the sole newsagent in Killeshandra against a supply to a second shop in the town. Applications for a supply were very carefully considered. In the Dublin area this often involved a study of surrounding shops and of the existing business of the applicant. Eason's considered the views of the Association, but where it was not convinced that there was a valid objection to a new applicant, it gave a supply even against the views of the Association. In the case of representations made to Eason's about one applicant who had been refused supply, J.C.M. Eason, now effectively managing the business, explained in a letter of 16 October, 1924:

> The accepting of all applicants is really impossible because there are so many. The newspaper business is known to be one where risks of bad stock do not exist because papers can be returned. It is regarded as an attractive means of bringing people into a shop and is therefore often taken up by shopkeepers who have no real intention of doing their best to encourage it, and it is not profitable for us to handle petty accounts on trade terms where the margin of profit is exceedingly small, and where the number of parcels to be despatched must, if papers are to be received in time by an agent, involve deliveries three times a day on every day of the week.

However it was not in the interests of Eason's to be as restrictive as the Association might have liked. In May 1925 J.C.M. Eason wrote in exasperation to the secretary of the Association that it was disappointing to find: '.... in connection with a matter regarding which, under certain circumstances there must obviously be considerable differences of opinion, that our views on all these applications which one might regard as being doubtful, have not at any time found acceptance from your members.'

A meeting and a long correspondence followed on from this particular instance, and the upshot of it all was that the applicant's case was granted. By 1925 the policy of the house was well-defined. Newspapers were supplied at agents' rates only if a total weekly order reaching twenty-five shillings per week at published prices was involved. In towns or villages where Eason's had no existing newsagent they were prepared to consider weekly orders of not less than twenty shillings at retail terms less 10 per cent. A small number of orders were serviced at full retail price, in which case the sole benefit to the retailer was carriage-free delivery.

Another feature of this period was the rapid growth of street vending, meeting a demand for casual newspaper purchase. It first became a source of complaint at the outset of the 1920s. In September 1923 the *Newsworld* contrasted the situation with England and noted that 'in most of the large centres the street vendor is master of the situation .... the great bulk of the sales are of as casual a nature in the country as a whole'. The *Irish Newsagent* had commented in the previous year that the growth in street selling had increased out of all proportion and that newsagents were cutting down their supplies. This was particularly true of Sunday papers which were sold outside the churches and of evening papers, where shop sales had fallen 'almost to vanishing point'. Even a non-trade journal, *Irish Society*, complained:

> The newsboys of Dublin are becoming more of a nuisance every day. They almost knock you down when you are coming off a tram; you have to fight your way through hordes of them at a railway station; and they put your heart jumping with their unearthly shrieks from morning to night.

One of the newsagents' complaints was that street vendors often sold newspapers at the very door of newsagents, and actually stopped customers going into the shops. The Newsagents' Association directed particular attention to this. Some vendors were prosecuted for obstruction, and the *Irish Newsagent* published details of one instance where it was claimed that the newsvendor earned from between £7.10s and £10 a week. Eason's shared the retailers' views in a qualified way. In November 1921 J.C.M. Eason wrote to Hart, the secretary of the Newsagents Association:

> The question of street selling is a matter upon which we would certainly express a strong opinion on your behalf, but you know how the publishers view this matter, and if this course is not prolonged for too great a period, may be of assistance in promoting sales and generally helping the trade.

Although the question of outlets was important, it was not the main source of contention between the wholesalers and the retailers in the years of inflation during and immediately after the war. Delivery charges for papers proved to be a much more explosive issue, and ruffled relations between the two sides. Owing to the greatly increased cost of living and working expenses, the Association had recommended in September 1917 a charge of 1d per week on the delivery of newspapers to customers in the Dublin and district area. But while prepared to surcharge its own customers, the retail trade viewed things differently when the two wholesale houses, Dawson's and Eason's, decided to follow the existing practice among British wholesalers and to introduce a charge on deliveries by the wholesalers' vans to retailers.[8] As early as April 1920 a note in J.C.M. Eason's hand read: 'Rents up, rates up, high wages. Delivery of papers — boys' wages going up'. Further wage increases took place in July, and a later note by J.C.M. Eason commented that delivery costs were the heaviest of all. Previous increases in costs had not been passed on, but the introduction of a delivery charge was decided upon starting from 1 September 1920. At two meetings between the sides a delivery charge seems to have been agreed upon, and the wholesalers even offered, at one stage of the discussions, to scale down their demand from 1s 6d per week to be paid by each newsagent to 1s if agreement was achieved there and then.

The *Irish Newsagent* was hopeful of a successful outcome, so J.C.M. Eason was rather taken aback at the end of the month to have a request for the deferment of the charge, especially as the wholesalers had already sent out their circulars, and some charges had even been paid. Another inconclusive meeting took place on 14 October and the matter was complicated by a new demand from the retailers that they should be given terms of 13/12, i.e. a free thirteenth copy. To J.C.M. Eason, this seemed to widen the issue and to conceal the inability of the Association to get the necessary cooperation among its own members. On 25 October he wrote that: 'We certainly feel disappointed that you should suggest going back upon the arrangements which you made on September 14 regarding the delivery charge which we had found it necessary to make and which we find it is impossible to give up.' The failure of the Association's representatives to carry its own members was largely due to a dispute between *The Irish Times* and the newsagents which came to a head in September 1920. The newspaper had refused to give trade terms of

8 The carriage charges seem to represent a war-time reintroduction of charges which had frequently been paid by the publishers in the pre-war decade.

thirteen copies to the dozen which other papers had agreed to since early 1918, and it also refused, unlike the *Irish Independent*, to credit newsagents with unsold copies. A strike took place in which the Association claimed the support of three quarters of the Dublin trade. It was eventually settled in October 1920. The *Irish Newsagent* commented that it was '.... the first appearance of a strike in our trade in Ireland'. Feeling was strong in the Association councils, exacerbated by the fact that the newsagents felt that the wholesalers had backed *The Irish Times* in the recent dispute. In the end, few newsagents refused to pay the delivery charges. Ten chose to collect their parcels, and eight either stopped getting supplies or said that they would refuse payment. Two hundred and sixty five newsagents paid the charges. Eventually a compromise was worked out with the Association after a meeting with J. C. M. Eason in late November. From 4 December onwards the Association offered to pay 1s per week. In the long run the wholesalers had prevailed, but there was a price for victory. Some ill-will had resulted, and the question of terms had been ventilated publicly.

The *Irish Newsagent* in its issue of 4 December gave news of the settlement and commented that 'the wholesalers one knows are indeed badly hit over the present heavy expenses in wages and extra carriage charges'. Elsewhere in the same issue it observed that 'if it can be arranged for a new wholesaler to come to Ireland and in this case I mean Dublin as Ireland — the trade will be well pleased'. There were already two wholesalers in Dublin, Dawson's and Eason's. Eason's remained the larger business. In the negotiations with the association in 1920, the meetings with both wholesalers, i.e. Eason's and Dawson's, were held in Eason's. J.C.M. Eason took the initiative in drafting the responses and on the whole seemed the dominant character on the wholesalers' side. In a letter to Hart, the secretary of the Association on 7 September 1920, enclosing a summary, he commented that the summary was 'perhaps not very complete owing to the extent which I took part in the discussion'. In the competitive conditions of the trade Dawson's claimed that they were 'the famous wholesale firm', a hint at the dual role of Eason's as wholesaler and a major retailer, and Eason's were well aware that in some cases where they stopped supplies, newspapers reached shops from Dawson's. This was an added factor in making them reluctant to accede too readily to the requests from the Association to refuse supplies to new applicants. In October 1920, in the heat of the controversy about delivery charges, the *Irish Newsagent* referred on several occasions to the possibility of a new wholesale house. It hinted first of all at the likely arrival of a further English house, and then at the appearance of another Irish house. This resentment directed against Eason's is reflected in the reference: 'I want to see competition by the retailers for the rights of having the Bookstalls at the railway termini. I want to see an effort made to compete for the Irish railway advertising. I want, in other words, to see fair play all round, and big monopolies smashed.' Porter's, the small but successful wholesale house in the north, was praised fulsomely.

Eason's handled the weekly edition of the popular papers published on Fridays. They did some business before the war through the bookstalls in true Sundays, i.e. weeklies arriving in Dublin or Rosslare on Sunday morning and going on general sale on Sunday. Eason's distributed them to the military garrisons and retailed them at the bookstalls on Mondays. Before World War I weekly as well as Sunday editions made up the purchases by the Irish readership. Even in 1911 the Sunday editions which reached inland districts around midday or in the afternoon on Sunday were being distributed. With improved distribution the true Sunday edition began to supersede the Friday edition, and as Eason's did not lay up news in their wholesale department on Sundays, this business passed into the hands of other distributors. Dawson's did wholesale Sundays, but they did not have the business to themselves. Several lesser agents had emerged to cater for the Sunday business, in some cases as early as 1911, The *News of the World* and the *People* were handled by Farrell of Temple Street, and the other Sundays were handled by Thomas J. Kirwan of Fairview. Dawson's therefore failed to make their mark in the one area where they had no competition from Eason's.

Moreover, according to the *National Newsagent* of 30 October 1920, Dawson's, 'because of some trouble, could not have supplies of the *Independent* except through Eason's,[9] and several other publishing houses in Dublin were also said to supply only through Easons.' Dawson's finally withdrew in the course of 1922, giving over their interest to Gray, who had been their manager. The withdrawal may have been prompted by the political change-over in 1922, but it seems more likely that trade considerations were uppermost, since the successor firm also ceased to trade within a year. The Association canvassed the leading wholesale firms in England to see would they set up in Ireland 'with a view to taking up the vacancy', although without a positive result. Eason's position rested unchallenged, and the uncertain political and economic situation almost certainly contributed to this. By 1925 the possibility of

9 Their taking over of other orders during the 1913 strike.

establishing a second large wholesaler seems to have been abandoned, and Craddock, the new secretary of the Association, wrote to Eason's on 30 March 1925: 'Certain small wholesalers supply *non-newsagents* with certain publications and [I] suggest that your firm and our association could possibly take joint action to prevent this becoming more common'. By this time the Association's enthusiasm for other wholesalers was tempered by an awareness that while they helped to guarantee better terms to newsagents, competition among the wholesalers also tended to multiply the number of retail outlets. This was particularly evident in the case of the trade in Sundays, where the new distributors had no loyalties to the established retail trade.

How true were the charges made by the retailers against the wholesalers? In 1920 they alleged that the wholesalers refused terms of thirteen copies to the dozen which the retailers maintained that publishers provided. Eason's sent out a circular anonymously in which they countered these charges. The circular claimed that when periodicals were charged in England at the rate of thirteen to the dozen, a lower rate per dozen of twelve was charged in Ireland, i.e. the equivalent in Ireland of the English price of 13 for 1s 7d would be 12 for 1s 6d. The circular also pointed out that since a newsagent had to order thirteen copies to get any benefit from the thirteen per dozen rate, the benefit in Irish conditions was an illusion since very few newsagents could order so many copies, and charging on a copy basis put all newsagents on equal terms. In addition the circular went on to claim that higher priced papers were never sold at the 13 for 12 rates, and asserted that 'the principal illustrated weeklies are, for example, at present sold in Dublin at better prices than in provincial towns in England in spite of extra carriage costs'. The *Irish Newsagent* representing the more established retailers, did not share this view. In fact, while they may have overstated their case, the retailers had a point. On balance Eason's gained nothing from the position they took up, and might well have accepted the English price structure which would have given slightly better terms to the relatively few large retailers and less favourable terms to the many smaller newsagents. This was certainly the view of Rhys Thomas, then Circulation Manager of Alfred Harmsworth (Lord Northcliffe)'s Answers Ltd. Knox McKay, the Dublin agent of Answers Ltd. in 1924, relayed the fact that Thomas '.... strongly expresses his sympathy with the attitude of agents here who seek to get the same terms as the majority of the English retailers obtain.' Knox McKay, like Wallace of Odham's, who also tended to be critical of Easons' policy, represented the view of large publishers with mass circulations.

It is probable that houses like George Newnes, Pearsons and smaller houses, all selling a smaller number of copies at individual outlets, would have taken a different view.

Eason's were probably unduly obstinate in their view. But in fact Eason's had a well-defined reason for their policy of charging. J.C.M. Eason made it clear in the correspondence that, as Eason's saw it, a 13 for 12 rate would encourage retailers to increase small orders to thirteen copies with a subsequent rise in returns of unsold copies. In the case of the fashion journals there were only 53 agents getting more than 12 copies, as against 419 getting less than 12. In response to criticism they proposed to offer the 6d *Answers* papers at a wholesale rate of 4¼d instead of 4½d. This would mean a reduced profit for them, but would provide a uniform profit for every retailer. Eason's stand exonerated then from the charge they they wished to profiteer, but it may be that they held to their point too grimly. In correspondence with Odham's in the previous year, Eason's explained that although they received publications at the same rate as wholesalers in England, they charged 5½d instead of 5¼d as they never charged farthings on invoices.[10] This prompted Wallace of Odham's to respond that 'perhaps little matters like this have caused certain enquiries to be made in certain quarters as to possibilities for competition in the

TABLE 15 *Dublin Wholesale news supplies and returns*

	Town*		Country*		Bookstalls**	
	Supplies	Returns	Supplies	Returns	Supplies	Returns
	£	%	£	%	£	%
1921	59,224	5.1	139,278	1.2	51,698	11.0
1922	61,101	5.6	154,637	1.7	52,934	12.7
1923	65,487	7.5	138,307	3.4	46,318	15.0
1924	71,158	8.6	134,116	3.9	44,955	15.7
1925	74,668	9.2	132,604	4.5	44,832	15.4
1926	78,142	10.2	135,847	4.7	45,097	15.3
1927	72,527	11.1	126,325	5.1	42,756	17.8

* at wholesale prices
** at retail prices

10 Charging in farthings was a standard practice in the house as late as 1945-50 and even after. It would seem therefore to have been introduced, or reintroduced (assuming that war-time inflation had caused its abandonment), at this stage.

wholesale trade on your side'. Net profits of the wholesale division remained at a high level in the 1920s, reaching their peak so far in 1923/4 and 1924/5. Trading profits as a whole were disastrously low in the mid-1920s so that the wholesale news business was subsidising other parts of the business. Trade customers were therefore right in their complaints about Eason's, as the profits were in a sense at their expense.

Newspaper and periodical sales held up well throughout the post-war period. Even though they fell from the peak in value in the year 1921/2 to a lower level in 1926/7 they were still satisfactory. The fall in prices implies there must have been a rise in volume. The drop in wholesale news sales in the Dublin house was not paralleled in Belfast. There the turnover actually rose continuously from 1921/2 to 1924/5 from £71,834 to £82,559. However there were significant contrasts within the Dublin total between town (i.e. City of Dublin and suburbs), country and bookstall components. The largest component, country sales, seemed to be fairly stable, while town sales tended to rise. Competition was reflected both in a much larger proportion of returns in town than country sales, and in a very marked rise in returns over the decade. Bookstall sales were less healthy. The fall was significant, and returns were a much higher proportion of total supplies. The figures foreshadow serious difficulties at the bookstalls, which became increasingly evident in the years of stable prices from 1927 onwards. While demand from town and country combined rose, newspaper and periodical sales at the bookstalls declined heavily.

Dailies and weeklies were in roughly equal proportions. A typical pattern of supply can be seen in a note of figures for a week ended 23 February, probably in 1920 although undated. The value of dailies for the Dublin area was £667 and of weeklies £773. The number of newsagents was 326. Three shops took no dailies. The average value of all news supplied in the week was £4 8s 10d, per newsagent. There were twenty-six agents who took £10 or more per week, and one, Duigan of Baggot Street, who took £34. Even as late as 1924 the number of newsagents in country centres was quite small. Eason's had none in Cork city, where News Brothers monopolised the market. They had eleven in both Dundalk and Wexford, ten in Sligo, nine in Limerick and Galway, six in Roscommon, five in Waterford, where Harvey's and later Croker's were rivals, four in Tipperary and two in Ballinasloe. In the Belfast region there were said to be between three and four hundred newsagents at this time.

The category of weeklies of course included not only newspapers in the usual sense, but a large and growing body of serious and light literature, especially titles at low prices of 1d, 2d or 3d. The business with Answers Ltd, for instance had grown a great deal since the 1890s. By 1924 there were at least sixty-three papers published by this company, and no less than 1233 quires (of 26 copies) were supplied of the eight most popular of these. Their names are a clue to the market and its nature at the time (see Table 16)

TABLE 16 *Popular news sales, 1920*

Name	*Quires*	*Name*	*Quires*
Answers	320	Picture Show	106
Home Chat	238	Comic Cuts	101
Rainbow	142	Popular Music	100
Woman's Weekly	126	Tiger Tim	100

J.C.M. Eason noted in 1924 that: 'We believe that in connection with farming papers, and papers dealing with matters of new interest such as will be required in connection with the development of wireless and broadcasting, opportunities arise for expansion.' At that stage, weeklies were clearly more important in the country trade than in the Dublin trade. While in Dublin weekly orders of twenty-five shillings were to contain not less than ten shillings worth of weeklies in addition to the dailies, the terms to small agents in the country related to fifteen shillings of weeklies in a total order of twenty shillings. J.C.M. Eason considered that: 'Our view of the country trade is that on the whole great expansion is possible and should take place as the public become more accustomed to reading....' The pre-printed sheets distributed to agents for their weekly orders had grown greatly in size over the years. In 1878 they included 14 named dailies and 121 weeklies and periodicals. By 1908 this had increased to 28 dailies and 249 weeklies and periodicals.

THE STRUCTURE OF PROFITS

As far back as 1884 Eason had observed to Smith that capital invested turned over in newspapers as frequently as ten or twelve times in the year, four to five times in books and magazines, and more slowly in other lines: three times in stationery, and two and a half times in retail news and news advertising, and railway advertising. The consequences of this are clearly seen in the inflation in the war and post-war years. Inflation was becoming evident in 1917 and 1918, and it became more marked in 1919. In 1920/21 cash turnover rose dramatically, so that by 1921 cash receipts in the Dublin Wholesale side were 38 per cent higher than they had been in 1919. While prices were rising, the profits for the company improved. The net profits rose from £4,342 in 1916/17 to £9,766 in 1917/18 and further to £12,990 in 1918/19. They plunged to £5,302 in 1919/20, in part because of a net outlay, allowing for government grants, of £12,665 on new buildings. Heavy liabilities arising from the re-building were part of the reversal of fortunes in the financial year 1919/20. The reversal preceded by up to one year the general deterioration which set in in Irish business as the post-war boom collapsed in 1920. In 1920/21 Easons' financial position began to reflect fully the combined impact of the widening recession and of the accumulated indebtedness arising from the rebuilding programme, which was by this point completed. In the year 1920/21 the profit was £3,801. Liabilities on account of the new buildings amounted to £40,000.

When prices began to tumble, profits contracted dramatically. Net trading profits were a mere £962 in 1921/2. High priced stock was slow to sell and dependence on credit to finance inflated purchases raised costs further, and reduced profits. In the largest division, News, gross profits dropped slightly but net profits as a percentage of turnover in news in Dublin fell sharply from 3 per cent in 1917/18 to 2½ per cent in 1918/19 and to a mere 1 per cent in 1919/20 and 1¼ per cent in 1920/21. Only in 1922/3 was the 1917/18 level restored. As the auditor observed in 1920, the company was short of working capital at this stage. The shortage of capital was resolved in part by an increase in cash deposits up to £17,848, by members of the family and some members of the staff, and also by an increase in bank borrowing. Between 1921 and 1922 liabilities were reduced by £14,000, mainly in bank borrowing, but they were still historically large in March 1922:

Trade creditors etc.	£62,136
Bank overdraft	£28,399
Cash depositors	£17,848
Mortgage loan	£5,000
Total liabilities	£113,383

The auditor's report in July 1922 stated that:

> These liabilities are of course very heavy, and but for the cash depositors it would be impossible to carry on without increasing the

> capital. That the capital of the company is really inadequate is apparent from the fact that the fixed assets stood at nearly £80,000 while the capital and reserve amount to £50,000.

When a separate Belfast company was created in 1924, the existing assets were made over to it, and the transfer was matched by the allotment of 7,000 Ordinary shares of £1 each in the new company to the Dublin house, and by a payment of £10,000. The latter payment was in the main applied to the reduction of deposits. The financial position of the Dublin house gradually improved. The minutes of the directors in February 1926 noted that not more than £15,000 was required by way of overdraft.

The accounts of the firm had always been audited internally. Hallett, the accountant, was auditor, and an outside auditor was not appointed until June 1901, when the new Companies Act prohibited servants of a company acting as auditors. George Herbert Carpenter of the National Museum, who became professor in the College of Science in 1904, was appointed auditor. In fact, he continued to be auditor until 1917. At this point the directors reported to the general meeting of 1917: 'The destruction of the premises and stock in April 1916 raised so many difficult questions in the preparation of the Balance Sheet that Mr G.H. Carpenter informed the directors that he felt unable to undertake this work any longer.' At this point the work was entrusted to G.H. Tulloch of Craig Gardner & Co. It was characteristically still a family arrangement. George Hill Tulloch was married to the widow of William Waugh Eason. The audit was entrusted to him in a personal capacity rather than in his capacity as a partner in Craig Gardner & Co., and his reports on occasion even had a slight tone of business conversation within a family circle.

The introduction of professional auditing was a consequence of the destruction of the main premises and stock in 1916. It was also the occasion for the first time of serious attempts to estimate net profits at departmental level. Before this, attempts at costing had been made only for the railway advertising and stationery businesses. The attempts were imperfect. As no totals for overheads had ever been made up, the allocation of overheads for railway advertising was purely notional. Until 1909 there had been no attempt to separate the cost of sales of stationery goods purchased from outside suppliers and those manufactured in the firm's own factory in Gloucester Street, and there was in fact no method of deducing whether the factory itself operated at a profit or at a loss. No division of sales categories existed before 1909 and factory production was calculated only from 1911. In the firm at large expenses were not allocated to departments, although J.C.M. Eason was already working towards this end. Years before the outside auditors came in, he had provided for the collection of such data, although no analysis was attempted till after auditing was introduced in 1917. From that time forward, costing began to give a very clear picture of profit and loss within the firm. The most dramatic example of the inflation switch-back was in stationery. Stationery stocks appreciated rapidly in the years of scarcity. On the other hand stock purchased at inflated prices suffered a catastrophic depreciation when prices collapsed in 1920. Receipts soared and then collapsed, and this was reflected in profits. In 1919 profits on stationery were £3,198, almost as large as profits on twice the turnover in the news department. A huge net loss of £3,017 was experienced in stationery in 1920/21 and an even larger loss of £5,380 in 1921/2.

The company as a whole made profits of £3,801 and £962 in those years. Profits from sales of newspapers and periodicals, which didn't involve stocks, were immune to the adverse consequence of falling prices. This flexibility, combined with the growth of independent retail newsagents which required wholesaling, meant that the pattern of departmental profitability changed. Not only did profits in news wholesaling rise, but once the inflationary profits of other divisions collapsed after 1920 profits increasingly depended on the news division. The drop in profits in the wholesale news section in 1920 must reflect the impact of war which disrupted distribution systems. The economic strains of the early 1920s are reflected in nominal profits or in losses in most divisions and a profit in news which carried the persistent losses in several divisions, notably stationery. The rapid turnover of capital in news wholesaling compared with other divisions can also be seen in the fact that the division is much less prominent in the departmental breakdown of gross profits than in the breakdown of net profits.

The change in profitability was dramatic and abrupt. The long-term trends in profits also help to explain for instance the enormous importance attached to the railway contracts in the pre-1914 period. In fact, until the early 1900s, railway business provided most of the firm's profitability. In 1888/9 bookstalls and advertising accounted for 46 per cent of total profits of £5,971 and for 57 per cent of £7,508 in 1898/9. Bookstalls were a minor component of combined profits in advertising and bookstalls, and only in the expansive new market of 1895-1905 did they acquire a larger significance. In terms of profits, the jewel of the pre-1900 firm was the railway advertising business. Given this position the change in its fortunes was quite startling. The rise in railway rents was one reason for the change, and the directors were aware of this from the start. The directors'

TABLE 17 *Net profits in the 1920s*

Year	Net profits in Dublin wholesale news house	Total net profits in Dublin*	Belfast net profit**
1919	£3,804	£12,927	£2,324
1920	1,718	5,927	2,648
1921	3,545	3,801	2,351
1922	5,946	962	1,816
1923	7,486	2,366	
1924	8,560	6,650	
1925	8,991	1,193	
1926	8,220	470	
1927	6,958	1,090	
1928	8,440	3,082	

* includes transfer from Belfast (i.e. profit and payments) up to and including 1922.
** included in total net profits of Dublin house.

report to the general meeting in June 1900 anticipated a less favourable situation in the immediate future: 'As the profit for the new railway contract will be considerably less than formerly we think it wiser to reduce the dividend by 5 per cent.' A year later they noted that: 'The decrease is further accounted for by the increased sums payable to the GSW and GNR companies under the new contracts.' These are the only general comments that the pre-1914 minutes venture into, a measure of the weight attached to this aspect of the firm's business. In 1901 £3,100 was charged in rents under the contracts between Eason's and the railway companies for advertising rights, and the minimum payment was increased year by year up to £3,900 in 1909, and £4,000 in 1910. Increased 'rents' were thus a factor in reducing the profitability of the railway advertising.

There was a fundamental and totally unexpected factor which Eason's, judging by the surviving documentation, inexplicably missed. The company apparently failed to understand the implications for outdoor advertising of advertising in the popular press and periodicals whose sales swelled the receipts of their own wholesale news division. Railway advertising lost all buoyancy and the figures of 1902 were only marginally exceeded in subsequent years. The decline in railway advertising accelerated during the war years. A loss was incurred despite the fact that the railway companies waived the enforcement of the minimum guarantee. The year 1919/20 showed a recovery but in 1921/2 there was once again a loss.

One of the most striking features of the firm in the twentieth century is the decline in profits and in rates of return on capital. In the early 1900s in the wake of the successive changes in the profitability of advertising and bookstalls they contracted (in the main because of the greatly increased rents under the railway contracts). In 1905/6 the profits of the house were a mere £3,273, compared with £7,508 in 1898/9, and it seems clear that the determined effort to get direct supplies and better terms was a response to the slide in profits in the formerly prosperous area of advertising. In fact, a deep gloom and a sense of crisis pervaded the house in 1905.[11] Profits rose steadily in subsequent years to 1911, though they fell back after that again. In 1916 they were £6,486. If they were below the 1910/11 peak of just above £9,000, at least they were twice the 1905/6 nadir. It was still a disturbing fact that with the increased investment in the house, the return on capital had fallen dramatically. In 1886 £5,384 had been earned on a capital of some £15,000. In 1916 only a slightly larger profit was made on more than twice the capital. The situation worsened by the early 1920s, and the growing indebtedness of the Dublin house on an inadequate capital base was reflected in high interest payments and in meagre profits. Allowing for the 80 per cent rise in the price level since 1914, the real level of profits was painfully low, and the outlook of the Easons personally was one of narrow material expectations.

The low overall profits concealed the profitability of newspaper and periodical sales. More sophisticated costing after 1917/18 showed that the rate of net return on turnover in the News division was at its historically high point. It is likely that the business was already being carried by this division before that date and that poor profits in other divisions had concealed large profits in News sales. Moreover, even in News real profits had fallen. As bookstall profits only averaged about £1,000-£1,200 in 1906-14, and advertising was losing, the greater part of the net profits of £9,000 in 1910/11 derived from Wholesale News. In real terms, this level was probably never exceeded between 1919 and 1928. Before 1924 profits included a substantial amount in respect of profits transferred from Belfast. These profits, as a percentage of local turnover, were larger than those of the Dublin house. This was partly a consequence of the fact that

11 This comes out very clearly in a letter from Albert Brunton to Charles Eason on 6 July 1905. Eason's Belfast, Private letter book of Albert Brunton, 1905-6.

Dublin carried overheads which Belfast did not have to carry, such as senior management staff and interest on borrowings and deposits, and partly a consequence of the fact that Dublin carried the stationery and factory business in which losses were largest. In 1922/3 an effort was made to attribute costs more accurately between the two houses, and in 1924 a separate company was incorporated to provide for the needs of the Belfast house under a separate fiscal jurisdiction.

None of the branches of the business recovered all their old buoyancy between the wars. Railway advertising receipts in Dublin recovered somewhat from the depressed levels of the war years. They rose from £8,398 in 1918 to £12,796 in 1924, to which a little earned by the separate Belfast house should be added. But it did not exceed that figure in the next three years. Allowing for the rise in the price level since 1914 the fall is disastrous. Stationery was consistently the largest division of the company after News. It expanded its relative position during the inflation of the war years and in the aftermath of the war, but then contracted quite sharply in the 1920s. Cash receipts virtually halved. In 1922 it passed from the second to the third division of the Dublin house, and in 1924 it slipped to fourth place, after News, Books and Retail. The auditors' report as late as July 1925 noted that 'the wholesale stationery and books departments are feeling the effects of the depressed state of trade and of competition.' Between 1924 and 1929 the stock-in-trade in stationery was steadily reduced from £15,000 to £9,000. This was reflected in the fact that by 1927/8 the loss had at last been converted into a profit, but it was achieved of course at the price of a greatly reduced stock. As there is no evidence that consumption had fallen, it can only be assumed that Eason's were now progressively surrendering the dominant position that they had once held in wholesaling in stationery. Its position in that market now depended more than in the past on sole agencies for patented goods.

Chapter 10 The heyday of the bookstalls

THE BOOKSTALLS HAD THEIR TIME of most sustained growth in the eight years after 1899. Cash receipts (at retail prices) for the entire system rose from £31,287 in 1899 to £50,460 in 1905. After that the impetus to growth was slight. Sales reached £55,934 in 1911 and had not exceeded that level in 1913. Receipts grew more rapidly in the north than in the south with the recovery of the Great Northern Railway and Belfast & Co. Down Railway contracts in 1900. Between 1900 and 1901 receipts from the north doubled, and between 1899 and 1905 they rose from £2,984 to £11,604. Despite the especially strong rises in the north, growth was country-wide; less than half the actual increase in receipts between 1899 and 1905 was accounted for by receipts in the Belfast office.

In these years bookstall sales outpaced wholesale sales and turned Eason's for a while into an important retailer. The total number of bookstalls grew to ninety-five. Fifty-nine of these were under the Dublin office and thirty-six under the Belfast office. In the south a bookstall had even been established at Cahirciveen at the extremity of the Iveragh peninsula in Kerry, and no less than five bookstalls appeared on the burgeoning Donegal railway system, excluding the Lough Swilly stations in Derry and Strabane. Only Connaught and Clare were untouched; the stalls at Athlone, Athenry, Galway and Sligo, stood in splendid isolation. Cash receipts benefited from the war and post-war inflation. Overall, they peaked at £83,154 in 1923/4. Dublin peaked in 1921/2 and Belfast in 1923/4. After that they fell in both centres.

The growth in the bookstall network had taken place under the influence of some optimistic assumptions. This is reflected in the fact that when Olley's, who had been a major competitor in the north, went bankrupt in 1899 Eason's paid a high price for the new contract, which in turn influenced the GSR contract, which was renewed at a high rate. In entering into the contract with the GNR, Eason's had been influenced by two things. First, such figures as were available about the business conducted by Olley's were unreliable, and they led Eason's to overestimate the outcome. A second and even more important factor leading them to make a high bid was the desire to keep out cross-channel competitors. The conditions of the new contracts were particularly onerous on the advertising side, and converted profits into loss as early as 1906. As far as the bookstalls were concerned, a profit remained, but it was not buoyant.

Within the first decade of the new century, bookstalls receipts had fallen as a proportion of total receipts, and even in absolute amount had lost momentum after 1905. Some retrospective calculations by J.C.M. Eason suggest that in the 1900s as much as half the net profit was accounted for by railway advertising and bookstall profits combined. In 1906 and 1907, when railway advertising profits had changed into losses, the bookstalls accounted for 40 per cent of profits in 1906, and almost 50 per cent the following year. This abrupt change provides the rationale for the phenomenal rise in the bookstall network in these years. The dramatic rise in bookstall receipts up to 1905 apparently fully justified the expansion in the network, and the profitability of the bookstalls made good the collapse in that of advertising.

In the long run, however, the optimism proved unfounded. Bookstall sales did not maintain their momentum; the future was in wholesaling to independent newsagents. Even as early as 1899 it was recorded that: 'We might by dropping prices at bookstalls compete with retail traders in country towns but on the contrary we have trade constantly taken from us by agents who undersell us, and we get no thanks from the trade.' Sales at bookstalls fell during this decade as a proportion of cash receipts. Net profits from bookstalls peaked at £1,726 in 1901; between 1906 and 1914 they fluctuated within limits of £1,000 — £1,200. Even in the inflated

TABLE 18 *Bookstall Profits, Dublin, 1922-8*

Year	Bookstalls	Curragh
1922	£1,068	£522
1923	580	342
1924	348	129
1925	562	235
1927	537	(164)
1928	100	142

( ) = loss

receipts of the late 1910s the net profits of the Dublin bookstalls and the Curragh Shop were only £1,947 in 1919, and £1,538 in 1920/21. In the 1920s the profitability of the bookstalls and the Curragh stall subsided in a dramatic way (Table 18).

WHOLESALING BOOKS

In the 1920s the wholesale book division, whose turnover included monthly magazines as well as books, was thriving. Between 1918 and 1924 turnover rose from £44,047 to £82,871. Its progress closely paralleled that of newspaper and periodical sales. The main driving force in the department was almost certainly magazines. In contrast to newspaper and weekly sales, which peaked in 1922, book and magazine sales peaked in 1924, and the dip afterwards was slightly sharper than in news. Because of the importance of magazines, the Books division, although a distinct department, was very much affected by the same forces that had made weeklies the most expansive dimension of the news department. Turnover was, however, slower than in news and profitability was less marked. The division ran a loss in 1920/21, then made fairly good profits in 1922-24 and turned in marginal profits or losses in the next four years. Magazine sales fairly consistently accounted for one-third of the division's turnover between 1899 and 1918 and it is likely that this proportion was subsequently higher.

The importance of magazines as a component of turnover is illustrated by the phenomenal success of *Our Boys*, of which Eason's were the distributors and nominal publishers. Turnover rose from £798 in 1915/16 to a peak of £7,386 in 1923. In that year the journal accounted for 9 per cent of the turnover in books and magazines. Its sales exceeded 40,000 copies per issue, reaching 70,000 for special issues. The sales of *Dublin Opinion*, which first appeared in the early 1920s soon exceeded 40,000 also. *Easons' Monthly Bulletin* in April 1925 noted: 'this we believe to be the greatest number ever printed of any similar Irish publication.' These were unparalleled sales for any magazine in the Irish market. The two magazines on their own probably accounted for 20 per cent of turnover in the entire division. (Sixty years later, the best selling magazine on the Irish market, the *RTE Guide*, sells 120,000 copies per issue.)

With a very wide range of publications, many of them specialised, profits were much lower in this division than in the Wholesale News area. The slow movement of book stocks was another factor in keeping profits down. Unfortunately there is not enough evidence to permit a close study of wholesale book supply trends, but it is clear that popular editions of best sellers at as little as 6d were a feature, and that hardback authors like Edgar Wallace, Agatha Christie and Sabatini were the best sellers. Ethel M. Dell, Bertha Ruck were popular, as were Zane Grey and other 'Wild West' authors. The popularity of the motor car and the advent of broadcasting in 1925 led to a demand for books on cars and wireless respectively. The cinema was also becoming a potent force in the sale of books. The sale of Sabatini's novels was promoted by the film versions of his books, and Eason's noted in 1925 that the historical novel was coming back. The appeal of the cinema was reflected even in the stationery department where cards of film stars and of their homes were becoming popular. In July 1925 they advised the trade that 'we anticipate a steady sale for both these lines, particularly in towns and districts where there is a picture theatre.' The impact of the cinema is reflected in a greater emphasis on the visual element in books, notably in the jackets which were now becoming a selling force. Eason's regretted in April 1925 '.... the increasing number of suggestive book-wrappers which are being issued. There are a number of volumes which really contain nothing of a harmful nature, but unfortunately one cannot stock them.'

Eason's were not of course the only wholesaler in books. Hely's were also in that market in a limited way, claiming in 1905 that they stocked 'prayer books, and a cheap class of stories, for sale in our wholesale department.' News Brothers were also wholesalers of books in the Cork area from the late nineteenth century. But because retail booksellers tended to buy directly from the publishers and from the great London wholesaler Simpkin Marshall, Irish wholesalers could really only significantly affect the market for the cheaper mass market products where small quantities could be distributed through their own travellers and through the news distributive system. Easons' importance in the book market derived also from their position as a retail bookseller in Dublin. Bookselling itself was not a large business in Ireland at the end of the nineteenth century, and it can hardly be said to have flourished in proportion to the population of Dublin. It was going through a difficult time in Britain as well. The demand for books, particularly novels, was increasing, but the system of pricing that had been established since Sir Walter Scott's time was under attack. In the old system original novels were priced at extraordinarily high levels such as 31s 6d for three volumes. In practice most novels were bought by the subscription libraries such as Mudie's and Smith's who in effect supported the publication of novels by buying most of the first edition, but also had a vested interest in maintaining the artificial standard price. Booksellers got trade discounts from the publishers, and often allowed discounts to the public of between 15 and 25 per cent on the list price.

The demand for cheap reading led non-specialist retailers to use heavily discounted books as loss leaders. Thus the drapers Clery's in Dublin were selling books to the public at a discount of 3d in the shilling off the list price. To compete, specialist booksellers had to slash their own margins, and to increase profitability by selling stationery, wool and other goods. At the same time they demanded greater discounts from publishers, who thus began themselves to feel the squeeze. As Eason wrote to Macmillan's in 1890: 'the trade is year by year getting more demoralised. Publication price is very nominal and publishers discounts increase as the only alternative.' Solutions to the 'underselling problem' were being proposed on all sides. In March 1890, Frederick Macmillan had written to *The Bookseller* suggesting that a system of 'net books' be set up. By this he meant retail price maintenance. His idea was that publishers should announce to the trade and to the public that certain books were not to be had except at list price. Macmillan & Co. published the first book under this system, Marshall's *Principles of Economics,* in July 1890.

In April 1896 Dublin booksellers met at Easons' premises at 40 Sackville Street to consider '.... how best they could make a stand against any English publishers facilitating drapers or others in Dublin who are cutting prices.' In the same year they resolved 'not to alter the present practice of allowing only 2d in the shilling discount to the general public' and requested publishers to refuse to supply any firm giving a larger discount. In this way they sought to mitigate the effects of uncontrolled competition. In fact, as there had been no previous agreement on discounts in the trade, they were creating one, not so much as an end in itself, because competition among established booksellers did not pose serious problems in 1896, but as a means of distinguishing between orthodox trade outlets and others.

Publishers did not always accept the distinction. Longman's held out against the suggestion of cutting off Clery's, and a long dispute between the Dublin trade and the London publisher followed. At one stage, Longman's proposed that the Trinity historian and MP William Lecky, who was one of their authors, should arbitrate the matter. This was courteously declined by the booksellers, and in January 1898 a letter was received from Longman's informing them that on the advice of Mr Justice Madden and Lecky they had closed Clery's account. Clery's however continued to get books from various sources.

In 1894 the two largest subscription libraries, Mudie's and Smiths, had announced that they no longer supported the three volume novel system. The effect was immediate. In that year, 184 three volume novels had been published. Three years later the figure was down to four. Novels increasingly began to be issued in single volume form, priced at 6/-. This instantly focussed further attention on discounts. A discount to the customers of 25 per cent off a book at 31/6 still leaves a certain return: the same discount off a 6/- book left too little.

The Associated Booksellers of Great Britain and Ireland was founded in 1895, and immediately took up Frederick Macmillan's net book idea. After some years of discussion, the Publishers Association (founded in 1896) and the Associated Booksellers reached agreement, and the Net Book Agreement was despatched to all booksellers for their acceptance, in the summer of 1899. Its basic aims were to limit the allowable discount on 'non-net' books and to prevent discounting at all on 'net' books. Over a thousand booksellers soon expressed their acceptance of the scheme, and those who hesitated were quickly brought into line by a statement from the Publishers Association that supply would be refused to discounters of net books.

At the first meeting of the Dublin booksellers in 1896 there were only eleven firms represented, and in the Dublin branch of the Associated Booksellers, as it became, the number of members never exceeded fourteen until 1935. In Belfast, where a branch of the Associated Booksellers was formed in 1901, there were six members, including Eason's. By 1912 a Cork branch was affiliated but in June 1914 according to a circular of the Associated Booksellers this branch had ceased to exist 'owing to the apathy of its members'. Charles Eason explained to the Council in regard to an application from Cork that '.... there were not many booksellers in the district. He recommended that the writer of the letter be invited to remain a member not connected with the Parent Society'. In 1918 the Secretary of the Dublin Associated Booksellers noted that 'I am afraid that there is no scope for extending our membership as I know only one other bona fide bookseller; they are mostly newsagents and stationers, and most of them obtain their supplies through Messrs Eason's or other wholesale houses.' Clery's, who had been a source of contention in the 1890s, eventually signed the Net Book Agreement in 1904, but Dublin booksellers were very sore at subsequent recognition of Clery's for trade terms by the Publishers' Association. They continued to disregard them as booksellers, and Clery's never became members of the Irish booksellers group. In 1903 the Dublin booksellers protested against an offer of a book by Macmillan through a newspaper stating that 'if this matter is allowed to pass now without protest a very dangerous precedent will become established.'

In most years, meetings of the Association were few. After the conversion in 1902 of the Dublin Booksellers Association into a branch of the Associated Booksellers of Great Britain and Ireland, meetings were perfunctory for five years, and in two of these years there was no occasion to hold a meeting. Matters erupted in 1908-9 when no less than four of six meetings were devoted to 'problems of publishers extending terms to firms not engaged in bookselling, properly so called', and in the following year another four of seven meetings dealt with the same subject, which by now revolved around the 'Cafe Cairo affair'. Ostensibly this was a question of objection to large discounts by the seller to the public, but at heart it revolved around the recognition of outlets such as cafes or restaurants for trade terms. Most publishers withdrew trade recognition, but Methuen's held out. The attitude of the Associated Booksellers of Great Britain and Ireland was much less whole-hearted than the Dublin booksellers wished, and it took a lot of lobbying, helped by the support of north of England booksellers, to get a Council resolution passed, that 'in the opinion of the Associated Booksellers of Great Britain the supply of books to cafes is against the interests of authors, publishers and booksellers'.

The issue of trade outlets was far and away the dominant theme of the meetings, and indeed the only consistent one. Discounts were an issue but not a major one. The Net Book Agreement had divided books into net books which should be sold at net price, and 'subject books' which were subject to discounting from the list price. Educational books were among the latter, and the Irish publisher M.H. Gill's for instance in their lists of 1903 had only three net books as against twenty subject books. The Dublin booksellers sought to hold discounts on such books to the public to 2d in the shilling, although discounts of 25 per cent to schools were regarded as an established practice. The temptation to offer larger discounts was evident even among members of the Association itself. McGee, chairman of the Association, breached the agreement himself in 1902 in regard to school books by offering school terms directly to parents. Others broke it either by granting discounts on net books, or by exceeding the discounts limit on non-net books to the public. In 1905 even the discount of 25 per cent to colleges and schools had to be confirmed, but Combridge's refused to be bound by it. This situation prompted O'Carroll of Duffy's to observe in 1905 that 'a number of us are rather small in our views of business methods. There is a lot of petty jealousy .... we are not as closely associated as we might.' In 1916 when publishers' conditions changed, new and more restrictive terms were introduced, with discounts not exceeding 10 per cent.

Eason's took an active part in the Associated Booksellers, although they were careful not to let their dominant position in the Dublin book trade, wholesale and retail, be reflected in an overbearing prominence. However both Charles Easons, senior and junior, and William W. Eason were regular attenders at early meetings, and the fact that the meetings from the start were in Easons' premises is a further indication of the firm's active interest. Charles Eason, junior, became chairman in 1906 and remained in this position until 1930. It was in this year that the *Publisher and Bookseller* noted that Eason's were the largest retailer of books in Dublin. On some peripheral issues, Eason's seem to have abstained when matters were pressed to a vote. When the issue of copyright copies for libraries came up in 1927 some booksellers wrote in against it, but both Gill's and Eason's supported the proposal. The general view prevailed however, and the report of the Association for 1927 commented that their endeavours against the Bill had not found favour before the Dail.

The one occasion when Eason's took a prominent initiative was significantly in relation to magazines, in which they were not only major wholesalers, but where their role was more central than in books. At a meeting in September 1897 Charles Eason reported that the firm had sent a letter some months earlier to principal newsagents inviting their cooperation in maintaining prices for magazines with a form for signature stating that 'I am in favour of charging full price for all magazines, and will undertake to do so on learning that the trade generally are willing to combine for this purpose'. One hundred and fifty letters were sent out, and one hundred and ten returned assents. Forty did not reply. In March 1902 the booksellers agreed to make an effort to get all booksellers and newsagents to agree to charge full price for magazines. One newsagent, who had already made his position clear when the original circular had been distributed in 1897, held out, and at the following meetings it was agreed to endeavour to ascertain the source from which he got his supplies. The inference from this may be that he had been refused supplies in the interval by Eason's.

WHOLESALE STATIONERY AND THE STATIONERY FACTORY

Stationery sales could be divided into plain goods, fancy goods and post cards. This actually grossly over-simplifies a wide range of requisites which included not only stationery but many writing and office materials. Before the First World War one of the most important areas of business was the Bevis *Hand and eye training* contract which Eason's secured for several thousand schools. Much of the material they contracted from manufacturers, but in time some was made in their own factory. J.C.M. Eason also retrospectively recalled an 'unusual' sale of Science Note Books — some fifty or sixty gross were sold annually in the autumn. From 1927/8 onwards stationery sales also included £3,600 per annum worth of sales of tobacco and sweets at bookstalls, which had been formerly carried in the accounts of wholesale books.

J.C.M. Eason had reckoned in 1921 that a wholesale house had to carry upwards of seventy-five designs of Christmas and New Year greeting cards. Much of the ordering of stationery was done as much as a year ahead, particularly for Christmas items and a circular after the 1916 Rebellion about their temporary premises referred to 'very large orders with Japanese, French, Danish and British makers towards the close of last year and the early months of 1916.... Deliveries are still coming in almost every week from Japan.'

In 1906 it was felt that profits were lower than they might be, and that one factor contributing to this was the handling of such a wide variety of goods often in small quantities. Buying had to cope with an enormous range of items, though subdivided between several individuals. F.T. Eason bought cards and fancies. Coghill handled the plain stationery and also looked after the picture postcards as that trade developed. By 1901 he had far too much on his hands. Because of the demands on him, Coghill bought picture or view postcards in a wholesale fashion — Eason's were to sell every publisher's product. While Christmas cards, and comic postcards were a mass product in which Easons' role, in line with Coghill's thinking, was a passive wholesale one, viewcards had an essentially Irish and local topographical connection. However, as sales of individual scenes were slow, stocks had to be held for periods that big houses would find unacceptable. Travellers for the publishing houses were therefore not responsive to suggestions for cards, and as a result both the Irish house of Lawrence and the Scottish house of Valentine had little time for wholesalers. Indeed, this was reflected in Valentine's opening a Dublin house of their own in 1905. This situation created a market gap which Eason's themselves filled with the launching of their 'Signal' range of pictorial views in 1905. It was one of the first ventures by J.C.M. Eason himself. Easons' venture was successful, and between 1899 and 1915 card sales trebled, selling strongly after 1907. During the war years pictorial cards outsold Christmas cards and Eason's took advantage of this trend by producing special series of cards, e.g. the rebellion views. This in conjunction with the rise of other categories made the postcard department a buoyant one.[1]

More than in any other division of the firm the need to be able to follow the fates of a large and various stock made stationery a pioneer of more sophisticated accounting. Before 1909 sales of cards and of plain and fancy stationery were not analysed. All that existed was a crude division of purchases in which factory wages were used as an estimate of house-made goods. A first analysis of sales was made in 1909 and two years later factory output was calculated for the first time. In that year, 1910/11, sales were valued at £27,806, divided into *plain*: £14,141 (of which the factory made £8,255) and *fancy* £13,655.

Factory output was almost wholly in the range of plain stationery, such as the highly successful Terra Cotta exercise books. Before 1914 Easons were competitive in these areas. As Charles Eason, junior, wrote in 1899: 'Our travellers are always looking to see what copy books etc. are preferred to ours and we then try to produce books equal or superior to our rivals.' In fancy goods and comic cards, however, Eason's were unable to compete against the very long runs possible to specialist manufacturers. The Eason series of picture cards for instance were commissioned from other houses. As explained already, these cards were part of a response to the problem of competing in the stationery line in which profits were largest.

The earliest calculations of gross profits are from 1908/9 and factory profits were added in 1910/11. Unfortunately not all the sales calculations survive, and from 1920 we are reliant on the transfer component from the factory in purchases or supplies to study the position. Factory output had held its own during the war years, maintaining the proportion of about two-thirds of supplies of plain stationery, but factory supplies then collapsed in 1923, falling to a half of supplies of plain goods by 1924 and

1 For details of picture postcards by Easons and others, see F. E. Dixon, 'Pioneer publishers of Dublin Picture Postcards', *Dublin Historical Record*, September 1979 pp 146-7. Some years ago Easons presented their own collection of negatives to the National Library, Dublin.

to less than a third by 1927. As gross profits were fairly well maintained on plain stationery, it is clear that it was primarily a switch out of unprofitable house-production into more profitable imports. Gross profits were lower as a proportion of turnover on fancy goods, no doubt because of the great range carried; the smallest department of all, cards, had the highest profit ratio in the stationery division.

LIBEL

A perennial problem for Eason's, whether in their role as distributors, publishers or printers, was that of libel. It came up, for instance, as J.C.M. Eason noted in a memorandum in 1939, six times between 1907 and 1914. Since publication is effective only through distribution, the law holds that the distributor as well as the publisher and the printer can be held responsible for a libel. The basic position was settled in such cases as *Emmens v Pottle* in 1885. Counsel's opinion for Eason's in 1913 set out the law regarding newsvendors' liability:

> Assuming that a periodical distributed by a newsvendor in the course of his business did in fact contain a libel on the plaintiff, the newsvendor is not liable in respect thereof if (i) he sold the paper in *ignorance* of the fact that it contained matter defamatory to the plaintiff, and if (ii) such ignorance is not due to his negligence, that is to say to the neglect of such precautions as *in all the circumstances* should *reasonably* be expected.... As the law stands at present a newsvendor will not escape liability by 'wilfully closing his eyes'. There may no doubt be some papers of a character so 'notorious' that a newsvendor's only safe course in regard to them is not to sell them at all. I am however clearly of the opinion that in certain cases at least in regard to periodicals, there is no duty on a newsvendor to take any precautions by way for example of providing for a perusal in the absence of notice that a particular issue does in fact contain defamatory matter, though after such notice he would probably be liable in respect of any copies of that issue subsequently distributed by him.

Surveying the position in 1939, J.C.M. Eason set out the distributor's experience over long years:

> Broadly speaking it is seldom that the distributor is chosen as a mark for damages: the publisher and the printer are the first objective, and the publisher of repute (who alone can establish justification of the libel) is unlikely to let down the distributor. The publisher who is

> taking chances deliberately, and who is without adequate resources must be dealt with on his merits by the distributing trade.

The files of the house bear these observations out. No single award seems to have been made in the courts against them. A high number of the cases in which proceedings were threatened related to minor publications or publishers. However all cases of threatened proceedings were treated gingerly. They took up a lot of time, and legal costs could be high.

The most important of the six cases that occurred before the First World War was that concerning *The Throne* in 1912, which recurred in 1913. This was the largest single case in the history of the house, and the sole instance in which it made a settlement out of court. *The Throne* was a unionist and imperialist periodical of ardent views, published in London, which launched a violent attack on the Ancient Order of Hibernians in September and October 1912, and repeated the onslaught in subsequent issues. Six actions were taken by individual members of the Order, but five of them were rejected by the court on the grounds that individuals could not take libel proceedings where the matter complained of did not sufficiently identify them personally. In the sixth instance, relating to a Mrs McDermott, the court held that there was sufficient identification, and subsequent reporting in *The Throne* represented a repetition of the libel. Eason's settled with Mrs McDermott out of court, because they might have been held negligent, since the issue had already come up. In addition, because of the quasi-religious and political nature of the libel, a decision in favour of the plaintiff was all the more likely in a jury action. The costs of settlement were high. Easons' legal expenses came to £169 1s 7d and £120 was paid to Mrs McDermott. These were large sums in 1913.

Legal costs could be high even where a settlement did not arise, and where the basis of the allegation was slight. In 1932 a Mr Farrell, a former Lord Mayor of Dublin, took an action against Batt O'Connor, the author of *With Michael Collins through the fight for Irish freedom*, which was first published in 1929. This book repeated a tale that when Farrell's house was raided by British forces, he confronted the soldiers with the remark: 'You are raiding your friends. Do you know that I received the king? I had twenty minutes conversation with him.' Despite the fact that J.C.M. Eason considered that the libel was flimsy and that the damages were likely to be slight, the book was withdrawn. No judicial decision was ever made, and O'Connor's sister continued to sell copies of the book in her shop, and a new cheap edition was brought out. Easons' costs had been sizeable, and Robert Eason recalled years later: 'I don't remember what the amount was — but it was my first experience of legal costs and I remember thinking at the time that it was a lot to have to pay.' The firm's solicitors were cautious, and advised against running risks by circulating the book again.

The threat of libel proceedings was unquestionably inhibitory. On the other hand while a threat made the firm instantly cautious, they sought as a matter of policy not to take the possibility too much into account in day-to-day running of affairs. J.C.M. Eason emphasised this point in a letter to George Best, manager of the Belfast operation, in 1937:

> I want to warn you not to be too meticulous with regard to papers of a responsible character which may contain libellous matter. We must be in a position to assume the role of 'innocent distributor'.

One purpose of taking a libel action was to inhibit distribution. In the case of *The Throne* Eason's had continued distribution after proceedings had arisen, and this was the basis for fearing an unsuccesful defence if a case against them came to a court hearing. A plaintiff could achieve the end of stopping circulation by a threat of an action. In one case in 1965 a threat of proceedings was made against Eason's if they distributed a French weekly likely to contain an alleged libel against an Irish businessman. Few copies were distributed and as Eason's noted, 'from our point of view you can understand that it would simply not be worthwhile contesting this claim, whatever its merits may be.' Another reason for citing Eason's was to establish a jurisdiction for proceedings against an overseas publisher or printer. This led to Eason's being involved in the beginnings of cases, only to be dropped later. This situation was commented on by a legal advisor in connection with a case in 1932:

> Mr Binchy also considers that it may create a wrong impression and possibly may be a bad precedent in so far as it may lead plaintiffs in other similar cases of libel to join your company as a matter of course in the belief that they can discontinue against you at any time without incurring any penalty.

Chapter 11 Eason's and the Troubles 1916-1924

THE MOST DRAMATIC OF ALL EASONS' corporate experiences was the destruction of their premises in the 1916 Rising. They were near the GPO in O'Connell Street, so they were inevitably affected by the destruction of centre-city property in the Rising.

Monday 24 April 1916 was a bank holiday, and Charles Eason's visit to the office was a short one. He left town by train at 10.45 am to return to his home in Dalkey, with no suspicion of what was about to happen. The first intimation of trouble was a phone call at 2.30 pm from Davis, one of the clerks in the wholesale department, to say that there were disturbances in Dublin. Charles Eason requested Davis to go to the office and to telephone again from there. He himself went at once to Kingstown, where he arranged with the clerk to distribute papers as usual that evening, and to have the parcels for Dublin stored at the station. At 4.00 pm Charles Eason phoned the office in Abbey Street and learned that three of the staff were there, and would stay the night. He was told that Abbey Street itself was quiet. There were no police or military to be seen. However, the signs were ominous. As trams returned to the sheds, they suspended their runs, and train services to Kingstown had been halted from around midday. Phone calls from the office at 7.30 pm and 10 pm assured him that all was right there.

The following morning, Tuesday 25 April, Charles Eason learned at Kingstown that the steamer had not even left Holyhead. He got into Dublin by taking a train to Bray and then another train to Harcourt Street. From there he walked to Fred Eason's house in 30 Kenilworth Square. Some members of the staff who had been into town had bought *The Irish Times* there, and they were able to report that one of the directors, Albert Brunton, was at the office. A number of men, and thirty of the women and girls, had reported for duty. Some one volunteered to go across to *The Irish Times* office, and came back with 200 copies. None were sold, and no newsagents called for copies. The staff were all sent home, apart from two or three who were to stay on to look after the premises. Brunton saw the streets being barricaded, and watched the shops being looted until 3.30 am the following morning. Communications were now difficult, because the telephone operators would generally only take messages for military purposes. While the men on the premises of Eason's were getting their tea at 6 or 6.30 pm, they were surprised by the insurgents who had made a hole through the wall from the adjoining Metropole Hotel. They turned the Eason's men out of the premises and out of Abbey Street, saying that 'they would not do any injury unless firing took place, then they could not say what might happen'. Charles Eason learned all this the following morning. An unsuspecting member of staff, called Devitt, had reported for duty on Wednesday morning. His keys were taken from him, and he was sent off, but he was able to phone Charles Eason at 7.30 am with news of the position. Telephone communication seems to have closed totally only later that day.

Fred Eason's house in Rathgar now became the temporary headquarters of the firm. It was decided to put an advertisement in *The Irish Times* on Thursday requesting staff to report there. It was also envisaged that if cash could be withdrawn from the bank, their wages would be paid there. Charles Eason slept at Fred's on Wednesday night, and did not get back to Dalkey again to spend the night until Saturday. Civilians were still passing under the barbed wire in the city centre. They brought reports of looting, and news concerning the Abbey Street premises to the effect that 'our lower windows have not been broken, but the upper windows have been broken to shoot through them'. By now a fairly accurate picture existed of the disposition of the rebel garrisons in the city, but the picture was still uncertain as to the provinces:

> We believe that the Provinces are quiet. There have been wild rumours of outbreaks but no reliable reports. But several persons coming from South and North report all quiet. Sligo is mentioned as an exception. The soldiers are reported to be shooting men who surrender, but it is not worthwhile to record the numerous rumours.

On the following morning (Thursday 27 April) Charles Eason could get no nearer the centre of the city than Portobello Bridge. He recorded what he saw, the eerie uncertainty of a city in the grip of rebellion:

> A fair number of people about but quiet. No police to be seen. I don't quite understand this. Their being withdrawn from the streets in Dublin is natural as they would be shot at, but outside the city there is no body of men armed. Meantime the food problem is getting serious, great scarcity is becoming apparent, and unless some steps are taken to supply food to the masses, food riots are probable.

The parcels of the *Daily Mail* addressed from London to the Kingstown bookstall had arrived in the morning. All the other parcels had been returned from Holyhead to the senders. On the morning of Friday 28 April, Charles Eason was able to go 'along Harcourt Street as far as I choose'. He proceeded as far as the public house at the corner of St Stephen's Green. This had been held by the insurgents, and as he could hear occasional shots, he thought it best to proceed no further. By now news was beginning to filter out from the centre of the city, bringing details of destruction and of buildings on fire.

The supply of newspapers through Holyhead was becoming more normal. A good few parcels arrived on Friday morning. Some were opened and distributed to agents in Kingstown. Others were sent to Dalkey and Bray. A pass was also obtained to take papers daily from Kingstown to Kenilworth Square, and the first transfer under its authority was executed. Cash was obtained from various sources, and Mr Hallett, the accountant, paid wages to any of the staff who came between 4 and 6 pm. On Saturday morning the car arrived full of papers from Kingstown:

> In the meantime Albert (Brunton) and I opened the parcels which we got on Friday evening, and had them ready for sale spread out on the floor of the motor house. We got 2 trestles from the loft and put on top half a door of the old hen house. A number of the staff turned up and we supplied the agents, who came back for more, time after time, till all were sold by about 1 o'clock.

On his way home to Dalkey on Saturday Charles Eason received reports that the rebels had surrendered unconditionally. The following morning, Sunday 30 April, Charles and J.C.M. Eason queued in the town hall for permits to go to Dublin. They were fortunate enough to be spotted by an officer who had been in their employment, and their wait was greatly reduced. J.C.M. Eason went into town by bicycle, and brought home reports about 5 o'clock. The surrender of the insurgents was partial, and he was unable to get right into town without running too much risk: 'So many houses are occupied by rebels that the work of clearing them seems likely to take a considerable time'. The Easons were still without definite news about their own premises. Finally on Monday 1 May, it was possible to go by car as far as O'Connell Bridge, and from there to Abbey Street, where they saw their premises totally destroyed 'but the return building, consisting of the 3 strong rooms was standing and the iron doors were closed'. The precise time of the destruction of the premises was not known, but it was taken to be Friday night 28 April and Saturday morning 29 April. The only good news was that inspection further afield found that Brunswick Street (Pearse Street), and Gloucester Street (Sean MacDermott Street) were all safe. On Tuesday 2 May, it was possible to inspect the premises, and in the evening Coghill and Brunton sadly watched the fire brigade pull down the front of 79-80 Abbey Street.

Meanwhile the shuttle by car from Kingstown to Kenilworth Square continued. This remained the only premises in operation until the following Thursday, by which time supplies were being carried by four-ton lorry. On Friday 5 May the railway advertising department at 174 Great Brunswick Street was made the headquarters of the firm and the centre of the newspaper and magazine business. By 15 May Eason's were able to take possession of two other temporary premises: 56 Dawson Street for stationery, fancy goods and postcards, and the Antient Concert Rooms, 42 Great Brunswick Street, for books. On 2 May Charles and George Jacob offered to put some of their premises at Easons' disposal. In fact Eason's seem to have made use of part of Jacobs' premises up till mid-October, which eased the pressure while the other premises were being fitted up. As accommodation was made fully ready, its use changed to some extent. The bulk of news distribution, as well as postcards sales, transferred to the Antient Concert Rooms, and the shop was combined with the stationery at 56 Dawson Street. On the empty site in O'Connell Street a temporary wooden hut was put up and used for newspaper and magazine sales. When the builders began to work on the site, accommodation was secured in No 50 O'Connell Street.

Eason's were quick to take advantage of the Rising by issuing a book of photographs in June 1916 entitled *The Rebellion in Dublin 1916*, which continued to sell for several years. In two towns, Carrick-on-Suir and Clonmel, two newsagents were ordered to remove them from display. There was no basis for such intimidation, although as Eason's explained, 'we are not ourselves showing them in our windows.' The booklet had been prepared in haste, and in 1919 Eason's became the subject of a minor controversy because of a statement in the foreword that the Volunteers had fired on the Fire Brigade and that this had contributed to the fire danger. In fact, as the booklet had appeared in June, it preceded the statement by Captain Myers of the Fire Brigade in the autumn about the real facts. However Eason's had failed to take this into account in subsequent editions, and it was only corrected in the edition in hand in June 1919.

The extent of the damage to the premises can be measured by Easons' claim for compensation. In respect of buildings a total of £32,626 was claimed. The award made was £27,252. For fixtures, £10,126 was claimed, and the sum actually paid to Easons came to £9,156. Stock losses were estimated at £20,577 and the amount allowed was £19,442. The total claim came to £63,329 and the amount allowed was £55,850. The contract for the new buildings was signed with the contracting firm of J. & P. Good on 7 January 1918. Occupation of the new wholesale premises began in October 1919 and was completed in March 1920. The retail premises were opened one month later. The new buildings were designed by J.A.C. Ruthven, an engineer by profession who was manager in the railway advertising department and had for a long time been in charge of repair, upkeep and rebuilding of premises.

The Abbey Street and O'Connell Street premises were rebuilt as a single interlocking group of buildings: the O'Connell Street frontage was enlarged in the rebuilding as No 41 was acquired. One novel feature in the rebuilding was the raising of the floor level in the O'Connell Street premises so as to keep a uniform level throughout the entire area of the O'Connell Street and Abbey Street premises. This also provided adequate headroom for the basement. One unusual consequence of this feature of the new plans was the necessity for steps from the street to the retail shop. In all, the new premises cost about £55,000, a good deal more than the value of the old premises, not only because they were conceived on a larger scale, but because wage inflation added to the cost. The cost of fixtures amounted to about £22,000, thus being more than double the compensation received. The expenses of stocking were heavy, as prices were rising rapidly.

The four years between the Rising and the inauguration of the new premises were difficult ones for the staff. The business was being conducted on several different premises, none of which were designed for the purpose and which were modified to meet the requirements of business at a not insignificant outlay. This was particularly true of the stationery department whose business was handled in no less than four separate premises. Yet the period was one of great economic prosperity, especially in the immediate aftermath of the war.

The years from 1918 onwards were crowded with problems. There were financial problems, because the firm was overextended and had to call heavily on deposits from the family. There were practical problems because the business had to be conducted for four years in scattered, makeshift accomodation. On top of this, strikes and political upheaval added to the difficulties. From 1918 onwards labour unrest, partly in Ireland, but frequently in England, disrupted train and boat schedules, and culminated in the general strike in England in 1926, which played havoc with newspaper deliveries from Britain for several weeks. More serious than these problems, though, was the political unrest which intensified in Ireland from 1919. While it may have helped to stimulate sales of newspapers, the drawbacks outweighed the benefits, and the anti-English feeling engendered was reflected in widespread opposition to English publications, which accounted for over half the turnover of the news department.

The English railway strike from 27 September to 8 October 1919 was the first external upheaval experienced by the firm. There were many more disruptions by strike later on, but they were overshadowed by the emerging war in Ireland. The first hint of how the firm would be affected came in a report from the Killarney bookstall on 12 September 1919, intimating that: 'The police and military authorities searched this town today for seditious literature. Afterwards they came and asked me to allow them to inspect the stock in the stall which they did. After a few minutes they retired, leaving everything as they found it'. Reports of searches elsewhere in stalls or in the shops of agents came to hand from time to time. There is no complete list of them. Eason's advised one newsagent who had particular nationalist literature seized on 15 March 1920 that 'we do not find these are seized in very many places'. But police or military attention could be considerable in individual cases. One agent in Belturbet reported in May 1920 that for several weeks past the police had been calling into his shop and taking away without payment any copies of the *Watchword, Old Ireland* and *New Ireland* that were lying about. The Limerick Junction bookstall was raided on at least three occasions in 1920. Once, the clerk, Miss Frewen, was taken to the barracks before she was released. J.C.M. Eason recalled later: 'We had a suspicion that this particular clerk might have been giving some assistance but nothing ever came to light, and she did her work efficiently and satisfactorily so perhaps it was quite unfounded'.

An agent in Limerick city on 30 September 1920 reported that picture postcards of Terence MacSwiney and Dr Fogarty had been seized by the Black and Tans who threatened that the newsagent would be 'blown sky high if I stock any more of this muck'. There were other incidents, but not many. Yet the unpleasant intimidatory atmosphere created by these instances (a correspondence with the Inspector General of the RIC drew admissions that the sale of these items was legal) was reinforced by instances of intimidation elsewhere. Some of this intimidation was directed against English papers and some against individuals. In June 1921 a note signed IRA warned a newsagent in Killeshandra against supplying papers to a man 'as he is a police spy'. In October 1920 Easons were themselves warned against keeping 'a spy's daughter on your premises.... And now that our wishes have not been complied with, the principals of this firm were doomed.'

Eason's at times found themselves in the position of having dealings both with the legal authorities and with Dail Eireann, which was now extending its illegal jurisdiction. As early as March 1920 a letter from Charles Eason revealed his fear that an occasion might arise when the firm would have to publicly take the side of the law against Sinn Fein. A circular from the Trade Department of Dáil Éireann on 20 April 1921 intimated that a prohibition of Christmas pictorial cards of British origin was under consideration. The circular advised stationers not to place orders for British goods 'which it is likely they will not be permitted to sell'. A draft letter survives from Eason's setting out the arguments against the proposal, which eventually came into effect on 4 January 1922. A similar order against pictorial calendars had come into effect on 18 May 1921. On another occasion, a communication from the Dublin City Brigade of the IRA intimated knowledge of plans to rob the regular weekly Friday consignment of cash to the Gloucester Street premises, and advised Eason's to take the necessary precautions.

Direct interference with publications was limited. There is no evidence that seizures increased in 1921. Disruptions of deliveries for other reasons became serious as time went on however. Apart from the English railway strike in 1919, there was a prolonged disruption of the Irish railways between 20 and 30 September 1921. In 1920 the most serious disruption was the politically motivated refusals by railway men to handle trains with military, or military supplies, aboard. This had a serious effect on news distribution. Charles Eason wrote in a private letter on 21 November 1920 that:

> We have notified our staff that stoppage of trains will lead to loss of business and dismissal of staff. Kerry has now no railway running. Supplies to 32 agents and 3 bookstalls in Killarney, Tralee and Cahirciveen have stopped from yesterday. One hopes the railway men will realise the tremendous loss they are bringing upon all Ireland....

As the security situation deteriorated in Dublin, a curfew was introduced on 24 February 1920. Some fifty-five permits for staff were obtained from the Dublin Metropolitan Police. Tighter requirements were introduced on all movement in an area to the east of Sackville Street, which affected the stables, and hence created problems in moving the early morning vans from the area for collections and deliveries. Eason's suggested either blank permits or an instruction to the officer on the spot to permit vans to leave the area:

> Under ordinary circumstances a delay of an hour or two in getting permits to leave the area would be of no importance, but in the early morning such a delay would be fatal to our day's work. We commence the distribution of the morning papers as soon as possible after 5 am. Before the curfew, our staff were here by 4.30 am, now they do not arrive until 5.15 to 5.30. In consequence of this there is even now very great difficulty in catching the early trains with our parcels of papers. Any additional delay would involve the parcels being late....

A friendly reply from the Castle intimated that 'as I get my papers from your firm, and many of my relations have for years past done the same, an effort would be made to arrange the passage of the vehicles.' The post was erratic, and one letter from Newry written on 7 May 1921 complained that 'Posts are getting very irregular, and letters are often 2 and 3 days on the way.'

On one occasion Easons' Dublin premises were raided by the military, late in the morning and again in the evening of the same day. The premises were surrounded by a cordon at 10.30 am on Monday 8 November 1920. All exits were blocked, and male employees, some 160 in all, were questioned individually in the board room. Four employees were taken away, although they were subsequently released. According to the *Freeman's Journal*:

> Each employee when brought to the board room was asked the following questions —
>
> What did you do in 1916, '17 and '18?
> Are you a member of a club?
> What club are you a member of now?
> Were you ever in the Volunteers?

The second search of the premises was made at 6 pm on the same day. On this visit, according to a contemporary note of J.C.M. Eason, 'they stated openly to all seniors that there was ammunition on the premises and that they had the information from secret service.' The morning raid was a pretty tense occasion:

> The occasion led to a considerable amount of tension throughout the premises; those conducting the search of the premises and of the staff were not very punctilious and it was natural that everybody should feel a little nervous. At the same time, the members of the staff with

> cool heads succeeded in calming the others, and it may be of interest to note that on this occasion permission was given for smoking, and I think that had some beneficial effect; who was responsible for suggesting it to me, I do not remember, but it was a good move.

Four men had already been taken away in the morning raid for questioning, though later released. Three men had absented themselves in the afternoon without permission and later they 'practically admitted that they had definite reason to expect the military to return. Brennan (one of the three) said they were told by *their organisation* not to stay.' A difficult situation ensued within the firm. Several years earlier there was already evidence of the Republican sympathies of some of the members of staff. Charles Eason wrote to Daphne Clare in August 1917 that 'several of the staff were mixed up with the rising, of whom some were taken to England for some months. Most of them were allowed to resume work.' An anonymous phone call in the afternoon of 8 November 1920 had preceded the second raid. Rumour circulated within the house that one of the staff, who had a brother in the RIC, was responsible for the raid, and that he had gone through the house with his brother when the military were present. Three apprentices from the factory were under detention from the end of 1920 until well into 1921 in Ballykinlar. The trade union would not allow the firm to take on other apprentices in their place. Coghill, manager of the factory, commented in May 1921 that the situation 'is unfair to the employer and it is very hard on the boys.'

One of the continuing problems the firm experienced related to the distribution of such newspapers as drew the adverse attention of the IRA. These were the English papers generally, Belfast papers, and to a lesser extent the *Freeman's Journal*. The earliest instance seems to have been a decision in August 1920 by Pembroke Sinn Fein committee to ban the sale of English Sunday papers. According to Hart, the then-secretary of the retailers' association, the wholesalers' vans were held up at gun point on 'the bridges leading to the outskirts of the city' on two successive Sundays.[1] This became the subject of negotiations by the retailers' organisation with Sinn Fein headquarters, and an assurance was received from Arthur Griffith that the embargo would be withdrawn pending consideration of the issue. The matter next came up on 19 October 1920 when Easons' traveller, Toms, reported from Tipperary that a notice was being circulated telling agents to cancel all English papers. He had himself been told that papers on their way from Limerick Junction to Tipperary

1 J. J. Hart, 'The early history of the Irish Retail Newsagents' Association', part 5, *Irish Retail Newsagents Gazette*, April 1944

had been burned. In December 1920 Mrs Harnett in the Lismore stall sent on a copy of a notice which she and several newsagents had received in Lismore from the 'Customs Dept IRA':

> You will have noted our determination to wipe out English literature. Please see that the following papers are no longer sent to you by Easons
>
> Lloyd News — News of the World
> Reynolds News — Daily Sketch
> Mirror and Graphic.
>
> Some people do not seem to realise that there is a war on and that these are enemy newspapers as well as being immoral in tone. We shall take any action necessary to enforce this order. Please spare us any further trouble by doing the right thing at once.

While none of the supplies to the stall were interfered with, a press report referred to the burning of papers at Lismore. Eason's were aware of objections by Sinn Fein groups in a number of places to English papers.

As far as the distribution of news was concerned, the problem was very much secondary to the impact of the boycott on the distribution of Belfast papers. The Belfast boycott began in late 1920, but was very ineffective in its earlier stages. Charles Eason commented to his brother, Benjamin Macfarlane, on 25 November that 'also the Dail tells us not to get goods from Belfast — we pay no attention to the notice'. The first direct approach to Eason's seems to have come as late as March 1921. Eason's purchased very few items from Belfast apart from news, and their reaction at this stage, after reviewing the small scale of Belfast purchases, was not to buy goods from Belfast, but to continue to buy newspapers. As might be expected, the response to the call was stronger in the north. The first letter about it was from the Sligo bookstall on 15 March, informing the head office that in response to the order all Belfast papers should be stopped from the next day. The area to be boycotted was defined by the Belfast Boycott Central Committee to include Belfast, Newtownards, Lisburn, Dromore and Banbridge. The boycott also extended to firms outside this area who distributed through Belfast, and it also included newspapers elsewhere which accepted advertisements for Belfast products. The list from the Derry Committee in November 1921 included the *Derry Standard* and the *Londonderry Sentinel*. Supplies to the Sligo bookstall were halted for some time, but in Donegal town only for a few days. By the end of the year Eason's and a number of stalls in the north were on the black lists. The reaction of the Dublin house is illustrated in a letter of 19 November 1921 to Ballsillie in the Belfast house:

> On first thoughts we do not see any advantage in dealing with the matter in a partial way — if we are going to get into trouble and be blacklisted we may as well keep on all suppliers. If our name is going to be taken off the list, then we should not continue to sell any copies.

In Omagh the boycott had fallen through by the beginning of December. In Strabane the clerk reported on 2 December that, 'I have lost some of those who are in sympathy with the boycott so I have made up the loss with Unionist customers who have started to get their papers from this stall'. The first boycott was not very effective,[2] and even within the north itself newspaper supply was not greatly dislocated. Apart from the initial approach in March 1921, the first direct approach to Easons' Dublin office to observe the boycott was on 9 December 1921 at 6.30 p.m. when a young man called, saying 'that he had been sent in a hurry to inform us that by order of Dail Eireann we were to cease the sale of all Belfast papers'. According to a later account by Charles Eason, representatives of the committee had called to the premises, and he went to the Mansion House and discussed his request for permission to sell Belfast papers: 'we were not further interfered with nor notified that we were not to sell.' In 1922 the boycott began to acquire teeth, and also to spread more effectively in the south. A communication on 31 March 1922 from the Boycott Committee referred to a decision made at an IRA convention on 26 March, and announced, 'that the boycott will be more rigidly enforced from this date.'

At this stage the whole atmosphere in relation to newspapers became more strident. The matter had already come up in the Sinn Fein convention. A Dail debate, according to a press report on 2 May, suggested a good deal of animosity towards Irish papers, especially, in the words of the President de Valera, because the Irish papers were not giving sufficient publicity to the atrocities in the north. One voice was applauded when it shouted, 'burn them at the railway station'. This drew a comment from Collins that

> If you are for that kind of freedom, I have no use for it. If the advice of one delegate from the body of the hall is to be taken that newspapers are to be burned, these are the conditions I foresaw when I advised from out side that we ought not to have a discussion on this question....

The *Freeman's Journal* had in the past been the subject of intimidatory

2 Its termination was one of three points in the Craig-Collins agreement in January 1922. D.S. Johnston, 'The Belfast boycott, 1920-1922' in J.M. Goldstrom and L.A. Clarkson, ed., *Irish population, economy and society* (Oxford, 1981), p. 295.

letters to Eason's from loyalists. In 1920 it was beginning to run foul of Republican feeling. In January 1922 an agent in Tubbercurry received an order not to sell the *Freeman's Journal* 'owing to remarks made about President de Valera.' In April notices of this kind were received in Clonmel. In Dublin on the morning of 1 April 1922 vans and parcels were searched constantly, as were parcels at Broadstone station to see if they contained copies of the *Freeman's Journal*. On 21 April the offices of the *Sligo Champion* were entered, and the type for the week's issue was destroyed. Early in May all imports of Sunday papers were seized on arrival in Rosslare Harbour, and were thrown into the sea. A Dundalk newsagent had his issues of the *Belfast Telegraph* burned on six successive days early in April. On 13 April copies of Belfast papers on the retail counter in O'Connell Street were seized. A peremptory letter of the same date from the Director of the Boycott informed Eason's that they were fined £100 for this and other breeches of the Dail's regulations, and summoned them to pay the amount forthwith. Eason's undertook to withdraw Belfast papers, and, when efforts failed to have the fine remitted, they paid it. They refused to sign the written undertaking which the Director of the Boycott tendered for signature, and which would even have involved them in refusing to handle the Belfast papers within the north-east. A spirited letter was sent to the Lord Mayor, intended for Arthur Griffith, on 26 April 1922:

> We object most strongly to the attempt to interfere with the trade of a Dublin house having a Belfast branch in the six county area. We can understand the interference with trade — however wrong we may think it — in Southern Ireland, but these books are supplied from Belfast, and the boycott is not extended to Belfast firms, our competitors in the six county area. The result would be to penalize a Dublin firm doing business in that area.... This involves possible seizure of our premises, and almost certain interference with the distribution of our goods. In this connection we have to advise you that during the last fortnight some £150 worth of papers dispatched from our Abbey Street premises to the country agents have been destroyed on account of our carrying copies of the *Daily Independent* — while yesterday a Ford motor delivery van was taken, and so far has not been returned.

They wrote again on 3 June, this time referring to the problems they faced in towns near the border where their rivals were distributing the papers, and urged that 'boycott of the Belfast papers should be removed as a special case owing to the importance of free distribution of newspapers to all sections of the people.' There was one small irony; the Press Room Department of the Provisional Government complained on 23 May of the non-receipt of the *Irish News*, and J.C.M. Eason was able to refer them to their own ban. By this time the whole issue was to be overshadowed by civil war, an inevitable result of the brooding tensions of the intervening months.

In fact the prohibition lingered on. Indeed, it even played a part in the outbreak of the civil war because the incident that set it off was the arrest by the Free State forces of Leo Henderson, the first director of the Belfast Boycott Committee on 26 June, in a boycotting incident and the arrest of the pro-treaty deputy chief of staff as a reprisal.[3] The boycott survived as late as October 1922, and its effects were still experienced by Easons at that date. On 4 October 1922 Charles Eason wrote to General Beasley:

> May I also put in a word for Belfast publications other than the daily papers. Am I right in supposing that these publications are being stopped simply as a retaliatory measure on account of something which the northern government has done in reference to publications in the South.... If I might mention any one specially it would be the *Witness*, which is the organ of the Irish Presbyterians, and it does look bad that the Presbyterian should not be able to get his paper now that there can be no military purpose served by its exclusion.

In the first four months of 1922 there was a good deal of sporadic labour unrest. The most prolonged instance was a strike on the Great Southern Railway in late January and the first half of February. Political tensions were reaching a peak from April onwards. On 30 March the machinery of the *Freeman's Journal* was destroyed, and in April there were a number of instances of papers being seized and burned. The attack by Free State forces on the irregulars in the Four Courts on 28 June signalled the beginning of overt civil war. On that day the military operations were principally in the vicinity of the Four Courts.

Only a small section of the morning staff were able to turn up for duty. Country parcels of Dublin papers were sent on late trains, and there was a curtailed delivery in the city. On 29 June main line trains did not run at all. The van drivers returned to garage before completing their morning deliveries, as the streets were made dangerous by military operations. One van, with the London papers for Rathmines in it was seized by armed men. The following day, 30 June, no early morning staff turned up, and the premises only opened for a few hours. On 1 July some staff turned

3 Johnston, loc, cit., p. 297.

up. There were no cross-channel dailies, city deliveries were erratic, and the only main-line trains running were on the Great Northern line. At midday, Hallett, the accountant, was ordered by the military to shut up the premises. There was no work on 2 July, and on 3 July Hallett opened the premises and some workers came in from the northern side of the city. The premises were occupied by the Red Cross. Some dispatch work was transferred to Westland Row for the south side of the city. On 4, 5 and 6 July it was still not possible to resume work in the main premises. Only Hallett and a few hands were in the premises, and communication with the south side was impossible. There was fighting in the immediate vicinity, and the irregulars were driven out of Upper Sackville Street on 5 July.

The streets had become reasonably safe on 6 July, with people going about freely, and on 7 July for the first time since 27 June fairly normal working began again, with a near full morning turn-out of staff at 5 am. Work began to distribute the backlog of newspapers, but main line trains to the south were not running beyond Thurles, to the south-east beyond Woodenbridge, or to the west beyond Ballinasloe, Roscommon and Ballymote. In the factory in Gloucester Street the work force was reduced from the start of the hostilities. Four of the workers were called up for Free State Service, and others had difficulty in getting to work. On Friday 30 June the shooting became so alarming in the neighbourhood that work was suspended at 1 o'clock for the remainder of the day. The following day the factory was occupied by the irregulars at 1 o'clock and they remained in occupation overnight. Some work was done in the days that followed, but work was not resumed generally in the factory until Thursday, 6 July.

The civil war caused much more extensive disruption to the firm than the preceding Anglo-Irish war. Dislocation of rail and telegraphic communications was much more serious, and censorship posed particularly acute problems. As early as 3 July 1922 a provisional government proclamation in the daily papers ordered that no papers which had not been censored should be distributed. Charles Eason saw a Mr Hayes at Government Buildings in Upper Merrion Street and was told that the sale of English papers should be stopped at once. The large accumulation of papers on Dun Laoghaire pier and in the Coast Guard Station could not be cleared without permission from the censor, although by 7 July an understanding seems to have been established with the censor. However as the news continued to flood in every day, Charles Eason was reduced to writing to the censor on 12 July to say that the backlog of papers was 'now so great that we should like to take some steps to reduce the accumulation.'

One of the problems at the outset was that the principles according to which the censor was working were not clear and only began to emerge gradually as the days went by. Charles Eason wrote to the *Daily Herald* on 15 July that

> We are submitting your paper every day to the Censor and therefore we think it is quite possible it will be passed, but he appears to object to any telegrams coming from districts in control of the irregulars or any from Belfast. Of course he may pass telegrams from Belfast if he thinks the information therein is harmless. It is a strict military censorship.

On 18 July Charles Eason was able to be more specific, and advised the editor of the *Daily Express* that: 'I know he is specially determined not to permit statements to be made about military operations, positions of troops, or of leading officers — including of course the commander-in-chief.' Eason indicated that it would be necessary to give an undertaking not to publish telegrams which had not been passed by the censor, in order to be allowed to sell a paper without prior permission. *The Times* of London came to such an arrangement, and on 27 July Eason advised the *Manchester Guardian* that

> The exact nature of the undertaking which they have given we do not know but it amounts to this — I think, that they do not insert any telegrams which have not passed through the censor's office, and therefore you will see that they are not willing to pass papers which contain telegrams direct from Belfast or from Republican quarters.

In explaining the attitude of the censor to English papers, Eason made a distinction between military information which could be of value to the republicans, and political information. The parallel was close to measures effected by the English authorities during the World War in dealing with 'Pro-German' propaganda and with the literature issued by concientious objectors. By 28 July Charles Eason had prepared a memorandum on the operation of the censorship. This was his own rationalisation of what was happening, and as he pointed out in a letter written on the same date, 'The statements are purely my own, and not in any way binding on the Censor.' On 2 August Eason wrote to one of the London newspapers that

> The Censor acts primarily under the military authorities and therefore you might write to the Chief of Staff, but I think as regards political matters he is in touch with what is called the Publicity Department

— of which Mr. Desmond Fitzgerald is the head. I believe Mr. Fitzgerald sends communications to the newspaper reporters as they come in — that is to ensure that nothing gets into the papers without being passed by the Censor.

Charles Eason had not of course been told formally by any party of what undertakings, if any, *The Times* and four other papers had given to the censor, although he was able to tell the *Daily Telegraph* on 17 July that he had a copy of an undertaking submitted by the *News Chronicle*, but was not able to say whether the censor actually endorsed it. Easons were embarrased by the fact that they were quoted in one London newspaper as referring to an undertaking by the five papers. A vigorous letter of denial to Easons came from the Manager of *The Times* on 22 August. It is not clear whether *The Times* was being a little coy, but J.C.M. Eason replied to the letter on 25 August that

> Our information was derived from such direct contact with the censor's office during the past four or five weeks. The papers on the list given include some which enjoy a permit to which no time limit is attached and some to which a permit for a limited period has been issued and is being regularly renewed.... In your case we received a permit on 11th July and we have never had any interference with the distribution since. For a day or two prior to that each individual issue was being submitted and being passed.... It is a fact, at any rate, that your representatives here of the commercial, reporting and correspondence side, appear to have approached the Censor's office in a tactful way, and were amongst the first to assist us in our distribution work by looking after your interests in that quarter.

Three London dailies declined to give any undertaking. The *Daily Telegraph* and the *Morning Post*[4] treated the censor's requirements with disdain and were not at any time prepared to co-operate with the office. In fact, the *Daily Telegraph* and the *Morning Post* came to be totally banned. As early as 13 July Charles Eason had suggested to the *Daily Telegraph* that it should meet the censor's requirements. On 15 July the *Daily Telegraph* replied that 'it was quite impossible to accept conditions' and that it would continue to publish Belfast telegrams. Some of the weeklies also adopted a lofty attitude to Irish censorship. While the widespread hostility to English Sundays, and the occasional burning of papers might provide some reason for dislike of Irish attitudes, the main reason for their outlook was a contemptuous view that censorship by the Irish

4 The third paper was the *Daily Express*.

government was inherently unreasonable. Eason frequently reminded English editors and managers of the parallel with censorship in England during the Great War. As he put it to the *Saturday Review* on 24 July:

> I would suggest that you should write as carefully as possible in reference to what is going on in Ireland. I do not think you quite understand the situation — perhaps you would realise it best by considering the attitude of the Censor in England to publications issued during the War by conscientious objectors. You know quite well that both the Public and the Censor were very much opposed to anything by speech or writing which tended to discourage persons fighting against Germany, and I think that this is the explanation of a good deal of the Censor's action. Anything which would discredit the Provisional Government or exalt the action of Republicans, or which represents the Provisional Government as acting in the interests of Great Britain or at the suggesting of Great Britain, hampers the Government in dealing with the opposition. Personally I think they are too sensitive in some cases, but you must not suppose that they are acting blindly with the desire to stop English publications — the majority are let through without any questions.

In a few cases Eason made representations himself to the censor, when he thought that the censor was too sensitive or that action was unnecessary.

Newspaper burning, when it occurred, was not confined to the republicans. Free State commanders may on occasion have taken matters into their own hands. Possibly the most serious spate of newspaper burning occurred early in the civil war in Waterford, and was conducted by the Free State forces. John Toms, the traveller, wrote to Eason from Clonmel about this on 11 July:

> Yesterday I had an interview with Commdr. Cronin at the Barracks, Waterford, over the wanton destruction of papers, magazines, books and fashion papers taking place daily at Waterford. I gathered (without any admission) that this was being done with his approval but he professed ignorance as to magazines, books and fashion papers being included; [he] justified his action under the head of propaganda, [I] pointed out to him that the action was local and not under general orders and was likely to lead to trouble as the loss was to the State and not to the vendors. He promised to stop the Mag and B[ook] F[ashion] destruction and to reconsider the paper question.

In fact Eason had worked out a fairly good relationship with the censor's office, which was prepared to be flexible in relation to magazines without current news, and to leave a good deal of the initiative as to what should be considered for banning with Eason's. As early as 26 July a memorandum of a telephone call from the censor's office stated that: 'General Beasley will be satisfied if Mr. Eason will bring over a couple of copies of the magazine lists which he had over in the office this morning and gives an undertaking that any magazines with Irish articles will be submitted to him.' The evidence suggests that the actual amount of banning was limited. Between 7 August and 25 September 1922, seventeen individual issues of newspapers seem to have been banned, and on one single day all the issues of the Belfast papers.

The area affected by the civil war was very extensive, with much disruption of train services. By 15 July parcels were no longer being accepted by the post office for eleven counties. These included all the counties of Munster, the whole of Connaught, except for Leitrim, and King's County (Offaly). Even the postal service operated only with long delays. A letter from the Cobh station bookstall, dated 15 July, was received on 27 July, with the message, that 'I wish to inform you I received no monthly or weekly parcels since the 28th ult.' Toms wrote from Clonmel on 7 July:

> On the off chance of this reaching you I have held all orders taken in Ross and Wexford owing to insecurity in postal arrangements and having no duplicates of them. I went to Enniscorthy Wednesday evening but did nothing as the town has been closed since Saturday last. It was in a state of siege and the (?) and barracks surrendered to the republicans about 6 p.m.

A letter from Ballaghaderreen, dated 14 July, had been even more graphic: 'We did not get a paper since the 8th of this month no way of getting them and they would not be allowed in. Line broken up no trains running. No post. No nothing here and I do not know when it will end and our food running short.' Parcels to Waterford were suspended in the course of July, but were resumed on 24 July indirectly by means of the Dublin South East railway. Even as late as October, the GSWR was running trains only as far as Thurles and Buttevant, and its direct service to Waterford halted at Kilkenny, with a connection for Waterford. From 2 August services were restored to Limerick, Ennis and West Clare via Nenagh. But conditions elsewhere were still bad. Returns of the August and September issues of *Our Boys*, for instance, were large. J.C.M. Eason wrote to the editor of *Our Boys* on 10 November to explain that: 'owing to the disturbed condition of the railways it was impossible to distribute the supplies, and parcels came back unopened.'

Cork was the Republican stronghold, and together with Kerry held out the longest. Cork city was captured by Free State troops on 11 August, but the county remained for the most part in Republican hands. A letter from News Brothers in Cork city to a firm in Dublin, written on 19 August, reported that

> As far as the south of Ireland is concerned matters have become infinitely worse and as a result of the civil war we are entirely cut off from communications with the rest of the country and our customers generally. All railway and road bridges have been destroyed. Cork is now quite isolated and the Free State Army holding it is practically in a state of siege. Before evacuating the city last week the Republicans entered one of our offices and smashed machinery value £20,000 with sledge-hammers; similar outrages occurred in many places. Our business, except in the news departments is now entirely closed down as it is impossible to deliver goods or collect money, and we have no option therefore but to ask for a *moratorium* at present in regard to our debt to you.

In September Eason's were having parcels to Cork from England routed by boat and distributed by river steamer to Monkstown and Queenstown. News Brothers were willing to give every assistance, and offered Eason's 25 per cent off published prices on news in their hands, and distribution of papers by their motors to Fermoy. Kerry presented even greater difficulties, and a telegram on 30 August from the newsagents' association in Tralee (delivered on 2 September) asked Eason's to send news by rail to Limerick, and from there by steamer to Tralee. Rail communication was established as far as Mallow on 20 November, and into Cork city itself on 18 December.

By 14 October some degree of general order was restored, and censorship came to an end from that date. However problems still abounded. There was a partially effective strike on the GSWR line from 16 October until 12 November. The effects of this strike were compounded by the fact that so many telegraph wires had been cut and particulars were slow in coming to hand. Troubles continued well into 1923 with railway links on occasion still being cut. The Nenagh line was cut on 15 January 1923, the Cork line below Ballybrophy was cut on the same date, and the Waterford line was cut on 24 February. A press report on 11 May 1923 noted that in all between three and four hundred bridges had been completely or partially destroyed. Newspapers continued to be interfered with directly. On no less than three occasions in October and November 1922, Irish and English papers were burned on the Dublin & South Eastern line. Dailies were also burned on the Cork line near Mourne Abbey on 30 November 1922. In January 1923 Sligo and Monkstown stations including the bookstalls were destroyed by fire.

After 1923 incidents of this kind ceased, but violence lingered on and interfered with newspaper distribution. A few years later the seizing and burning of papers began again, but this time it was part of the campaign against 'immoral' papers. Charles Eason wrote to his cousin, Daphne Clare, in London on 22 November 1925 that 'Ireland is still unsettled. The blowing up of the picture house where Ypres film was exhibited shows that the unruly elements are not yet under control.'

Chapter 12 Publishing, printing and manufacture

ONE OF THE FIRST ACTIVITIES that Charles Eason expanded into during the 1860s, the decade when the firm developed virtually all the activities that were later to characterise it, was printing. The firm already used a lot of printed matter for wrappers and for forms for internal use, and Eason himself had served his apprenticeship as a printer. Family tradition states that printing started in 1868, in the Eason family home in Kenilworth Square, though there is evidence that some was being done in the house in 1863. An enlarged printing operation commenced on the top floor of 85/86 Abbey Street in 1874. The printing of forms for internal or house use could be extended to make similar forms for use by the public or by other firms, in other words, to start manufacturing stationery. A 'work room' to do this was already in existence by 1877, and premises were taken in Lower Gloucester Street in 1883.

As the operation grew, it was possible to expand from printing into publishing. Two major ventures into publishing were conceived by the first Charles Eason when the firm's printing was in its infancy. The first of these was the publishing of catholic prayer-books, which started in 1866. The second was the publishing of an almanac, which first appeared in 1874. They were an important although small part of the business activities of those years and doubly significant because they helped to create and sustain the national or nation-wide public image the firm was acquiring. With a printing base and a publishing image, it was inevitable that Eason's would do some publishing of other works, although this was pursued rather passively after 1902. The firm published little after this, other than diaries, though they frequently took on the contract printing of books for other publishers, or acted as publisher for authors who had commissioned their services. This activity was never very extensive or coordinated, but a sizeable number of books, some of them titles of consequence, appeared with Eason's imprint.

CATHOLIC PRAYER-BOOK PUBLISHING

The publishing of catholic prayer-books by a 'protestant' firm was quite astonishing in Irish terms. In a letter written in 1883 Charles Eason recalled the genesis of this activity: 'I took up this publication some thirteen years ago, at the request and urging of the late Bishop Conroy and my intimate acquaintance with the whole subject is the fruit of study and conversations held with him and many of the Catholic clergy here.' However, a few isolated sheets in a surviving ledger date the beginning of activity to the autumn of 1866. 2,000 copies of the *Key of Heaven* and 1,750 copies of *Catholic Piety* were printed in September and October 1866. Reprinting followed in 1867, 1868, 1869 and 1870. The same printer, Mullany, seems to have been used for all these editions. The frequent reprinting suggests that the books were in demand. A few other ledger entries give the impression that the stock was disposed of and accounted for monthly, through S. and A.J. Galwey, and it is probable that they bore the imprint of that house. No copy of these editions survives in the house, and they are not listed among the works donated by the firm to All Hallows College in 1972. It is possible that they simply wholesaled the books for Galwey, and that their own direct involvement in publishing grew out of this association as well as out of Eason's contacts with Bishop Conroy.

The early books under their own imprint were brought out in close association with Bishop Conroy. It is this activity which dates back to 1870, but no formal association seems to have been proposed before 1871. No book under the house imprint is known to have appeared in 1870, but surviving letters from 1871 give an impression of feverish activity. The Bishop wrote from St. Mel's in Longford on 18 April 1871 that 'I find here at my hand an abundance of literary power for the purposes of which you and I have often conversed. If you have not finished the *Treasury of the Sacred Heart* or the other books, they can be at once sent to me here.' Two days later Bishop Conroy wrote again, 'I restore you the proofs corrected. In the additional pages intended for the *Catholic Piety* I have marked at pp. 23-25 two prayers which belong to the English ritual exclusively and are not usually added in Ireland.' This appears to be a reference to the preparation of the first known edition of *Catholic Piety* under the direct imprint of the house. Charles Eason's success in getting his books accepted was due to a great extent to his close collaboration with the Catholic clergy. Even as early as August 1871 Bishop Conroy wrote to Eason that: 'I have not forgotten your request about having a priest named who might be of use in giving advice etc. concerning your literary ventures. But I must wait until I can speak with the authorities in the matter.'

In November he was telling Charles Eason that it would give him pleasure, 'to make known to others your sentiments as to the principles on which the business of a firm like Messrs. Smiths should be conducted.' In about 1873 Dr Donnelly, coadjutor Bishop of Dublin, was appointed as advisor to Charles Eason on catholic prayer-books. The books turned out to be an astonishing success. They were the major prayer-books in use in Ireland. Though there are no surviving figures for sales in the first few years, the earliest available figure for 1876/7 amounted to £2,880, and rose to £4,078 the following year. The books also acquired a ready market in England. One of the firm's travellers visited England every year, and apart from some stationery, the prayer-books were the only Eason product which had a consistent and significant sale outside Ireland.

Charles Eason personally arranged and revised the texts for publication and saw them through the press, correcting proofs himself. In moments of periodic depression, the volume of detailed work in which they involved him was one of the points made in letters to W.H. Smith. When Smith made over the prayer-book division to Eason, he was not only getting rid of a political embarassment, but also giving Eason ownership of an activity which already absorbed a great deal of his energies, judging by his letters. In order to fix the literary responsibility on a stated individual, the books bore both the imprint of W.H. Smith and the name of Charles Eason.

In 1883 Charles Eason explained that

> Bishop Conroy had warned me against the errors from carelessness of printers and those from unauthorised editions and I have studied at all times to preserve the original character of each book, whilst adding the devotions most recently instituted, and having the highest sanction. I have come to see how very valuable these devotional works and prayers are as a help to the Christian life. I am myself solely responsible for them, except for the text, and for these the priests who have advised me and corrected the proofs with the censors appointed by the Cardinal are my authority ....In all my publications I have striven to correct the text, by careful comparisons with older publications of the prayer books so as to correct mere misprints and errors of the printers, and where changes have gone beyond these to submit the text afresh to my clerical advisers.

Charles Eason referred to 'peculiar difficulties' to be overcome which it would take too long to explain by letter. As to what these were, they are hinted at in his correspondence in 1886 with Rosa Mulholland, who had edited some works of piety for the firm; she had recently begun a book of meditations. This was literary work with a wider scope than the editing of existing prayer books or the compiling of new ones: 'His Grace the Archbishop is I am told unfavourable to such works being in the hands of other than Catholic publishers and I have both heard and read expressions in his speeches which support this view.' Charles Eason seems to have had an interview with the Archbishop the previous year, and in requesting the interview he had said:

> I have felt a strong desire to hand down to Catholic control the continuance of this business and without seeking any immediate change, I desire it to be known.... Meanwhile and until such can be found, I desire to do as much good as possible, in the country of my adoption in whose welfare for more than 40 years, I have taken the deepest interest.

Archbishop Walsh respected Charles Eason, and writing to him from Bonn in September 1889, he mentioned that as he was going to speak on education reform on his return, he would welcome Eason's comments from a protestant perspective, and also asked him to keep for him any papers that might be useful to see on his return. In practice, Eason remained in personal charge of catholic prayer-books.

When the prayer-books were made over to Eason by W.H. Smith in 1885, they became Charles Eason's private property, as far as the firm was concerned. Figures for sales disappear from the accounts, and Eason took separate premises for prayer-book publishing at 13 Aston's Quay. Even when the Easons took over the business from W.H. Smith in 1886, the prayer-books remained distinct for another three years, and only in 1889 did they once again form part of the general business of the house. There are no existing sales figures for the years 1884-9. Profits from the prayer-book business in those years were entered into Eason's own records of income and expenditure. Although later recollection considered that the prayer-book division had been unprofitable, in fact it yielded an income to Charles Eason of several hundred pounds a year, which can be regarded as a very satisfactory return on the probable level of turnover in those years.

Sales fell rather sharply in the depression of the late 1870s and were only at a level of £3,563 in 1882/3. They do not appear to have recovered by 1889/90 when they stood at £3,412. After that they rose, reaching a peak in 1901/2, of £5,695. Sales then faltered, and from 1905/6 were below £4,000. They benefitted from a boom in 1918-21. In two of these years the cash value of sales reached a record, but in the 1920s generally sales settled at a level around £2,000. Whether sales figures are inflated with sales of other books is not clear — although probably not. In 1929 religious goods were transferred to the Prayer-Book Department, and figures after the Second World War certainly include sales of prayer-books other than Easons'. In real terms, the value of sales of their own prayer-books at this time was only a shadow of itself. Post-1940 figures, which are frequently much larger, include sale of other prayer-books as well as sales of their own, and offer no basis of comparison with the past. Prayer-books made large net profits in 1918/1921 and afterwards continued to make a small profit.

The prayer-book publishing was impressive in its volume. The first book under their own imprint was *Catholic Piety* in 1871. The *Key of Heaven* in 1872 was the next, and it was followed by the *Manual of Catholic Doctrine* and *Catholic's Manual of Prayer* in 1874, *Holy Childhood* compiled by Rosa Mulholland and the *Treasury of the Sacred Heart* in 1876, *Child's Book of the Passion* in 1877, *Path to Paradise* in 1878 and a *Manual of Instructions for Little Children* by de Segur in 1879. A catalogue dating from around 1880 lists thirteen publications in all. Between 1871 and 1885 there were no less than nine editions of *Catholic Piety*. In later editions the book was considerably enlarged, and the prices for the cheapest format varied from 4½d in the first edition to 2s 3d in the fourth edition. A wide range of prices above these rates was charged for more luxuriously produced versions of each edition. The early printing does not seem to have been done within the firm. In the 1890s their printing was mainly done by Ballantines of Edinburgh, but from the end of the century printing seems to have been conducted in their own factory. The prayer-books were however bound abroad. Details of sales for individual editions no longer survive. One of the exceptions is *Treasure of the Sanctuary* which was not an Eason publication, but one which was published for the Irish Sisters of Charity. Sales in the 1920s ran at around 3,000 per year, and thereafter were usually below 2,000.

Eason's were not the only publishers of catholic prayer-books. Duffy's for instance brought out their own edition of *Garden of the Soul* in 1878, and both Gill's and Warren of Kilmainham published editions of *Catholic Piety*. As late as the early 1930s there were no less than four Dublin firms who were both printers and publishers of catholic prayer-books, and three others who were involved in publishing only.

The success of the venture before 1914, in both commercial and competitive terms, seems in little doubt, but after the 1918-21 boom the enterprise lost ground rapidly. The main difficulty was the competition from cheaper imported editions of catholic prayer-books, mainly from Belgium. The large volume of printing in 1920-1922 was not maintained in subsequent years, and in only two years in the remainder of the decade, 1925/6 and 1927/8, was there a significant amount of printing of prayer-books. Gill's equalled or exceeded Eason's in output, and employed nineteen to twenty-four men in their printing department in 1920 almost exclusively on prayer-book work. By 1934 the number has dropped to five. Eason's had by that time practically withdrawn from publishing. A new printing of the *Imitation of Christ* in 1931, which ran to 7,600 copies, seems to be the latest printing that can be traced in the 1930s. Unlike other Dublin printers and publishers of prayer-books who sought tariff protection, Eason's as a firm never appeared before the Tariff Commission. Charles Eason did appear, but in a personal capacity as one of the representatives of the Dublin branch of the Associated Booksellers, who opposed tariffs.[1]

There was a definite upturn in activity as soon as the Second World War began. The *Treasury of the Sacred Heart*, which had last been reprinted in 1930, was reprinted no less than five times between 1941 and 1944, amounting to 65,954 copies in all. 15,000 copies of the *Imitation of Christ*, last reprinted in 1931, were produced in three printings between 1941 and 1944. *Holy Childhood*, last reprinted in 1929, was reprinted three times between 1942 and 1944. *Holy Childhood* was revised and updated by Archdeacon McMahon in 1943. The war-time boom in sales of home-produced prayer-books led Eason's to bring out new prayer-books, an aspect of their publishing which had atrophied altogether. Eason's Bulletin noted in October 1945 that, 'being thrown upon our own resources in the production of Prayer-Books, Missals and such books since 1940, had led to a vast improvement in the approach of Irish printers and binders to this type of work.' The *Child's Own Prayer Book*, of which they acquired the rights, was printed six times between 1942 and 1945. In 1944 they also brought out an Irish language edition of *Holy Childhood*. This consisted of 10,000 copies, and it must have sold reasonably well, as a further printing of 6,500 copies took place in 1953.

This new impetus lasted into the post-war years; and some completely new works appeared. *Nazareth*, translated from the German and edited by Archdeacon McMahon was published in 1948. Between 1948 and 1963 there were seven printings in all with a total of 45,470 copies. The only

1 Tariff Commission, *Report on books of Prayer* Report nr.15, 1934.

other book to rival it in the postwar period was *Holy Childhood*. Reprinted again in 1945, it was further reprinted on nine occasions between 1947 and 1962 making a total of 177,757 copies. But the prospects for their prayer-books were now ending, and these two books had a deceptive success compared with the others. The *Imitation of Christ*, one of the most popular books of all time, continued to have some success in the Eason edition. It was reprinted in 1945, 1950, 1955 and 1958. But the old prayer-books which had so long satisfied the Irish need for piety no longer met that need. The *Key of Heaven* was reprinted in 1945, and sheets printed in 1946 were brought up to date in 1953 by a new table of moveable feasts, and published. The *Treasury of the Sacred Heart* which appeared in 1948 was not reprinted until 1962. The 1953 edition of the *Key of Heaven* — made up from 1946 sheets — was the last of the old books to be reprinted in the 1950s, apart from the *Imitation of Christ*, which was reprinted again in 1955 and 1958, after two editions had come out in 1945 and 1950. The last venture was in 1962 when *Rosary novenas to Our Lady of Fatima* was printed under licence by Cromo of Milan — 20,000 copies. *Holy Childhood*, the most successful of the post-war prayer books was last reprinted in 1962 and 1965, and *Nazareth* in 1963. With the 1963 and 1965 printings of these works, a long history of publishing prayer-books, which had begun with *Catholic Piety* a hundred years previously, was at an end. By this time also, the progress of the Second Vatican Council had significantly changed the kind of books that catholics wanted to read. As Sean Feehan of the Mercier Press put it in 1969: 'Very soon after the Council began its deliberations it became apparent that the years ahead could offer only doubt and confusion, and that the vast unsettled mass of Catholics would cease to buy the kind of books they had bought for years past.... The warehouses of many religious publishers today are crammed full of hundreds of thousands of pounds of unsaleable titles.'[2]

EASON'S ALMANAC

The only other significant and sustained publishing venture by the firm was *Eason's Almanac* which first appeared in 1874, and whose last edition appeared in 1885. Once again, it was a project entirely thought up by Charles Eason. From the start the book reflected not only Eason's publishing flair, but his interest in Ireland. Charles Eason was the compiler

2 Feehan, Sean *An Irish Publisher and his World*, (Cork 1969), p 132

as well as the publisher of the *Almanac*. The address at the front of the first edition in 1874 stated some of the objectives of the *Almanac*:

> This is an attempt to supply, at a very moderate price, an annual work for Ireland, which shall detail from year to year the principal matters common to almanacs, and added to these, give some information on the social, agricultural and mercantile condition of the country.

In the second edition he told the reader that 'Proceeding on the lines begun last year, I have sought to supply further information on the social, agricultural and industrial condition of Ireland.'

His aim was stated even more explicitly in the third edition:

> My aim in this publication had been to supply a concise hand-book of Irish facts in which, at a trifling cost, anyone interested may read the story of Irish progress from year to year; and which may be an especial channel for conveying to the British public information upon Ireland both useful and interesting.

Perhaps it was in response to this that W.H. Smith wrote to Charles Eason on January 3 1877 that 'the *Almanac* is on my table as a book of reference and I like it much.'

It was intended to be a cheap convenient little book, not a rival to *Thom's Directory*, whose value Eason recognised in declaring it to be 'The best and fullest annual record of the trade, commerce and finance of Great Britain and Ireland that is before the public.' The *Almanac* was an immediate success. The first issue ran through three printings, and was very well received in reviews in the press. It retailed at 1s 6d. From a very early stage, the routine work passed over to Eason's son, Charles Eason junior, who entered the business in 1875. Charles junior assembled the statistical information. By 1880 the acknowledgement of the work of Charles Eason junior on the *Almanac* was quite explicit. The address in the 1880 edition noted:

> The compilation and arrangement of all the tables of statistics, as well as by far the larger portion of the details of this work, has been done by my son, Charles Eason, jun., and upon him, in the future, the progress of and authorship of this Almanac will mainly depend.

In the 1883 edition the address appears over the signature of the son, and in fact the emphasis in that year shifted away from Ireland. Charles Eason junior noted in the address that 'In the statistical portion of the Almanac I have introduced further tables relating to the United Kingdom generally.' The father's intention had been mainly to confine himself to

Ireland, and to provide figures which would be useful to those specifically concerned with Ireland and Irish affairs: 'Though the process be difficult and the lesson hard to learn, it is only by active reflection upon the phenomena of our country's life that we shall be able to plan wisely for its future welfare.' In retrospect years later, the son admitted that his father's design had been the wiser one, and that he had made a mistake in extending the coverage of English data.

A good deal of pains were taken to bring information on affairs up to date, and the *Almanac* also incorporated reference information such as the programme for the Intermediate examinations. From the start there was information on exports and imports, even if much of the information was not precise, and could be given only approximately. An effort was also made to keep the *Almanac* lively. The 1877 edition commented that: 'The form of some of the facts given in the Statistics is varied, so as to permit of a wider range of view, and to prevent the sameness which creeps into tables which are repeated frequently in one style, and which from want of fresh treatment, often deter examination.'

The *Almanac* was particularly enlivened by short features or articles on particular topics, which varied from year to year. In the second issue there was a report on drainage, and in enlarging the range of topics in 1876, a preference was given 'to those which are of general importance'. The 1877 issue included an analysis by Professor Baldwin of the 1876 agricultural returns, a paper on the 'Ocean-side watering places of Ireland by an English visitor', a statement on the valuation of Ireland, and sketches of parliamentary papers. In 1878 the address drew attention to a short paper dealing with the 'scientific phenomena of reclamation of bog-lands, and an account of stock pedigree which it is hoped may become more perfect by the voluntary co-operation of breeders all over the country'. Topical as always, the 1879 issue of the *Almanac* even included an article entitled 'Peasant proprietorship, or how to increase the number of landowners in Ireland'. The quality of some of the pieces is quite high. The analysis of the Irish crisis in the 1881 issue entitled, 'The Irish distress of the Winter 1879-80' is still worth reading by students of those years, and the railway statistics give much retrospective information on the building of the Irish system in a more convenient form than is available elsewhere. In the early 1880s these statistics involved Eason's in a legal action. The compiler of a compendium of railway statistics in England felt that the similarity to his was a violation of his copyright. The issue of 1884 had a short feature on 'The amalgamation of Irish railways', followed by a longer feature on 'State aid to Irish railways', very obviously written by Charles Eason junior, proposing a greater involvement by the state in the financing of railway building.

The last edition of the *Almanac* was in 1885 when the rights were sold to Purdon's. The reasons for abandoning the *Almanac* are not clear. An obituary notice in the *Publishers Circle* in November 1899 for Charles Eason senior stated that the reason for discontinuing the *Almanac* was that, 'The preparation of it was found to require too much time and labour, and the sale of the *Almanac* was not increasing.' While it lasted, the *Almanac* was an interesting expression of the outlook that was characteristic of the Statistical and Social Inquiry Society of Ireland, and there are indications in the *Almanac* of the influence of the Society and its members on the two Charles Easons, father and son. From its nature, it must have demanded a lot of time, and significantly its disappearance coincided with the great change and challenge of 1886, when the house became independent. Charles Eason senior's own drive in publishing was also diminishing, as his health grew weaker. As early as October 1883 he had expressed reluctance to Rosa Mulholland about a new prayer-book project: 'There is a further reason special to me, my health during the last year has not been good, and I should not like that, in the event of my death or my having to give up business, I should have an obligation to publish absolute upon me.'

However, the end of the *Almanac* had no bearing on other publications, as the extension of publishing into other fields can be dated to 1886. Significantly, much of the new publishing was done in association with other houses, or simply involved new editions of existing texts. The labour-intensive preparation of the *Almanac* was dropped and the success of the catholic prayer-books rested on the sale of the established favourites, not on the publication of more speculative texts, which the eccesiastical authorities would have been reluctant to encourage from a protestant house.

OTHER PUBLISHING ACTIVITIES

Apart from prayer-books and the *Almanac*, the firm did little original publishing. What it did fell into three categories. One was the publication of a number of books on their own account. The second was the provision of distribution facilities for books and magazines which did not necessarily involve their imprint. The third was regular trade materials, especially *Eason's Monthly Bulletin*.

Eason's did have a publication department, or at least referred to one, although it was a shadowy affair in the sense that it had no separate staff, judging from staff records. The term was really one of convenience. There are no records of publication, and the development of the activity can only be traced from surviving copies of books in the archive, whose range is not complete. In addition to books, Eason's published diaries and ready reckoners as well as street maps of some cities. They attached importance to this activity and an exasperated correspondence between Charles Eason junior and the Presbyterian Association on one occasion shows that their protection of their copyright was a determined and strict one. The first distinct extension beyond catholic prayer-books and the *Almanac* appears to have been in evangelical literature, when in 1886 Charles Eason brought out *How we got our Bible* by Paterson Smyth, who had impressed him so much. This line of publication seems to have been undertaken in conjunction with Bagsters in London. Samuel Bagster was a distant family connection of Charles Eason's, via the Toms, some of whom worked in the firm on the printing side. The second edition of *How we got out Bible* bears the imprint of Samuel Bagster alone. In all twelve editions came out between 1886 and 1897 involving a total of 62,074 copies. Other books by Paterson Smyth were also brought out jointly. *The divine library: suggestions how to read the Bible* was brought out by the two houses in conjunction with Simpkin Marshall in 1896, and another edition in conjunction with a New York house came out as well in the same year. Paterson Smyth's *The old document and the new Bible* under a joint imprint was in a fourth edition in 1894. The link with Bagsters seems to have been intended to be a wider one, as a new edition of W.F. Stevenson's *Praying and Working* was brought out by the two houses in 1886, and the ninth edition of J. Dymond's *Essays on the principle of morality* in 1894 came out in association with Simpkin Marshall. There is no clear pattern in the matter of imprint. In some cases Eason's is the more prominent. In some cases it is in smaller print below that of Bagster.

Around 1890 there was a slight widening of publishing activities beyond religious and near-religious books. Before 1886 some of the material in the *Almanac* had been republished, under the name of Charles Eason junior, under the title *Manual of railway, agricultural and other statistics for politicians, economists and investors,* in association with Simpkin Marshall. In 1890 in association with Longman's, Eason's brought out a cheap edition of O'Brien's *When we were boys,* which Longman's had originally published earlier that year, and later in the same year, under their exclusive imprint, a 6d edition of it. Later correspondence shows that Eason's had acquired the rights in the book. There seems to have been a design in 1890 to widen their publishing activity, as the few books published cover a wide range. M.E. Blake's *A summer holiday in Europe* was brought out in association with Bagster in 1890. In 1891 Eason's themselves brought out T.F. Sullivan's *Blanaid and other Irish historical and legendary poems,* and with Bagster's in 1898 they brought out a very plush little volume entitled *Jack Ahoy or talks with sailors* by W.J. Mathews. An undated volume by A.W. Samuels entitled *The financial relations report* came out at some time after 1898, and a topical book was brought out in 1902 by J. Muldoon and G. McSweeney, entitled *Guide to the election of county and rural district councillors in Ireland*.

The fragmentary evidence suggests that there was a conscious attempt to move into a wider field of publishing in these years, but the impulse was not sustained. After 1902, what publishing was done, was mainly commissioned by the author. But some caution in regard to this had emerged by 1905. In that year they advised Tempest's that if their name appeared in the title page of a particular work, it was to be as agent not as publisher: 'our reason is that in the past we have more than once been brought into legal troubles by authors registering their productions as published by us, as for instance in the case of 'Irish Bee Guide.' ' A stray file of 1918/9 reveals that *The Practical Bee Guide* had been published for the Rev. J.G. Digges of Lough Rynn, Mohill, Co. Leitrim. The correspondence related to the pricing of a new edition, and suggests that it was a good seller. It is likely that there were other similar works of which we know nothing. The correspondence referred to Easons' 'commission department' — a department which, like the publication department, had a phantom existence merely as a form of words to cover one of the house's minor activities.

In the 1920s publishing largely consisted of printing under the house imprint the addresses of the Easons to the Statistical and Social Inquiry Society. They were also the publishers in 1947 of the *Centenary Volume* 1847-1947 of the Statistical of Social Inquiry Society of Ireland, which reflected the active role of both Charles Eason junior and of J.C.M. Eason in its proceedings. Charles Eason's research work into the Douai Bible was published in 1931, and on the Geneva Bible in 1937, and a few other items were brought out such as E.K. Eason's *Our defective calendar and the remedy,* and Senator J.G. Douglas's *President De Valera and the senate: speeches delivered in the senate,* which came out in 1934, a result of the close contact between the Easons and J.G. Douglas. In some cases the printing was arranged in their own factory, and in other cases it was arranged with other printers.

Little of the pre-1902 printing seems to have been done in the house. After 1902 some, although not all, of the printing was done internally (prayer-book printing in the house had apparently just occurred in 1890), and this points to the development of technical expertise in book production. Ideally, publishing could be combined with printing, thus mopping up some of the overcapacity of their printing works, but the total volume of publishing was small. The Earl of Dunraven's *Cheap food for the people at large; an open letter from the Earl of Dunraven to the people of Ireland* was published in 1925, and the two volumes of Mick's *Congested districts board*, of which they were not the printers. In 1926 they printed and published F.M. Laird's *Personal experience of the Great War (an unfinished manuscript)*, and in 1932 C.R.L. Ronayne's *Yacht racing*, and in 1934 they published but did not print E.W. Proud's *A Guide to the Road Traffic Act, 1933*. In the same year they printed the *Irish Baptist Hymnal* for the Baptist Union of Ireland. Their publishing activity had ceased to be concerned with building a proper list, but the tradition of this activity has never died, and is currently most evident in the *Irish Heritage Series*.

OUR BOYS

Eason's were nominally publishers of periodicals in a number of cases where they were only in fact either printers or distributors. One such instance was the *Irish Naturalist* where the obvious link was the editor Herbert Carpenter who had married one of the Eason daughters and was auditor of the company until 1917. An outstanding instance of this arrangement was with *Our Boys*, and the vicissitudes of the relations between the Christian Brothers and the firm illustrate vividly many aspects of this part of the company's work. Eason's had always had some relationship with the Brothers. Brothers' boys were readily employed, and an undated pencil note referring to some criticism of the Brothers reads: 'Still the Christian Brothers are entitled to great credit and I believe have done good work.' *Our Boys* was launched in 1914 as part of the clean literature campaign of the period, and was intended to provide an Irish journal which might take the place of the English literature which was coming into Ireland.

The fact that the Brothers approached Eason's is a tribute to the entirely non-sectarian reputation that Eason's bore. The relationship with the editors of *Our Boys* was uneventful for the first eight years of the agreement made in 1915, but it proved a serious problem for the last four years of the association. By 1921, when the magazine sold more copies than any other Irish publication, and the circulation had reached 50,000 copies an issue, Dawson's 'whose manager', according to Brother Craven 'was accompanied by one of the directors from London' had apparently made an offer to handle *Our Boys*. Since Dawson's were soon to pull out of the Irish market altogether, this may have been a last ditch attempt by them to revive their finances.

Brother Craven used the offer to seek better terms from Eason's, and stated that '.... nor does the [present] arrangement exist in writing.... We therefore feel that we have paid a large amount in excess of the contract entered into with your firm'. Because of rising costs, the agency commission had been raised (by agreement) from 10 per cent to 12½ per cent in 1917, and carriage costs outside Ireland shifted from the wholesaler to the publisher. The Brothers did not appear to have — or had lost — a copy of this agreement, which they persisted in treating as merely temporary. Craven intimated that he would consider a new offer from Eason's but that the manager of *Our Boys* wanted to know if Eason's were prepared to make a refund of the 'overcharge resulting in the change from 10 per cent to 12½ per cent.' Eason's contested this, but at the same time they were clearly anxious not to lose a prestigious and at that stage moderately profitable customer, especially to a rival. On 11 March 1921 Craven wrote that 'We are not bound to accept the lowest tender. By making an offer you will save the situation, and probably hold the distribution, as in that case, we could make a suitable reply to Messrs Dawson.' Eason's made an offer after an interview, and reduced the terms again to 10 per cent. At the time it could have looked that the Brothers were simply astute and possibly sharp bargainers. But while agreeing to the terms in order to retain *Our Boys*, Eason's must have appeared, despite their formal dissent, to have accepted Brother Craven's version of events.

All was still superficially well, and Brother Craven wrote to Eason on 21 March 1921 that 'the management are much pleased that the work of distribution is to remain with your firm.' The circulation grew rapidly, and the sales, as reflected in Easons' cash receipts, soared. At their peak in 1922/3 they amounted to over 9 per cent of the book and magazine department turnover. The October 1922 issue of *Our Boys* sold 53,000 copies, and in the same year the double numbers in July and December sold over 70,000. In fact the December issue in 1922, with a sale of 74,944 copies, proved to be the peak. Sales of ordinary numbers through the Dublin house peaked in the spring of 1923, and then fell sharply. Ominously, the fall was concentrated on the wholesale trade, and was at first less evident in Eason's agency distribution through schools and other outlets. Between December 1922 and December 1924 wholesale sales to the trade through Eason's had fallen from 33,605 to 22,169, while distribution through schools, the Brothers headquarters and other outlets, fell only from 41,329 to 37,817. Much of the sale through the non-trade outlets was a captive one, either to schools or to individuals, who were then compelled to dispose of all their copies, as no returns were allowed. In some cases, these distributors were taking to street sales to dispose of their copies, and as early as November 1921 Hart of the Retailers Association had protested to Eason:

> The feeling in the trade is that the management should be requested to refrain from the present arrangement of turning their pupils attending school into competition with the legitimate trade, by allowing them to sell on commission in all parts of the city and suburbs of Dublin.

Hart noted that retailers had no objections to sales within schools. Many of the non-trade distributors took the publication on a non-commercial basis, and with no returns allowed, unpaid accounts built up in Easons' ledgers. As early as January 1923 Eason commented on the mounting debtors list and underlined to Brother Craven that Eason's were only to pay to him what had been paid to them. While good relations had existed up to this, things now began to change. In a letter of 15 January 1924 Brother Craven wrote to Easons about hitches in distribution, not all of which were the fault of the house:

> 'The clock has struck.... Now, any action that we may take in this matter, you may blame yourselves for it. There are certain interests that, as I am informed on reliable authority, you take good care to protect. Now, we must take care to protect ours. Surely, it is time for Catholics to sit up.'

In April 1924 J.C.M. Eason strongly advised the Brothers against bringing *Our Boys* out as a fortnightly, and against reducing the price from 3d to 2d, stating that 'Increasing the number of pages, or improving the publication in whatever way you think would make its hold upon the boys more secure would, we think, be the wisest course.' In July J.C.M. Eason pointed out: 'We will get 1s 9d for 12 copies instead of 2s 8d, and as there would be two issues against one, it means 3s 6d in the month, which is an increase of not quite one third, but the cost of handling will be exactly double'. Eventually a new agreement was confirmed by Brother Craven on 22 August 1924 for a year until 31 August 1925, giving the firm a 12½ per cent agency fee, and a flat payment of £130 per year to cover country carriage charges.

Things might have continued more or less quietly, if the change to publishing fortnightly had been a success. As J.C.M. Eason had foreseen, the change was a failure. In the autumn of 1924 the circulation was still around 50,000 per issue, but a year later it was only 40,000, and in the spring of 1927 it was down to 35,000. Brother Craven had apparently envisaged that the circulation would actually double. The management of *Our Boys* began to run into difficulties. The Brothers had formerly acquiesced in long credit, but Brother Craven was in search of cash, and started a stream of enquiries in 1925 relating to individual accounts. Correspondence in October 1925 shows that there was serious trade objection to the total disallowance of returns, in place of the restricted returns which had applied from January 1925. On 15 October 1925, Craven admitted himself that returns of late had been so very heavy, and on 21 October commented that 'So far, the fortnightly issue has not been as successful as we expected.' Schoolboys began to make an appearance outside churches selling copies. When J.C.M. Eason pointed out that such forced sales were self-defeating, and that they would simply mean a shift of sales into new hands or other outlets, and a consequent rise in returns from newsagents, Craven dismissed the recent correspondence on circulation '.... as a pile of letters from Messrs Eason prophesying disaster to *Our Boys* if we pursued our propaganda.'

By now the Brothers' financial problems were serious, and Brother Craven had to admit in December that they were £150 overdrawn with the bank. The agreement between the two sides setting out the terms for the fortnightly issue had expired on 31 August 1925 without Brother Craven having taken any steps to alter or cancel it. Easons proceeded on the assumption that in the absence of any instructions to the contrary, the Brothers wished to continue on the same terms. Brother Craven took the view that at the end of this period the agreement had reverted to the old terms, and sought a refund of the carriage costs. Eason's took the view that in the absence of any new understanding, distribution continued after August on the same basis as in the temporary agreement.

Brother Craven was nothing if not transparent. A letter of 31 December 1925 makes it clear that the similarity between the annual figure for carriage in Ireland that he had agreed in 1924 to pay — £130 — and their liability to the bank was the attraction of the course he was taking. J.C.M. Eason agreed that if any new agreement was reached, it should be made retrospective to September 1925.

In December a bullying element in the relationship, which had always been on the fringe, now became explicit. On 21 December 1925 Brother Craven wrote to J.C.M. Eason that:

> It would not be wise to set the Christian Brothers' backs up against your firm, especially as there are big events, in which your firm are deeply interested, that must be settled in the near future. I had a letter from an influential member of the Dail a few days ago which is very significant'.

This was a reference to the committee on 'evil' literature, which had just been appointed by the Dail. In the meantime Brother Craven refused to grant J.C.M. Eason an interview to discuss arrangements, and wrote on 23 January 1926 that when he had,

> taken counsel with those interested in and possessing expert knowledge of the distribution of clean literature, I may be able to see you.... Enclosed you will find the two centre leaves of *Pear's Annual* 1925. When I saw the paper I sent out scouts to buy up all the unsold copies in Dublin. I also bought some other obscene things, paying £4 10s for all. The lot were then burned publicly in front of the *Our Boys* office, the blaze being photographed by the *Evening Herald*. Perhaps you would favour me with your opinion of verse 4 (marked) of *Pears Annual*?

Brother Craven attached to this letter a statement entitled, 'Messrs. Eason and *Our Boys*: Who owns *Our Boys*?' which was intended as a basis for publicity of their cause against Eason's. On 29 January 1926 Brother Craven wrote that they had taken up the challenge:

> .... in order to prevent Messrs. Eason from strangling *Our Boys* by putting the paper into bankruptcy.... Though £593 were paid in one year to Messrs Eason for distributing *Our Boys*, that firm hides the paper away in a back shelf in their premises while placing in a conspicuous position in their O'Connell Street shop cross-channel favourites of a well-known character.
>
> To have the whole business tested publicly, and well thrashed out, will be of service to: Newsagents (wholesale and retail) all over the country; Managers, principals, teachers and pupils of schools; Presidents and students of college; The members of the Dail and Seanad; Archbishops, bishops and priests; Fathers and mothers who desire that the children whom God has sent them should have pure minds and clean hearts; All who are in charge of providing healthy and national literature to reading Rooms, Clubs, Civic Guard stations, Soldiers' Barracks and Officers Quarters; In short, the public

> generally. For some years past, filthy literature has corrupted many pure hearts; brought shame to many homes; deep humiliation to many fathers and mothers; and disgrace on the whole island.
>
> Mr. Montgomery (the film censor) has done good work in regard to indecent pictures. This test case may do better still by ridding the country of literature full of brutalizing grossness.

The state of disorganisation of Brother Craven and the Christian Brothers at this stage had become very evident. On 5 February a letter from Brother Craven called for a copy of the March 1924 agreement, and three days later another letter requested a copy of the original agreement of 1915. On 12 February J.C.M. Eason wrote to them: 'We cannot afford to be left in a state of complete indefiniteness as to your position.'

Acrimonious correspondence continued through 1926, until finally in March 1927 the Brothers made arrangements for *Our Boys* to be published by the Educational Company. Brother Craven, however would not let matters rest, posing a whole series of short questions, each in a letter of its own. This continued through July and August. In September he wrote:

> I am now fully supplied with the required material for a 24 page pamphlet which I am preparing showing the methods adopted by Messrs Eason in carrying out the agency of *Our Boys*. Beginning with the original contract which was in every respect a legal document stamped with a six-penny stamp, and signed by both contracting parties, I pass on to the devices used in making alterations in some of the articles of agreement, and in the total removal of others. The letters lately received from Messrs Eason in reply to short, straightforward questions, clearly show the necessity for investigation.

Brother Craven revealed that the claims on the part of the Brothers amounted to £1,200. In February of the following year, during some routine business, a friendly exchange took place between J.C.M. Eason and Brother Craven. Eason wrote with reference to Brother Craven's having been ill that he was, '.... very pleased to see that you are signing letters again.' However in May another letter from Brother Craven made clear that the old issues were still on his mind.

Initially *Our Boys* had been an astonishing success. The Brothers' problems arose both from the cost of converting the magazine from a monthly into a fortnightly, and from carelessness over details of management as they pushed sales. The Brothers had made two mistakes. First, they were careless on a financial front. Secondly, in pushing sales, they were over-optimistic, both in allowing long debts, and when sales were flagging, adopting a fluctuating policy about returns. They never really appreciated the significance of returns being their own financial responsibility, and the costs of unprofitable distribution. They added to their own confusion and that of others by their fluctuating policy on returns, as J.C.M. Eason pointed out to them on 12 May 1927:

> Your position with regard to the acceptance of returns from agents has not been uniform, you have changed your instructions to us at various times. At one time we were instructed to accept no returns, afterwards were allowed to accept returns without limit; then on a 10 per cent basis and recently the magazine was made non-returnable again.

In the last analysis the financial plight of the Brothers was probably more directly the consequence of changing the journal to a fortnightly than of any other factor.

Luckily *Our Boys* did survive. Miss O'Farrell transferred from Eason's to the Educational Company, and no doubt as previously she helped the work along. *Our Boys* was an astonishing success, whatever the reversal in its fortunes. Its sales of 70,000 for its double issues was an unprecedented achievement in the Irish market, and no other publication, English or Irish, came near it, with the exception of *Dublin Opinion*. *Our Boys* proved that there was a market for good publications that had a distinctively Irish appeal, and that the problem was a shortage of such publications, rather than a lack of demand for them. Roughly half of the total sales were distributed through Easons' wholesale channels, and so were outside the agency terms which had proved so contentious, and Eason's could certainly take some share of satisfaction for the success of the magazine. Wholesale sales of *Our Boys* continued to be important to Eason's, although there is no measure of them after 1927. In May, when publication passed from Eason's to the Educational Company, Eason's made a point of stressing in the *Monthly Bulletin* that they were still wholesale distributors, and could continue to supply the magazine to the trade on the same terms as before. *Our Boys* was very significant not only in Eason's own books and magazines department but in Irish sales generally. This is reflected in a comment in the house's *Monthly Bulletin* of December 1930 which contained the news that *Our Boys* was now being provided on a full sale or return basis. It was hailed as '.... the most interesting and important event in the magazine world.'

Some profit figures exist for *Our Boys* along with *Virgo Potens* which the firm handled for the Irish Sisters of Charity in the mid 1920s. The profits on *Our Boys* had been £142 in 1917/8 and £166 in 1918/9. These figures are small but they explain why Eason's were quite keen to keep the publication when the Brothers broached the matter of the Dawson's offer in 1921. In fact, these profits were never approached again in the course of the relationship. The figures appear to relate to the agency only, that is to say, to copies supplied to agents, houses, and retail outlets outside the news outlets normally supplied by the Wholesale Books department. On 1 January 1926 J.C.M. Eason noted: 'Our records for past year shows clearly that the agency has never been a source of substantial profit to us — in fact at times it has actually been worked at a loss — and that all through it has called for supervision and attention to an exceptional degree.' If the exceptional management effort had been costed in, the arrangement was unattractive. Sales to trade customers through the wholesale books department are of course not included in these calculations. It would have been one of the most substantial magazine items and a solid contributor to the turnover and profitability of that department.

Easons were distributors, although not publishers, for two publications, *The Kingdom* and *Our Girls*, which were published by the Kingdom Press. The proprietors of this house were Ernest Gordon of Mary Street, publisher, and Thomas Maguire of Bullock Castle, Dalkey, solicitor. The original agreement was signed in December 1930 and it was terminated in 1932. *Our Girls* seems to have had a substantial circulation of almost 20,000 in 1931, and *The Kingdom* a circulation of around 12,000. There is no indication of the reason why the agreement came to an end. The circulation figures point to a significant market, whatever the success of the venture, for any publication seriously attempting to meet the interest in Irish publications. A stray sheet with some profit calculations seems to suggest that a combined circulation of about 40,000 had been envisaged. There is no evidence that sales had fallen off at the time the distribution through Eason's was ended.

The third kind of publishing activity was information to trade customers, of which the major example was Easons' *Monthly Trade Bulletin*, which first appeared in April 1925. It carried advertising by Easons' suppliers, and generated some revenue for the house as a result. It also carried a certain amount of comment and some features, such as profiles of prominent members of the firm. A single reference to it in the Board minutes in 1926 suggests that 1,500 copies were distributed. It suspended publication during the war years, and reappeared as *Eason's Bulletin* in May 1945. When it reappeared, it was in a smaller format, and it also concentrated to a large extent on books. Its book comment at this stage was extremely lively, well-informed and well-written.

A series of articles entitled, 'Irish Authors' was launched in the first issue, with a profile of Annie M.P. Smithson. The total number of profiles reached eighty-two by the time the series ceased in September 1953. Many of them were lively and informative, often on little known or obscure authors, and some have revealing insights, particularly when they were written by the authors themselves. Of Irish authors of the period, perhaps only James Stephens is missing. His publishers, Macmillan, wrote to him for biographical information, but a month later they had to admit that they had had no reply to their letter, and further letters to Macmillan bore no result. The character of the new series and its liveliness seems to have been mainly due to Paddy Hughes, who left the firm in 1949, and was later to go to the Mercier Press. While Robert Eason was head of the book division, the *Bulletin* retained its momentum, and he was personally responsible for its content. John Menzies of the Edinburgh wholesaling house congratulated Eason's on the *Bulletin* in a letter of February 1952: 'May I take the opportunity to congratulate you on the excellent little bulletins which you put out, samples of which you enclosed. They are so much more comprehensive than the monthly news-sheets which we issue.'

PRINTING

Easons' printing works were an important part of the business. With so many house forms, printing on the premises was a great advantage. The works grew very rapidly in the second half of the century, but though the volume of printing was sizeable — it kept eight compositors occupied in 1882 — it was subsidiary in importance to stationery manufacture which expanded rapidly in the course of the 1880s. Printing gained in importance at the end of the century when it was extended to cope with the demands for high class printing including Easons' own prayer-books.

Manufacturing was already a sizeable activity in relation to the pre-war turnover in Dublin. The importance of the factory was such that a good deal of attention was devoted to its activities, and it is clear that from 1910-11 onwards, J.C.M. Eason, who worked in stationery, spent a considerable amount of time in analysing the figures in order to arrive at a picture of the situation in the factory. The output was calculated on the basis of wages plus purchases, and it was divided into broad areas of production (see Table 19) The impression received is that stationery production accounted for more than half of the output in peacetime.

TABLE 19 *Manufacturing output, 1911-1920*

	Stationery*	Printing*	Others	Total
	£	£	£	£
1911	4858	3178	219	8255
1912	5201	3666	212	9079
1913	5565	3107	228	8900
1914	5669	3122	161	8952
1915	6002	2999	140	9131
1916	5373	4193	136	9702
1917	5086	6378	239	11723
1918	5645	8593	362	14600
1919	9466	9725	380	19571
1920**	7072	9337	1819	18228

* These are not the categories used by the firm. *Stationery* is made up of the analysed categories 'manufactured stock' and 'ordinary stock', and *Printing* of the categories 'trade jobs', 'wholesale house' and 'interdepartmental' whether for outside clients ('trade jobs') or for in-house use.

** The *Others* category in this year includes a sum for retail which is not given in previous years

The factory employed 111 people in July 1914. It was particularly important for the manufacture of plainer ranges of stationery and for prayer-books. The rise in output during World War I for the most part reflected rising prices. In December 1916 in their return to the Board of Trade, Easons stated for the first time that 'our machines are not running to full extent of their capacity owing to lack of orders.' This became a refrain which was repeated in subsequent returns. It began to change somewhere in the middle of 1917 when references to shortages seem mainly to concern the manufacture of stationery, while printing remained unaffected. In June 1917 'shortage of brass eyelets, paste, sheet strips, cutting knives (punches), straw boards, wood, greaseproof paper, restricts output. Only a proportion of orders offered can be accepted.' By June 1918, one year later, the situation had become even more serious: 'We have difficulty as to materials as mentioned in previous returns as the further restrictions in supply of paper must tend to a reduction of business, but we cannot say definitely when such effect will be felt or to what extent.' The year 1918/9 saw a sharp rise in output, although shortages were still posing difficulties. The number of persons employed had fallen off, but by July 1918 it had recovered to the 1914 level: 'The demand for our stock has increased, but as priority certificates cannot be procured for the papers necessary for our work, our output is restricted to what material we are able to procure.'

The importance of the factory is reflected in the fact that it followed the prestigious and crucial railway advertising department in the firm's attempts to measure profits accurately. From 1910/11 onwards calculations of gross profit were made by Hallet. These were adjusted further by J.C.M. Eason by calculations of other expenses, in order to arrive at a net profit. These figures did not include an item in respect of interest until 1916/7 when £500 was added for this purpose, a figure which rose to £700 in 1917/8. Even if the interest were not charged, the factory was already running at a loss from the time of the first calculations. A profit was recorded only under war conditions in 1916/7, 1917/8, 1918/9, and again in 1920/21, when the firm benefited from exceptional stock appreciation. In the year 1919/20, a year in which there was some lack of orders and a strike occurred in the printing works, there was a loss.

TABLE 20 *Profits and Losses in Factory*

	Profit £		Loss £	
1911	—		1267	
1912	—		810	
1913	—		707	
1914	—		656	
1915	—		771	
1916	n/a		n/a	
1917	992	(492)*	—	
1918	1797	(1077)*	—	
1919	325*		(375)	
1920	—		468	(1168)*
1921	575*		(125)	

* Figures in brackets include an allowance for interest.

Printing and stationery manufacture was doubtfully profitable. Even during the war, stock appreciation failed to make the activity very profitable except in one single year. J.C.M. Eason noted on a loose sheet, apparently in 1921, with regard to the Christmas cards, where the variety was enormous: 'Irish firms have not the necessary plant and machinery the procuring of which would involve the spending of thousands of pounds, and it would be very questionable if anyone would be found willing to undertake the risk...' He observed that 'Cards can only be produced at a moderate price by very large editions.' Precisely the same problem applied to the printing even of the prayer-books, which were the only standard publication which Easons printed in quantity. Their runs were much smaller than those of their rivals in Belgium and elsewhere. Although wages in the 1930s were higher than in England or on the continent, it was the relatively small number printed of any one item rather than high wages which meant that books could no longer be priced at an economic rate.

In the 1920s the difficult situation was reflected in an overall decline in output. As valued for the first census of production in 1926, output was only £9,720. Even in cash terms this was no higher than pre-war levels, and in real terms it was far below the pre-war level. It is reflected in the comment on the return that if the factory has been working to capacity, it could have produced 150 per cent more. The total work force was halved compared with the pre-1920s. In 1926 the number employed varied from 50 to 61, and it never exceeded 60 in the next census (1929). The difficulty in competing seems to have been concentrated in stationery, where output dropped very far below pre-war levels even in nominal terms. Within stationery, it was probably more evident in some lines than in others. The economics of the situation were such that not even the technical ingenuity of Coghill, the manager of the works, could counterbalance these trends.

In post-war days the works was no longer competitive, and this became even more marked in the 1930s. The firm could attract little extra jobbing printing work, though a rise in book and more particularly magazine printing gave the printing side some boost. Apart from the Eason's *Monthly Bulletin*, which is included in these figures, *The Irish Free State Farmer (Irish Farm Life)*, *TCD*, and *Irish Golf* seem to have been printed regularly in the 1930s. Efforts to capture other printing were disappointing. The *Baptist Hymnal* was printed in 1934 for £393. For some reason this was included in the total for magazines and periodicals. The only book printed in 1935 was a *History of Inishowen*. The book print sales

TABLE 21 *Components of Printing Turnover*

Year ended March	*1926* £	*1929* £	*1931* £	*1932* £	*1933* £	*1934* £
*Manuscript Books**	2808	3341	2227	3955	3457	3450
Printing — Printed Books	—	408	75	52	—	521
Periodicals/ Magazines	—	1785	1834	1620	1381	1048
Job/General Printing	6876	8177	7488	6544	5595	9217
Other	37	—	—	24	3120	2669
Total	9720	13711	11624	12195	13553	16905

*i.e. Stationery

Year ended March	*1935* £	*1936* £	*1937* £	*1938* £	*1939* £	*1940* £
*Manuscript Books**	2489	3490	3888	1431	1208	2054
Printing Printed Books	93	159	440	—	—	—
Periodicals/ Magazines	1580	1105	1140	925	785	537
Job/General Printing	10471	11357	10428	8118	9363	9979
Other	3118	4343	2773	4179	1589	2753
Total	17751	20454	18669	14653	12945	15323

*i.e. Stationery

in 1936 are made up entirely by 1,485 copies of the *History of the Firm,* or 'House Souvenir' which was brought out to celebrate the fiftieth anniversary of the house as Eason & Son Ltd. The last book production in the history of the printing works was 2,383 copies of a book commissioned by *Dublin Opinion* in 1937. This output was meagre in the extreme. It seems likely that publications such as the *Baptist Hymnal, TCD* and *Irish Golf,* all of which were related to interests of members of the house, were probably attracted as much by contacts as by competitiveness. The job or trade printing which had languished in the 1920s picked up very significantly in the 1930s, roughly doubling between 1933 and 1936. This activity was a direct beneficiary of protection, but even protective barriers were not enough to give it a sustained growth. Output fell in the next four years. The rubric, 'Other', in the table above included in the main various printed stationery for other commercial firms. This was an entirely new line, and it seems to have been made possible by tariffs on imported printed matter. It was a fairly sizeable figure and outweighed the importance of the more traditional lines of Eason's in exercise books, account books, jotters, duplicate books and so on, which increasingly found themselves in a precarious situation.

The profitability of the factory became more doubtful as time went by. In the years before 1914 when costs were low, losses were small. In the altered cost structure after the war, the factory was much less competitive and losses mounted alarmingly. Even without taking interest into account, losses became massive in the 1920s, extending to £3,000 p.a. in the late 1920s. A good deal of the loss must have been in stationery production, which got into a vicious circle. Losses led to reduction in output, which in turn put up unit costs further. Later, as stationery output was greatly reduced and printing volume expanded, losses must increasingly have centred on printing. There had probably always been over-capacity in printing from the start of the enlarged operation. The sharp rise in losses in the 1920s, on a higher real volume, suggests that it was inherently uncompetitive. It was unspecialised work, done on a small scale for a variety of sources, and therefore unit costs were high. Underused capacity meant inevitably that if there was any significant upturn, losses should be considerably reduced, as happened in fact after 1932 because of protection. In the early 1930s losses fell in absolute amount, and even more significantly as a proportion of factory turnover. Small runs inevitably meant that unit production costs were high, and even the recovery in activity in the 1930s failed to achieve profits. The critical condition of the factory is revealed in the fact that the rise in output in the 1930s was achieved with little rise in the labour force, and so reflected a chronic overcapacity. The increase in output between the years ending March 1933 and 1935 involved a rise in the October work force from 54 to 57 between 1932 and 1934. In 1936 the staff in October was 63, and at one point during the year it had reached 78. But this was short-lived, and corresponded to a temporary upturn in job and general printing. After that employment declined steadily. The decision to close became more and more inevitable. Interestingly, the story of printing in W.H. Smith's in London was a story of tribulation and losses, with closure in 1937 preceeding that in Eason's by four years.[3] The closure of the factory in March 1941 was the end of a long tradition in the house. In the end it demonstrated the difficulties that a general firm encounters in running profitably a specialised activity.

3 Wilson, *First with the News*, pp. 228-34, 255-6, 277-8.

Chapter 13 ❧ The problem of 'Evil Literature'

FROM THE BEGINNING IT HAD BEEN a key object of W.H. Smith's bookstall strategy to provide the travelling public with 'respectable' literature. Consequently the company in England had always operated some form of internal censorship, and the Irish business both before and after 1886 followed the same pattern. In the nineteenth century it was books rather than periodicals that were the principal object of censorship. The house reserved the right to refuse to circulate freely a book which it deemed unsuitable, although it recognised that its dominant position made it mandatory under normal conditions to provide a copy to any one specifically ordering it.

This censorship was taken for granted, and far from attracting hostile criticism, was considered one of the proofs that the firm was discharging its moral responsibilities seriously. In the 1890s this situation, which had been an easy one for Smith's and Eason's, began to change. Books exploring moral or sexual issues more explicitly began to appear, and the right to do so also began to be asserted. W.H. Smith's were involved in controversy in 1894 when they refused to circulate George Moore's *Esther Waters*. Eason's found themselves in the eye of the storm the following year. In February 1895 Eason's refused to circulate the *Review of Reviews* of that month on account of the 'Book of the Month' review by W.T. Stead, with long extracts from Grant Allen's book *The woman who did*. The reasons for their decision were set out in a letter by Charles Eason jnr., no doubt acting for his father:

> Allen's book is an avowed defence of Free Love and a direct attack upon the Christian view of marriage. Mr. Stead criticises Allen's views adversely but we do not think the antidote can destroy the ill effects of the poison. We decline to be made the vehicle for the distribution of attacks upon the most fundamental institution of the Christian State.

An article by Stead in the *Westminster Review* reprinted in full a letter which Charles Eason senior had written in reply to a letter from Stead. In it Charles Eason has asserted that 'we are more and more confirmed in the belief that its influence had been and is most pernicious.' The affair was widely reported in the press in England, and Eason also received several dozen letters from both England and Ireland congratulating him on his stand.

On this occasion censorship was challenged. The Easons' moral tone was perhaps out of place in taking the decision that they took, especially as the immediate subject of controversy was related to a review and not to the book itself. It seemed to give some justification to Stead's charge of the dangers of 'censors ....(who) do not owe their existence to Act of Parliament or Imperial ukase'. The *Book and News Trade Gazette* in the following month ran a feature entitled 'The Dublin Veto', concluding that 'beyond all doubt, the position of Messrs. Eason is a very strong one, and it is extremely doubtful whether it can be assailed with anything like success. At the same time no harm can arise from publishers having had their attention drawn to the matter by the recent autocratic behaviour of the firm.' It went on to relate that they had received a communication from a Mr James O'Hara who had wished to borrow *Napoleon and the Fair Sex* from Eason's circulating library:

> Mr O'Hara sends a communication which shows that if Messrs. C. Eason and Co. are ostensibly very solicitous for the morals of the reading public they are not consistently so. Mr O'Hara asked to be supplied with the volume, and it was refused him on the ground that Mr Eason considered it improper, and therefore had decided not to circulate it. Three days afterward Mr O'Hara saw a young man ask for the same book, and it was presented to him with a low bow. He mentioned this to Mr Charles Eason, who told him that he had issued it to this one subscriber only, because he was the Prince Francis of Teck. Mr O'Hara remarked that the book was not less likely to be injurious to a young man like the Prince Francis of Teck. Mr Eason replied, 'Oh, these high-up people are different. Besides, they are so influential we cannot refuse them.'

Whatever the freedom (if any) the writer may have taken with the actual happenings and sayings in Eason's circulating library on that day, the validity of the point was unassailable.

However, events such as this related only to books, which circulated narrowly, and to a relatively cultivated readership. After 1900 the problem became more general, as popular periodical publications began to become common, and as photography opened up new and more alluring forms of appeal. Publications which were withdrawn on occasion from the book stalls included periodicals such as *Photobits* and *McFaddens Physical Development*. Objectionable plates were also beginning to appear in some periodicals. These plates were still expensive, but the occasional withdrawal of the Christmas numbers of certain periodicals was a sign of things to come. More important still, in the sense that they reached larger numbers, was the emergence of wide-circulation Sunday papers drawing on the courts for crime reports and especially on reports on divorce proceedings for columns of titillating detail. As early as 1899 the Irish bishops denounced 'bad' literature in their Lenten Pastorals, and Charles Eason wrote in a letter to his youngest brother, Benjamin, on 4 March 1899 that he had received three letters from Cardinal Logue on the subject. Concern was becoming widespread, and the resultant call for censorship was in no way specifically Irish. Lord Aberdeen, the lord lieutenant in Ireland, had been president of the National Vigilance Association in England for a decade, and pressure was already gathering towards some sort of clean up. W.A. Coote, the secretary of the National Vigilance Association, was able to write to Eason in January 1910 that 'There is no question that there is at the present time a great improvement in some publications, especially in connection with the cheap illustrated papers.' A joint select committee of parliament had reported in 1908 and had recommended that the law be strengthened by better definition of what was objectionable.

There was extensive controversy in England over improper books in 1909, and Smith's were taken to task in the *Academy* over a departure from the standards of 'Old Morality'. The main focus of controversy revolved around the decision of the Circulating Libraries Association not to circulate books which they thought would be objectionable to a large number of their readers. Charles Eason took an even harder line than the English circulating libraries. He excluded some books altogether, and other books were available only on request. Wells' *Anne Veronica* was freely available in England, but not in Ireland. Charles Eason had to admit:

> Perhaps it is on account of the views on 'marriage' held by Anne that I have a good deal of hesitation as to *Anne Veronica*. I exclude it on the grounds that it contains a direct attack on marriage. It adopts the view that a married man may leave his wife and live with another woman because their temperaments agree. The effect is to tell all young men and women that they may at any time form a ....

The question mainly revolved around the availability of books in libraries, because this raised the question of discretion in stocking. Though he regarded it as necessary, Eason disliked the Libraries Association approach, because he felt that it created the impression that all other books in a library were safe, and released the manager and the reader alike from any responsibility. Debate was now joined. A Conference of London Societies interested in public morality came out, at least as early as 1910, on the side of control or censorship. This led to the formation of a National Council of Public Morals, which waited on the Home Secretary in January 1912 to request legislation, and more vigorous police prosecution. On the other side of the debate was the literary viewpoint, as expressed by George Moore in February 1912 in the aftermath of the deputation to the Home Secretary: 'Literary morality varies every ten years; it is the prejudice of the moment....' Lord Aberdeen relayed back to England favourable reports on what was taking place in Ireland.

Charles Eason himself took a vigorous part in the discussions raised by these issues. He set out his views at length to the editor of the *Athenaeum* in a private letter written in February 1910, and he was also in correspondence early in 1910 with W.A. Coote, chairman of the Conference of London Societies interested in public morality. Coote was himself Secretary of the National Vigilance Association and the International Bureaux for the Repression of the White Slave Traffic, of which Aberdeen was also the president. In January 1910 Coote wrote to Charles Eason: 'I wish that all the publishers would take the stand you have always, and still do take, it would simplify matters, and prevent the circulation of much unwholesome reading. We know we can rely on you.' In 1913 the banning of three books by Hall Caine, Maxwell and Compton Mackenzie gave the issue a new life. A controversy ensued in which H.G. Wells also got involved. Charles Eason was in correspondence with Hall Caine, who sent Eason a copy of his novel *The woman thou gavest me*. Eason replied to Hall Caine that, 'people who ask for it must of course get it but [I] don't suggest it promiscuously.'

Concern in Ireland took on a distinctively Catholic and nationalistic form. In England the matter which took up most interest was the principle of censorship, which was discussed at great length in the serious periodicals in 1909 and again in 1913. The question of more popular literature and its discouragement or purification never led to a national movement, although it was one of the objects of reformers in the National Council. In Ireland a national campaign against popular English Sunday newspapers did develop, and the objections centred on the reporting of divorce proceedings. This question was already under consideration by the Divorce Commission in England, and in Ireland objection to such reporting was soon to take on a forceful and popular character. In 1913 when Charles Eason refused to put the cheap 7d edition of *Ann Veronica* on sale, he was able to refer in a letter of 12 June 1913 to the fact that 'there is a strong feeling in Ireland against books and papers which attack the Christian view of Marriage.'

The campaign was started in 1911 in Limerick by a Father Gleeson, director of the 5,000 strong Holy Family sodality. The local newsboys were organised under the auspices of the Confraternity, and a vigilance committee was set up under the chairmanship of Father O'Connor of St Michael's parish. Pledges were secured from twenty-nine newsagents not to supply objectionable newspapers. The *Leader*, D.P. Moran's weekly, on 18 November 1911 reported that a large crowd gathered outside the shop of a man selling Sunday papers 'who found it difficult to keep his word' and that 'only for the presence of the priests serious consequences might have resulted.' The *Leader* had quickly identified with the movement and supported it strongly.

The first direct contact between Father O'Connor and Eason's was in a letter received from him on 27 October 1911 which expressed the hope that Eason's would sign the undertaking which had already been signed by the Limerick newsagents. Eason's replied the same day that they had instructed their clerk in Limerick 'not to expose for sale the papers we understand are objected to' and in a further letter on 30 October they set out their policy ideas at length for Father O'Connor. This drew a reply from him in a letter dated 1 November: 'I don't think there would be much use in my discussing them — at least on paper. Your outlook is purely commercial — ours purely moral .... they have now practically ceased to be sold in Limerick. There seems however to be a good deal of work yet before us, but we mean this to be a fight to the finish. It will not be, as some hope, a mere flash in the plan.'

Lord Aberdeen welcomed the happenings in Limerick. As reported in the *Freeman's Journal* on 26 October, he commented to the National Vigilance Association in London that 'the fine example of Limerick may well be quoted as illustrating that there is no need for any community to submit tamely to the injurious incursions of an evil trade.' These comments on the Limerick movement were unfortunate, as they added to its authority, and were ruthlessly exploited. According to the *Leader* report already cited:

> A Mission which was being conducted by the Capuchin Fathers roused great enthusiasm on the subject of indecent literature. Moreover, Father Gleeson, at several of the meetings of the Men's

> confraternity preached on this subject and also on the necessity of supporting the Catholic press, special mention being made of the *Leader*. In addition, on one Sunday, reference was made at each Mass, in the city churches, and the people appealed to, one and all, to end the circulation of the reptile press in Limerick. The result was the people were finally stirred to action, and the difficulty was to keep them within the bounds of the law.

An ugly atmosphere of intimidation now hung over Limerick. In October, as orders from Limerick fell, the *News of the World* suggested selling through protestant agents, to which Eason's replied that 'we do not keep any note of their religion, and we may say that one agent who has stopped the papers is a Protestant who very strongly objects to being obliged to do so.'

On Sunday 22 October a large crowd assembled at the station as the Sunday papers arrived. There was no violence, but one representative left Limerick taking seventy dozen copies of his paper with him by the next train. The following Sunday the crowd gathered again. The day's incidents were reported by the *Freeman's Journal*:

> The Rosslare train, which arrives at 12:30, brought two parcels of a Sunday paper, one for an agent, who alleges they were not ordered, and another for the military barracks. The first of these came into the possession of a crowd, which, headed by the Boherbuoy Brass Band, set out for the People's Park. At the Spring Rice Monument addresses on the evils of bad literature were delivered, and the papers were solemnly burned, amidst a scene of great enthusiasm, the band playing hymns while the obnoxious journals burned, and then the Dead March (Saul) over their ashy remains. Loud cheers were given as the people moved away quietly.
>
> At half past three when the Dublin train arrived, two soldiers of the York and Lancaster Regiment, now stationed in Limerick, appeared at the terminus (at which a large crowd had again assembled) and took away the papers that had come by the early train. When the men made their appearance in front of the station, the papers were removed from their possession, torn into tiny small pieces, and pounded into the mud. The soldiers offered no resistance and were not in any way molested.

An account also survives in a telegram from Easons' bookstall clerk which confirms the accuracy of the press report, and puts the crowd at five hundred men and boys, adding — which illustrates the political tensions underneath the incident — that, 'I must say it was a very fine sample of Home Rule'. A comment the previous week in a letter to Eason's on the Sunday's events in Limerick had been less political, saying that 'this is a horribly priest-ridden town but must put up with it. What about your bookstall here? They are determined to make it very hot for anyone selling these.' Eason's bookstall handled the order for the garrison, and on the Sunday afternoon both the bookstall clerk and the army still seemed determined to get their supplies for the following Sunday. The Easons' nerve did not however prove very strong in these daunting circumstances, and the reply to the clerk in Limerick instructed him to state that no papers could be delivered on the following Sunday. This led to the Regimental Sergeant Major cancelling the order in a letter on 1 November 1911, adding pathetically: 'Will you kindly mail me a copy of the *Referee* that contains the football news of next Saturday as our colonel is anxious to see if the paper is a good one for the men.' Eason's replied the following day that: 'we felt bound to execute your order, but we are glad that you see your way to fall in with the views of the people in that town.'

Viewed from London, it must all have seemed quite outlandish, and one of the news managers observed in a letter to Eason's: 'It seems an extraordinary thing that any agitation can be got up even in Ireland to stop English soldiers from buying any paper they want.' In emphasising the availability of suitable Irish alternative reading material, the reformers overlooked the fact that much of the demand was not for stories about sex or broken family life, but for up-to-date news and entertainment, and that alternative literature did not in itself answer the relatively novel interests that the Sunday papers met (and had to some extent created) for sports results and light entertainment. An Irish equivalent — *Sunday Freeman* — only appeared from 22 June 1913. The success of these English papers was quite striking and in 1911 was of very recent origin. An editorial in the *Freeman's Journal* on 6 November 1911 commented that 'a few years ago these journals had only a limited circulation in this country. Now they flood every Irish city on Sunday morning.'

Within a few years their circulation had become quite large. One newsagent in 1911 estimated that no less than 40,000 copies of English Sunday newspapers were sold in Dublin alone. The papers were usually referred to as 'Sundays', but the Irish trade and public opinion before World War I made little distinction between weekly editions of dailies and Sunday newspapers. In fact, before the first world war, the only English papers which could be distributed in time for sale in the Irish country towns and provincial cities on a Sunday morning were the weekly editions published on Friday evening or Saturday morning. True Sunday editions, i.e. those published on Saturday evening, could not be delivered before the early afternoon. The papers Eason's handled for the army garrison on the occasion of the Sunday riot at Limerick station had significantly only arrived at half past twelve midday. Eason's also handled weekly editions of English papers, and although they did not put papers on sale on Sundays at their own bookstalls, they arranged parcels of Sunday editions for garrisons, and also disposed of a limited number of Sundays on Monday morning at the bookstalls, and in the retail shop on Sackville Street. For the garrisons, with the keen following of British sports results among the officers and men, the true Sunday edition was essential.

The movement against the Sundays now began to gather pace elsewhere. In particular the *Leader* gave it unqualified support week after week. At the annual meeting of the St Columba's branch of the Catholic Young Men's Society in October 1911 it was decided to form a vigilance committee in Dublin. A meeting for this purpose was held on 5 November, and a provisional committee met on 10 November. By the beginning of December eighteen parochial committees had been formed. From the start, while there was some lay membership on the Dublin committee, the general membership was heavily clerical. A meeting was held in Clonmel to form a committee on 26 November. One of its decisions was to call on the barracks to prevent the sale of papers in the barracks by an itinerant vendor. The adjutant general agreed to the committee's request, but the Eason's bookstall was instructed to ensure that papers were delivered in wrappers. A committee in Galway opened a vigorous correspondence with Eason's from 30 November. Other committees followed in December in Waterford, Carrick-on-Suir, Kilkenny, Athlone and Westport. In Mullingar representations were made to the bookstall by the parish priest. While they did not make representations to Eason's, similar committees were in existence in Cavan and in Cork in November. Eason's were invariably requested to stop the distribution of the papers. They in turn objected to the unwarranted intrusion on their rights, but agreed not to expose the papers objected to on the counters of the bookstalls. As 1912 went by the movement became more general, and as in 1911 Eason's were called on by the committees not to stock the Sundays. At its peak, according to an editorial in the *Freeman's Journal* on 9 June 1912, the movement seems to have had about one hundred vigilance committees scattered throughout Ireland, with a central body in Dublin.

The officers' mess of the Surrey regiment at Moor Park outside Fermoy approached Eason's in January 1912 about getting newspapers. Eason's proposed the same arrangement that had been proposed in November 1911 to supply the soldiers in Limerick, that the papers should be supplied to a named person in the garrison, without going through the Eason's bookstall at all, and that the account should be charged directly by Dublin and not by the bookstall. The letter hints that the arrangement had not been carried through in Limerick because the people had approached the officers. The order in Fermoy marked time for a while, but a letter of July 1912 from the bookstall clerk shows that military business was booming:

> I may state that although the order was sent to the House it was I who procured it by canvassing in the ordinary course. I have also got the Regimental institutes and Sergeant Mess of same regt. but the officers mess probably sent their order through the House as they may think it would receive more attention. I am quite prepared to supply all orders for Moor Park (three miles from Fermoy) and I cycle out there every day and help to deliver papers to the Leinster Regt. etc. The competition in this business in Fermoy is unprecedented and I have held my own remarkably well for so far I would scarcely get a single order but for corresponding with the military before they came here and trade rivalry and jealousy had gone so far that the *News of the World* was burned on Sunday last under the guise of morality, but in reality in furtherance of the existing competition.

The Dublin provisional committee had first appointed a censor committee to draw up a list of objectionable Sunday papers and other publications. It met monthly, canvassed newsagents, and gave newsagents who agreed to observe the ban a card of approbation to display for the guidance of the public. In addition all the Dublin newspapers were asked to cooperate by not publishing unwholesome details of divorce proceedings and similar cases, and according to the first report of the Vigilance Committee in January 1913, all the Dublin papers agreed to extend their cooperation. The campaign was welcomed by the Archbishop in his Lenten address in 1912. At a meeting in April of that year in the Oak Room in the Mansion House attended by delegates 'from every Catholic organisation in the city including delegates from sodalities and confraternities', a new organisation was decided on, and its officers and committee elected at a further meeting on 1 May. Some sixty meetings were held in all during the remainder of the year, including some twenty public meetings to administer pledges to 'crusaders' throughout the city. The biggest event of all was the monster demonstration against 'pernicious' literature held in the Mansion House in July 1912. From the start the new committee was in touch with Charles Eason, who assured the secretary McMahon on 19 June that: 'we are most willing to cooperate with you in checking the circulation of objectionable publications.'

In July Eason agreed to receive a deputation from the committee. Eason's entertained complaints from the committee, and made representations to offending publishers. The committee was increasingly concerned about advertisements for 'literature' and for 'medicaments'; in other words for contraceptive literature and appliances. On 12 July 1912 Charles Eason referred to the fact that evidence was being submitted to a committee of the Commons sitting in London and suggested that: 'you might perhaps use your influence with the Irish members of parliament to get them to support any action which may be taken in this direction.' Earlier, in December 1911, Charles Eason had noted that: 'the priest who took a leading part in starting this movement told me that he was very much influenced by a pamphlet received in reply to such advertisements.'

The progress of the movement was confirmed by the holding of a monster meeting in the Mansion House on 1 July 1912 attended by the Lord Mayor and no less a figure than the Lord Lieutenant. The adoption of the committee's report was actually proposed by the Lord Lieutenant, who went on in his address in a somewhat extraordinary fashion:

> His excellency said he was not going to criticise any co-religionist, but so far as he and his house were concerned they would not have act or part in anything that could offend the feeling of any catholic (applause). They would not participate in anything which approached or came under the head of — he would say — proselytism (loud applause). There were times when one could speak for oneself, and he was now speaking for himself and Lady Aberdeen and stating their fixed attitude and conscientious position.

The *Irish Catholic* estimated the overflow audience outside as over 20,000, and when he left the Mansion House, Lord Aberdeen addressed them also. On 17 August the Vigilance Committee decided to map the city out into districts in order to ensure that there was an active committee in every district, and that newsagents were systematically canvassed. The success of the campaign can be judged from the newspaper reports which were assiduously encouraged by the movement. According to an editorial in the *Freeman's Journal* on 9 June 1913 about one hundred associations had allied themselves with the central body, and a report earlier in the same year 26 February noted that a large meeting of two hundred newsagents had adopted the pledge. On 8 June 1913 a procession and a monster meeting of the societies, sodalities and confraternities who supported the 'noble object' of the committee was held. At the meeting it was claimed that over 100,000 had signed the pledge against 'pernicious' literature. In May the *National Student* noted that the campaign was 'backed by practically the whole Catholic hierarchy, high and low, in Ireland.'

The movement drew on a strong feeling of nationalism and triumphalism. Publications which had already expressed an interest in censorship included the *Catholic Bulletin* which in November 1911 noted that it had repeatedly called attention to the growing circulation of English Sunday and weekly papers. Another was the *Irish Rosary* whose editor for four years had been the Rev. Coleman, OP. Later on, following a lecture in 1914 by Coleman on 'the so-called terrible oath of the Ancient Order of Hibernians' in which he referred to a book entitled *Intolerance in Ireland* 'by an Irishman' which had been on sale at Easons' bookstall in Kilkenny, Coleman himself entered into correspondence with Charles Eason, alleging that 'if there were any reply to that published or anything in favour of Catholics they would not find it in the bookstalls.' Later Coleman admitted to Eason that he had spoken 'much more strongly in fact than I was reported'. In the course of a long correspondence with the reverend gentleman it emerged that the real source of his grievances was that a pamphlet by himself entitled *Grievances in Ireland* was not on sale at the bookstall:'It strikes me as curious how the books giving the opposite views are sent round so readily and abundantly to the stalls and that this penny pamphlet which has been a year in existence and would sell readily to Protestants as well as Catholics cannot get around.'

In his defence Charles Eason pointed out that they did not distribute penny pamphlets, except by special arrangement, as many did not sell well. Since they were the publishers themselves of catholic prayerbooks they could hardly be accused of a hostile attitude to catholic publications. This brought a retort from Coleman:

> As you have mentioned your publication of Catholic Prayerbooks I may say that the general feeling amongst priests is that in that matter you have got hold of a source of profit, legitimate of course but outside the natural lines of a Protestant publisher, and I have often heard remarks to that effect. The feeling is that owing to this matter especially you should exercise great fairness to Catholics.

This attitude, nationalist and triumphalist, by a figure in the censorship movement, represents not unfairly the outlook of many catholic clergy at this time. The nationalist element was as strong as the religious. As early as 15 April 1911 the *Leader* had noted that the question of objectionable papers was being raised and a boycott of shops proposed:

> Sheer anglicisation lies at the root of the matter; English civilisation, with its literature and mental outlook, is, to say the least, non-catholic, and the current literature of the present day agnostic. It is the antithesis of the Gaelic Catholic mind, with its faith and imagery....

This was an almost classic expression of the catholic view which was often to be reflected in later utterances even into the 1950s. Despite the predominantly catholic tone of the movement, protestant clergymen were on the platform at several of the original meetings (at least those in Waterford and Athlone). Indeed, there was a Protestant White Cross Association in Dublin which was concerned with the problems of literature. But even at these two meetings the press reports had hints of sectarian tension. At the meeting on 5 November 1911 which set up the Dublin Vigilance Committee, one of the speakers made it clear that the terms of reference were wider than the issue of the Sunday newspapers, and that only catholics were admitted. After the suggestion had been made that members of other denominations should be co-opted, Father MacEnerney PP, City Quay explained:

> They were not confined to the Sunday papers; they wished to stop the evil in the evening papers, which were full of rottenness. Should they confine themselves to newspapers only? A great many people read these things in the newspapers because their strength had been sapped by the low periodicals and novels. Then, were they to confine themselves to matters of purity? Were they to take no notice of newspapers which sapped the foundations of society (applause), papers which sapped the Christian feelings of man towards man, which generated hatred between class and class, and which made a hell upon earth? He thought they were just as bad (applause). From that arose a difficulty that if they brought in people of other creeds they might be members of a Rationalistic Society, who would not go along with them all the way in their object. As to the public meeting, he was afraid they had not got to that state of unity in Ireland when they could unite everybody.

In the case of correspondence between Charles Eason and the Vigilance Committee in Galway, the source of complaint in one instance was that a catholic sacrament had been referred to in 'a disrespectful manner'. In Limerick in December 1913 there was an intimation, according to a newsagent, of opposition to the *Daily Sketch* 'unless there was an improvement in a certain daily periodical which had a story in a neighbouring county with the inhabitants as if they were belonging to a low English town.' The aims of the movement emerge more significantly, in the light of what happened after 1922, when Father Cullen, head of the Pioneer movement and chief speaker at a meeting under the auspices of the Dublin Committee on 18 May 1913, said that 'one of the first things he hoped to see carried through in the new Irish Parliament was a measure constituting a censorship on the Press, and if that were accomplished, they would no longer see vile and filthy publications imported into Ireland.' The emotional atmosphere in which the movement was conducted meant that intimidation was inevitable. As early as 10 February 1912 the *Leader* reported that:

> In Waterford a priest had to strip a shop window of its picture cards, or some of them, and his lordship the bishop has instructed his clergy to read out the names of Catholic newsagents who break their pledges not to sell dirty papers. The dirty evil calls for such measures. It may happen that English law is apparently incompetent to preserve Ireland from English dirt, so Ireland must take the matter into her own hands. It may happen that a few newsagents' windows have to be broken, and the dirt extracted and publicly burned out, and as a consequence, it may be necessary for soldiers in the crusade to go to jail.

The first instance of picketing in Dublin was noted in the *Freeman's Journal* of 25 November 1912. A shop in Terenure was picketed from 9 a.m. till 3 p.m. by pickets who walked up and down outside it, and distributed handbills. The first annual report of the Dublin Committee in January 1913 referred to picketing which had taken place at some offending newsagents, and noted that 'in the near future it is hoped to perfect a system of picketing that will make the selling of pernicious publications an unprofitable trade.' Outside a shop in Dorset Street on 3 February 1913 there were wild scenes. Windows were broken and the incident culminated in the prosecution of two picketers. They had been part of a crowd of two or three hundred who had refused to leave the footpath, and insisted on giving their names and addresses in Irish. In Tralee the local committee set up intimidating pickets outside shops, and customers of one shop were asked not to buy anything there. Two newsagents were humiliated in May 1913 by having to insert apologies in the press for selling papers forbidden by the committee, and they had to undertake to sell none of the publications declared objectionable by the committee.

Throughout the campaign Eason's continued to make the papers available, asking committees to specify their objections. Where the objections were valid, Eason's corresponded with the publishers of the papers concerned to see if the objectionable feature or advertisements could be withdrawn. In some cases Charles Eason disagreed quite sharply with committees and their sweeping demands, and pointed out that the committees were undiscriminating in the very way they included acceptable as well as objectionable papers in their ban. There is little doubt that Eason's themselves were intimidated. In general they sought to meet local pressure by not exposing the more objectionable papers, and only supplying them to order. But their attitude after the episode in Limerick lacked courage and conviction, despite the official help Eason reported in a letter dated 2 December: 'I went up to the Castle, saw the Assistant Inspector General of Constabulary and arranged with him that steps would be taken to prevent such a thing occurring again.'

While he emphasised his willingness to service the London publishers, in his letters Charles Eason never disguised his own view that some of their publications did have highly objectionable features and that he shared some of the feeling in Ireland. On one occasion he had even told Fifoot, the circulation manager of the *News of the World* that it made 'unhealthy reading'. Fifoot certainly had doubts about Charles Eason's commitment to sell his paper. Eason had to give him an assurance that 'my personal expression of opinion has had no influence at all upon the conduct of the News Department, who indeed knew nothing of it.' In a letter dated 30 November Fifoot suggested to Eason that the fall-off in sales of the *News of the World* had preceded the start of the campaign, insinuating that Eason's were responsible for this. He referred fairly bluntly to the fact that the *News of the World* had so far refused to service direct parcels, and had declined offers from 'opposition wholesale agents, who are anxious to establish themselves in Ireland'. Fifoot ended his letter with an ultimatum: 'If we cannot maintain and improve our sales under present conditions, we must seek reluctantly to take other means and methods of distribution.' Charles Eason responded to this at once with a letter on 2 December in which he assured Fifoot of their best efforts, and continued: 'You can feel sure that in towns where we have bookstands the sale of your paper cannot be stopped, and our action will tend to induce agents to follow our example.' At the same time he advised Fifoot that he did not think that 'it would be wise to take any special steps to push the sale of your paper at present.'

It is easy to appreciate the intimidatory atmosphere of the time when it is recalled that late in 1912 Charles Eason corresponded with Cardinal Logue about charges made by the Cardinal in a speech in September 1912 that 'publications of a very questionable character' were on sale at the bookstalls of the Great Northern Railway. The correspondence established that this charge related to a date prior to 1900! (Cardinal Logue had been in correspondence with Charles Eason several times in the course of 1899.) However, the bookstalls left Easons vulnerable to pressure, even though Charles Eason had assured Fifoot that they were the strong point of Easons' distribution. On 30 January 1914 the Dublin Vigilance Committee wrote to the shareholders of the Great Southern and Western Railway to state that: 'It is considered that the question might be suitably raised at the meeting more especially if Messrs Eason and Son apply for a renewal of their licence to use the railway stands.' They were seeking 'support and sympathy' from the shareholders for a resolution authorising the directors of the line to remove any objectionable matter from the bookstalls. There is no evidence that this move had any effect on Easons' relations with the railway company. At the same time the railway contracts were the most jealously guarded activity of the house, and even the hint of a threat was probably more effective than the Vigilance Committee appreciated.

After 1914 the movement petered out, as far as Eason's were concerned. It was only in December 1919 that Charles Eason had a protracted correspondence with the Rev. P. O'Halloran CC of the Nenagh Committee who admonished Eason:

> It is not your view that matters but the view of the public at large, and healthy public opinion in Ireland is now thoroughly alarmed.... The Vigilance Committees throughout the country will take the action the pressing nature of the evil demands. Rest assured the matter will not end there. It cannot be disposed of by a letter setting out your 'views'. Commercialism cannot [upset?] the commandments of God.

On 12 December Father O'Halloran intimated that if Eason's did not fall in line: 'I venture to predict that you will find the result to be that it will no longer pay to keep a bookstall in Nenagh.' Illustrated papers such as *Eva, Pan* and *Tatler* were a comparatively new source of complaint. A few years later on 24 January 1925 the *Irish Catholic* commented: 'Seductive pictures in some illustrated papers are a more or less modern development which is doing a great amount of harm.' A month earlier a memorandum from Kilkenny advised that the picture on the front of *Pan* was considered 'very objectionable to a certain class — Catholic priests especially who have threatened to bring Vigilant Committee on the scene.' Charles Eason noted in a letter to Wallace, the circulating manager of Odhams Press that: 'Matters which would not have been published in newspapers twenty or thirty years ago are now freely admitted, but much more freely in England than in Ireland.'

The activity gathered pace again in the 1920s, though now inspiration was drawn from a concern with the low quality of the Sunday papers which was rising also in England. Many commentators, and not just those on the right, were disturbed at what they saw in some of the Sundays, whose circulations were now larger and were pushed more aggressively than they had been before 1914, and whose quality was at best no higher. The *New Statesman*, whose perspective was vastly different from that of Irish catholic opinion, and which did not favour censorship, wrote on 26 August 1922 about the *News of the World*:

> A rough estimate of its contents show that about fifteen columns are devoted to ordinary news, about ten columns to sport, about fifteen to serial matter, and over forty columns to reports relating to crime or divorce. About 25 out of these forty columns deal with matrimonial causes, sexual crime, and minor sexual misdemeanours, adultery, homosexuality, indecency, attempted rape, improper or criminal treatment of girl children, venereal disease and so on.

The circulation of English Sunday newspapers in Ireland expanded rapidly after 1917. The circulation in Dublin was said to have been 40,000 in 1911, and the national circulation by 1920 was probably about three times that figure. By 1926 the circulation of the *News of the World* alone was said to be 132,444 and of all the other English Sundays, 220,358.[1] In 1925 the circulation of the *News of the World* was said to be larger than that of all the Irish morning papers put together (*Irish Truth*, 6 June 1925).

It was inevitable that this growing circulation combined with the continuing low moral quality of the Sundays would lead to rising resentment. Some of this drew on the old vigilance committees where they had lingered on. The new wave of agitation owed much to the monthly magazine *Our Boys*, and in particular to its editor, Brother Craven. The magazine had been specifically founded, in 1914, by the Christian Brothers to provide healthy reading. The first signal from this new force came from Ballyhaunis, where in December 1921 a newsagent cancelled a large number of comics as well as other publications. In January 1922 *Our Boys* published a pledge taken by four newsagents in Ballyhaunis not to sell 'any publications calculated to lower the Catholic mind of the youth of the parish'. A resolution was also signed by thirty-

1 M. Adams *Censorship: the Irish experience* (Dublin, 1968), p. 28

eight newsagents in Dublin. In February 1922 the Newsagents Association passed a resolution:

> This Association as representative of the newsagents and booksellers of Ireland are quite prepared to cooperate with any movement to stop the circulation of objectionable literature and would suggest that a Committee composed of members of the Retail and Wholesale newsagents, the Vigilance Association, and the Board of Film censors be formed forthwith to take effective steps to accomplish this object.

The source of inspiration for this step is hinted at in the fact that the editor of *Our Boys* was one of the five persons to whom a copy of the resolution was sent. *Our Boys* launched a vigorous campaign, drawing up black-lists of unsuitable literature, and using Christian Brothers pupils to canvas support. Boys were organised at parish level in divisions of 12, or 24 or more, in Christ's Young Army, and their objective was, in the words of Brother Craven, 'to lend a hand to drive the damn and impure literature out of Ireland and to maintain National Virtue'. A letter in the *Evening Telegraph* on 16 June 1924 commended the use of children 'in such a manner as the devoted Christian Brothers have done in many localities.'

Judging by the evidence in Easons' files, the former vigilance committees were not active as they had been in the past. On one rare occasion in Nenagh, according to a memorandum from the local bookstall, a newsagent who had been selling Sundays on the streets had the papers seized and burned. The Vigilance Committee in Nenagh had been reconstituted in May 1923 by Rev. P. O'Halloran. Those letters of cancellation which were received in 1923, 1924 and 1925 give the impression that the campaign at that time owed more to the drive of individual clergymen than it had in the past. Eason's continued to sell Sunday papers, but direct involvement in their distribution was much smaller than formerly. In March 1922 Charles Eason wrote to Hart, the secretary of the Irish Retail Newsagents Association, who had now taken up the cause of clean literature, that while Eason's could not refuse to handle the *News of the World*, '.... at the same time we give it as little publicity as possible and though not absolutely confining the supplies to definite orders, the returns are very low.' As early as 1920 Toms, who was travelling in the south of Ireland, regarded the ban on the Sundays as much less serious to Eason's than 'the loss of the weekly illustrated papers .... [which would be] too serious a loss to run for the sake of a few 2d papers.'

In the autumn of 1924 there was a very aggressive correspondence from the command chaplain at the Curragh Training Camp, who threatened drastic action if the sale of certain named papers stocked at the Eason Curragh Shop was not dropped. When asked about the basis of some of his objections the chaplain stated that 'I have not the time nor the opportunity to go into the items that I object to.' The chaplain was able to prevail on the colonel commanding the camp to ban the papers from the outset of 1925. This was a taste of things to come. The Tuam Vigilance Committee, for instance, cast its net widely. A newsagent in Tuam in August 1925 told Easons that 'all 2d novels are stopped here — not to be got any more'. Correspondence during 1925 from places as far apart as Tipperary, Kildare and Cobh pointed to the Catholic Truth Society as the driving force. At the Catholic Truth Conference in the presence of Cardinal O'Donnell, (as reported by the *Irish Independent* on 10 October 1925), James Geoghegan KC called for the control of distribution of printed matter and for the elimination of the newsboy and the small trader selling newspapers as a sideline. The idea of government action was gaining ground, and in February 1925 the Irish Commercial Travellers Federation supported the call. On several occasions in 1925 and 1926 Frank Duff, founder of the Legion of Mary, acquired copies from Eason's of some of the publications which were considered objectionable.

It was in this context of mounting demand for interference that the Evil Literature Committee was appointed in the Dail at the beginning of 1926. Charles Eason advised Odhams Press, the publishers of the *London Mail*, on January 30 1926 that 'it would be unwise to do anything which might give a handle to the objectors at the present moment.' The findings of the committee, which were published in the spring on 1927, and which were in favour of censorship, gave a new lease of life to the agitation. The *Irish Independent* noted on May 22 1927 that 'the work of the committee on evil literature has resulted in a hardening of public opinion on the question.' The Catholic Truth Society had been increasingly active throughout 1926. When Charles Eason, in a letter in the *Irish Independent*, suggested that the papers banned in Canada could be kept out of Ireland without additional legislation, he drew down on his head a reply from the secretary of the organisation on 20 October 1926:

> Is Mr Eason not in favour of strengthening the existing law in the matter of all this objectionable literature? As one of the largest distributors of Catholic prayer-books in Ireland, I should have expected him consistently to be one of the most emphatic in favour of banning printed matter advocating foul practices condemned by the Catholic Church.

Widespread intimidation was now becoming the order of the day again, and newspaper burning once more made its appearance. When papers, including the *News of the World*, despatched to a newsagent in Kanturk were destroyed in March 1926, the Department of Justice finally reported to Eason's that the Gardaí found: '.... that they can secure no information from Mr Heffernan who does not appear to desire that any proceedings should be instituted and he is not prepared to assist the Garda in the matter.' At a Mission in Charleville in September, the Rev. Moran OMI declared with reference to an undertaking by local newsagents not to sell papers, that 'if the young men of the town had sufficient courage, they should burn the papers .... jail would be better rather than to allow such imported filth to circulate in their midst.'

The intellectual issues of censorship inevitably appealed to Charles Eason, and as illustrated in his letter to the *Irish Independent*, he was prepared to run into argument in print. Charles Eason not only had a life-long interest in the matter, but appeared before the Committee on Evil Literature himself and had submitted evidence and recommendations. A letter to his clergyman brother Benjamin on April 2 makes clear his own views on moral matters. He considered the unrestricted circulation of books dealing with birth control amongst young people as 'very pernicious' and equally felt that 'the attitude of some novels to marriage and sex relations outside marriage is very pernicious.' His submission to the Committee made it clear that he thought that voluntary action was the only complete remedy, although voluntary action in his view had a broad interpretation, and included a role for the clergy and a return to religion. He commented: 'It is obvious from what I have said that I am not in favour of absolute prohibition of sale of publications except in extreme cases', but at the same time he was in favour of the prohibition of the sale of unsuitable literature in the streets, and of the exposure of it for sale in shops. It is clear that the appointment of a censorship committee was acceptable to him, as he gave his opinions on its formation and functions. As a convinced liberal, however, he was not happy with the bill which the Government finally put before the Dail. Some disjointed notes on the bill in his hand refer to his anxiety because there was no provision for evidence being heard against a proposal to prohibit a publication, and in the case of birth control, he felt that a distinction should have been drawn between publications that habitually inserted advertisements for birth control, and those that only occasionally did so.

Charles Eason also felt very strongly about films which were based on objectionable books, particularly where an effort was made to promote the sale of the books in towns where the film was being shown. He described in a letter to T.P. O'Connor on 24 January 1917 the efforts which he himself had made in 1913 to prevent the showing of a film based on a book:

> To give a concrete case — the book *Five Nights* by Victoria Cross was filmed and the publisher, Mr John Long, sent out notices two months ahead giving a list of the towns in which the film was to be shown. I at once got a copy of the book and examined it and decided that it would be very injurious if such a book should have attention drawn to it. I first wrote to Mr Long, remonstrating, but he stated that he was not responsible as the arrangement was made by the author with the Picture Houses and that it was his business simply to sell the book. I then wrote to the London County Council and the Municipal authorities in Manchester and Birmingham and also to the Police in London. The result was that in London and in Birmingham a special exhibit of the film was arranged, and the authorities decided not to interfere with its production. I brought the matter under the notice of the Lord Mayor and the Police in Dublin and the former took the matter up and the film was not allowed to be exhibited in Dublin. I also took the matter up in Rathmines as the film was advertised to be exhibited there in one of the picture houses. The secretary of the Rathmines Council wrote to me — of course confidentially — to say that they did not think they could interfere once the licence had been granted. I contested this, pointing out that the owner of the Picture House might be warned that although the Council might not be able to prevent an exhibition of the film, yet if it were exhibited it would be considered as an act on his part which might be such a reflection on his character that the renewal of the licence might be refused. Other persons took some steps also, and the film was not exhibited in Rathmines.

During 1917 Charles Eason continued to discuss this issue with a number of people, because the question of films was then being pursued in parliament. Eason was concerned even in cases where a morally good film might help to sell the original, objectionable, book. He was nothing if not determined. In 1918 a play based on a book was to be produced in the Gaiety. Eason made representations to the Manager of the Gaiety to prevent its production, and he also sought to enlist the good offices of the Lord Mayor and the *Irish Times* and *Freeman's Journal*.

In 1926 Charles Eason recalled that 'thirty years ago we remonstrated with various publishers upon the insertion of advertisements relating to Birth Control, and succeeded in getting them excluded from certain papers.' The earliest case which survives on file was in April 1911, when Charles Eason wrote to John Dicks Ltd. regarding advertisements in a column headed 'Marriage' that 'If the paper is to be freely circulated by us it will be necessary to exclude such adverts. in future.' His action in this case would seem to have stemmed from comments in the *Leader* but his views were firm and expressed a personal outlook as well. A month later, in May 1911, still some months ahead of the 1911 newspaper campaign in Ireland, Charles Eason wrote to Carter of *Reynolds News*:

> Can we arrive at any rule for guidance in the insertion of advertisements? Would you agree that a book which offers means of procuring abortion or preventatives of conception should not be advertised? These are certainly practices hardly known in Ireland and which we desire to keep out of the country.

In the same year he was in correspondence with W.A. Coote of the London Conference of Societies interested in Public Morality about some of the problems raised by the advertising of unsuitable books. As late as September 1928 he was in correspondence with the secretary of the London Public Morality Council, to whom he sent the text of the Censorship Bill, and to whom its terms were pleasing.

Charles Eason felt that it was important that a news wholesaler should be careful not to impose his own views by the exclusion of unsuitable books altogether from the circulating library, or by a refusal to handle particular papers at all. His comments to the management of some papers were quite as blunt as those to the *News of the World*. On 25 January 1926 he wrote to Wallace of Odhams Press, publishers of the *London Mail*, which was found objectionable, to point out that feeling in Ireland was 'no doubt sometimes carried to extreme lengths, but we approve of it to a certain extent.' He had a long and revealing correspondence with George Russell (''AE''), in 1929. Eason brought to AE's attention a report on censorship in the Tralee County Library, which was receiving attention in the *Irish Statesman*. Eason thought that Russell might not have seen the report. He considered that Russell's Tralee correspondent, Sheehy, was not reliable, and he hoped that the *Irish Statesman* might 'sum up the matter in a more reasonable way than has been done hitherto'. Eason's dislike of the reporting by Sheehy was inspired by more than an objective assessment of the situation in Tralee:

> I think Mr Sheehy weakens his case very much by referring to the books of William O'Flaherty and James Joyce. There are certainly far more novels of a suitable character that should be put in the library before these. We have O'Flaherty's novels but they are very coarse,

> and I would keep them out of any local library. As to James Joyce, I need not tell you we have not got his 'Ulysses', nor have we got any other works of his.

Subsequent letters show that Eason and Russell were very far apart on the matter of censorship. Eason was not correct in relation to the accounts from Kerry. Subsequent comments by Russell himself, and the fact that the books banned by the Dean of Kerry and his committee included the *Playboy of the Western World* leave no doubt that George Russell and the *Irish Statesman* were right to express concern about what was happening in Kerry.

In November 1926 some newspapers were seized on arrival in Cobh by the Rev. Wigmore of the Cathedral. Other papers were seized by young men and burned. The atmosphere became more charged in 1927. A letter from the Drogheda branch of the Catholic Truth Society at the end of April referred to the possibility of violent action by others. A report in *The Irish Times* on 2 May 1927 related how masked men had seized some thousands of copies of eleven Sunday papers the previous day. On 8 May, five hundred weight of Sunday papers were seized and burned at Killiney station by twelve armed men. In the spring, stormy scenes took place in Cork. Newspapers, including the *News of the World*, were seized by four members of the Cork Angelic Warfare Association on 13 February 1927 and proceedings were brought against the four defendants on 16 March. A number of clergymen were in court including the Dean of the diocese as character witnesses. One of the clergy, the Rev. Barrett OP claimed that 'whatever contradicts the natural law cannot be rational; cannot claim the dignity of law; is a mere abuse.' He even admitted to similar activities himself:

> Passing up the quays a few Sundays ago I encountered a youth who was selling Sunday papers. I examined the papers; detached the copies of the *News of the World* and dropped them into the Lee — the only congenial place for such filth. There was no violence ....we are proud of the Civic Guards. We know that there are a few among them who have much of the mentality of the Black and Tans.... Yet in this case, they are asked to protect the circulation of these infamous papers. And what is that but to create crime?

The clerical response to the court case was to arrange a monster meeting in Grand Parade on 20 March, at which the Dean read a letter from the Bishop. The first resolution was moved by J.J. Walsh, Minister for Posts and Telegraphs, and called for the extension of the proposed controls to native newspapers.

Brother Craven's campaign as editor of *Our Boys* reached its peak in 1927. In the spring he had no less than 100,000 leaflets printed, and in the *Irish Independent* of 11 October 1927 he took a whole front page advertisement entitled 'Satan, Smut & Co'. directed against 'pamphlets and newspapers, any of which would be quite sufficient to change an angel into a devil'. The advertisement took particular exception to what was described as a 'blasphemous Christmas carol' and it reported one of Brother Craven's well-published exploits: 'We considered it so devilish that we sent our messengers on bicycles to buy up every copy that could be found in the city, and had them publicly burned outside the office door. The whole pile cost £4 10s and a gallon of petrol.'

Some seizures of newspapers continued in 1928. A less violent type of action was also in evidence. The *Irish Statesman* of 25 August 1928 recalled 'the attempts in Dundalk and Cork to prevent the poster of a nude baby reaching for soap being used as an advertisement, and the solemn way in which the bill-posters went to paint breeches on the baby, though in every household in the country the washing of nude babies is a daily occurrence.' Earlier in the year in a repeat of the experience at the Curragh bookstall, the Kilkenny barracks cancelled its order from the Eason bookstall. As the clerk reported on April 7: 'This must be the work of Rev. Father Drea who is capable of influencing a new staff of officers and some of the old officers left. This is finishing what he undertook about three months about turning out any boy in books dealt with by you . . . .'

It was in this atmosphere that the Censorship Act was discussed and finally passed in 1929. The Committee on Evil Literature had been sweeping in its report, not only proposing a committee to advise the minister on banning, but recommending also extensive powers of seizure and dealing with a wide range of publications: books, papers and magazines. A report on 10 September 1928 in *The Irish Times* claimed that: 'With the exception of Mr Cosgrave himself and Mr Fitzgerald, his Minister of Defence, it is understood that the entire cabinet hate the bill. . . '. An indication of this lack of enthusiasm in the cabinet can be seen in the fact that Patrick Hogan, the Minister for Agriculture, was a critic of the bill in the Dail debate. However the suggestion of widespread prohibition had been implicit in the campaign, and at times explicit. Unlike the campaign in 1911, the campaign in the 1920s both by the Christian Brothers and by the Catholic Truth Society was not confined to censorship of Sunday papers. It was unlikely that a cabinet would wish to go against widespread public opinion. Apart from *The Irish Times*, AE's *Irish*

Statesman was the only Irish paper to hold out against the bill, and it was not typical or representative. The *Irish Statesman* proclaimed that 'we will have book-leggers where they [i.e. Americans] have boot-leggers.' According to the *New Statesman* on 1 September 1928 the ministers of the cabinet were not anxious to qualify their stand, in case they might give de Valera an opportunity of demanding stronger measures than they proposed to take. This was a point of substance in assessing the cabinet's action. As *The Times* of London pointed out on 14 September 'one fact, however, we must recognise. The proposed legislation is extremely popular in Ireland.' An editorial in *The Irish Times* on 29 September noted:

> Ministers are exceedingly unhappy about this bill. Most of them dislike it; they are afraid of the educated criticism which it will provoke and of the abuses it must engender; the bill has been redrafted a dozen times. Nevertheless, they are unable to resist the peculiarly effective pressure which is being put upon them by various religious organisations. The Fianna Fáil party will support the bill and even may demand its prohibitions shall be strengthened.

After the passing of the Censorship Act, and the setting up of the first Censorship Board, day-to-day running of censorship matters fell to Robert Eason, who was in regular contact with the Secretary of the Board. Despite his decreasing involvement in the business in the 1920s, Charles Eason had retained a close interest in this issue throughout the decade, and it was only in the 1930s that J.C.M. Eason became the final arbiter. His attitude to censorship was quite different to that of his father. He committed no views to paper, and was not inclined to waste his own time, or that of others, on the consideration of borderline cases, where he tended to advise against distribution. He followed the new censorship law carefully, and cooperated faithfully with the Department of Justice. At the same time he advised publishers pragmatically on the situation affecting their publications. Unlike his father, he never let his personal views on censorship obtrude in his business letters. In a pragmatic fashion he could even see the benefits of the Act which removed the responsibility from a private firm and he made no bones about expressing this view. On one occasion only J. C. M. Eason expressed his personal views on censorship in public. In February 1947 his brother Keith Eason was the guest chairman at a debate of the College Historical Society in Trinity College, Dublin. The subject of the debate was censorship. In a subsequent report on the debate, Keith Eason was quoted as saying, somewhat recklessly, that the Censorship Board was 'useless and was damaging to the reputation of the country'. This became the subject of an editorial in the *Evening Herald* the following day, and drew a reply from J.C.M. Eason in the next issue in which he gave a sharp rebuttal to Keith Eason's remarks:

> The policy of this firm is and has been to accept the working of the Censorship Act without question and as necessary in principle. We have cooperated with the Committee in achieving rapid and effective application of its decisions.
>
> It has prevented the circulation of many publications and books which are wholly objectionable. Prior to its operation we had abstained from handling many such, but found that individual action was too limited in its effect and was open to criticism in many directions.

While he complied loyally with the Act, there is one indication that J.C.M. Eason was less than happy with the situation. This is in a private note, which refers to books rather than magazines, that appears to refer to 1942. The note is entitled 'Object — secure wise administration of Act':

> Ministry of Justice has erred.
> Books are not borderline cases.
> Many books would not have been banned if examined properly.
> Flaws are in regulations.
> Marking of passages prejudices its examinations
> may lead to nothing else being read.
> Books listed on Register suggests that other reasons than
> prescribed have been really the cause of banning.

Keith Eason's rather naive intervention in fact gave voice to some misgivings felt within the house.

From the time it came into operation the Censorship Act posed many practical problems for the house. For one thing it meant a vast amount of correspondence both with the Department of Justice and with publishers. It also meant accepting losses when newspapers or popular periodicals were banned. The banning of some of the women's periodicals with large circulations in October/November 1957 meant a loss at trade prices of at least £6,000 in turnover. Care had also to be taken that books which had been banned by the Censorship Board should not be sold in Eason's shops or bookstalls or distributed wholesale to retail booksellers and newsagents. This task proved so formidable that over a number of years Eason's compiled and printed their own lists of books which had been banned by the Board.

On occasion, when only a single article was the source of offence, it was cut out of the magazines by Eason's. This procedure was rarely resorted to and was scarcely satisfactory as it roused the anger of both the reader and the publisher. For the wholesale news department, distributing newspapers and periodicals, and for the wholesale and retail book business of the firm, censorship was one of the facts of life which added to administrative costs and took up a great deal of time for the service management of the business. From the start however both through Easons' readiness to cooperate and the straightforward attitude of the officials in the Department of Justice, a fairly satisfactory working relationship was established. As early as 12 July 1931 the Secretary of the Department of Justice wrote to Eason that: 'The Minister appreciates the assistance which you have given in connection with the administration of the Censorship of Publications Act. The Minister is anxious that the enforcement of the Act should involve as little inconvenience as possible to wholesalers.' In the early stages Charles Eason had suggested some informality in handling periodicals, and his suggestion was taken up in a letter of 14 June 1930:

> Some time ago you suggested that in cases in which the Censorship of Publications Board found periodicals to contain some objectionable matter it might be possible, if you were informed unofficially of the facts, that you might be in a position to take the matter up with the Publishers and to secure the removal of the offending matter.

The Censorship Board was prepared not to proceed against them if assurances could be obtained that the offending matter would not appear in future. This applied in particular to advertisements for birth control and literature advocating family planning, advertisements which frequently appeared among the advertising matter in publications that were otherwise perfectly harmless. In fact these advertisements were not in themselves a major source of revenue to journals, and English periodicals circulating in Ireland were in many instances quite ready to take up the advice not to publish them. Even *John Bull* in November 1930 was prepared to arrange to drop all advertisements relating to 'sex and birth control'. The *Spectator* had an Irish circulation of only 200 copies through Eason's, plus a few direct postal copies. In response to complaints from the Department of Justice about advertisements for Marie Stopes' books, it gave an undertaking to Eason's on 29 April 1931 as they 'very much value our Irish circulation'. A month later Roche, the assistant secretary of the Department of Justice wrote to Eason referring to the advertisement of a book, not by Stopes, entitled *The facts of life*, and again the *Spectator* 'gladly' provided an undertaking. In the previous year *Pearson's Weekly* consulted Easons on their own initiative and excluded doubtful advertisements. Throughout the 1930s this point came up again and again, and many English publishers were anxious to conform to the Act. Roche's attitude, as set out on 2 June 1938, was as cooperative as it had been at an earlier date: 'I am anxious if at all possible to avoid referring the complaints to the Board and I should be glad if the publishers of these periodicals could give an undertaking that similar matter will not appear in the editions sold here. Do you think this could be arranged?'

From the outset the Sundays and some weeklies, which had been the cause of so much of the agitation in the preceding two decades, were in conflict with the new law. By June 1930 three Sunday papers, *News of the World*, *Empire News* and *People*, and one weekly, *Thomson's Weekly News*, had been banned. Two of the papers sent representatives across to see the Minister and the Censorship Board, and as a result the ban was revoked on the *People* and the *Empire News*. According to J.C.M. Eason in a letter of 4 July to Bezant, the circulation manager of the *News of the World*, this step was 'very severely commented on in certain quarters here.' Earlier in a letter to Bezant on 11 June, J.C.M. Eason had commented that 'considering the history of the whole movement I think it would have been a very extraordinary situation if the *News of the World* had escaped. Rightly or wrongly your paper was selected for years as target of attack.' The *News of the World* sent a representative to Ireland to interview the new Minister for Justice.

Eason's do not seem to have been closely involved in arranging any of these meetings. This reflects the fact that Easons' involvement in the distribution on Sundays was small as more efficient transport arrangements had made it possible to replace the weekly editions published on Fridays with the Sundays, throughout the Irish market. This fact enabled the specialists in the wholesale distribution on Sunday newspapers to expand their business, which had been quite limited as long as weekly editions predominated. Few figures survive, and the only precise ones relate to Easons' requirements in 1930: 4,644 copies of *Thomson's Weekly News* and 176 quires (4,752 copies) of the *News of the World*.

The first ban was for a period of three months. If banned a second time, the ban became permanent unless revoked by the Minister, and until 1946 no provision for appeal existed. The *News of the World* was promptly banned again when it reappeared in September 1930. *Thomson's Weekly News*, of which Easons distributed over 4,000 copies, was published by D.C. Thomson of Dundee, and from the outset this publisher refused as a matter of principle to make any concessions to the Censorship Board.

Although the first ban on *Thomson's Weekly News* expired, the publisher remained deaf to all entreaties by Eason's to resume supplies. This refusal continued even after the introduction of the Censorship Appeal Board in 1946, and it was not until the publication had changed its name to *Weekly News* that its distribution was resumed. Another paper, *World's Pictorial News,* was banned for an excessive coverage of crime, and Charles Eason advised the publishers, Allied Newspapers, on 22 May 1930 that during an interview at the Department of Justice:

> I saw at the office the copies of the *World's Pictorial News* which had been submitted for censoring, and I noticed at once how much the items relating to crime had been reduced in recent weeks, but I also noticed that articles on 'Mormonism' had been pencilled. Of course this does not necessarily mean that they are counted as 'crime' but it just shows that the term 'crime' requires to be somewhat widely interpreted. And I think it would be well for you to be specially cautious about general items for a few weeks at any rate.

Books of course could be seized by the Customs under an 1876 Act, and in 1934 there was a good deal of complaint or comment about excessive interference with book consignments at the ports and of variations between one port and another. Croker's, a newsagent and bookseller in Waterford, were irate about what appeared to be an excessively officious officer in Waterford, and the issue was also aired in the Senate by Sir John Keane. J.C.M. Eason commented, in a letter of 8 June 1934 to both Croker and Sir John Keane, that Easons' own experience had been satisfactory: 'Our report shows that in two years we have only had 8 cases; in one, the books were released; in six they were subsequently banned; in one case the consignment was not intended for us, or indeed the Free State at all, and it was reshipped to its proper destination.' Eason reminded Croker that in Dublin they had eight or nine members in the Booksellers Association who had not experienced trouble. Croker's complaints from Waterford and the raising of the matter by Sir John Keane seem to have been related, and in fact Sir John Keane obtained his knowledge of the legal position from Eason. This correspondence shows Eason's precise, fair and careful mind at its best, and his ability to take in all aspects of a complicated matter. Neither Croker nor Keane had precisely the same approach, and in fact Keane does not seem to have heeded Eason's advice in the terms in which he raised the issue in the Senate.

In 1937 the *News of the World,* which now boasted a circulation of over three million, decided to return to the Irish market, and sought J.C.M.

Eason's advice. It is a measure of Easons' standing in the Irish market that not only did they decide to consult Eason's (in contrast to 1930 when the London papers acted on their own) but they were guided by him, and also proposed making all the distribution arrangements through Eason's. Through 'being fortunate in being able to interview a friend', Eason was able to advise them on 24 September 1937:

> Write to the Secretary of the Minister for Justice stating that you contemplate publishing a newspaper called the 'Saturday News of the World' Irish Free State Edition, that you realise that while there is no prohibition on a paper of such a name, you do not wish to take a purely legalistic view of the matter and you think it better to approach the Minister, advise him of your intentions and ask whether you are not right in assuming that there is no prohibition on such a paper.... Quite privately, I may say I derived the impression that there is a preparedness after seven years' prohibition to give you an opening, but I think it would be preferred that the prohibition order should not have to be formally revoked, and that the description of this paper with a new title would enable those who are willing to give you the chance to defend your position against criticism because there undoubtedly will be some people who will raise questions.

Eason himself had an interview with the Secretary of the Department and on 5 October 1937 the news of a favourable decision was conveyed to him. A proof of the heading of the new edition, a point which had been heavily emphasised, was submitted later to the Secretary and approved.

At the end of the 1930s a new feature was the emergence of general circulation illustrated periodicals such as *Illustrated* and *Picture Post*. These were profusely illustrated, and as a result of their choice of pictures they were liable to run foul of the law. They raised prickly issues which had come up previously and more acutely in the case of *Photography*. On 16 May 1938 the Department of Justice had written that:

> When recommending that this periodical should be prohibited the Censorship of Publications Board requested the Minister to inform the proprietors of *Photography* that it is with the greatest reluctance that the Board recommended this publication for prohibition. The Board recognised the artistic and technical excellence of *Photography* but were of opinion that the space and attention given to the female nude was altogether out of proportion to the position which this branch of photography occupies.

When the ban expired Eason sought the opinion of Roche of the

Department of Justice on the August and September issues. Roche noted that the magazine had tried to carry out the suggestions of the Board and that 'studies of the female nude are almost completely absent', but the pragmatic and experienced Eason noted that he did not propose to continue importation.

In the case of *Picture Post*, the *Irish Catholic* was quick to note that 'we were more than usually alarmed when we had occasion to note the vulgarity and suggestiveness of the illustrations which appeared in it almost every week' and on 16 November 1939 called for the banning of *Picture Post*. The following month it was banned. As 26,000 copies were normally sold each week, Eason's tried without success to have the next issue distributed subject to the examination of the advance copy. Although it was the photographs in *Picture Post* which caught the attention of the Censorship Board, the *Irish Catholic*, which had led the campaign against it, also objected to articles in it by H.G. Wells which were critical of the Catholic Church and of Ireland. The issue of *Picture Post* of 13 July 1940 distributed in England ran a feature headed WE ARE BANNED IN IRELAND, and declared: 'that the Eire authorities should now ban *Picture Post* without having the courage to admit the true reason for the ban seems to us the heaviest blow they could strike at their own country.'

Distribution was resumed when the ban expired, and for some time *Picture Post* was sufficiently careful to avoid trouble. However in 1948 a new problem arose. An issue in June carried an article SHOULD A FAMILY BE PLANNED? which Easons were advised 'advocated' contraception within the terms of the 1929 Censorship Act, so that the article was *per se* illegal, quite apart from the fact that it rendered the publication as a whole liable to be banned. In the face of this obvious dilemma, which required a quick decision, Eason's decided that the lesser evil was to remove the offending article and distribute the publication. The publishers expressed the sharpest condemnation of Easons' action, and in a subsequent issue ran a short feature article headed MUTILATED COPIES IN EIRE. Nevertheless they did print a letter from Eason's, whom they described as 'the firm mainly responsible for the distribution of *Picture Post* in Eire', explaining the legal position. In Easons' view the publishers of *Picture Post* either did not recognise, or did not want to recognise the legal constraints, and Eason reiterated this point in a letter to the circulation manager of *Picture Post* on 28 June 1948: 'I still feel that you do not grasp the significance of the reference to contraception: there can be no question of anything doubtful in that matter; it is definitely prohibited and must be excluded if you want circulation here.' In 1949 *Picture Post* introduced an Export Edition which according to J.C.M. Eason's note 'represents effort of editor to curtail features which might be objected to: we await result with some element of doubt as to the effectiveness of the policy. Not wholehearted enough.' The problems were not too long in arriving. A memorandum from Robert Eason to J.C.M. Eason on 22 June 1951 informed him that: 'I spoke to Mr R. Boyd of Hultons on the 'phone. He told me next week's issue of *Picture Post* contained a two paged feature entitled BEHIND THE BEADED CURTAIN. He said that the two pages consisted largely of pictures of nudes. The feature dealt with the subject of 'Life in a Harem'.' In fact one of the pictures was an Ingres painting, and by later standards the whole could hardly be considered serious. Given the importance attached to nudes and the record of *Picture Post*, the publishers decided to avoid possible difficulties and did not send the issue to Ireland.

The reasons for banning were often vaguely expressed, and calculated to bring censorship into disrepute. *Exchange and Mart* was banned in 1930 on the grounds that it had 'usually or frequently been indecent'. This led J.C.M. Eason to protest that there must have been 'some mistake in assigning as a reason that the paper was generally indecent', as the inclusion of advertisements for contraception in an otherwise unobjectionable journal could not justifiably be so described. When *Modern Woman* was banned in June 1954 Robert Eason could only get vague grounds for the decision:

> So far as I could learn, the objection to *Modern Woman* was mainly on account of the stories which were described as the general kind of 'triangle stuff'. The Secretary of the Censorship Board also referred to the 'picture of the He-man', also to a feature regarding Bathing Suits. He may be referring to a picture on page 21 of the July issue and to pictures on page 41 of the July issue.

At this point censorship verged on the lunatic.

It is generally believed that the Board acted largely on books referred to it by the customs officers. Easons' experience in Dublin suggests that customs interference was minimal, and J.C.M. Eason's view, as conveyed to Colonel Lawson of the *Daily Telegraph* on 10 June 1938 was that 'generally speaking I would assure you that we have found the official attitude here helpful — not obstructive and with an appreciation of the difficulties involved.' Adams suggests that the Council of Action on Censorship (1942-4) were incorrect in regarding the Secretary of the Board as responsible for many of the complaints.[2] However, a press report of

2 Adams, op. cit. p. 235 (note 5)

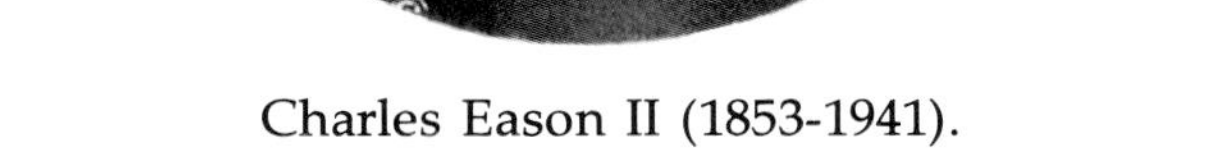

Charles Eason II (1853-1941).

Albert Brunton (1868-1921).

Above: The Board in 1936. *From left:* J. C. M. Eason, W. M. Calwell, Charles Eason II, Keith Eason, Fred Eason. *Below:* The Amiens Street Station bookstall in 1928.

ADVERTISING
ON DELIVERY VANS

These smart little Delivery Vans may be seen daily in all the principal streets of Dublin and Belfast. Each Van is fitted to carry three Contents Bills—one at the side and two at the back—also a display board on top to carry a Streamer, size 5 ft. 4 ins. x $7\frac{1}{2}$ ins.

RATES for Contents Bills are 5/- each per week, and for Streamer spaces 7/6 each per week, less 10 per cent. discount for three months' order and 20 per cent. for 6 months, or longer.

Only Publishers' advertisements are accepted for these Vans.

EASONS
17 DONEGALL STREET
BELFAST

BROADCASTS ALL DAY

Above: The Belfast market was extremely competitive in the 1930s, and every asset was used to its fullest extent. *Top right:* The news lay-up room in 1951. *Bottom right:* The wholesale book department in 1951.

PRAYER BOOKS

Above: J. C. M. Eason (1880-1976) was President of the Dublin Chamber of Commerce in 1927. *Top right:* The Cork No. 1 bookstall in the 1950s. *Bottom right:* The Board in 1970. *Back row:* F. Nixon, J. R. O'Donnell, W. H. Clarke*, E. B. Walmsley*. *Front row:* E. J. Kelliher*, J. A. Walmsley (Chairman), R. B. Eason. (* denotes subsequently Chairman of the Board.)

GLORIOUS FULL COLOUR
ILLUSTRATED
EVERY WEDNESDAY
PLATFORM Nº2
EASON & SON. Ltd. DUBLIN
PLATFORMS Nos 3 & 4
The Listener
THE POLICE AND THE PUBLIC
RADIO PROGRAMMES
RE BBC AFN
LUXEMBOURG
TIMES PICTORIAL
WOMANS LIFE
4d
EVENING PRESS

The modern front of the O'Connell Street shop, with the new clock, erected to mark the Dublin Millennium.

20 October 1942 of evidence given by Roche, now Secretary of the Department of Justice before the Public Accounts Committee stated that;

> The Board .... in nearly every case acted on its own initiative in the banning of books. The Secretary had access to a big circulating library and he brought books to the notice of the Board.... Customs officers occasionally and perhaps some particular customs officers more than others, hold up books and refer them to the Board.

The Censorship Board maintained no contacts with the Home Office or other British agencies.[3] Its complacency was all the greater, because its censorship was even on its own terms no more effective than the action of its secretary. The consequence was that in default of such action quite unsuitable publications could circulate readily. When the English National Association of Wholesalers formed a committee to deal with and ban undesirable literature (with Home Office backing to prosecute) in England, a situation arose where publications liable to prosecution in England were being distributed by Eason's and other wholesalers in Ireland. This was brought to J.C.M. Eason's attention early in 1938 through W.H. Smith's and he then moved to get the cooperation of the other Irish wholesale houses, the Dublin Wholesale Newsagency and Porter's in Belfast, so that the Irish wholesalers would cease to handle such publications.

Where birth control was concerned, all advocacy was illegal, and there was no discretion for the distributor as to how to act, or for the Board, if the publication came before it, in deciding to ban it. This explains the extreme caution of Eason's, who were quick to act for fear of prosecution. The case involving the excision of pages from *Picture Post* was an incident which achieved some notoriety in 1948, and the problem came up again from time to time. In 1958 a member of the firm noticed that an article in *Everywoman* could be construed as a possible contravention of section 16 of the 1929 Act which prohibited the publishing, selling or distribution of publications advocating contraception. Following consultation with the publishers, the 2,000 copies distributed were recalled so that the pages in question could be removed. The essence of the problem was that the distributor had to take quick action one way or another and the legal advice was to act cautiously even where fair comment was involved. Easons' solicitor advised them in May 1963 in regard to an article in the *Saturday Evening Post* that:

> The article in my opinion is a well balanced carefully considered article from a medical point of view, but I fear that technically speaking it

3 Adams, op. cit. p. 235 (note 4)

> contravenes the provisions of Section 16 of the Censorship of Publications Act 1929, though I cannot see any reasonably minded person objecting to it or claiming that it advocates the unnatural prevention of conception. It is, as the article endeavours to point out, a planning article to guide married people on family planning. It is not, in my view, an attempt to alter the course of nature by unnatural means but rather to guide families. It makes the strong point, which I think is taken by any body of christian people, not Catholics alone, i.e. that the primary purpose of marriage is not the creation of children but the creation and education of children. Be that as it may, my view is that you should withhold publication.

Within the same week he gave similar advice in regard to an article in *Life*.

The most famous of all the incidents involving reference to birth control concerned the issue of 31 March 1956 of the *Observer*. The non-distribution of this issue led to a violent and protracted controversy in Ireland, and at the time it was unclear what exactly had happened. The *Observer* noted the following week that 'responsibility has been disclaimed by every official quarter.' In *The Irish Times* and in the correspondence about the matter the suggestion was made that it may have been impounded illegally either by the Customs, or by the exercise of their powers under the 1876 Act relating to material which was indecent or obscene. The *Observer* raised the question; 'Could the answer be that the trade would not handle the papers?' and went on to dismiss that explanation at once: 'The trade so far as it will speak at all insists that the answer lies with the customs authorities.' In his book on censorship Michael Adams concluded that 'the ins and outs of this curious affair are still a closed book', but felt that the balance of probability lay with Sean Ó Faoláin's conclusion at a meeting in the Mansion House organised by the Irish Association of Civil Liberty that the distributors (Kirwan's Sunday Wholesale Newsagency) had decided not to distribute the issue.[4] Seven months afterwards, in November, J.C.M. Eason wrote a resumé of the episode 'as it is desirable to have a record of what took place.'

> It was known on the 25th March that the next article (in a series on 'Sex and Society') was to be by Mrs Joan Malleson and that it would deal with Birth Control. On account of the authoress it was considered most likely that the article would cause trouble since it would infringe the sections of the Censorship Act of 1929, part IV, by advocating the use of contraceptives.

4 Adams, op. cit. pp. 140-145

On some day during the week Mr Kirwan, who acts as Importing Agent for the *Observer* received some information regarding the contents of the articles. On some day during the week Mrs Stanley, Chairman of the Newsagents' Association, had knowledge of the impending article, and at some date the Censorship Office was communicated with, by either or both of these parties.

On all these points our information was largely secondhand and on the Thursday Mr Kirwan did advise Mr R.B. Eason of what was impending and asked for some advice. Without knowledge of the article it would be impossible to give any advice.

What is quite obscure is the extent to which Mr Kirwan really instructed the *Observer* Editor as to the legal position here. Unless the *Observer* deliberately misrepresented its position it had no knowledge at that time, or even later, of the existence of part IV of the Censorship Act.

On the Sunday morning when the paper arrived at Collinstown Mr Kirwan obtained a copy before accepting delivery. It is understood that he communicated with other people, possibly the Censorship Office, as to the appropriate action, and he refused to take delivery.

Comments in the newspapers, not excepting the *Observer* itself, seemed deliberately confusing. An article as late as April 7 referred to the Censorship Board, but in fact the Censorship Board was not involved.

There is a high degree of probability that the following factors tended to increase the amount of publicity to which this incident gave rise:

(a) Mr Kirwan was (perhaps understandably) very reticent as to why he did not take delivery.

(b) The action which led to the stoppage appeared to originate with Mrs Stanley, who was a member of the League of Decency.

(c) The *Irish Times* in its comments may have been influenced by its editorial connection with the *Observer* as its Dublin representative.

(d) The confusion between the regular course of banning under the Censorship Act which takes place under Part I partly arises because the existing Act is not comprehensive and does not repeat parts of the earlier Act including Part IV of 1929.[5] There is a difference of

5 The Censorship of Publications Act 1946 was the most up-to-date act relating to censorship, but although most of the provisions of the preceding Act, the Censorship of Publications Act 1929, including section 16, were not repealed, their terms were not repeated or referred to in the later Act.

> opinion regarding whether the article infringed sections of Part IV of the Act, but only a few people seemed disposed to argue on those grounds.

J.C.M. Eason's reference to section 16 of the 1929 Act is crucial to an understanding of this episode. Few of the parties in the controversy seem to have appreciated its mandatory character. Eason, on the other hand, had explained this to British publishers time and time again since the beginning of censorship. He always took its character to be mandatory in its application to Eason's. Over the years many possible episodes had been avoided by prompt action on the part of the firm, and by its advice to publishers about the legal situation. J.C.M. Eason could recall no parallel to the *Observer* incident apart from one involving the *Sunday Times* in December 1931:

> On that occasion the police seized copies of the offending paper: took them from the newsagents: prosecuted them, but no punishment was inflicted for everything pointed to the fact that the newsagents were ignorant. In that respect it differs entirely from the *Observer* case, where there was a wide range of knowledge regarding the probability of trouble under the act, which meant that few important newsagents — certainly not Mr Kirwan or ourselves in so far as we were selling it at Waterford or at the Retail — could have pleaded ignorance.

Seizure by the police was involved in the 1931 case. Such powers would have been under the 1876 Act, as the Censorship Acts 1929 and 1946 conveyed no powers to seize periodicals as opposed to books. The absence of confusion about the matter in the trade (as opposed to the gross confusion evident in the media and among critics) and the absence of other seizures, particularly bearing in mind the large number of periodicals which touched on forbidden topics or were banned, is in at least some measure a result of vigilance on the part of Eason's. Without such vigilance, and the caution that went with it, the Censorship Board's work would have been more difficult, and the public controversy engendered by the act would have been even more confused. Michael Adams noted that 'birth control censorship has never been a major issue' and that 'even in the decade after the passing of this Act (1929) comment and controversy about this question are extremely difficult to find'.[6] Behind the scenes, as far as periodicals were concerned, questions as to what advocated birth control took up more of J.C.M. Eason's time than the other aspects of censorship, and presented the most delicate issues.

Some minor incidents occurred which did not receive any public

6 Adams, op. cit. pp. 138 and 145

attention and which made it clear to Eason's, although not to the public, that the Customs did at times use a narrow definition of the term 'obscene or indecent', in seizing publications which contained anything relating to birth control. In June 1935 when the *Small Trader* was seized, Eason protested to the Department of Justice:

> The action taken by the Customs Officer at Rosslare raises an issue which seems to me of some importance, and I was wondering whether it comes within your jurisdiction. It implies a definite clash between two Departments and it certainly makes our position more difficult. It seems to me that the Rosslare Officer must surely know that the Censorship Board deals with such matters as these.

The reply to this letter from the Department left no doubt that such seizures were tolerated by the Department: 'As regards the detention of the periodical by the Customs it is usual for the Customs Authorities to hold up books or periodicals which seem prima facie to be indecent, or to advocate birth control, so that an authoritative decision may be obtained from the Board.'

The unequivocal support of the Department of Justice for such steps significantly enlarged the scope of the 1929 Act in practice, and it was a further justification of the caution which distributors had to observe. The comparative secrecy in which such action was taken was a basic reason for the confusion evident in the 1956 controversy.

Censorship was a controversial issue, both because some of its rationale could be disputed, and because of the way in which the Censorship Board operated. The point raised by Eason in 1935 touched on a real point of principle. The failure of the Board to advance adequate grounds for action against inoffensive publications, and the too ready refuge in the 1876 Act when the Censorship Act itself did not provide scope for action, were factors which tended to discredit censorship in the public eye. The difficulty of assessing its work is that its decisions covered a wide range of publications from the most corrupting to the most trivial.

The real key to the decisions of the Board lay in the stature and independence of the men appointed to it, and on that score it must surely be regarded as having been deficient from the outset. When the writer 'Lynn Doyle' (Leslie A. Montgomery) was appointed in 1937 the other members refused to sit on the Board with him until he withdrew publicly charges he had made earlier against the Board.[7] He did not even take up office before resigning. The Board had been long given to defending itself against criticism in a self-righteous manner, and on one occasion

7 Adams, op. cit. p. 73

even threatened a newspaper with libel.[8] This is in itself an indictment of the calibre of the membership. A new appointee in 1949 resigned after six months.[9] The biggest resignation debacle in the history of the Board in 1957 led to a reconstruction of the Board. As Michael Adams has noted the results were that: 'The attitude of mind of the Board seemed to be quite new .... one could say that they regarded their task in the same way as a British or French Board would have regarded it: as one of making it difficult for the average person to read books which were pornographic and had no literary merit.'[10] The outcome of the collapse was a more liberal regime, which took censorship out of the realm of public contention. This meant effectively that censorship ceased to pose serious problems for Eason's. But for thirty years it had posed many serious problems, and entailed much extra work. The results of this work were reflected in the publication for the trade by Robert Eason of Easons' list of banned books, which was relied on by the Censorship Board itself. By their continued attention to the mandatory requirement not to circulate literature advocating contraception, Eason's had played a vital role in making the Censorship Act workable. They prevented the public controversy and confusion which could arise if literature likely to create offence under the Act were not detected before distribution. The controversy that was occasioned by the issue of the *Observer* of 31 March 1956 revealed the potential for confusion that clause 16 of the 1929 Act contained.

With the possible exception of the pharmaceutical industry, publishing and news wholesaling are unique in the ethical issues associated with the products they sell. Censorship, at first self-imposed and later increasingly administrated by the enforcement of new or existing laws, posed a range of problems. In the Irish case the wholesaler found himself in a central position, required to observe the law, and at the same time one of the vehicles for its efficient administration. Attitudes too reflected sensitively attitudes in society. A growing body of concern from 1911 onwards was followed by very strict legislation in 1929. Later the discrediting of existing censorship and more liberal attitudes in society were followed by distinctly more liberal attitudes on the part of the Board from the end of the 1950s. From that time, censorship ceased to occupy the large part in the day to day affairs of the company which it had held over the preceding thirty years.

8 Adams, op. cit. pp 136-8
9 Adams, op. cit. p. 117
10 Adams, op. cit. p. 122

Chapter 14 From Paternalism to Unionisation 1880-1920

BY JANUARY 1891 THE TOTAL NUMBER of Easons' employees in the Dublin house, excluding bookstall staff, was 209, up from 175 in December 1886. However this growth was not evenly spread over the firm. Two-thirds of the increase was due to recruitment into the factory. In 1886, factory employees amounted to 33; by 1891 there were 56. The rest of the house hardly grew at all between 1886 and 1891. In the 1890s growth resumed, and between January 1891 and July 1897 the numbers grew from 209 to 262, and by January 1901 they had increased to 311.

These figures do not include the Belfast house, which had started in 1868. The number there remained small, and the staff numbered only 18 in 1873, and 17 in 1896. The Belfast figures do not include railway advertising staff stationed in Belfast who were part of the Dublin division. The number involved around 1900 was four. Between 1895 and 1915 staff numbers grew rapidly in Dublin, in Belfast, in the factory and in the bookstalls (see Table 22).

TABLE 22 *Number of Employees 1896, 1907 and 1915*

	1896	1907	1915
Dublin, general staff	181	229	307
Dublin, factory	69	116	112
Belfast	17	12	54
Bookstalls	96	na	195
Total number of employees	363	na	668

The impetus to growth was nearly spent by 1915. In Dublin, for instance, excluding the factory, and the new staff dealing with motors, the total number of employees in 1925 was 354. Thereafter there was little change in the number of staff until recent times. In particular, the run-down of the factory and then of the bookstalls prevented any rise in overall staff numbers in the Dublin house.

The structure of the company in 1900 was much as it had been in 1875 (see Table 23). The wholesale functions were divided into departments for news, books and stationery: the factory handled both printing and stationery manufacture: other departments included the Retail, which included the newspaper advertising business, and the two railway departments, bookstalls and advertising. The Belfast house was always counted separately.

TABLE 23 *Structure of the Company c.1900*

Department	*Managers*	*Departmental Manager*
Wholesale	McDowell, Brunton	
— News		Fitzgerald
— Stationery	F.T. Eason	
— Books		Stephen
Factory	Coghill	
— Printing		
— Stationery		
Railway	Ruthven	
— Bookstalls	W.W. Eason	
— Advertising		Stokes
Retail	Digges	
— Shop		
— Advertising		
Prayer-books		Miss Byrne
Accounts	Hallett, Butler	
— Cashier		(Butler)
— Accounts		C.M. Brown

The key department was that of Wholesale News, from which the long-serving James Dignam retired in 1893 after eighteen years as head. He was eventually succeeded by William McDowell who was largely responsible for the growth of the wholesale division in the 1900s, and for the increase in the practice of direct purchase from publishers rather than through W.H. Smith's. In J.C.M. Eason's later recollection, McDowell was heartbroken by the fire in 1916 and retired on pension later that year. He seems to have lived on into the 1920s. H.C. Harris, who had entered the firm in 1891, became manager in 1916. He had the distinction of serving under all three preceding heads of News. The profile of him in *Eason's monthly bulletin* in January 1926 noted that 'he takes great interest in musical matters, is a vocalist of ability, and a member of one of our leading Dublin church choirs'.

Philip Brown, who had been recruited in 1909, became head of the wholesale news department in 1933, and died in 1956. His coming to the headship of a department was a significant event in itself. Most departmental heads at the time were protestant, but in fact Eason's recruitment was liberal in the general sense. Both catholics and protestants were recruited, and it is clear from the wage books that clerks included both religions. In Belfast as well, the firm was unbiased in the matter of religion. In October 1913, when it looked as if labour trouble in Dublin would spread to the Belfast house, a correspondent in the Belfast house reported in a letter to Dublin the rumours which were circulating that ...the poor Catholics will be getting the sack,' but he added in a later letter that, 'any sensible man in Belfast knows that you don't look to a man's religion when engaging him.'

Henry Digges, who had entered the firm in 1866, can only have been in his late twenties when he became head of the retail section. He was obviously liked and respected, although one would suspect that he must have been missing in some vital quality, since his early success did not lead to greater things. But his salary level was of course sufficient to give him an assured and comfortable social position. Even including the firm's directors, his salary in 1917/8 at £331 was the eighth highest, and the fourth highest of the non-directorial staff. In 1926/7 he was still on the salary list, earning £420.

In 1917-19 Coghill's salary as head of the factory at £530 per year was, along with Ruthven's of railway advertising, higher than that of any of the directors, with the exception of Charles Eason himself. Coghill's salary in the late 1910s seems to have risen despite the fact that he was now free of responsibility for the wholesale stationery division, a fact corresponding to the growing place the factory had assumed in the business. The responsibility for stationery seems to have been devolved onto a Mr Lothian at a much smaller salary. However, the importance attached to the wholesale stationery department at this stage is reflected in the fact that in the early 1920s Lothian's remuneration exceeded that of all staff except Ruthven and Coghill. Lothian retired in 1923/4. For a long time Lawson had been number two in stationery. In 1934 John Rowland recalled of Coghill that,

> He was in charge of the stationery department. Had an inventive mind and was a bit of a musician too. Started a band in the factory which for a time was quite a success. His daughter Rhoda became a pianist of some note in the city, swept all before her in the Academy of Music.

As already mentioned, he had shifted in later years to the factory exclusively, and his mechanical genius marked him out specially for that purpose. Significantly, Coghill's salary, which had risen so steadily over the years, did not rise at all between 1916/7 and 1924/5, although salaries generally rose sharply in these years. The reason is not clear. A diminution of his overall responsibility may have been one of the reasons. Another may have been some reduction of work load as his retirement approached. He retired early in 1925, and some of his responsibilities were shifted to J.C.M. Eason.

There is no doubt of Coghill's immense standing. In 1890 he was the second highest paid member of the house, following Cherry who was on £500 per annum. Ruthven's swift rise in the early 1890's left Coghill and Ruthven on a par at £9 per week. After Cherry's death in 1893, they were better paid than any members of the family apart from Charles Eason himself. At no time since the days of Dewar had any non-family member held such a position within the house, and it was only in 1920 with the advancement of J.C.M. Eason that this pattern began to change. In 1919/20 Jack Eason's remuneration passed that of Ruthven, and Albert Brunton's that of Coghill.

A few further words are warranted on two key figures: Albert Brunton, whose loss like that of McDowell ranks among the personal tragedies of the twentieth-century house, and Keith Eason, whose task was the unobserved and silent business of introducing modern accounting techniques, with few preliminaries, into what had been an efficient but highly conservative counting house. Albert Brunton married Frances Eason (who was the first of the Eason daughters to work in the business), having entered the house in 1884. He had many of the qualities which would have marked him out for a leading role in the house in the 1920s, and in the recollection of Digges, he had 'a bright and buoyant optimism'. Within a short time after entering, Brunton's salary was raised by 2s to 12s, the first of many salary improvements. In 1887 he was moved from books to stationery. In 1890 in a period of six months his salary was increased from £1 12s to £2, and he was promoted at the same time to the category 'miscellaneous', which meant that he was included in the handful of really senior men in the house. In 1896 his salary was £4 and it increased to £5 10s in 1898. He was now emerging as one of the best paid men in the house and he became a director in 1904. He combined the management of the stationery department with responsibility in Dublin for the Belfast branch. Almost nothing of Brunton's written work survives. The exception is a confidential letter book which he kept when he was on the spot in Belfast in 1905 to deal both with competition from Porter's and the new dispatch arrangements for the *Daily Mail*. The warmth and intimacy of his short and effective letters to Charles Eason confirm his position of trust in the inner councils of the firm. They showed interests outside the business: two letters from Brunton in February 1906 discuss the embarrassment caused for the General Fund of the Presbyterian Church in Dublin by its being ground landlord of a public house in Rathfarnham and how the problem might be dealt with.

Two of Charles Eason junior's younger brothers were in the business, Fred and William Waugh. Of the younger generation of Easons, J.C.M. Eason's younger brother Keith also entered the business in 1908. Keith Eason was a mathematician by training. He served under Hallett, and his main interest within the firm continued to be the accounts and records. The destruction of many records in the fire in 1916 made reorganisation at that stage imperative, all the more so as professional auditing was introduced then for the first time.

To the work of reorganisation Keith Eason brought much original thought, sometimes ahead of its time, and not always practical, although his interest and knowledge of early accounting and calculating machines and methods was of considerable value to the firm. His interest lay in the accounting procedures and the records which they produced, rather than in the trading results which they represented. Outside the business, his interests had a similar trend, centred as they were on the reform of the calendar (on which he wrote a small book), proportional representation, and the teaching of mathematical concepts. When expounding his views on any of these subjects, as he would to all and sundry, he had little sense of time. In many ways he would have been much more at home in the computer age than in his own time.

In 1890 thirteen women were employed. At the turn of the century female employees were still mainly concentrated in the wholesale stationery department, which accounted for 21 out of 29 women in January 1902, excluding the workroom. Of the remaining eight, two were in retail, one was in accounts, five were in books and prayer books combined. By December 1911 the number of female employees had increased to 53. The main concentration was still in stationery where they accounted for 35 of 44 employees. They had also become numerous in retail (12) and had made an appearance in the prestigious news division, where there were five. Their importance continued to grow. By December 1917 there were 117 women employed, and they outnumbered male clerks and assistants in retail (20 as against 13), and in accounts as well, (14 as against 9). In books they accounted for 8 out of a total of 26. Stationery now accounted for a minority of the female employees within the firm (51 out of 118). Roughly one-third of the staff in the head office in Dublin were women, and this figure would have approached one half if all-male categories such as porters and 'morning men' were excluded. The cash office, all male, and the news division, two-thirds male, still remained the male bastions of the firm. Nevertheless, the rise in the number of female employees, from 13 to 118 in less than thirty years, represented a dramatic turnabout within the firm. While females tended to concentrate in the less well paid areas and jobs in the firm, and to be paid lower salaries, the creation of a large amount of employment which did not exist previously must have had wide psychological and social consequences.

These consequences would have stemmed from the creation of jobs in the first instance, and secondly, from the tendency for female employment to concentrate within well-defined areas. In other words, female clerical employment had patterns both of novelty and of conformity to existing norms, a conflicting development which must have raised problems for women as well as opening new horizons to them. The higher echelons of the business generally remained male. Although the stationery division continued to be managed at the top by men, at least one woman reached the position of being head of a department within the stationery division. Miss Kingsman entered the firm directly from school, and learned the business from Fred Eason. She succeeded a man, Mr Lawrence, as head of the fancy goods, leather goods and toy department, when Lawrence became a traveller for the firm. As head of the fancy section, she was responsible for buying a wide range of goods on behalf of the firm and had thus quite a senior position. She rated a profile in the series on senior figures in the firm which *Eason's Monthly Bulletin* ran in 1925/6. According to this 'At one period the firm had practically decided to give up the sale of dolls, but Miss Kingsman induced the firm to continue, and the sale of dolls is now one of its greatest features.' In 1920 Miss Kingsman was the first woman who achieved the socially significant distinction of being paid by cheque. Important though her department was, her salary remained a relatively low one. It varied between £222 and £234 a year, and showed no rise over the 1920s. As the salaries of many other cheque-paid staff did not vary over the period either, this was not in itself significant, but as head of a section, one would have expected some once-for-all change to have taken place at some stage.

The overall long-term trends in wages and salaries are more difficult to interpret than they might appear at first sight. On the one hand, as experienced men and women accumulated in the firm, earnings tended to rise; or the other, periods of rapid recruitment increased the number of young or inexperienced people which reduced the average age and salary level. Another technical factor is illustrated by the 12 per cent drop in average (weekly) wages which occurred between 1904 and 1906. This was a result of an increased move of senior personnel out of the wage totals, into monthly payments by cheque. Also the structure of the house, in terms of departments, shifted over time with the consequence that wage levels compared at particular times are not necessarily very meaningful, since trends can be obscured by the shift towards or away from more remunerative activities. In the early twentieth century with the mechanisation of many tasks — typing, the use of addressograph machines — a large number of specialised routine jobs were created which supported the activity in other divisions. The increase in such tasks plus the allied increase in female employment tended to dilute the rise in average earnings.

The figures show average earnings per head rose between 1857 and 1877 and then they fell until 1886, very probably because of the significant increase in women employees in stationery. By 1904 they had risen quite sharply. The rise in earnings between 1886 and 1904 is in large measure a consequence of the emergence of a well-defined management structure, and the rise in earnings of a growing personnel. If wages in individual sections are analysed, as for instance in the Retail department, and in wholesale news, expansion in the second half of the 1890s was reflected in a fall in average earnings. Average weekly wages were close to or above £1 between 1891 and 1898, but they fell below it during the expansion of the next three years, to 18s 6d.

The payment of monthly salaries by cheque, accounted for separately, had happened quite early in the case of the head of the firm. In 1883/4 Charles Eason junior and Cherry were withdrawn from the wage totals. At a later stage the earnings of directors were also accounted for separately. In 1906 the number excluded seems to have risen sharply.

Apart from four directors, seven members of staff were excluded: Butler, Hallett, Coghill, Ruthven, Digges, McDowell and J.C.M. Eason.

TABLE 24 *Average weekly earnings (Dublin)*

Year	Average weekly earnings £ s d	Number of employees covered by the average*
June 1857	0 17 2**	22
Jan 1858	0 17 11¾	28
Jan 1860	0 16 2	34
Jan 1866	1 0 1	64
Dec 1868	0 19 1	80
Dec 1877	1 1 10½	140
Dec 1886	0 16 0	142
Dec 1904	1 2 3	218
Dec 1906	0 19 8½***	223
Dec 1908	0 17 2	214
Dec 1912	0 17 9½	250
Dec 1913	0 17 1	281
Dec 1915	0 17 6	287
Dec 1916	0 16 10	322
Dec 1919	1 11 10½	330
Dec 1920	2 0 11½	321
1925 (average for year)	2 6 4	354****

* Excludes employees in workroom and factory and bookstalls
** Excluding Charles Eason
*** 7 senior members of staff excluded by transfer to monthly payment by cheque
**** Excludes factory and motors

A combination of a sharp rise in numbers and the allied factor of increased employment of women was responsible for the marked fall in average earnings between 1906 and 1916. War-time inflation however gave a spur to rising wages. In December 1919 they had risen to an average of £1 11s 10½d per week, and they rose again to £2 0s 11½d in December 1920. Following the first world war, the rise in wages was quite phenomenal during a period of raging inflation. The weekly wage bill literally rose almost month by month for a fairly static staff. Thus between January and December 1919 the total wage bill rose 43 per cent; by June 1920 it had gone up a further 18 per cent. This unprecedented rise in an era unused to dealing with the problems of inflation makes it easy to understand the dilemmas of the house at that time.

TABLE 25 *Rise and Fall of Wages and Salaries 1917-31*

Year to March 31	Wages	%*	Salaries	Total
	£		£	£
1917	17,111	74	5,947	23,058
1918	19,913	76	6,461	26,374
1919	24,917	77	7,453	32,370
1920	35,750	78	9,880	45,630
1921	43,654	79	11,460	55,114
1922	42,226	79	10,986	53,212
1923	38,731	75	12,888	51,619
1924	38,380	75	12,848	51,228
1925	41,254	75	13,600	54,854
1926	40,850	75	13,408	54,258
1927	38,509	75	13,029	51,538
1931	39,407	73	14,241	53,648

* Wages as a per cent of total payroll.

Over the period 1917 to 1931 the rise and fall of wages and salaries can be seen in the total wage and salary bill. with a very moderate increase in the labour force. In fact wages, which had risen very sharply in the late 1910s, fell very little in the 1920s, despite falling prices. In 1925 earnings averaged £2 6s 4d (excluding the factory and motor staff). The fact that many were on incremental scales meant that widespread recruitment in the decade before 1914 was reflected in an upward drift in per capita earnings, though wage rates themselves had turned down after 1920. As prices had risen only 80 per cent, as against a rise in average wages of 171 per cent since Dec 1913, real earnings had improved immensely. The rise in costs was thus a serious one.

The lowest wages were paid in the factory. The wages of the twelve 'workshop' employees in December 1877 averaged only £0 6s 2½d a week. In December 1886 the average wage of 33 employees was only £0 7s 4d.

Even in December 1906, when they were inflated by an increase in the number of compositors, well paid and in regular employment, the average was only 10s 9½d for 116 employees, almost half the average for the rest of the house. From the 1870s some women earned little more than 3s a week, although such extremes were for part-time work and most women earned more. But the low wages in these unskilled tasks were little better than domestic work or cleaning and can only have been appealing because of its comparative regularity and some flexibility in the reduced hours offered. Charles Eason's clergyman brother Benjamin expressed some unhappiness with these wage levels, and Eason responded to him on 25 March 1899:

> It is not easy to judge whether wages are unduly low or not. For instance we have two married women to whom we pay 7s and 6s a week. Of course this is not enough to support a woman but would you say that we are bound to pay more. The work is there to be done — it is merely packing shavings — sorting them so that we get a somewhat higher price for picked rather than for unpicked shavings. The woman whose wages are 6s in fact only gets 5s 9d as she does not work full time (that is her own choice). The cost of labour enters as an important element into the cost of most articles we manufacture, we cannot afford to pay more than the usual rate of wages. If we did the price of our goods would rise and they could not be sold. I find we have about 47 females who have been with us less than 5 years, their wages range from 3s (2) to 10s (1). The one at 10s and another at 9s are working two machines, a pageing and folding machine, and this labour, involving some skill, commands a better price.
>
> We have 18 females who have been with us more than 5 years. Wages range from 6s 6d to 22s paid to Miss Saurin the fore-woman. One gets 12s 6d on piece work, with us ten years, one at 13s, also on piece work with us 12 years, and 1 at 13s with us 15 years. The value of work does not increase after a sufficient number of years to acquire a certain skill. There are four earning 7s to 8s, who have been with us over 5 and under 6 years.

In a list of 24 workers in the factory in January 1898, whose wages were increased that month, five had been earning 3s 6d, two 4s, three 4s 6d, and four 5s a week. The remainder earned various figures in excess of that.

Individual earnings cannot be judged solely by averages based on aggregates. There was a very large turnover in staff, and hence the prospects of individuals who remained on in the firm were much better than the comparatively low per capita figures suggest. Clerical staff and assistants were typically recruited at 6s a week throughout the second half of the century. It was rarely more, unless they were already experienced. A typical instance may illustrate the pattern. Shields was recruited at 6s a week in Retail in September 1887. Fifteen subsequent adjustments (two in 1891 and again in 1901) brought him to £1 16s in 1902. He went on to serve 67 years with the firm, eventually retiring in 1954. In fact, the early stages were probationary and reflected a long, formal apprenticeship, the details of which we unfortunately lack. Employees in clerical and shop assistant categories were on an informal incremental scale. Permanency offered real prospects of advancement to a salary of around £1 16s a week over a period of around 15 years, in other words, at about thirty years of age.

This was a salary which guaranteed modest comfort in nineteenth-century conditions. A clerical employee could look forward to marriage, housing himself, and maintaining a modest competence. Many of the clerical employees lived in the central districts, as is evident from their addresses. Even in the 1880s social segregation was still imperfect. However, advancement beyond a salary of about £2 a week depended upon promotion into the higher ranks of the company, and the great bulk of the staff were below £2. To take a single example, the retail department in January 1893 had Digges at its head at £4 10s, but only one other employee had a level of £2, while there were three at £1 18s and nine below that figure again, at various salaries from 7s to £1 10s. Salary increases took place twice a year in January and July. Charles Eason senior and subsequently, Charles Eason junior, kept a series of books in which the dates and amounts were carefully noted. Increases only rarely took place in other months. The number of salary adjustments within the year in the 1890s and early 1900s amounted to about a hundred. Few received two adjustments within the same year. As the staff amounted to something less than 200, it meant that roughly one half of the staff received an increase in wages or salary within the year. There was clearly from the earliest days a well defined system of progression in wages on the basis of age and experience, coupled with a considerable discretion in the hands of the management in granting or withholding increases. Two adjustments within a year, or the converse, the absence of adjustments, tell their own story. The normal size of increments tended to be 2s at a time. For individuals recruited at higher levels of salary, increments tended to be larger and less frequent.

A system of pensions was introduced, apparently in 1888. It provided a pension on retirement, or to a widow, or to a long-serving employee who had to retire prematurely through illness. This provided some protection against the distressful conditions evident in contemporary employment in Eason's as well as elsewhere. A surviving list suggests that twelve such pensions were granted between 1888 and 1902. James Fitzpatrick, who had been foreman in the railway advertising department, earning £2 a week, was granted a pension of £1 a week in 1888. James Dignam, manager in the wholesale news department, was granted a pension of £2 a week in 1893 on his retirement. Widows or dependants were granted pensions in several cases, and the family of a porter who died earning 17s a week were granted a pension of 3s a week from August 1900 to December 1901. Patrick Kelly, a clerk in wholesale news who had been employed since 1873, and who was earning 34s in 1900, was struck with paralysis, and was granted a pension of £1 a week. In 1902 an elderly porter was transferred to the pension list, and his wages which had been previously reduced from 21s to 14s on account of his age were henceforth debited to the pension account. By 1916/17 there were no less than eleven named persons plus 'sundries' on a pension list, which amounted for the year to £377. In 1921/22 the list embraced fourteen individuals plus 'sundries' at a total cost of £595.

In 1918 Charles Eason recorded in *Notes re wages* that employment included pension — '.... no contract but in fact no old servant turned adrift .... pay that comes to full wages during illness.' Good though this was, it had faults. First, while the Board provided pensions readily for employees with long records of service, it was not willing to do so for employees whose service though substantial was shorter. As late as 1936 one employee who was sick for two months lost her job, although the firm would reconsider employing her if she recovered. She was paid four and a half weeks wages while ill. J.C.M. Eason proposed a pension for her, but the Board in fact granted only a lump sum of £25. Especially in the case of long-service employees at the lower level, the sums were inadequate, and could only alleviate but not prevent destitution. As one employee put it to J.C.M. Eason in 1946: 'My knowledge of the usual retiring allowance made by the firm made it clear to me, that in my case at least, it would mean penury and actual want.' The provision of allowances at discretion was advanced enough at the time it was introduced, but it was archaic by the 1930s for such a large firm. In November 1938 the possibility of arranging for a pension scheme for staff was actually discussed by the Board. W.H. Smith's in England had introduced a pension fund as early as 1894 — Eason's finally introduced one in 1946.

Strikes of staff in or outside the house were unknown before 1911. The first labour trouble was in August 1911 when short strikes occurred on the railways, and among the newsboys demanding better terms from the *Daily Mail* and *Evening Herald*. On 21 August 1911 Eason vans moved under police protection. The outstanding feature in the labour history of the house before World War I was the industrial dispute of 1913. This grew out of the activities of James Larkin's Irish Transport and General Workers' Union, whose expansion since 1911 was particularly resented because of its use of the sympathetic strike to further its ends. By 1913 its spread had begun to encounter determined employer resistance, especially from William Martin Murphy, the head of the Dublin United Tramway Company, *Irish Independent* newspaper, and a host of related business interests.[1] Murphy refused to recognise the Union, and dismissed members from his employment. By August 1913 militancy had become the order of the day in Dublin labour relations, culminating in the famous lock-out of Larkin's members by a large number of employers on 26 August. Eason's was inevitably affected as the conflict between Larkin and William Martin Murphy developed, since they were the distributors of Murphy's newspaper, the *Irish Independent*. The first ominous note was struck as early as 15 August when one of Eason's boys was involved in a minor incident at mid-day. He was:

> followed by four boys from the Pillar to Sackville Street Club and Rotunda Hospital — and was struck by a stone at the corner of Upper Sackville Street. They followed him back to the Pillar — where he spoke to a policeman who brought him back to the shop. From his description one of the boys appears to have been Ball who he saw previously delivering Strike Hand Bills — in Abbey Street.

The direct involvement of the firm in the dispute followed soon. It had already affected Larkin's men in the despatch section of the *Irish Independent*.

On the morning of Tuesday, 19 August, an interview took place between Charles Eason, accompanied by his son Jack, and Larkin and P.J. Daly of the Transport Union. The subject of this meeting was the distribution of the *Irish Independent* by Eason's. Subsequent versions of this meeting by Larkin and Eason differed radically. Larkin claimed that Charles Eason had 'agreed not to distribute such papers during the dispute, and to increase their wages later.' Larkin claimed in addition

1 On William Martin Murphy, see Dermot Keogh, 'William Martin Murphy and the origins of the 1913 lock-out', *Saothar* vol IV, (1978), pp 15-34.

that when Eason had been given an assurance of motor transport for distribution by William Martin Murphy, he went back on his word not to distribute the *Irish Independent*. There is in fact no record of what transpired at that meeting, but a letter written by Charles Eason a month later discussing the course of events would suggest that the approach of the Easons had been conciliatory, and the likelihood is that Larkin assumed a greater degree of agreement than was in fact the case:

> What happened was this. On Tuesday evening, 19th August, after an interview with Mr James Larkin, we informed our staff that they would not be asked to handle the *Independent* the next morning, but gave no promise that we would not put the paper on sale or handle it by other men. We carried out this promise, and the men worked as usual.

The *Irish Independent* therefore appeared on the Eason bookstalls the next day. James Larkin called on Eason's to cease distribution. Eason's declined to do this, and Larkin called out his union members at 5.30 pm on Wednesday evening. Of the 56 members of the wholesale news division who answered Larkin's call, there were 23 porters, 17 messengers and van drivers, and 16 clerks. Six clerks or assistants in other branches of the business also answered the call.

Larkin had not a habit of strict accuracy. It seems that the statement that his members were locked out, made in a later speech, was not accurate. Likewise his suggestion that a wage increase had been promised later does not seem correct, as a remnant of a 1913 diary, which survived the fire in 1916, notes that apart from the distribution of Murphy's newspapers, there was no dispute with Larkin's union, and no other demands had been made upon the firm. Later J.C.M. Eason made it very clear that the Transport Union and Larkin had not been at any time in dispute with Eason's beyond their refusal to break their contract for the distribution of the *Irish Independent* when Larkin requested them to do so.

Eason's were now drawn into the dispute prominently and publicly. Larkin circulated a handbill advising newsagents to order news from the other Dublin wholesaler, William Dawson & Sons, who were not handling the *Irish Independent*. Goods for Eason's were blacked. Some of their suppliers would no longer deliver to them. In most cases, Eason's were able to overcome this by sending their own vanmen, although on 26 August Charles Eason noted in a letter that 'Bewley & Draper have declined to supply us with any ink, they would not even give it to our vanman to bring here.' More seriously, their news distribution was affected. An undated longhand note in Charles Eason's handwriting records that: 'Agents are being threatened with injury to their shops if they receive any parcels from us. Some have already withdrawn their orders rather than run the risk of injury and loss of business.' This threat to newsagents can be dated, from other references, to late August. Larkin's handbill had laid heavy emphasis on the transfer of business to Dawson's, who were Easons' competitors as wholesale newsagents, being a subsidiary established as recently as 1911 of one of the principal London wholesalers. From the surviving correspondence it seems that it was this aspect of the strike which caused most concern to Eason's. It is clear that Eason's considered that Dawson's had broken employer ranks by refusing to handle the *Irish Independent* during the dispute. They also inferred from Larkin's propaganda that Dawson's had an understanding with the Transport Union. On 25 August 1913 Charles Eason wrote to W.H. Smith's in London:

> Is there not an Association of London wholesale agents of which you and Dawsons are members? If so, I would strongly urge that the matter should be brought before the executive body; and that you would ask that the Association should approve our action and disapprove of Dawsons.

It was usual for supplies for Dawson's and Eason's from the Amalgamated Press to be sent in bulk to their Dublin agents, Carr & McKay. Dawson's sought to have the parcels separated at despatch in England. Eason's sought to have them left combined. Carr & McKay declined to have them separated, although of course as usual their clerk allowed Dawson's to withdraw their supplies from the parcels on arrival. Eason's took particular exception to Dawsons' proposal, as they held that by informing publishers that parcels for Eason's would be stopped, Dawson's were interfering with the normal channels of distribution. Dawson's took the view that since 'it was commonly rumoured about town that Eason's and Carr & McKay's goods would be stopped', they were only seeking to have their own supplies secured by despatch under their own label. The Federation of Newsagents at last on 20 September 1913 replied to Charles Eason's letter, to the effect that Dawson's Dublin house denied having any understanding with the union, and in fact had requested the *Irish Worker* to withdraw their circular on the subject. This letter was less than pleasing to Charles Eason. On 23 September he wrote back: 'We stated that Messrs Dawson & Sons have ceased to sell the *Daily Independent* and *Herald*, that we continue to sell them and we said we should value the opinion of other wholesale agents on this matter.'

The rights or wrongs of the Dawson affair hinge on this question. To

Eason's, the attitude of Dawson's must have appeared opportunistic, as there was in Easons' view a matter of principle involved. As Charles Eason put it to W.H. Smith's in a letter of 26 August: 'It would be a disgrace to all concerned, Railway Companies, publishers and newsagents if Mr Larkin were to succeed in compelling us to discontinue the sale of the *Independent*.'

Apart from the competitive angle, under which Eason's were in danger of losing sales and agents to Dawson's, the direct impact of the strike on the house was surprisingly short-lived. The first effect was experienced on 22 August, when the regular carters would not deliver papers arriving at the North Wall by the L.&N.W. Railway Co. This problem was overcome by Eason's collecting the supplies themselves under police escort, although 'necessarily with serious delay and disorganisation of our work'. The most alarming disruption came on 26 August when the City of Dublin Steam Packet Company refused to accept supplies for Eason's at Holyhead. The railway company however arranged despatch by an express boat for the North Wall. The refusal by the packet company seems to have been on orders from the company headquarters, but in the afternoon new orders were issued, and supplies henceforth came normally by the mail steamer. There seems to have been no further disruption at Holyhead, although uncertainty and the possibility of blacking lingered on. Jacob's goods, for instance, were not being handled in Liverpool. Through redeployment of staff and the engagement of new staff, Eason's were able to manage to move their goods. On 1 September Charles Eason reported to the Secretary of the Chamber of Commerce:

> During the course of the week we have had to collect goods from the B & I, SP Co, the Laird Line, Messrs G & J Burns, Midland of England, Silliott Line etc for none of their regular carting contractors would deliver goods to us. Some of these companies indeed have had difficulty in getting the cargoes unloaded, but united action on their part got over this difficulty.

A large amount of work fell to be done by the redeployment of existing staff, or by the engagement of new workers. By 9 September Eason's had engaged 30 new men, although 'many of them are not much use at present'. By the middle of September the number had risen to 60, and within a further month it proved possible to proceed without much help from other departments in the firm. Even as early as 20 August Eason's were able to insert an advertisement in the morning papers to the effect that:

> They are executing all orders without very much delay, and making

> arrangements by which they expect shortly to resume all distribution at the usual times. They would repeat that they have no dispute with their staff nor have they locked out any men. The sole cause of the strike is that they continue to sell newspapers published by the Independent Newspapers Ltd. They feel sure that in doing so they will have the approval and sympathy of the public.

The only continuing consequence of the strike by this stage was some extra work in handling goods. Right into January 1914, 'We had special work (motor lorry etc) arising out of the fact that we are a tainted firm.'

In fact apart from a short-lived period of a few weeks in August 1913, and the more long-lived competition which developed from Dawson's, the impact of the strike was very slight. In some respects the most significant feature of the strike was that it brought Eason's into a position of prominence in the Dublin business community. Larkin's charge that William Martin Murphy had prevailed on Charles Eason to change his mind is not true, in the sense that Eason was too independent in his outlook to be easily prevailed upon, but Larkin was correct to the extent that Eason and Murphy did actually meet on 20 August, as indicated by a surviving letter from Murphy dated 21 August, and addressed to Charles Eason:

> I thank you very warmly for the stand you have made against the forces of disorder. I am sure you are making a great sacrifice but it is for principle and I am confident that in the end it will not involve you in consequences so serious as you thought yesterday.

An executive committee had been formed by the Council of the Dublin Employers' Federation on 29 August, to deal with current and future labour disputes. It is not clear whether Eason was a member of the committee at this stage, although it is highly likely, as at the meeting of some four hundred 'prominent' employers which the committee arranged on 3 September, the crucial resolution, whereby employers pledged themselves not to employ any person who continued to be a member of the Irish Transport and General Workers Union, and to dismiss workers refusing to carry out reasonable instructions, was, according to the minutes, '.... proposed by Mr George Jacob, seconded by Mr Orr, and supported by Mr C. Eason'. Charles Eason was also a member of the deputation from the Dublin employers which had a series of meetings from 5 September with a deputation from the Trades Union Council. In a letter to W.H. Smith's, Charles Eason reported that at the meeting which took place on 8 September, prior to an adjournment for one week, he was asked, 'whether we would reinstate the men on strike as a preliminary to a discussion of permanent arrangements. I said no, not ''en bloc''.'

Charles Eason's new-found prominence in employer circles was confirmed by his inclusion in the permanent executive committee which was formed on 10 September at a meeting of the signatories of the agreement adopted at the employers' meeting on 3 September. The employers' committee built up a sizeable fund. Some £22,519 was disbursed up to 1918, mainly no doubt in the period of the 1913 strike. Thereafter disbursements were few except between 1923 and 1925. Charles Eason became Treasurer of the Fund in 1923. In 1924 the issue of employer organisation came to the fore again. Larkin was once more at the centre of the Dublin labour trouble. He was now in conflict with the Transport Union, and was seeking to organise a union of his own, the Workers' Union of Ireland. Larkin attempted to conduct his campaign against individual firms with which he was in dispute, by selectively disrupting traffic through Dublin port. An emergency committee of Dublin employers was created, with some funds provided from the employers' Executive Committee fund, to fight this threat. One of the methods pursued by Larkin was to refuse to handle goods tendered by members of the Transport Workers Union. The object of the committee was:

> To insist upon their employees carrying out all reasonable orders irrespective of the Union to which they belong. They wish to impress upon those who are forwarding goods to Dublin the necessity for using the existing means of transit and under no circumstances to avail themselves of any offer which may be made by owners of independent vessels to convey goods to Dublin. Such an arrangement would be against their best interest.

The prime movers in this committee seem to have been J.C.M. Eason and George Jacob. A manuscript note in Eason's hand refers to Jacob 'coming here at 3.45 to draft with me a circular to send across to merchants on other side re goods coming forward'. A draft circular survives in Eason's hand for signature by employers of an undertaking agreed at a general meeting, noting that employers had acquiesced in the workers' behaviour in declining to do certain work, because they had been waiting for evidence that they (the employers) could count on general support. A form of resolution survives among the papers dated 19 December, proposed by J.C.M. Eason and seconded by George Jacob, which proposed 'to consider the possibilities of a complete organisation of employers in Dublin'.

Thus labour trouble led the Easons to identify themselves closely with the employers' interests, and to take a leading place in their activities. As a result the Eason family was now prominent in the Dublin business community, in contrast to the past, when they had been content to play a low-key role quite at variance with the scale of the business. With a total labour force of roughly 450 workers in Dublin alone, Eason's was a large employer, exceeded in scale only by the transport undertakings, and by two or three factories. It only required a prominent role such as that played by Charles Eason, and later by J.C.M. Eason, to stamp them publicly as among Dublin's leading business figures. As a result, from 1921 for the first time in the history of the firm, one of its directors, J.C.M. Eason, was nominated to a leading position in the world of Dublin businessmen.

The Dublin business world itself was of course changing. It was no longer dominated by the arch-conservative Arnotts, Guinnesses, Gouldings, Martins, or the largely unionist and anglican group who sat on the boards of the railway companies and banks. William Martin Murphy, a catholic whose main interests were in municipal transport undertakings and newspapers, was representative of new business forces, and the leading part played by the Easons, news wholesalers and dissenters totally disassociated from the old establishment, is a further illustration of the way in which the leadership of Dublin business life in a subtle way was shifting away from the old anglican and establishment mould. In fact, some links between the Murphys and the Easons began to emerge outside business: in the aftermath of the 1916 rebellion, when newspaper distribution was disrupted, newspapers were dropped off on the run from Kingstown pier to Fred Eason's house in Rathgar for one of the Murphy family. William Martin Murphy's son, who was elected to the Council of the Chamber of Commerce on his father's death in 1919, constituted with George N. Jacob and J.C.M. Eason a triumvirate who were to dominate the Chamber of Commerce in the early 1920s: between them they provided the presidents in three of the four years 1924-7.[2]

The immediate significance of the 1913 strike in the present context was not the events themselves, but the fact that unionisation had now begun to spread within the firm. The future could never be quite the same again. No settlement was made with Easons' men who had gone on strike. Only some of the old staff were re-employed. Hereafter both old and new members of staff were required to sign an undertaking not to belong to the Irish Transport Union. The first reference to union negotiations —

2 L.M. Cullen *Princes and pirates: The Dublin Chamber of Commerce* (Dublin, 1983), pp 88, 91-2.

and indeed the only one in the Board minutes — came on 5 December 1916, when it was minuted that 'The question of our relation towards the threatened binders' strike was discussed and decision postponed.' Traces of labour troubles between 1917 and 1919 in the factory can be found. The return to the Board of Trade for January 1917 referred to 'six men out owing to strike of binders and cutters'. Their resumption of work is referred to in the return for March. In October 1917 it was reported that 'the printing staff of 12 went out on strike on Oct. 12 and are still out'. In July 1919 the printing plant was again said to be idle because of a strike. But intimation of the spread of demands came quickly enough. Already in January 1918 Charles Eason wrote that:

> We have now increased wages very largely during the past year, especially women's wages, but I don't think we have done all we might yet. Yesterday Jack and I had an interview with a trade union Sec. who came to represent the packing staff of our news dept. in reference to an appeal for more wages. We found him a reasonable man to deal with and his demands were moderate, but if we grant them it may be a starting point for staff in other depts. to join this or other unions, and total demands will be considerable.

What was feared did in fact happen. Four wage increases were conceded between October 1917 and July 1918, amounting to an increase of 23 per cent on preceding levels. But this did not forestall a demand from the Irish Clerical Workers Union on 27 July of that year for an increase of 60 per cent retroactive to 31 March 1918, and for improved rates for overtime. Charles Eason seems to have been prepared to concede the increase demanded, but was opposed to retroaction. He himself addressed the men on Tuesday, 27 August 1918 at 6 pm. He did not deny the increased profits from 1917/18, but argued the demands of financing the business, and the fact that dividends and directors' payments had not been increased:

> In the last resort the question between us comes to this. Do you believe what I say? Do you trust us? You cannot know all the circumstances. Do you think I am keeping back essential facts which might tell against my position?
>
> Though we do not feel able to give a bonus at the present time we undertake to give one as soon as the facts warrant such a distribution. I might say we won't increase our dividend till we have paid such a bonus, but though this might have an appearance of a concession, it would not be really important. Our main idea is not to draw as much as we can out of the business, but to build up an

> assured business based upon the confidence of our customers, that we think of their interests as well as our own, and upon the good will of our staff and their confidence that we will share our prosperity with them. Wage earners desire most earnestly security of employment and that we desire to give. We have given it in the past and it would be a serious matter if the staff were to take up a position which would impair the ability of our business — theirs as well as ours.

From the perspective of the demands on the business and the likelihood that prices would fall back, Eason's case was very reasonable. Equally, the union members had a case — prices had soared and at the time the firm was in a position to pay wage increases from profits in the immediate past and in the present. His appeal fell on deaf ears, and it was the death throes of the old-style paternalism. The union turned its face against any compromise, and on 25 September 1918 Charles Eason wrote to his brother that: 'We settled with the Clerks' Union without a strike but we gave them their demand for 20 weeks back pay.' No sooner was this claim met than one was made by the union which represented porters and stablemen. Eason noted that:

> The men seem to expect that every demand be conceded without argument. This is what I particularly resisted on the part of our clerks and I got a meeting with some of the representatives of the Union and some of the staff belonging to the union. We talked the matter over and the men put their case very well and we stated our difficulties. The discussion we think was useful and paved the way for further exchanges of views.

In 1919 a further increase in wages was sought; the driving force, in the Easons' eyes, was Mr Logue, the Secretary of the Irish Clerical Workers Union. Exactly how unionisation developed in the firm is obscure, and the vagueness of the surviving records tells its own story about a somewhat confused pattern in the early years. Larkin's ITGWU already had a foot-hold in the news department in 1913 but an Irish Clerical Workers Union or 'Clerks' Union' was the main focus of attention from 1918 to 1923. A long-term pattern of two unions — ITGWU and IBATU (Irish Bookbinders and Allied Trades Union) — was the ultimate development in the Dublin house. As a generalisation, craftsmen in the factory and males in the wholesale department tended to be in the ITGWU, women in the factory and in the wholesale department in the IBATU, but the precise line-up of staff within the firm in the early decades is in fact obscure: in each early episode, the attention of management seems to have focused on a single union.

Working conditions, especially in the wholesale news department, were demanding. By 1920 some workers seem to have began at 4:30 am.[3] When Sean O'Casey referred many years later to an hour of 3.45 a.m. as his starting time in the 1890s he must have confused it with his time of getting up rather than the time at which he entered Easons' wholesale premises. London morning papers arrived in the late afternoon, and even when they began to arrive in time for a morning distribution from the first decade of the twentieth century onwards, they only reached Dublin at 8 am. It was the earlier printing of the Dublin dailies which made an earlier opening hour essential, and in the 1920s the earliest edition of Dublin dailies was available from 1:45 am. The starting time in wholesale news was therefore pushed back to 1:45 am.

In 1919 arbitration machinery was in existence, and an advance in union strengths is illustrated by the fact that the arbitration was based on submissions from the Union on the one hand and from the Dublin Stationery, Bookselling and Allied Trades' Federation, representing the employers, on the other. At this stage the main role in negotiation had passed from Charles Eason to his son J.C.M. Eason. Some notes taken by J.C.M. Eason during the arbitration proceedings survive. One of the points made by the union was that special consideration should be given to the difficulty that girls from the country had in living in Dublin at current prices; Eason contested this, and considered that the average employee should be taken. What the negotiations established in effect was a rigid incremental improvement during apprenticeship in place of the more discretionary one that had applied in the past. Wages above the minimum level for a qualified assistant were left untouched by union demands. Eason's notes read: 'Future progress must be left to employer. Depends on opportunities — business done — capacity — may improve or may actually diminish — circumstances vary.'

One of the most significant achievements of the union was not simply an increase allied to a formal incremental scale of apprenticeship, but the establishment of a standard or minimum wage for qualified assistants, male and female. Eason noted that events 'have reached a stage that Mr. Logue has defined rather obscurely as his objects as regards the minimum and yearly rate of progress to that standard.' This was itself a major development, which circumscribed the employer's powers more than the

3 See pages 119 and 335.

incremental scale in apprenticeship which was a formalisation of an existing practice. Eason's notes continue: 'Origins of enquiry desire to reach a standard — have agreed to the principle of a standard — not without feeling that we have given up something valuable namely the incentive to progress for sake of uniformity — means a great deal to Mr. Logue's union.' He added in pencil 'large number above the minimum', which is correct, but this implied the exercise of the power to withhold the minimum level, which was now to be removed from the management. For employers the new situation was traumatic compared with the immediate past. Eason noted: 'difficulty of dealing with vague reasoning of Mr. Logue — no limit to his wants.' Elsewhere he wrote: 'not antagonistic — open to new ideas' but an addition in pencil again suggests a measure of exasperation: 'Struggling against difficulties, yield nothing to Mr. Logue.'

The Union seemed to take Hely's as their base, stating that junior male shop assistants started there at 9s 3d a week, and proceeded to about 23s at the end of five years. They claimed an increase of 50 per cent and minimum of £3 for all qualified employees. The union also claimed the same rates for males and females. The award — the so-called 'Barton award' — was for 10s rising half-yearly to 30s at the end of five years, and to 55s at the end of eight years. The minimum for qualified assistants was set at 55s. Female assistants had a five year apprenticeship period, rising from 12s 6d to 35s, with 35s set as the minimum for a qualified assistant.

The union sought to have the period of male apprenticeship reduced to five years. The employers had claimed that skills were low, had been diluted, and that the best type of labour was not attracted. To this the arbitrator observed that 'if this be so, ten years would appear to be an unnecessarily long time for apprenticeship.' The arbitrator reduced it from ten to eight years.

Unlike other houses, Easons' were not the subject of a demand for retroaction, which suggests that the increases in the preceding year must have been in advance of those elsewhere in the trade. In August a demand was made again for 20s to adults, and 10s to juniors. The figure eventually agreed was 2s 6d to those on three years, and less than five; 5s to those on five years and 7s 6d to those on seven years. In the case of women, scales were not changed, but 2s 6d was added to those in receipt of the maximum. In December, by direct agreement between the Federation and the Union, a further increase of 2s 6d was granted to all junior males, and 5s to males in receipt of 55s and above, but only as an addition to wages, without reference to the scales which were affirmed on the existing levels.

Constant increases of this sort were alarming. In October 1919, Charles Eason noted that 'The increase in wages in the past half year (April-Sept) is very great and has cut most seriously into the margin of trade.' The settlement in March 1920 was said to add £2,000 to the wage bill. In May 1920 Charles Eason noted that the wage bill was up £10,000 in a year.

Chapter 15 Charles Eason II

THE ERA OF CHARLES EASON JUNIOR'S DOMINANCE in the firm, from the 1890s to the 1920s, was one of social, political and business change. After much political and military strife, the Irish Free State emerged from the Anglo-Irish Treaty of 1921; by the 1920s the influence of the landed class in the political world had gone; catholics were also beginning to assert themselves in the business world. After 1905 mass-circulation newspapers such as the *Daily Mail* developed new markets for reading; in Ireland William Martin Murphy's relaunched *Irish Independent* reached a sale of 100,000 copies by 1917. By the 1920s total sales of morning dailies in the Irish market probably exceeded half a million copies. Book publishing also changed radically. Many new publishers came into the market in the 1890s, and in 1926, the year Charles Eason resigned as managing director, radio broadcasting began in Dublin.

Charles Eason presided over the growth of the business in the first decade of the century, the second of the major expansions in its history. During this time the number of employees throughout the company went from just over 200 to nearly 700. The growth was most marked in the growth of the bookstall chain. The number of bookstalls doubled, and they became the feature of the business which made Eason's a household name throughout the entire island. He supervised the ordering of newspapers direct from the English publishers rather than through W.H. Smith's in 1905, and carried through the rebuilding programme after 1916.

As a man, Charles Eason was very like his father. It is clear from an incomplete autobiographical note how much he was under his father's influence and how much he respected him. Even as a young man he was serious: on the occasion of the fiftieth anniversary of Charles Easons' association with the house in 1925, Henry Digges, the manager of the Dublin shop, described 'a very vivid recollection of a studious small boy who when home from school for the holidays always found his way to our library.' He made a similar impression in 1875 on the Scot William

Barclay Peat. Peat, who was destined years later to become the head of the accountancy profession in Britain, was a cousin of Anna Thomson, whom Charles Eason was shortly to marry. Referring to Eason's trip to Germany, Peat wrote: 'I am rather surprised that you have taught yourself to drink German beer but then that is almost excusable, considering the goodness of the German beer.'

His intellectual energy was enormous and restless, greater than that of his father or of his own son, J.C.M. Eason. In the 1890s, and in the first two decades of the twentieth century, he was able to combine the wide range of his intellectual interests with the demands of his full-time occupation in the firm. His correspondence with his clergyman brother, Benjamin McFarlane Eason, ran across a wide range of interests, including intellectual and religious topics, and the moral implications of business from the 1890s onwards. The correspondence with Daphne Clare (a grand-daughter of the original Eason to settle in Australia) from as far back as 1914 is particularly striking because it was between a man of nearly seventy years, and a young woman who finally arrived in England in 1922 to pursue a career in journalism. He discussed books with her and commented on her newspaper articles, and advised her on sources of information.

His vitality comes across very clearly in the tone of all his surviving correspondence. It is also reflected in the number of interests he combined, and in the variety of meetings he attended. Even in February 1896 when the sole burden of conducting the business was falling on him, as his father's health was failing, he was able to remark that 'I am busy — almost too busy with matters outside the business.' Later that year he became a founder member of the Philanthropic Reform Association. On another occasion in October 1897 he remarked that with winter meetings beginning he had been out four nights in the previous week. In November 1907 he wrote to his brother Benjamin:

> I am much pressed with work and have not had time to send you anything about Street Trading Act but will do so on Thursday if possible. In addition to business I have had to prepare
>
> 1. Note as to the history of the Presbyterian Association for a meeting on Friday;
>
> 2. Arrangements for appointing actuary of Dublin Savings Bank;
>
> 3. Meetings in connection with report of Social Service Co.

At the Presbyterian Association he read no less than twenty papers from 1887 to 1931. Many were on religious or intellectual or partly political subjects, but they ranged far afield to include a talk on a papal encyclical, and even a paper in 1908 on Lafcadio Hearn, the Irish scholar greatly admired in Japan whose work is still scarcely known in Ireland.[1] He also read nine papers at the Statistical and Social Inquiry Society between 1881 and 1931. His connection with the Dublin Savings Bank was one of his earliest external associations. He was one of the managers in 1888, elected a trustee six years later, and appointed vice-chairman in 1904. In 1919 he became chairman, a position he relinquished only in 1937 through ill-health.

In all, according to a list of 'work in hand' in 1903, he was a member of no less than eleven bodies, and in a number of cases either in a secretarial or financial capacity. He was co-opted to Dalkey Town Commissioners in 1894, but as had been his father's case, his public life was low-key, and did not last long. But just as his father had taken a keen interest in the arrangement of the park in Kenilworth Square, Charles Eason, junior, was one of the residents of Dalkey who were responsible for the transfer of the Vico Road into public ownership. Although he supported William Martin Murphy staunchly in the employers' stand in 1913, and his support was undoubtedly a factor in the emergence of a new group within the Chamber of Commerce, his role in the day-to-day activities of the Chamber was minimal. He was not on its Council, and at its general meetings, he seems characteristically to have made a contribution only when purely intellectual issues were debated.[2]

His formal education was more extensive than his father's. Not only had he been to university, but he enjoyed the distinction of being the first presbyterian to win a Foundation scholarship at Trinity, after Fawcett's Act in 1873 had repealed the tests. In 1874 he got a first class Moderatorship. Like his father, Charles Eason was religious, more so than would appear from the external record of his activities. He confided to his clergyman brother Benjamin in March 1918 that when he found it hard to sleep, fearing a German victory 'I try to quiet my mind by repeating verses of Scripture and of hymns with fair success.' Like his father his cast of mind was independent. As he put it himself in a letter to a Canadian relative in 1934, 'we are all Presbyterians — of a sort.' When he moved from Rathgar to Glenageary in 1881 he joined the congregation of Kingstown Church. He was very active in its Councils, but as he had doubts which prevented him from signing the Westminster Confession,

1 T. Matsuo, 'Lafcadio Hearn (1850-1904) — his Irish background and appreciation of Japanese Culture' *Hosei University Economic Review*, LI, i (1983), 51-9.

2 Public Record Office of Ireland, Minutes of general assemblies of the Chamber of Commerce.

he was debarred from becoming an elder of the church. He was a regular attender at Sunday church services, morning and evening; the minister, Rutherford, recalled in 1930 that 'there is seldom a Sunday evening when Mr Eason does not come into the vestry to discuss bits or a part of my sermon.' Although he was not a signatory of the Westminster Confession, he was much more closely identified with church activities than his father. He was elected a member of the Committee of the congregation of Kingstown in 1883, became secretary in 1883, and retained that office until 1919. He was a member of the Presbyterian Association from the 1870s and acted as secretary from 1886, and from 1912 to 1928 he was Honorary Treasurer.

Some of his interests stemmed from his church involvement, perhaps notably his interest in education. He also took a keen interest in missionary activities. An address made to him in 1933 when he had completed fifty years in the Kingstown congregation referred to his 'intense interest in foreign missions'. His correspondence with his brother Benjamin bears this out as well. In 1915 with Charles Jacob, Professor Trench and others he formed the Irish Layman's Missionary Movement. In 1918 they financed an abortive project for a hostel for oriental students. In the same year he sent his brother a copy of the *Far East*, a new Roman Catholic magazine:

> It shows the importance Roman Catholics attach to China and is an interesting effort to promote a distinctively Irish foreign mission. I think it is remarkable how the lines of the appeal follow so closely those of Protestant appeals. Nothing about the Virgin Mary or Saints and very little about the pope.

He himself started to teach in the Kingstown Sunday School in 1882 and from 1883 to 1912 acted as superintendent of the Sunday School. Even as late as 1922 in September — no doubt with winter coming on — he wrote that 'I am busy looking up my Sunday School children and preparing for winter work in our temperance and missionary associations.' He was also a member of the Trinity College Tenement Company from before 1900, and became a director to the Social Service Tenement Company in 1903. In 1898 he wrote to Benjamin Eason that 'no doubt drink does paralyse the efforts to improve workmen's dwellings — I hope to send you my paper on tenement houses in a few days.' He shared his father's passion for the temperance movement. The only occasion on which he expressed himself publicly at the Chamber of Commerce on a purely material issue was in 1917 when he was in a minority of three opposing a resolution supporting the malting, distilling and brewing industries, against the effects of government regulation.[3] Housing of the poor commanded a lot of his attention. He spoke to the Presbyterian Association in 1898 on the 'Housing of the poor in Dublin' and to the Statistical and Social Inquiry Society in the same year on 'Tenement houses of Dublin: their condition and regulation'. In the same years he took a keen interest in poor law reform, and was on the committee of the Irish Workhouse Association. In 1906 he wrote that:

> Poor Law Reform report is most important. I am considering it and attending meetings to discuss it. The changes proposed are in the right direction but are so enormous that there is no hope of carrying them at present but public opinion requires to be educated and some steps might be taken, eg. if all lunatics should be moved to auxiliary asylums. Labour houses should be established — the proposals as to unmarried mothers are most radical and some steps in this direction should be taken.

The Eason family was materially comfortable. Their lifestyle not only permitted the best education available, but annual holidays were taken as a matter of course, often in beauty spots in the British Isles, but to a much greater extent than before in Switzerland, Germany and Norway as well. They had two servants, and a pony and trap. Charles himself did not drive, and they were somewhat slow in adopting the motor car. The first holidays by car were in the 1930s. Apart from holidays and education, life was modest and almost frugal. Eason was able to invest regularly and a letter of 1907 illustrates his investment contacts: 'I have given up Carnegie & Co — since the old man died.... I am now giving my business to Mr Moffat Wilson — son of old Mr Wilson of Cookstown — one of our church veterans.' His approach to wealth was still the rigid dissenting one. He elaborated on his father's 'Golden Rule' in correspondence, and was against speculation, as he explained in a letter of 6 April 1899: 'speculation would come in if I took the opportunity given to me by the control of wealth to invest in shares of companies with the intention of selling them at a profit. This I have always abstained from absolutely.' The probate valuation of his effects at the time of his death in 1941 was £16,804,[4] not much higher, allowing for the rise in price level, than that of his father in 1899.

Few close friends outside the family circle can be identified. Charles Jacob seems to have been one. Senator Douglas, one of the most respected

3 L.M. Cullen *Prices and pirates: The Dublin Chamber of Commerce* (Dublin 1983), p 86.
4 Public Record Office of Ireland.

members of the Free State Senate, knew him on first name terms and seems to have been the main influence on the political outlook of the Easons. Charles Eason had no contacts with other political figures. Political events in 1896 led him to moralise that 'at the bottom of it all is the lust for gold — the mad race for wealth. The people must be christianised and taught not to reverence wealthy people. Teach simple living.' Entertaining at home was rare, and in January 1896 he wrote to Benjamin Eason that 'we had Mr and Mrs Ashly up with us last evening — he is the American consul. We like them very much, they are simple homely people.'

In the last analysis, a dissenter streak was more evident in him than in either his father or his son J.C.M. Eason. With his immense energy and intellectual interests, which were never allowed to be subordinated to business, he is in some respects the most attractive of the Easons. Brisk and impatient — the picture from Sean O'Casey's *Pictures in the Hallway* is considered to be not inaccurate[5] — the similarity with his father's temperament is only superficial, because he was serene, and never prey to the intense fears and worries which plagued his father. He was a small man, like all the Easons, with a short white beard, and full of nervous energy, a perfectionist. Despite his involvement in the church, he was dispassionate, keen to argue the intellectual issues, and not prepared to take sides in the more minor issues which often divide christians of otherwise similar views. In a rumpus over the introduction of the organ into services in the Kingstown congregation, he abstained. Ultimately there was a distaste for dogma. He observed in a letter in 1907 that 'nominally, Protestants do not claim to be infallible, but practically they continually act as if they were.' The old dissenter and urban dislike of the landed political establishment was evident also — though the feeling was by no means confined to dissenters. He observed to Daphne Clare in 1920 that, while some English aristocrats were admirable, 'unfortunately a large number are what Mathew Arnold called "barbarians"; they are interested in sport and the management of their estates but are not well-read.'

The latter point was a cardinal one in Eason's philosophy. He was an omnivorous reader, with a range even wider than his father's. The major intellectual, historical, philosophical and religious works of his age and culture had been read, and during the annual family holiday he made deep forays into English literature. Jottings in his notes seem to point

5 See p. 121.

to some of the significant works in his reading. We know that he had already read Lecky before 1894, but *Leaders of Public Opinion in Ireland* was re-read in 1901; the third volume of Lecky's *History of Ireland in the Eighteenth Century*, and the final volume of Froude's *The English in Ireland* both cropped up in 1897. He was familiar with Marshall's *Principles of Economics* shortly after its appearance in 1890,[6] and read Bastable's *International Trade* in 1903, Beveridge's *Unemployment* and the Webbs' *Poor Law* in 1910. Writing about Lecky in 1894 he observed that 'I do not think any English writer of consequence has ever seriously challenged his account of Irish history.' While he felt that a suggestion that England should adopt a policy of expiation for past misdeeds was a fantastic one, he thought that 'Englishmen may rightly be taught that it is their duty to study seriously the Irish problem and recognise that Ireland's feelings towards England have only too good a foundation.' He read Canon Sheehan's books attentively — the earliest reference to them is to *My New Curate* in 1900. They clearly influenced him. When recommending books to Daphne Clare in 1920 as an introduction to life in the British Isles, he observed that 'the late Canon Sheehan wrote a number of stories of Irish life — they idealize the Irish people — but not more than Marriott and Jack Maclaren did the Scotch Presbyterians.'

His reading, his dissenter background and the influence of his father all combined to give him a sympathy for Ireland and Irish issues untypical of his class at the time. He had a distaste for imperialism, and his dislike of such policies outside Ireland crops up from time to time. His correspondence with his brother in 1898 in regard to university education for catholics, a live issue at that date, is interesting. In response to his brother's apparent fears that catholics were priest-ridden and that their education would fall under the influence of the clergy, Charles Eason's reply was:

> I don't like Romanism but we have to face the fact that the people are Roman Catholics and I think that we must run the risk.... The grievance is palpable viz they can only get university education on terms which their Church declares to be dangerous to faith and morals. I do not think a priesthood can limit the effects of education. Competition will compel a fair standard of study, and the mind well applied to study cannot be controlled.

On the question of denominational education, which often came up

6 In reading this book in 1890 Eason would have been well aware that it was the first title to be sold under Sir Frederick Macmillan's 'net book' scheme — see p. 190.

in correspondence with his brother, he was in sympathy with the views of catholics and anglicans as against the narrow dissenter view: 'sacramentarianism I agree with you, is not true, but others think it is, and I cannot see that it is anything but tyranny to say I will force my view upon them.' Independently he expressed a high regard for the Christian Brothers. In 1897 he was anxious to see issues settled in relation to boarding out children so that their role could be enlarged.

The Easons' protestant background was sometimes to be held against them in post-1920 Ireland. But in pre-1914 Ireland, their association with catholics was the more likely source of criticism. A letter in July 1902 gives an interesting account of Charles Eason's having to give up the chairmanship of a public meeting because of objections from extreme Protestants, and of the subsequent lack of disapproval of their actions:

> The extreme Protestant party objected to my being chairman and threatened to make a public protest. For peace sake I withdrew. Objection was based on my publishing Catholic prayer-books and on sundry statements such as that Roman Catholic books and papers had preference over Protestant on the stalls, that I found fault with the Government over appointing a Protestant lady inspector of Boarded-Out children etc. I have waited for a month to see what might be said on the matter. Not one word has been said. What am I to infer? The conclusion is that although few found actually approve of the action of the .... (rest of letter missing)

His political liberalism was reflected in the fact that his preference among newspapers was for the *Manchester Guardian*, then in its great days. As early as September 1900, with an election approaching, he wrote: 'the South Dublin contest is a very interesting one. I shall vote for Plunkett and if no nationalist stands, he should get in early. Some will certainly not vote for him on account of his support of a catholic university but this is a point in his favour in my view.'

Charles Eason's political and social views were well-known. A British MP studying Ireland at close hand after 1916 called on him, but this is the only indication of actual involvement of any sort. As time went on, his views became more clear-cut. In March 1918, he read a paper on Morley to the Presbyterian Association. The discussion revolved exclusively around the Irish dimension, and he pointed out that 'a number of administration acts which he fought against in India have had parallels in Ireland and England during the war — excessive punishments, deportation without trial — arrests on suspicion — press control.' At the end of the year at the general election his position was unshaken:

> I voted at TCD today (17 December). Gwynn, Woods, Samuels and Jellet. I don't think Gwynn has any chance but it is well to let people know that there are some who want to see a settlement including Ulster even though she cannot be coerced under present conditions. It is illustrative of the difficulties surrounding the League of Nations, for other nations have their Ulster and the League would have to protect minorities from oppression.

In January 1919 he felt that Ireland's case should be submitted to the League of Nations: 'Why is separation from England not conceivable?' He felt that: 'Of course "Ulster" is wrong but I don't see how she is to be got to change her mind just now. I would go on — giving as much freedom as possible to Sinn Fein and working towards the gradual change of mind in Ulster by peacable (sic) means.' As the war of independence in Ireland emerged, Eason's view did not change. He disapproved of official reprisals, and although at first he was inclined to accept the official view that the mayor of Cork had been assassinated by dissidents on the nationalist side, he came quickly to accept the view that the authorities had been responsible. As the situation worsened, things began to look bad for business. In May 1919, he commented, 'wages are being forced up and where "Labour" ends and "Sinn Fein" begins it is hard to say.' Remarkably, his view of the political issues remained unaffected in 1920:

> I don't see how to get Ulster to change her mind. Ulster says she will not submit to the domination of the rest of Ireland. I think this is mistaken. They are not asked to come under the heel (as they put it) of the Sinn Feiners. In a united Parliament Ulster would exercise much power and would be supported so much by the moderate section of the Nationalists that they would be able to prevent any oppressive legislation — if it were attempted.

When the Free State came in 1922, unlike others of his class and background, he felt that while things could get worse, there was a real prospect of order being restored.

Charles Eason was now a man of 67 years, and the fact that advancing age did not lead to a more conservative or fearful outlook is in itself a comment both on his strength of character and his underlying resilience. The business had suffered a good deal — it had been physically destroyed in 1916, and the costs of rebuilding greatly exceeded the compensation, generous though it was. The living standards of the family had been cut back because of the need to keep money in the business. Family deposits in the business were greatly enlarged. All the profits of 1918 were left in the business, and even as late as October 1919 he wrote that 'practically, we directors have not drawn any of last year's dividends'.

By January 1920 Charles Eason had put £4,000 of his own profits into the business, and was selling investments in order to pay his income tax. In the course of the year deposits increased further. This may have been in part achieved by realising further investments, as he informed his brother Benjamin in May 1920 that he and Fred Eason (who was secretary of the company) would 'have to realise securities of one kind or another to supply part of the amount required.' In that year his thoughts on the family holiday ran to retrenchment. Most businessmen in Ireland did very well out of post-war inflation whereas the Easons found the task of financing the physical rebuilding of their business in a time of inflation a difficult one. Even despite their self-sacrifice the consequence in the 1920s was an undercapitalised business resulting in profits which in nominal terms were no higher than before the war and in purchasing power were substantially lower. However from the picture which can be pieced together from the accounts and, incidentally, from Charles Eason's correspondence, it is clear that he allowed neither business problems nor political uncertainties to prey unduly on him. His only really dark moment was in March 1918 when the German offensive seemed to presage an Allied defeat. Even the growing spectre of socialism left him argumentative rather than intimidated. In the course of a long letter written in February 1919 in which he discussed the shadow cast over the future by labour movements and by efforts to organize a Citizens' Sunday in Dublin, he commented on working class life as described in Robert Tressell's *The Ragged Trousered Philanthropists*. He thought the book somewhat out of date, as it described the condition of non-unionised labour, 'but if anyone still thinks no union is necessary, this book might show him the contrary.' He concluded: 'Much in the book is to my mind unsound, but the presentation of the socialist standpoint is often very good and it would afford a good subject for discussion as to the best answers to the various arguments.'

During the strike in 1913, Charles Eason's son Jack had taken on much of the work, and by 1920 it was accepted that he should in future carry the main work load. J.C.M. Eason still had at that stage little acquaintance with the day-to-day running of the news department, though he had often been the firm's trouble-shooter in a crisis such as the 1913 strike, or other special problems that arose in subsequent years. Indeed, it was at this troubled stage of the department's history — the War of Independence — that he first took charge of the news department. J.C.M. Eason's rising remuneration reflected the growth in his responsibilities. In 1916/17 his salary had been £500, a figure exceeded by Ruthven and Coghill, and equalled by Brunton and Fred Eason. In 1920 his salary was £600, exceeded only by Charles Eason himself. In 1921 it was £700, becoming £775 in 1922 and £950 in 1923. In that year J.C.M. Eason's salary exceeded Charles Eason's for the first time. He was now making the running in the firm, and the reduction of his father's salary from £800 to £500 represented a substantial withdrawal from day-to-day business.

In July 1920 Charles noted that 'Jack has heavy responsibilities in the business; in fact he is the leading one now.' However it was still a shared responsibility, in that father and son frequently handled the same correspondence at different stages. Eason always kept his father informed of major issues, and such matters were always referred to the father for a decision. Only in 1926 did Charles Eason hand over control completely to his son. This left Charles free to concentrate on what was most congenial to him — reading, often in history, and above all, on his work on the various editions of the Geneva and Douai Bibles which he eventually published. This provided infinite scope for what was the most pleasing of all his pursuits — the intellectual fringes of religion. His correspondence with Daphne Clare, who sometimes made enquiries for him in the British Museum, clearly illustrated the relish he took in this work.

Despite the firm's considerable achievements in his time, in the end the impression persists that Charles Eason was an able businessman rather than an innovative one. It is possible of course that the fate which has preserved some of his private correspondence and so little of his business correspondence in contrast to his father or son, has been unkind to him. But if he had applied the immense intellectual energy expanded on meetings, papers and issues to the problems of the business, it is unlikely that the resulting papers would all have disappeared, especially as his son Jack collected and listed such items systematically. So it is unlikely that a more positive impression of him would have survived.

Unlike his father or his son, Charles Eason never carried single-handedly the responsibility for the key department of wholesale news, and in the first decade of the century, McDowell, Brunton and J.C.M. Eason were already towers of strength. McDowell, the manager of the news department, seems to have been the driving force in negotiating direct purchases of English news, and Eason's son-in-law, Albert Brunton, gained his reputation in the same department. The first steps towards a fuller analysis of accounting information were taken in the years before

1914 by J.C.M. Eason, and modern auditing of the accounts was prompted only by the problems that arose after the rebellion. It was J.C.M. Eason who saw the need to broaden the personnel in the 1920s. The first attempt made to widen the business with outsiders at the top was made in 1925, when William Calwell, who had been secretary of the Chamber of Commerce, was brought in as a director. J.C.M. Eason had worked with him in the Chamber of Commerce for some years.[7] The development of a close liaison between Dublin and Belfast also seems to have been his son's doing, and it turned out to be the basis for the remarkably close contact between J.C.M. Eason and George Best in the 1930s which put the Belfast business for the first time on the plane of a department receiving the central attention of the Dublin office.

In fact, the growth of the business under Charles Eason has some of the character of British business generally in the decade before 1914. As in many sectors of the British economy, the bookstalls had mushroomed on the eve of their contraction, and the expansion of the factory, whose economics were quickly outmoded, had proceeded apace during the same period of time.

7 There were also some family as well as religious acquaintance. Charles Eason told Benjamin Eason on 25 November 1925 about Calwell that 'when a boy he was in Fred's Sunday School class'. This tells us more about Charles than about Jack Eason, whose interest in Calwell was totally pragmatic.

Chapter 16 ❧ The Belfast market — challenge and response

IN THE NINETEENTH CENTURY THE BELFAST BRANCH had grown only slowly — turnover rose from £11,528 in 1876/7 to £16,686 in 1898/9.[1] This was a distinctly slower rate of growth than that achieved in Dublin. After then, between 1898/9 and 1906/7, the turnover rose to £32,500, and by 1916/7 it was £57,320, much faster than the Dublin growth rate. The Belfast branch however merits separate attention not only because its operations were sizeable but because its hinterland was the only part of Ireland where the firm experienced sustained competition. Serious rivals appeared there earlier than anywhere else in Ireland, they lasted longer and presented the most expansive profile. In Cork the Tivy family, later trading as News Brothers, dominated the market from an early date, but they were content with their virtual monopoly there. As the Tivys showed no wish to expand, Eason's in turn were content not to challenge their position.

The first rival in Belfast was Olley's, who as already described, made serious inroads into advertising by capturing dramatically the valuable Great Northern Railway contract. Another rival, Porter's, emerged in 1899, the year in which Olley's failed. Charles Porter started as an ordinary retailer, who drew supplies from Eason's. He then began to distribute to other retailers. His rise was due to the fact that Eason's did not deliver newspapers to agents in the Belfast region, and Porter saw an opportunity in this to set up as a wholesaler. McNamara, the manager in Belfast, reported on 30 June 1899 that

> a Mr Porter, Donegall Road, is interfering with our customers and getting our orders divided as he delivers all goods having his own trap. He is making up a wholesale trade, having, I hear, 30 customers.... Our customers are not increasing their orders, nor, in

1 The Belfast branch opened in 1870. A Belfast warehouse had been opened in 1868 and moved to the new branch at 12 Waring Street two years later.

> some cases, are they ordering any new publications. This means that they are ordering elsewhere.[2]

Delivery had become an issue with the local newsagents, and Easons' indecisiveness in facing up to the implications, had given Porter the opportunity. As late as 16 June 1899 the Belfast manager wrote to Dublin that 'the delivery of our agents' parcels is an important matter that will have to be faced and it is not easy to work out a satisfactory, inexpensive plan, as our customers live North, South, East and West.' The source of Easons' reluctance was the fear that if agents did not come in to collect parcels, they might lose other business with them — as the manager wrote: 'also by delivery we would lose sales in the warehouse by the non-attendance of the customers who call for their parcels and inspect new stock of stationery or books.'

While the opening of Porter's business was prompted by local circumstances, its prospering was a result of external circumstances: the effort by the English dailies such as the *Daily Mail, Daily Sketch* and *Daily Mirror* to push circulation. Many years later in 1944 J.C.M. Eason vaguely recalled that 'until the Mail, Sketch and Mirror began to look for circulation (which was sometime after the Boer War) there was no daily distribution to be done in Belfast. I know there was no van distribution by us.' As early as 1904 the *Daily Mail* already appears to have had the largest circulation of any daily handled by the house in Belfast. Correspondence surviving from July 1905 shows that the *Daily Mail* had just launched national distribution in Ireland. Supplies for Dungannon and Derry came through Dublin, but parcels for Belfast were being sent by Stranraer. Some English dailies now appeared in the city in the morning, whereas previously they would have appeared via Dublin only late in the afternoon. With the push to expand circulation Porter's were able to extend business beyond the city itself and supply agents in towns immediately surrounding Belfast.

The fear of competition was sufficiently great for Albert Brunton to be dispatched north in 1905 for an extended visit. On 5 July 1905 he observed from Belfast that 'it goes against the grain to let him [Porter] into the country custom.' Brunton's visit established the tradition of surveying the Belfast house closely, instead of regarding it passively as a warehouse to be virtually ignored if problems did not arise. The crucial railway contracts had always been handled by the Dublin house and the small number of railway advertising staff in Belfast were regarded as staff

2 Correspondence now in Belfast House.

members of the Dublin house, not of the Belfast branch. However Brunton's presence in Belfast in 1905 was the start of a new policy. Belfast was now watched closely from Dublin, and a director was henceforth responsible for the Belfast business (in fact Brunton himself). A letter book which contains copies of a handful of letters regarded as too confidential to pass through the house provides us with some telling details of the circumstances of mid-1905.[3] Until his death in 1921 Brunton was a regular visitor to Belfast, a responsibility that then devolved onto J.C.M. Eason.

The English papers were the crucial factor in bringing about the increased competition in Belfast. The Belfast morning papers did their own distribution in the Belfast area. As early as 1916 a case was put forward for discontinuing an agreement made by both Eason's and Porter's with the Irish Society of Newsagents, Booksellers and Stationers in Belfast because it had 'increased the desire on the part of publishers to be represented by Wholesalers outside the two who agreed to act according to retail agents wishes three years ago.' It was noted that the publishers had assisted in introducing two wholesale agents to compete for trade with the two original wholesalers. These two agents must have been W. Norris for the *Daily Mail* and W. Fitzpatrick for the *Daily Sketch*, both of whom built up the sales of their own papers at the expense of Eason's and Porter's, who were left with a reduced share of the sales of dailies. As always when competition was fierce, discounts appeared. Porter was giving a discount of 5 per cent off invoices to newsagents in 1905. Brunton offered a 2½ per cent discount to Larne newsagents, who threatened to transfer to Porter: 'I do not think we should go further than the 2½ per cent unless we are prepared to fight Porter with his own weapons and that is against all previous principles with us.'

In these conditions, it is not surprising that Porter established a firm foothold in the wholesale news business in these years, although within a very restricted area. However, his business was still a very small one. Unlike Olley's, he did not bid for railway contracts in advertising or bookstalls. His staff in 1912 amounted to 22 persons, and it did not expand in the next five years.[4] It amounted to one-third of Easons' Belfast staff. Eason's was therefore a much bigger house, but was also providing many other services. Eason's supplied books and stationery, and serviced railway bookstalls. In January 1918 their staff totalled 62 not including

3 In the Belfast house.
4 Porters' wage book 1912-17.

staff in the bookstalls, and three staff in railway advertising. Eason's had 20 staff in wholesale news in January 1918, but to this figure should be added most or all of the eleven staff in the Counting House and the packers and messengers. Eason's therefore had twice as many staff in wholesale news as Porter's, who had 22 employees in December 1917. Wage rates in the two houses seemed broadly comparable (just above £1 a week in Porter's, just under £1 in Eason's). Porter's did not grow over the years 1912-17, nor did Eason's over the same period, so that a position of stability had emerged. Porter had secured a niche for himself in Belfast and in the immediately surrounding towns. Elsewhere in Ulster he had not challenged Easons' monopoly. Business through the railway bookstalls was still expanding in the north, and when this is taken into account, Eason's must probably have commanded about three quarters of wholesale news business.

Albert Bailie, who retired in 1976 after 56 years service, recalled that when he was recruited in October 1919 a small staff was required at the GNR station to meet the many trains from Dublin carrying English and Dublin dailies. Supplies for country and city customers were made up in a building at the station. Norris who handled the bulk supplies of *Daily Mail* and *Daily Mirror*, and Fitzpatrick who handled *Daily Sketch* and *Sporting Chronicle* established a priority in jumping into the railway wagon, and Easons' boys received rough treatment at times if their enthusiasm put them within reach of the opposition. With Norris, Fitzpatrick and Porter's gaining an increasing share of the sales of dailies by faster deliveries to newsagents, Eason's reacted by using a carrier (W.W. Kennedy & Co) to deliver newsagents' parcels. Delivery was still by horse drawn vehicles. In 1922 when rioting was not uncommon in some areas of Belfast, the slow open horse-drawn carts occasionally became a target, and at least one driver was personally attacked. To minimise this danger, a pick-up type of motor truck was used on really bad days with a delivery boy (Albert Bailie) in certain areas. Parcels were tossed on the pavement outside the shops and the vans moved on smartly. Although English dailies were a minor part of the news business and from Eason's point of view a small contributor to their revenue as compared with weekly and monthly publications, the newsagents could exert pressure on the wholesaler to give a fast delivery of dailies or threaten to give all or part of their business to the opposition wholesalers.

The competition in the north, at its most acute in the 1920s, meant that the branch had to be re-organised and its relationship with the Dublin house made clear. Superficially this was brought about by partition, which divided Ireland into two fiscal units, and led to the formation of a separate Eason & Son (Belfast) Ltd in 1924. However that was for legal and fiscal reasons. A more important issue was the actual management of the Belfast house. When Albert Brunton died at an early age in 1921, the question arose as to who should take on his responsibilities for the north. Competition with Porter's was becoming acute. Charles Eason had never been very interested in the Belfast business, and had been content to leave the branch to the manager on the spot under the general supervision of Brunton in Dublin. Horwood, the manager, must have depended a good deal on Albert Brunton for all but day to day management decisions, and it was virtually inevitable that J.C.M. Eason should take over Brunton's responsibilities in Belfast.

In the following year, the post of Bookstall Superintendent in Belfast became vacant, and J.C.M. Eason appointed George Best to this position. Best was a tough, competitive businessman who had been brought up in the hard school of making and selling handkerchiefs where as little as one farthing in a dozen handkerchiefs made the difference between profit and loss. For ten years he had been foreman and assistant manager in Sefton's, and had been let go in the depression of 1922. As bookstall superintendent he was given a salary of £5 a week (he had asked for £5.10.0). He had no experience of news or books, and it is a measure of his reputation that he was appointed to the position without any background in Easons' business. His testimonial from Sefton's stated that 'he is very honest, hardworking and attentive to his duties, he has a good control over those under him, and has identified himself in every way in the interests of his employers during the time he has been with us.'

Early in 1925 Eason received a telephone call from Joseph Doran, accountant in the Belfast house. As a result he went to Belfast immediately, and the manager Horwood retired forthwith, for reasons which can only be guessed. The impression which George Best had made on Eason meant that Eason had no hesitation after discussing the matter with Best in recommending to the Board that Best be appointed Manager. Best, who was now 38, was reluctant to take on the extra responsibility after such short experience in the Company, and he only accepted the appointment after Eason had agreed to visit Belfast at frequent intervals, if necessary once a week, until Best was confident that he had settled in to the new job. When he was offered the post Best wrote that 'bookstall work appeals to me, I like going after all the knotty little problems that crop up.' He noted that

I have fought shy of being placed in the position of manager because

> its a very important position to adopt and a vital one where the progress of a firm is concerned. If I had been brought up to this particular business I would have pleaded with you for the position, knowing that I could do it successfully, but as it is I am really frightened that through my inexperience it might go backwards, that would hurt me more than all.

The last phrase touches on a significant part of Best's character: his combative business sense. This quality is hinted at in his dismissive assessment of a would-be appointee to a post in January 1927: 'I don't think that he would be a "hustler" and that's what we want.' In February 1929 after Best had formulated his proposals for re-organising Derry, he wrote that 'I sincerely wish we had Derry working on a satisfactory basis not only in regard to ourselves but to agents, at the same time showing our competitor that when roused we are very much alive.'

A distinctive pattern developed. J.C.M. Eason travelled regularly to Belfast, every fortnight or so. In the interval he and Best discussed problems in an almost daily correspondence. This correspondence counted for much in the history of the house. Both in Belfast and Dublin many of the files were retained, and frequently the two sides of the correspondence have survived, which is a rare feature in business correspondence. This was a meeting of two sharp minds. Problems of terms and conditions of distribution were discussed at length, a vital concern because differences did arise in the terms offered by London publishers to Belfast and Dublin, and it was important to pick these points up quickly and pursue them. Best was a formidable man, and a respected one. Those who knew him thought well of him. He was not an intellectual — his hobby was breeding canaries, which he entered for competition.

Best and Eason were sensitive to all the currents in news in the north, and challenges in the trade were quickly identified and responses made to them. The correspondence between them, however, occasionally showed signs of exasperation on both sides. Best regarded some of Eason's interests as academic and gave way reluctantly. His practical mind meant that he had little time or inclination for the more refined statistical calculations, for the reduction of data to a few tidy tables that could fit neatly on a single sheet or for very fine niceties of language in a circular to agents. Eason, on the other hand, was precise in a relentless fashion, and was remorseless in these issues, which he pursued with assiduity, despite encountering a stiffness on the part of his northern counterpart. Eason liked to have situations summarised succinctly. On one occasion when he asked for a description of a position, he complained that he had been given a catalogue of detail. But Best himself had a clear mind, and his letters are fluent, written in a simple and unadorned style. Both men were reserved in temperament, both keenly interested in the detail of business, of which they had a thorough mastery and for which Eason clearly respected Best. Despite their frequent meetings and almost daily correspondence, the tone of the letters remained surprisingly impersonal, which is an interesting comment on the character of both men and on their direct and singleminded devotion to the immediate issues that arose. A measure of Best's standing is the fact that he became a shareholder of the Belfast house in the 1930s and was the only man from outside the small circle of family and Dublin directors to do so before the 1950s.

Best's appointment as manager took place when Eason's were encountering increased competition in the northern market, and it was prompted by the necessity of responding to that situation. Earlier deliveries in the 1920s were making it realistic for Porter's to extend the challenge to Eason's from Belfast and its immediate hinterland across Ulster. In the 1920s the railways apparently departed from the old flat rate for carrying newspaper parcels. This gave northern wholesalers a further incentive to expand their distribution. Deliveries through Dublin were now losing out on all counts. This competition was made all the more serious because in the 1920s the railway bookstalls were ceasing to be the mainstay of distribution, and as custom passed from them to retail newsagents, Eason's lost some of the business. Porter's systematically gave a discount of 2½ per cent on news supplies outside Belfast, whereas Eason's did not, or only on accounts exceeding £5 per week. The cost of delivery of newsagents parcels by train and bus outside Belfast was charged to the newsagents concerned, and the discount was referred to as an allowance against the cost of carriage, no doubt to forestall Belfast newsagents, who had a free delivery service, from looking for a discount as well. The growth of the English dailies accelerated in the 1920s partly because printing in Manchester combined with the chartering of special trains form Manchester to Heysham made it possible to get a wider range of papers to Belfast at 7 am in the morning. Early arrival made it possible to distribute to country agents by the later part of the morning. By the end of the 1920s between 100,000 and 120,000 copies of English dailies must have been distributed; approximately one house in two purchased a copy. Not only did these figures point to a near mass market, but they illustrate the dominance which the English papers were acquiring in readership in Ulster.

Eason's responded in various ways to this sharpening of competition.

In 1923 they produced a very attractive booklet, called *Newspapers in the Making*, clearly directed at the retail trade. Secondly, there was an effort in 1923 to organise delivery by air. This attempt was shortlived, but it was an obvious attempt both to win publicity and gain advantage. Despite these efforts, Easons' share in newspaper distribution was falling. Judging from staffing in wholesale news, Eason's could have had two-thirds of newspaper distribution, not including the railway bookstalls, during the second decade. By 1933 this proportion was certainly smaller. Of the bulk supply (excluding direct parcels) of seven English dailies received in Belfast in 1933 for town and country delivery amounting to 1,170 quires, Eason's took 255 quires, Porter's 252 quires, and the papers' representatives 663 quires. Figures for the *Daily Express* in 1942 reflect the position yet a decade later: of the total circulation of 2,000 copies, one quarter was handled by Eason's, 'very little more' by Porter's, and the remaining 40 per cent was in the hands of the representatives who according to George Best distributed to what were 'really street-sellers'. In March 1944 J.C.M. Eason thought that only the railway bookstalls gave Eason's more weight in the north than Porter's, and he commented to Best: 'On account of our bookstall position we may have a more favourable means of approach than he would have.' Easons' share of daily newspaper distribution was not an indicator of their share of the overall market. They did better in weeklies, although in 1933 Best reckoned that Porters' and Easons' supplies were on a par.[5] In the case of monthly magazines, Porter's supplies were only 75 per cent of Eason's.

Porter's were ahead of Eason's in opening a Derry branch. They opened in Derry in 1924. In October Easons' Belfast branch reported to Dublin with false optimism that

> Porter has no doubt suffered in Londonderry; his undertaking has not been a success, the success anticipated at our expense. He could not have expected to make the venture a success without getting a much greater volume of business than he had when he commenced, and the only way he could get further business would be to take Eason's customers....

The flavour of the intense competition in the north comes across in the letter:

> We have evidence, but I do not know how far we could prove it, that he himself as well as his employees have made remarks

5 By the 1920s Sunday newspaper publishers did not distribute through either Eason's or Porter's and frequently their retailers were different also.

> extremely detrimental to ourselves, not only in Derry but elsewhere.... The remarks are 'Easons are a Dublin firm — they are a big firm — I am a small man, one of yourselves, therefore you should support me — Easons do not give attention to their wholesale trade, but all their attention is given to their retail trade and their bookstall, this comes first with Easons'.

Porter for his part was threatening libel proceedings because of alleged slanderous statements to the effect that:

> Mr Porter is financially in a very bad way and as a consequence will have to close down his business in Derry, and threats have been made by the same employees to certain of Mr Porter's customers that unless these customers transfer their business to your firm they will not be supplied by you with goods when Mr Porter closes down.

By 1926 the loss of customers to Porter's was becoming serious. In August Best attributed the loss of customers to 'Porter delivering and collecting everything even *News Letter, Whig* etc', and concluded that 'I am afraid we must do something if we are to retain our business in Derry.' Eason's did their business in Derry through their bookstall. The only concession to the fact of competition was that a senior clerk had been put in charge of the bookstall. Best now saw that the only hope was to open a wholesale branch with a motor van for deliveries. He visited the agents in Derry himself in March, and the newsagents' comments made it clear to him how essential it was to change in Derry. One agent, for instance, 'wanted to know when we were going to open up the same as Porter in Derry, and it was a great convenience to have returns collected and extras delivered at any time required without being told that they must be ordered from Belfast House which meant a delay of one or two days'. At length premises were acquired in 51a Foyle Street, and in 1929 the branch opened. The first manager was Alexander Gordon, and he had four assistants. In 1926 Porter supplied 33 newsagents in Derry with approximate weekly invoices worth £107.10.0d. By the outset of 1929 Porter supplied 43 newsagents in Derry, while Eason's supplied only 15, although they were probably larger. Eason's certainly had the largest newsagent in Derry; fear of alienating him seems to have been the reason that Eason's decided against opening a retail business in conjunction with the new wholesale branch.

Competition remained very fierce. A report in March 1931 noted than when the manager, Gordon, 'managed to get in with one of Porter's agents, Leonard (Porter's Derry manager) sent word to Belfast and Mr Porter almost always came to Derry himself to follow up the business we had taken from him.' Charles Porter had been fortunate in his choice of manager to open his Derry branch in 1924. Robert Leonard went there as a young man and became a legend in his lifetime. The competition between Gordon of Eason's and Leonard of Porter's became so uncompromising that neither man was happy to go on holiday leaving the other a free hand in Derry. It was not unknown for the two to agree to go on holiday at the same time and for Leonard to break his holiday in Portrush and return to his business in Derry. Porter's was run less professionally than Eason's, but it combined informality with speedy delivery. In February 1928 Best had reported to Dublin that

> I learned that Porter had 52 agents in all to deal with at Derry; this means Derry (36?) and country districts (16?). He now has a staff of six to deal with the work, and on watching their methods yesterday morning, I would not be surprised if the business was carried on at a loss. Retail agents simply cut the parcels open, and took out their own supplies, simply a matter of speed, everything to be got rid of as quickly as possible. Apparently they do not make up parcels for the different agents. The whole supplies, as far as I could see, were taken in the Motor, and doled out accordingly from agent's sheets whilst at the door of any of their agents — this method is certainly speedy, saves packing etc., and to compete with this, presently we are not adapted for it. Even if we did adapt ourselves for it, and put on a motor service, the competition would be so keen that in the long run some one of us would have to retire. There are only a few of Porter's customers that I would care to do business with, the majority, in my opinion, would be very hard to watch in regard to payments.

Inevitably, as a late starter, Porter's newsagencies in established areas were smaller, and, as Best observed, not worth going after. More important was the likely fate of areas which were still largely untapped, and which could now be serviced for the first time through bus routes. Apart from Limavady and Strabane, Porter supplied newsagents at only six centres in Donegal, all of which were accessible from Derry. Best observed rightly in March 1929:

> There is a further field for development ie Donegal. The country is now being opened up with a bus service, the drawback from a commercial point of view, is the customs duty, or rather the border question. Derry business men, as a whole, are suffering severely through this, and do not like it. It will mean that agents, say, in Carrigans, St Johnston, Moville, Carndonagh, Culdaff, Fahan, Ramelton, Letterkenny, Burtonport, Killygordon, Stranorlar,

> Donegal, Killybegs, Ballyshannon and Bundoran have to pay 7d on each parcel. Even with this the savings in carriage per bus contract would be cheaper than per rail from the Free State. This, I think, is where our competitor is scoring in a number of instances. I know he is sending to Stranorlar, or rather Ballybofey, and I believe also to Letterkenny.

Porter's strengthened their Derry position by obtaining the wholesale franchise in Derry for the English Sunday papers and for the Dublin morning papers. In Belfast neither Eason's nor Porter's were interested in Sunday wholesaling at that time, nor did the attitude of the Sunday publishers encourage them. Sunday papers preferred to have the Sunday edition in the hands of a small wholesaler responsible for only one or two Sunday titles, even when their sister daily was distributed by the orthodox wholesalers who carried dailies, weeklies and magazines.

In the 1930s Eason's were cautious in going after business. The highly competitive Best would no doubt have been happy to do so, but J.C.M. Eason was conscious of the shaky economics of servicing a growing number of small retail outlets, and he was less enthusiastic about expansion. The war years led to a truce — a gentleman's agreement was made that neither wholesaler would look for the other's business or accept transfers during the war or for six months afterwards. The wartime shortage of newsprint resulted in a severe rationing of supplies of all publications in Northern Ireland, but the south was treated as an export market and some additional supplies could be obtained from publishers on the grounds that they were for export to Donegal or further afield. The truce lasted, but by February 1947 Best felt that it was not being observed by Porter's Derry branch and added that 'at the end of the period I made up my mind that .... we would make it as hot for him as we possibly could. We have steadily worked our way into Porter's customers and could do more if we had the supplies.' Thereafter Porter, who had consolidated his foothold in Donegal, spread into Connaught. Best warned Eason on 12 February 1947 that Porter had secured some orders in Galway and Westport: 'It is difficult to know what terms they have offered to secure this business, and how he is going to get supplies in at a lower cost of carriage than we are paying.' Eason's had one cancellation from Westport and another from Galway at this stage.

Where it was possible to obtain copy-invoices from a newsagent served by Porter, the terms of the invoice showed distinct differences from Easons' terms, although some things were not evident from the delivery sheets. Thus, although some papers were priced at the dozen rate, the thirteenth copy was in fact given. J.C.M. Eason in Dublin noted in February 1947 that 'there are very surprising differences in terms, and in many cases our terms are substantially better.' But Porter's operation was characterised by total flexibility, as Best pointed out in his reply to this observation: 'When an agent draws his attention to any difference between his list and that of Eason's he simply alters the price to that of Eason's and the agent goes away all pleased with himself.'

How successful were Eason's in meeting this competition? This question cannot be answered categorically, because there is a lack of adequate data about circulation and distribution. The impression is that Best and Eason succeeded in containing the competition, and avoiding a continuation of the erosion of Easons' hold which had been so marked in the 1920s. In 1930 the house's circulation of the seven popular English dailies in the second week of June had been 6,113 quires. By 1932 this had fallen to 5,075 quires, but had recovered to 7,319 quires in 1937. As the pioneers of news in the region, Eason's tended to have the larger newsagents to start with, and their strategy was to keep these rather than to expand into the small ones. In Belfast where turnover was largest they expanded the number of their agents significantly from 146 in 1922 to 192 in 1937. But the number of country agents changed little, and in Derry and Donegal in particular despite Porter's competition they were cautious about taking on extra small agents. This was still the policy in June 1947 when Best wrote:

> We suspect from the fact that Porter has made an application to open a number of accounts in the smaller towns in Donegal that we shall hear more about this point; it is an area which we may not cover effectively from here, and I do not see my way at the present time to enter into any competition on these lines.

The results were that in 1944 in the northern news region overall 339 newsagents were supplied by Eason's exclusively, another 58 were supplied by Eason's and another house (the 'split lists'), and 341 newsagents were supplied by other wholesalers. But there were marked contrasts in the different areas. Eason's supplied only 135 newsagents in Belfast compared with 157 supplied by other wholesalers (excluding 41 split lists). In the rural districts they supplied 86 newsagents compared with 87, and in Derry city 19 compared with 21. Of the country newsagents, a mere 14 seem to have been serviced from the Derry house: it had moved very sparingly into Donegal, and effectively left that geographically large but thinly populated and straggling county to their rival. In the case of towns with a population of 1500 and upwards, Eason's were in a dominant position: 99 retailers compared with 76. These figures do not take into account the railway bookstalls. They were still important, and would have been most significant in Belfast and the towns of east Ulster. If the large bookstall business in the Belfast region is included, Eason's must have had half the market. Eason's certainly held a significant place in the distribution in east Ulster and may have regained ground. In the more remote regions and in Donegal, they were content to hold their main customers, leaving it to Porter's to develop the smaller and more remote reaches of circulation. There is not enough data to measure their actual success in detail. Figures for four weeklies (*John Bull, Passing Show, Radio Times, Answers*) surviving from one week in September 1933, for which both Porters' and Easons' circulation survives, show that Eason's exceeded Porter's in all four publications in Belfast, whereas in three of the four publications Porter's led in circulation in Derry. The chance survival of a full list of the circulation of the *TV Post* for January 1960 confirms this pattern. In the Belfast region, Easons' circulation exceeded Porters': 47,000 copies as against 43,000. In Derry Porters' circulation was almost twice Easons': 1,300 as against 700.

Eason's strategy did not succeed in establishing a monopoly, nor was it intended to. It did succeed in holding on to the larger customers and in concentrating its success in the more lucrative parts of the province. In this way, despite intense competition, the Belfast house not only remained on balance the largest house in news in Ulster, but its profits were a vital component of the overall profitability of the Dublin house. The fact that the volume of business rose and some competitive ground was recovered between 1925 and 1937 is some measure of the success of both Best and Eason in difficult circumstances. The most delicate part of the operation and the ultimate test of the success of the two is that over the years from the early 1930s they were able to preserve their share of the market without enlarging their distribution network much outside Belfast itself, and in this way prevented the profitability of the house from being impaired even further by the many adverse circumstances of the 1930s.

The number of staff employed rose significantly with some growth in circulation. Even between January 1919 and 1920 staff in Belfast (not including advertising) rose from 62 to 66. With the impact of increased competition this figure had risen to 84 by January 1923, and to 100 by January 1925. The great bulk of the increase was in the years 1919-24. The growth was slower thereafter, reaching 117 by January 1937, including members of staff at the Derry branch. The rise in staff in Belfast contrasts with the near stagnation in staffing in the Dublin house in the interwar years.

Economic factors were important in establishing the northern company's position. Higher incomes, and a higher degree of urbanisation and literacy were factors making the per capita consumption of news greater in the north than in the south. Moreover while the north suffered depression in the interwar years, the service sector expanded over the same period, and employees in that sector had higher incomes and more highly developed tastes in reading than those in the depressed linen industry. Shipbuilding prospered, quite atypically for that industry through the 1920s, through the success of Harland and Wolff. Agriculture and the small towns in the north also escaped from the worst of the depression, and gained from British agricultural protectionism from 1933 onwards. Daily newspaper buying was probably not very different north or south, but crude comparisons would suggest that per capita consumption of weeklies (other than Sundays) was twice as high in the north. Moreover protection in the south sharpened the contrast because it virtually annihilated the trade in cross-channel daily news to Dublin. In the north on the other hand, during the period of severe competition in distribution, the circulation of cross-channel dailies in the Belfast house rose over the 1920s and 1930s.

These circumstances were to be reflected in the relative financial results of the Dublin and Belfast houses. While Dublin easily outshone Belfast in the age of selective readership prior to the first world war, the Belfast house was better circumstanced to profit from mass circulations as they emerged in the 1920s. Even the railway bookstalls fared better in Belfast than in Dublin in the interwar years. During these years Belfast benefited from favourable factors, and the weight of the house, both in news circulation at large and as a contribution to Easons' share of the total volume of business, increased very significantly. Belfast profitability was helped by the fact that both turnover per stall and turnover per newsagent was higher than in the south. This was partly a function of denser population, higher incomes and a high degree of literacy, but it was also helped by caution in expanding news outlets despite the competition. The ratio of Belfast news turnover to Dublin turnover was 31:100 in 1926/7 and rose to 48:100 in 1936/7. This helps to explain why the Belfast house remained profitable and why it became the keypoint of the overall profitability of the parent house. Belfast's place in the strategy of the firm, and J.C.M. Eason's and Best's interest in the northern market can be seen not merely as a reaction to very real local problems but also as a response to greater opportunities.

The consequences of their labours were reflected in the turnover. Eason's northern turnover rose continuously through the period from 1898/9 to 1916/7, indicating the limited impact of Porters at this stage. Between 1916/17 and 1926/27 however the rise in news turnover in Belfast fell short both of the rise of total turnover in Belfast, and of the rise in news turnover in Dublin. These figures exclude sales at the bookstalls, but in their case also buoyancy had disappeared between these dates. It was within this period that the impact of competition in the north became serious, and the appointment of Best in February 1925 was made at a crucial moment in the fortunes of the northern business. Between 1926/7 and 1936/7 news turnover in the north rose by approximately 50 per cent, whereas news turnover in Dublin stagnated.

Especially significant was the contribution that the Belfast house made to the profits of the Dublin holding company. The dividend from Belfast to the Dublin house rose from £934 in 1924/5 to £1,785 in both 1929/30 and 1930/31. The dividend from the north exceeded the net trading profits in Dublin in no less than four of the seven years from 1924/25 to 1930/1. Superficially the Belfast house already seemed the more profitable part of the enterprise in 1921/2 and 1922/3 but this was due mainly to the extraordinary post-war losses in Dublin in stationery and the factory. The contribution of Belfast is also somewhat overrated in the sense that Dublin carried more of the overheads than Belfast did.

The regular profits of the second half of the 1920s and early 1930s were a consequence of successful management by Eason and Best. Belfast profits slipped somewhat in the 1930s and even more in the war years. When they recovered later, their importance in the overall profits of the house were again very evident. In the 1950s the dividend from Belfast was the equivalent of up to a half of the final dividend paid by the parent house, and this serves as the best measure of the importance of the Belfast house. This solid contribution was most valuable in the late 1920s and early 1930s when Dublin's profits were meagre, and again in the late 1940s and early 1950s when Dublin's profits were once more very disappointing. Dublin's trading profits stagnated from 1947/8 to 1952/3 while the Belfast dividend more than doubled.

Chapter 17 The decline of the railway connection, 1920-40

BY 1920 J.C.M. EASON WAS THE PRINCIPAL EXECUTIVE in the firm, as his father described him. He had joined the company in 1901, and until 1916 he had been mainly concerned with the wholesale stationery side of the business, and with the printing factory in Gloucester Place. However, since 1913 or thereabouts he can be seen as sharing some of the general managerial functions of the firm with his father, and thus greatly widening his knowledge of the house at large. The destruction of the Abbey Street and O'Connell Street buildings in that year drew him into the wholesale news management in its temporary home in Great Brunswick Street (Pearse Street). The Belfast business was looked after by Albert Brunton until his untimely death in 1921. Thereafter J.C.M. Eason became responsible for that area as well and in 1926 he formally succeeded his father as Managing Director, a position which he held until 1950. By then he was aged seventy, but he continued as Chairman of the company until 1958. His years of management equalled his grandfather's in duration, his association with the firm from the time he entered was even longer.

The character of the period during which J.C.M. Eason managed the firm was very different from the era of his father's dominance. There was no repetition of the growth experienced in the late nineteenth and early twentieth centuries. From as early as 1887/8 annual profits had reached £6,000, and were well above this figure in many years during the late 1890s. In 1897/8 the dividend alone amounted to £5,400. But after World War 1 the profits were not remotely comparable to the earlier period. The immediate post-war recovery in 1922 was succeeded by a deep depression in the 1930s. The profits in the 1920s and the 1930s were in many years lower than before World War 1, and rarely much above the pre-war level, although the volume of turnover in money terms was much greater. Average net profits from all sources amounted to between £5,000 and £8,000 in the 1920s and 1930s, and did not exceed £10,000 until 1934/5.

As the capital had doubled and the price level almost doubled, the fall was sharp in real terms. The dividend in the second half of the 1920s was only £2,625, and even in 1938/9 it was no more than £3,964.

In the early 1930s net trading profits from all Dublin departments were low, a mere £934 in 1931/2, £3,027 in 1932/3 and £2,426 in 1933/4. In 1935 the loss-making factory was made into a separate company, and in 1941 factory operations were abandoned altogether. The bookstalls lost ground continually. In 1931, looking at bad results in the wholesale news department, J.C.M. Eason was prompted to observe that 'between 1921/2 and the current date the results were at times exceedingly good and it is the combination of falling sales with increased expenditures which has led to the serious reduction in the final profit.' Later in the 1930s the wholesale news business became distinctly less favourable. The introduction of tariffs on newspapers and magazines in 1932/3 handicapped sales, and the vigorous implementation of the new censorship laws also affected turnover. Net profits as a percentage of wholesale news turnover in Dublin fell from 3.7 per cent in 1928/9 to 3.0 per cent in 1929/30, and then to 2.6 per cent in 1930/31. This figure was exceeded, but then only fractionally, in just two years during the 1930s.

In the early 1930s a decided change took place in the contribution of different departments to the net profits. Net profits in news fell from an average of £8,146 for the four years ended March 1928 to £5,610 for the four years ended March 1934. From 1933/4 onwards the wholesale books section (which still at this time included monthly magazines) began to turn in a profit, and this was followed in 1935/6 by the wholesale stationery section.

The rise in costs since the early 1930s was a sustained one. The high net profit ratios, which could even exceed 3 per cent in the 1920s, were not reached again before 1963/4. The main reason was simply the rise in costs. Man hours were taken up in distribution as the network grew, and the hours of delivery from the publishers became earlier. In the 1920s staff began to come in at 1.45 am to handle the Dublin dailies, compared with a starting time of 5 am in preceeding decades and 4.30 am in 1920.

WEEKLIES AND MAGAZINES

The number of weekly titles, which was some 250 before World War 1, was about 400 in the 1930s, and, if fortnightlies and monthly magazines are included, was well over 1,000. By 1960 these figures were even larger.

No breakdown of the categories and circulation survives for the Dublin house before the late 1950s but such a breakdown survives for the Belfast house since the 1920s (see Table 26)

The general rise in circulation in Northern Ireland (apart from the war years) is very apparent. There was a steady rise from 1928 until 1939. The rise of girls' and women's weeklies, and after World War II, of wireless weeklies, is the most striking feature. The rise in women's and girls' magazines, first evident as a widespread phenomenon in the 1920s, was even more dramatic between 1949 and 1959 when they represented a cultural as well as major business innovation. The rise in illustrated weeklies by 1939 reflected the success in particular of *Picture Post*. The pattern in the south was similar, although censorship had a limiting impact on the sale of women's weeklies, while English wireless weeklies would not have had the same prominence. In the case of magazines (fortnightlies and monthlies) there were 61 in all in the fiction category distributed through the Belfast house in the 1930s. The best sellers in 1939 were, in order: *Lilliput, New Moon Novels, True Love Stories, True Story Magazines, Schoolgirl's Own Library, True Confessions, Strand Magazine,* and finally *Sexton Blake,* coming in valiantly at the end. The total number of copies rose from 8,184 in 1933 to 12,206 in 1939. There was, moreover, a striking change taking place in the range handled by Eason's in Belfast in the 1930s. Sales of magazines such as the *Strand Magazine* and *Wide World* were halved, while the more popular sort of the *True Love* variety doubled. The rise in the number of boys' and girls' papers was due almost exclusively to the appearance of *Schoolboy's Own Library, Schoolgirl's Own Library* and *Sexton Blake.*

Comparative data do not survive on the Dublin side before 1957. The Dublin pattern for weeklies in 1959 is similar to the Belfast pattern of the same year. The most striking feature is that the total number of weeklies in Dublin in 1959 is somewhat less than in the north, 476,885 as compared with 513,759. Allowing for the difference in sales of radio and television programme weeklies, the total circulation was much the same. Relatively, women's and girls' periodicals were more important in the southern figures. These and religious publications were the only groups in which Dublin totals exceeded Belfast circulation. Mass circulation women's weeklies were a novel feature of the inter-war years. The most important were *Woman,* from Odham Press, *Woman's Own,* from George Newnes Ltd., and *Woman's Weekly* from the Amalgamated Press. At their peak these publications had a total circulation of two or three million in these islands, and Eason's would have distributed over 30,000 of each

TABLE 26 *Belfast House Circulation Figures for weeklies (last week in Feb.)*

	1928	1932	1939	1941	1943	1946	1949	1955	1959
Children's papers	6,049	3,619	31,130	20,701	21,100	31,500	53,548	92,838	85,189
Girl's and Women's			65,385	37,731	40,200	64,340	76,397	154,864	170,180
Boys	94,813	86,138	19,911	10,249	9,260	13,650	13,501	25,234	23,685
Family			15,073	9,191	8,700	15,200	20,075	23,752	25,350
	100,862	89,757	131,499	77,872	79,260	124,690	163,521	296,688	304,404
Literary & General	22,625	33,738	31,196	24,158	24,660	34,660	64,534	88,879	68,841
Competition	2,444	4,066	12,337	6,374	6,130	9,790	1,672	—	23
Wireless	7,332	11,189	28,161	19,627	21,000	34,880	60,539	65,689	82,409
Film	—	—	2,159	1,097	860	1,370	2,851	5,001	2,954
Illustrated	1,281	1,062	10,626	15,148	11,730	15,940	21,773	15,744	915
	33,682	50,055	84,479	66,404	64,380	96,640	151,369	175,313	155,142
Agriculture, etc.	2,869	3,569	7,491	4,378	4,240	5,160	6,137	7,801	8,333
Commerce	725	1,313	793	817	1,030	1,450	1,140	2,521	3,398
Motors	2,292	1,880	1,578	690	700	930	1,286	5,006	4,690
Religious	13,760	13,530	18,413	14,851	15,300	20,480	21,929	22,709	21,986
Sporting & Racing	6,110	7,884	6,313	624	1,500	6,000	16,695	6,002	9,904
Technical	2,429	2,758	3,058	2,551	2,430	3,370	3,906	5,765	5,902
Part Publications	—	—	1,846	6,903	2,950	2,530	—	—	—
	28,185	30,934	39,492	30,814	28,150	39,920	51,093	49,804	54,213

of them through the house. These figures do not include weeklies published in the Republic, which had a circulation of 117,595 copies in the Dublin house. Of the total wholesale circulation of weeklies through the Dublin house, Irish published materials accounted for 20 per cent. In religious publications there was an even balance between Irish and English publications.

THE CONTRACTING BOOKSTALL CHAIN

Like the wholesale news department, the bookstalls were generally closely affected by changes in the market for news, which was their principal product. However, while wholesale news sales and profits were well maintained in the 1920s, the bookstall sales went into a permanent decline. Bookstall sales in Dublin peaked in 1920/21. The Belfast stalls bore up better. They operated under different conditions and were concentrated to a much greater degree than in the south on a densely populated region. Turnover per stall was higher than in the south. Cash receipts grew more rapidly, the peak came later in 1923/4, as against 1920/21, and the fall thereafter was much less than in the south.

TABLE 27 *Bookstall receipts in Dublin and Belfast**

Year to March 31	Dublin	Belfast	Total
	£	£	£
1893	20,979	8,246	29,225
1919	57,569	25,609	83,178
1921	71,612	30,819	102,432
1924	61,677	31,632	93,309
1934	40,423	22,944	63,369
1941	40,092	28,578	68,670

*Dublin figures include receipts for Curragh

Railway advertising, the factory and somewhat later the bookstalls were the only branches of the firm in respect of which figures of profit and loss had been worked out carefully. Much later J.C.M. Eason regarded the bookstall calculations, some of them apparently retrospectively worked out, as reasonably adjusted with regard to overheads, especially in the case of the Dublin house. The figures showed that the bookstalls had shown a profit consistently before the First World War, and in 1918/19 the net profit was no less than £2,879, by far the highest level of profit experienced so far. In the early 1920s the profits contracted. They were negligible between 1923 and 1927 and a small loss was incurred in 1928/9. In the following years the loss became larger, though the Curragh branch did succeed in remaining modestly profitable in most years.

The problems affecting the bookstalls were two-fold. The first was the shift in business away from the bookstalls to shops conveniently located in central districts of towns. The second was the change in transport with the growth of bus transport and of the private car. The railway termini in particular were from now on much less important relatively in total bookstall receipts. Other factors also affected profits. The decisive changes afoot had not been anticipated either by the railway companies or by Eason's, and railway contracts had been optimistically renewed on onerous terms, notably in 1925 the Dublin contract with the Great Southern Railway (GSR) and the Belfast contract with the Northern Counties Committee, LMS (NCC). What was even more striking by 1931 was that the firm was still wedded to the belief that the bookstalls were inherently profitable, and actually paid an increased guaranteed minimum rental (£10,000 as against £9,000) in renewing the GSR contract. North and south, receipts were at their lowest in 1933/4; in Dublin there was a loss of £1,775. Over five years the loss totalled £6,800. In Belfast, the corresponding loss in 1933 was £623 and over five years it amounted to £1,777.

More flexible contracts were negotiated as they came up for renewal. New contracts with the Great Northern Railway (GNR) in 1935 and with the GSR in 1936 had more advantageous conditions, and in the exceptional conditions of the war, the GSR contract was renewed in 1940 for one year only at a reduced rent, and in the following year was renewed on a half-yearly basis without any minimum. As a result a profit began to be returned on the southern bookstalls. In the north, in contrast to the neutral south, the war led to a rise in economic activity which boosted receipts and the GNR contract was renewed in 1942, but without a minimum rental.

The impressive bookstall network which had been built up in the first twenty years of the century was now contracting. The 59 stalls in the south at the end of World War I had been reduced to 43 by the end of 1939. In the north there had been 29 bookstalls in 1920, plus 3 in Donegal. There were 36 stalls in 1930; only 30 in 1939. Seven more bookstalls in the south were either closed at the outset of the war, or were open for only part of the year. The crisis was now evident. In 1942 J.C.M. Eason made a searching analysis of the bookstalls, and his conclusion, based on a long-term survey of their performance, was, 'that there seemed to be no factors to offset the continual loss in gross receipts.' He went on:

> The fact is that for justification of the policy which would accept heavy losses in certain years we have to look to the close connection between the bookstall work and the output in the News and Book Departments. Taking the business as a whole the possession of the Bookstall Contract undoubtedly strengthens our position with publishers, materially assists the trading departments in meeting their overheads, and, at certain points, facilitates distribution services to the agents which, otherwise, could not be made available. It has never been possible to measure their value in any precise manner, but throughout the period it has influenced the firm in making the maximum offer that seemed reasonable when our renewal terms were being discussed.

Even in the uncertain conditions of 1942 J.C.M. Eason thought that,

> It remains a good policy for us to keep up the combination as long as we can .... the fact that News Brothers, Cork, have a small contract with the G.S. Railway keeps the possibility of the Bookstall Contract before their minds.

ADVERTISING

Like the bookstalls, railway advertising was a significant component of the firm's income before 1914. In the decade before 1900 it was in fact the most lucrative single branch of the firm's activities. It was also the only branch at that time in which costs were closely analysed and the concept of departmental profit was well developed. Profit and loss figures for the department exist from 1887.

Everything changed after 1900. Until then display advertising at railway stations was regarded as the most economical way of getting a message to the public, for whom the railways were the only form of mass travel. Thereafter the growing demand for daily newspapers and magazines provided new media for the advertiser. The display advertising on the railways, which was the core of the firm's advertising business, began to feel the competition. Advertising income lost its buoyancy, and it was turned from the staple of the company's profit into an activity which made a loss for many years. It never recovered its former glory. Advertising revenue contracted heavily during the first world war, and the post-war recovery did not bring it back to its old level in real terms. In 1926/7 the combined advertising revenue in Dublin and Belfast was £16,867 compared with the pre-war peak of £14,415 in 1902/3. Revenue rose somewhat in Dublin in the early 1930s but it lost its momentum again in the second half of the decade, and in Belfast it fell heavily. The advertising portion of the GNR tender in June 1930 went to Slaughter's, while Eason's retained the bookstalls. Northern advertising sales did not show any recovery until the advertising portion of the GNR tender was regained in 1935. Dublin advertising revenue rose in 1929/30 due in large measure to permission in the new contract of that year to use roadside sites on railway property. This reflected the shift from railway users to road users, and in fact after 1935 the drop in railway revenue was compensated for by revenue generated under what was then the innovation of advertising on buses. Advertising on trams was added in Belfast in 1941.

With the decline in advertising revenue in the decade before the first world war came losses, both before and during the war. In the post-war period 1919-23 a loss was recorded in three out of five years. From 1924 the railway advertising, which had formerly been handled totally from Dublin, was separated into two departments located in Dublin and Belfast. In the second half of the 1920s both houses turned in a modest profit in advertising, but a loss was registered in Belfast in 1929/30 even before the effects of the surrender of the GNR contract to Slaughter were felt. Both divisions suffered losses in 1930/1. The largest net loss in Dublin was £1,133 in 1934/5. In Belfast, on a much smaller turnover, the proportionately much larger loss of £662 was registered in 1931/2. Railway advertising was more volatile than the bookstalls, which meant that in good times its profits had been larger, and that in bad times they quickly reflected changing conditions. In the second half of the 1930s, under more favourable conditions — the introduction of bus advertising in Dublin, and the recovery of the GNR contract in the north — profits were returned in some years. This feature held even during the difficult years of the second world war. But the whole rationale of advertising was now open to question, and in his analysis in 1942 J.C.M. Eason noted that, as opposed to the bookstalls, 'when it comes to justifying the acceptance of losses in the case of the advertising department, the position is somewhat different. It is much more detached from the other activities and in fact, it is not an assistance to any of them.'

Eason noted that though advertising and bookstall management had traditionally been combined, the precedents for dividing them had been becoming more frequent on both sides of the Irish Sea. Slaughter's contract for the GNR was a case in point at home, and the fact that the Belfast & County Down Railway had made a tentative move to invite Allen's (who had a controlling interest in Slaughter's) to tender for advertising only, was a material factor in influencing the level of the offer made by Eason's to secure the renewal of the contract in 1937. Eason recommended that it was in the interests of the company to secure its advertising 'as any large change of ownership might lead to a more active policy being pursued: it remains a good policy for us to keep up the combination as long as we can.'

BOOK AND STATIONERY WHOLESALING

In the period from 1927 onwards, while the wholesale news department was essentially stagnant in volume and was contracting in profitability, the firm depended increasingly for turnover and profits on the other wholesale divisions. The contribution of the other wholesale divisions to total wholesale turnover rose from 35 per cent in 1926/7 to 39 per cent in 1936/7 and to 50 per cent in 1946/7.

Books (which included monthly magazines) and stationery had both recorded losses during the 1920s. In the 1930s books fared better than stationery, and achieved profits, and during the second world war years, as paper shortages made it easy to sell reading matter, continued to do better than stationery, which was in an equally advantageous market. Magazines seem to have been the main source of these profits, as recorded profits fell abruptly in 1948/9, when magazines were no longer included in the department. Books and stationery were both major activities of Eason's throughout this period, although they were not areas of exciting growth, and returned poor profits for part of it. In both cases, Eason's were the major wholesalers in the Irish market, and in many lines, the dominant ones.

The role of Eason's in general trade books was limited as in the past by the fact that both customers and traders could obtain supplies from the publishers. Eason's had an advantage in the field of cheaper novels, which were acquiring a mass sale, and which were most effectively distributed through the news distribution channels which Eason's commanded. Eason's themselves made up assortments of books for retailers, who did not wish to specify their own choice. When censorship made its appearance in 1930, Eason's assured its retailers that 'Agents can rely upon our exercising stringent precautions to ensure that they will not receive such papers or books in any parcel from our warehouse.'

Increasingly in the 1930s Eason's were acquiring the sole distribution rights for popular books, north and south, a recognition of the dominant position they already held and of a service which no publisher could provide for himself. In the 1930s, for instance, among the many books for which they became sole distributors, were the popular *William* books, issued by Newnes and Pearson at 2s 6d. Eason's purchased these at the slightly better price of 1s 5d, as opposed to the more usual 1s 6d (43 per cent as opposed to 40 per cent discount). Popular book prices had come down sharply in the 1920s. The paperback books priced at 1s appeared, and eventually the 6d novel. The first 6d novel in the series known as the Reader's Library, was sold exclusively by Woolworth's, and was only later made available to the trade at very narrow terms — 2s 9d per dozen copies. Finally, there was a positive flood of 6d paper-backs from the Hutchinson Group, with attractive pictorial covers in red, and this was followed by Hodder & Stoughton with a 9d range.

After 1932 a duty of 1d imposed on novels meant an addition of 1½d to the prices of 2d, 3d, and 6d novels, once trade margins were allowed for. An extra 2d was added to 1s novels. This could have threatened sales of some of these lines, and one of the consequences was the printing of some of the cheaper fiction in Ireland for London firms such as Pearson's, Mellifont Press and Wright & Brown. The comments in Eason's *Monthly Trade Bulletin* and to a greater extent the advertising by publishing houses in the *Bulletin* give a good idea of the range of sales, and of the concentration of sales on the cheaper and more popular books. It should be added that from the trade statistics, it seems that the number of novels imported in the first half of the 1930s was at a level which was not greatly exceeded till the end of the 1950s.

The popular demand for books is reflected in the success of circulating libraries, the so-called '2d a read' libraries, in the inter-war years. Eason's responded to this demand by establishing the Torch Library in 1929, which was started at the suggestion of Hodder and Stoughton, who gave an extra 4 per cent discount on 7s 6d novels for the purpose. They also set up the associated Lens Library, which provided a stock of books to retailers who wished to have a library. There was a widespread demand for popular books supplied through lending libraries in the 1920s and 1930s. In 1933 two civil servants in their spare time established such a library supplying books to a small circle of retailers in Dublin, which was soon followed by an associated enterprise in Limerick. Eason's bought them out in 1936, not so much in order to acquire their customers as to take over their stock of books. The Torch library grew in the 1930s, and in the post-war period its subscription income rose from £4,000 to about £5,000. Though neither profit nor turnover was large, it made a small profit for much of its existence. The book stock rose from 16,281 volumes in 1930 to 46,684 volumes in 1939. It held its own in the post-war period at first, recovering to a level of stock near pre-war levels. Despite many competitor libraries, Easons' Torch and Lens libraries reached a peak of about 150 branches. In 1952 Dublin Corporation objected to shops selling milk and ice-cream running lending libraries, and this led to the closing of many of the branches. The paperback revolution in the 1950s caused a decline in business and led finally to closure in 1968.

Easons' role in the distribution of Irish books is of interest and in fact they went out of their way to give emphasis to such books. This was partly to support Irish endeavour, but in fact Irish books also sold very well, and the problem for Eason's as wholesalers was not so much the sale of such books as a shortage of suitable works. Popular Irish books, or books by Irish authors, did very well on the list of best sellers introduced into their *Bulletin* in 1949.[1] In months when good books on Irish subjects or by Irish authors were available, they appeared high on the lists, which in the intervening months were dominated by outside literature. In the Bulletin of November 1931 they observed that, 'there has been unfortunately a great dearth of books published in Ireland in recent years, and it becomes more pitiful still....' The only exception was the Talbot Press which stood out in the 1930s as the only Irish publisher bringing out a substantial number of books. The writer in the Bulletin noted,

> The one exception I have in mind is the Talbot Press.... It was the Talbot Press who introduced to the reading public Miss Annie M. P. Smithson, whose stories have charmed the hearts of thousands, and who has as big a reading public in England and elsewhere as in Ireland; it is they also who published Dan Breen's book (which turned out the best seller of the year in Ireland) when it had been turned down by others, and it was the same firm who took over the publications of Martin Lester, and thus prevented a number of valuable works being forgotten.

1 The *Bulletin* was edited by Paddy Hughes, who was described by Robert Eason, his immediate boss, as 'an ardent Irishman' — it was also not unknown for titles that were 'sticking' to be written up in the *Bulletin*.

Dan Breen's book *My Fight for Irish Freedom* which quickly sold out in 1928, and Beasley's *Michael Collins* in 1937 are two such examples. Dorothy Macardle's *The Irish Republic* (Gollancz, 1937) was also a best seller. In 1949, when Tom Barry's *Guerilla Days in Ireland* appeared, Eason's alerted traders to the fact that, 'hundreds of orders are being received weekly and customers are urged to re-order at once while the first edition is available.' Thousands of copies were sold in the first week, and it was out of print within a few weeks of publication. But the demand was not confined to books on the war of independence. The book most in demand in Christmas 1931 was H.V. Morton's *In Search of Ireland*, whose *In The Steps of the Master* also did well a few years later. Fiction with an Irish appeal could meet with a ready response. The success of Maurice Walsh's books is an example of this. It is clear that there was a demand which needed to be satisfied.

As in the case of books, Eason's had a dominant position in the stationery market. The sheer variety of items they stocked gave them a special advantage over rivals, and as in the case of cheaper books, this factor limited direct sales by the manufacturers to retailers, particularly outside the metropolitan Dublin area. However, selling costs were high, as most of the wholesale stationery business was brought in by travellers who covered the entire country, visiting virtually every town about four times a year.

In addition, annual shows or 'Christmas stock rooms' were held in up to fifteen principal towns, usually in the course of the summer and early autumn, when for a week or sometimes longer, the traveller for the area would have samples of the goods which his customer might expect to sell during the pre-Christmas period, including toys and gifts, greeting cards and Christmas cards as well as conventional stationery. Travellers at this time frequently worked long hours, particularly in the evenings, as they might expect visits at almost any hour after their customers had closed their own shops for the day. To this day Eason's stationery business reflects its origins. Its wholesale activity is geared to the newsagent, stationer or retailer, and sales of business and office stationery are relatively insignificant.

The advantages which Eason's could offer are reflected in the fact that in the inter-war years they were frequently appointed sole distributors in the Irish market for certain items. The range of products tended to widen progressively. In the inter-war years, gramophone records were added, and in 1929 an even more heterogenus item, toilet goods and hairdressing supplies were introduced at the instance of William Calwell.

This later became a separate department. In 1930 Christmas crackers were reported to be an increasingly popular line. At the same time stationery and writing and office requisites were the staple of the department, the range carried was very wide, and many of the items were intended for traders other than stationers. Even electric light bulbs were added to the list of goods traded in the 1920s. Sweet bags for retailers was one item on the list, and in May 1930 it was reported that, 'owing to the increased demand for white sweet bags we have decided to stock them also in brown.'

Stationery covered a wide range. Although there were Irish produced brands, the experiences of Easons' own factory, which was closed down in 1941, illustrated the economic problems in this field. The second world war gave home producers some advantages, given the shortfall in imports, but Eason's reckoned in 1945 that they accounted for only 20 per cent of the level of pre-war sales in envelopes, which were one of the great staples of the stationery department. 'Fancy goods' covered an extraordinary range, including more exotic items such as cribs and imitation jewellery. The card department was separate from the plain and fancy stationery, the two main sections. Cards covered a wide range of goods also: comic cards, Christmas cards, calendars and picture postcards. With delays of ten to twelve weeks, Eason's provided local view cards, at the request of retail customers. These were primarily a summer trade, and individual customers in some holiday resorts ordered picture postcards in lots of 5,000. During the 1930s cards expanded and in time greeting cards became even more important than Christmas cards.

The period between the wars did not provide the company as a whole with high profits; in part this was because of the problems of the world and Irish economies during that time. But also the character of the market which the company had been so successfully structured to supply changed rapidly. The most fundamental change was in the economic position of the railways. After the first world war they ceased to be the predominant mass transport system. As a result Easons' bookstalls and advertising sites no longer straddled a key artery as they had done twenty years before, and so the profitability of the railway business as a whole declined. The development of the mass readership for newspapers in the 1920s, supplied by 'high street' newsagents and other retailers, was another development with longterm significance, which is discussed in the next chapter.

Chapter 18 ❧ The growth of retail outlets for news

IN THE 1920s THE POPULAR ENGLISH NEWSPAPERS were beginning to enlarge the very small share of the southern market which they had previously held, and at the same time, Irish papers were facing increased competition from each other and from the English papers. Eason's handled four popular London papers in their morning despatch in 1926. The *Daily Express*, locked in combat with the *Daily Mail* in England, entered the Irish market in 1927. The total number of London dailies had risen to seven by 1931. The daily circulation through Eason's rose from 49,119 copies in 1926 to 60,707 copies in 1931. Because of distribution through publishers representatives and news vendors these figures are only an indication of the rise in their circulation. The *Irish Press* at the time of its launching in 1931 claimed that 300,000 copies of English dailies were distributed in Ireland (presumably 32 counties).

At the time of the imposition of duties on dailies in the Irish Free State in 1933, it was generally stated that the circulation of the English dailies amounted to between 180,000 and 200,000 copies. It is clear from these figures just how much the Irish market for daily news was penetrated by English newspapers. The situation would be still more striking if the even more dominant role of the English Sunday papers were taken into account. The picture would not change greatly if the circulation of Cork and Belfast papers was reckoned. In Belfast the stronger position of the English newspapers in the market is not evident in Easons' own sales since so much was sold directly by the publishers to newsagents and street vendors. In fact, in 1931, the whole of Easons' supplies in Belfast of all English dailies was only a little more than the Northern Ireland circulation of one single London daily, the *Daily Express*, which then sold 19,000 copies. The modest rise in English dailies supplied through Eason's in Belfast between 1928 and 1932 would confirm that their share in total circulation had slipped further between these dates.

An important strategy in the publishers' hunt for circulation was to ensure availability of their publications by the development of retail sources of supply to the customers. A growing proportion of distribution was handled by the English publishers themselves, and they retained effective control of new applications for supply.

The newest of the Dublin papers, the *Irish Press*, launched in 1931, was the one which made the greatest efforts to increase its circulation, by vigorously pushing its sales and seeking new outlets. In 1936 it was in conflict with the Newsagents' Association because the paper had opened new outlets 'indiscriminately'. The Association and its members struck for some months against taking the *Irish Press*, and refused to carry posters advertising it. In 1943 J.C.M. Eason observed with reference to the competitive character of news wholesaling that 'if the problem is studied in relation, for instance, to the *Irish Independent* and the *Irish Press*, it is fairly obvious how we as wholesalers can do little more than distribute.'

During the 1920s the rise in newspaper circulations compensated Eason's on balance for a tendency by both the Irish and English publishers to sell directly to the retailer. The competition of these years also meant that percentage discounts to the retail trade tended to widen somewhat. The longterm results were very different. The rise in percentage margins which publishers were prepared to concede to wholesalers, for the sake of achieving a larger circulation, was offset by the general fall in prices which bottomed out by 1927. Publications tended to be heavier, which increased carriage costs and to a lesser degree handling costs. The net sales value of the Dublin dailies distributed by Eason's fell in price by 20 per cent between 1926 and 1931, but rose in weight by a similar proportion. At the same time, the effort to retain existing trade in the face of competition raised administrative costs.

Returns increased in the 1920s as sales were pushed hard by publishers. This increased wholesalers' handling costs, and in addition there was an increase in the number of small accounts. This factor added to the costs of the wholesaler without creating commensurate extra sales, and the cost of handling unsold copies had to be met out of his own gross profit margin. In response to the competition from English newspapers the *Irish Independent* in 1927 reduced its price form 2d to 1d. This increased the number of copies sold, but Easons' business in money terms fell by £12,000. In fact, the total value of all Irish dailies distributed by Easons fell by £16,000 between 1926 and 1931.

During the 1930s publishers of popular English daily newspapers, particularly the *Daily Herald* the *Daily Express* and the *Daily Mail* encouraged by the falling price of newsprint, and driven on by the need for higher circulation in order to attract more advertising revenue, set themselves the target of attaining a daily circulation of over two million copies within the United Kingdom and Ireland. Various devices to increase circulation were introduced. House to house canvassing was used to publicise the merits of free insurance schemes and free gifts. Crossword puzzles with high prizes made their appearance, and the publishers were in keen competition with one another in the magnitude of their offers. The greatest excesses of this era did not reach Ireland, but the Irish market while small, was still attractive in the battle to widen circulation and thereby also enhance the advertising revenue. The competition between newspapers meant that their proprietors were impatient with the attitude of wholesalers like Eason's whose interest lay in moderating the rise in the number of outlets in order to keep down their own costs. From 1927 this became particularly evident when the *Daily Mail* and the *Daily Express* were fighting for circulation.

Newspapers sought to obtain direct accounts with Irish newsagents in the belief that they would obtain some advantage, and inducements were held out to newsagents such as subsidies for delivery by bicycle and for the cost of collection of parcels from railway stations. Many years later, J.C.M. Eason reflecting on what had happened over the years observed that 'we have accepted the control exercised by the publishers as being the most likely to arrive at a reasonable compromise between their own interest in increased sales and the interest of those newsagents who are already trading.' Eason's figures in the 1920s did not reflect the total growth in newspaper circulation as sensitively as they had done in the pre-war years. Even where wholesaling was left in the hands of the wholesalers, outlets were no longer determined solely as a result of individual negotiations between wholesaler and retailer.

The pressure to increase outlets alarmed existing newsagents. However the relationship between Eason's and the retailers' association was on the whole better than in the first half of the 1920s as wholesaler and retailer had a common interest in face of the pressure from the publishers to increase outlets. In May 1929 Eason's in Northern Ireland had a meeting with Porter's 'to discuss the situation arising out of the notification from the publishers of their determination to supply publications to certain agents who had failed to secure recognition from the (Retail Newsagents') Federation.' All these moves resulted in higher costs for the wholesaler — heavier papers, a higher percentage of returns, and frequent changes of accounts due to canvassing. On a static volume of business, wage costs in the news department were £1,600 higher in 1931 than in 1926. The pressure to increase the number of newsagents and the Distance Limits Policy, which had been largely a Dublin affair up until 1925, became a national issue. The Distance Limits Policy stated that a second newsagent should not be supplied in close proximity to an existing agent. In 1928 J.C.M. Eason noted that 'two developments tend to increase salaries etc. Pressures from competition — extra staff on lay up etc. and Newsagents Association D[istance] L[imits] policy involving extra time in enquiry, correspondence for Mr. Harris, Bryan, Jenkins etc.' In 1931 he commented further:

> Expenses constitute the real problem and there have been mentioned already certain reasons which have thrown extra work with a falling business. The other matter must also be noted — namely the development of numerous conferences and much correspondence with the Newsagents Association and also the cost of making inspections in town and country.

At least three representatives of the firm were responsible for visiting centres outside Dublin, both with reference to what was afoot, and in order to process applications under the Distance Limits Policy. This was a novel development, unparalleled in the pre-war history of the house and was a response to the novel problems of the 1920s. One problem was that decisions on applications were held up for so long by the Newsagents Association that the publishers opened up direct supplies, and the wholesalers lost business permanently. These delays gave the impression that the wholesalers, who were caught between the two interests, were not carrying out their functions properly as distributors, and were acting wilfully. As publishers were actively looking for business, the employment of representatives of their own gave them a means of canvassing directly for outlets. It is clear that competition left publisher, wholesaler and retailer alike unhappy in the second half of the 1920s and the cumulative dissatisfaction on all sides was greatly increased by 1929.

The rise in the number of Easons' retail newsagents was most noticeable in the Dublin urban region in the 1920s. In the country area served by Dublin the number fell to 546 in 1928 but rose to 568 in 1931. If outlets supplied by the newspapers directly were included, the total number of outlets would be significantly higher. In Northern Ireland, the local daily papers, the *Belfast Newsletter*, the *Irish News* and the *Northern Whig* had effective control of supplies to new newsagents. However they were all much more cost conscious than similar publishers in Dublin or London, and a strict control was maintained. As a result, the uneconomic increase in the number of newsagents was never as serious a problem in Northern Ireland as it was in the south. Competition between Eason's and Porter's, particularly in Derry, upset this pattern at times, but it did not affect the main trend. In Dublin both the *Irish Independent* and the *Irish Press* were at all times more willing, within certain limits, to supply new and often quite small traders, if they thought that even a few extra copies might be sold.

TABLE 28 *Eason's Newsagent accounts*

	Dublin			Belfast		
	Town	Country	Total	Town	Country	Total
1922	270	613	883	146	198	344
1930	334	556	890	168	211	379
1937	—	—	—	192	212	404
1944	—	—	—	176	221	397

No breakdown of how distribution was shared between different areas has survived. The one surviving analysis relates to weeklies supplied by the Dublin house in 1946, but it probably reflects a pattern which had emerged by the 1930s. The fact that Dublin and Dun Laoghaire combined account only for a third of the total is an interesting illustration of the development of this provincial market in preceding decades.

TABLE 29 *Distribution of sales of weeklies through the Dublin house, 1946*

	%	%
Dublin	33.0	
Dun Laoghaire	2.1	
Dublin & Dun Laoghaire Combined		35.1
Limerick & Waterford		8.8
23 Towns of 5,000 +		22.3
Remainder of the country		33.8

The competition between the publishers of English Sunday newspapers was particularly ferocious. Here Eason's were not involved (except to a limited degree in the Waterford area after 1931) because, as J.C.M. Eason remarked, 'there is a tradition against the use of the wholesalers' services'. There were however more specific reasons for the growth of small independent wholesalers in the distribution of English Sunday newspapers. The Road Traffic Act, which was designed to protect the monopoly of the public transport system, made it illegal for any except a licenced haulier to carry goods on hire. Sunday newspaper distribution in Ireland had of necessity to have its own transport and in effect this meant that the carriers had to be also wholesale distributors. In Dublin the *News of the World* (Sunday edition) was distributed by a wholesale representative named Farrell. Most of the others were distributed by J.P. Kirwan of Fairview, including the *Sunday Dispatch*, the *Observer* and the remainder, including the *Sunday Chronicle* and the *People*, were distributed by Dublin Wholesale Newsagency Ltd, run by Henry Hughes. The Dublin Wholesale Newsagency was also involved in general news wholesaling, having taken up some of this business when Dawsons withdrew from Ireland in 1922.Two further small wholesalers appeared in the Dublin region, two in Waterford, two in Limerick, one in Cork and one each in Urlingford and Castlerea. In Cork the Sunday newspapers were also distributed by News Brothers Ltd. (the Tivy brothers) which was also a distributor of daily newspapers and periodicals. J.C.M. Eason's own view was that smaller margins and fewer wholesalers would have been better for the trade in Ireland. In general, fragmentation in wholesaling was restricted to the dailies and Sunday papers. In the distribution of periodicals, where small lots of numerous publications had to be distributed over a wide area, publishers were content to rely on the wholesaler. Even in the fiercely competitive Belfast market, George Best observed to J.C.M. Eason in 1932 that: 'weeklies are a different proposition entirely. The publishers do not wish to deal direct at all, if they can avoid it, they desire the business to go through the wholesaler.'

One reason for Eason's dominant position in the Irish market was the negotiation, from as early as the 1850s, of a flat rate carriage charge with the railway companies, related only to the weight of the parcel and not to the distance travelled. As a result a provincial wholesaler in Ireland had no cost advantage in being nearer to his local market than the Dublin wholesaler. Eason's role in the Irish market was relatively greater than that of the London wholesalers in England, who faced the competition of powerful provincial wholesalers, especially in north Britain.

An exception to this dominance was in south-west Cork, where News Brothers Ltd. had a clear advantage over a Dublin distributor because parcels to that area from Dublin had to be carried across Cork to a second terminus, and had consequently to bear a second carriage charge. A similar situation arose in some parts of the north-west which could be more economically supplied from Derry, which, as we have seen, enabled Porters to establish themselves in that city. A favourite tactic in the competition for new accounts was for the wholesaler to increase the amount of credit given by the wholesaler to the retailer. The end result was that over the period 1920-50 much larger credit was given in Belfast than in Dublin. There also were no delivery charges in Belfast — another indication of the strength of competition.

In March 1944 J.C.M. Eason thought that it was only the railway bookstalls with their higher proportion of casual sales which gave Eason's more weight with publishers than Porter's, and he commented to George Best: 'On account of our bookstall position we may have a more favourable means of approach than he (Porter) would have.' Eason's and Porter's had an amicable relationship on issues of common interest. However caution remained the keyword. In April 1948 George Best wrote in relation to a particular magazine, and with the competition with Porters in mind: 'It is difficult to find out what Porter is charging unless we ask him the direct question. We generally refrain from doing so.'

In the south the disruption of communications caused by the civil war in 1922 had given News Brothers in Cork and Croker & Co. in Waterford an opportunity to expand their business at that time, while the belief on the part of the publishers that additional wholesalers helped to expand circulation also contributed. In the Cork area in particular Easons' interest receded rapidly after the destruction of the Mallow railway bridge, and soon they had virtually no retail customers for newspapers and periodicals in Cork except their own bookstall. In the north, when Porter's were in dispute with the newsagents in Derry in 1929 over the opening of a new newsagent, J.C.M. Eason was reluctant to take advantage of the situation and advised George Best in Belfast to refrain from attempting to secure any transfer of business: 'I told him I would not like to take any business from Porter under such circumstances, and that we should support him.'

In 1932 George Best wanted to compete with the representatives of the English daily newspapers who had become small wholesalers in their own right, and once again, J.C.M. Eason's approach was much more cautious:

> We have to remember that the support to be obtained from the publishers is not, at its best, very substantial, and unless we have the representatives with us in a thoroughly sympathetic manner we might be seriously embarrassed.

Eason's outlook illustrates the dilemma of the wholesaler caught between a competitive urge, and the desire to maintain an efficient wholesale service. In this particular case, since so much of the representative/wholesalers' business was with street traders, the established wholesalers like Eason's and Porter's who offered credit facilities and a delivery service had very little to offer to the street trader.

J.C.M. Eason was aware from the early 1920s how remote a Dublin wholesaler was from the conditions in the provinces, and a memorandum in 1929 studied the position in Limerick, one large urban market where Eason's were still totally free from local wholesale competition, and which it was crucial to protect:

> Bus transit will facilitate distribution to Ennis, Nenagh etc., at a lower cost than at present when publisher delivers carriage paid, and in Limerick itself there is probably more business to be done if supplies are on the spot. The question therefore is on what lines the matter is to be handled.... The one matter which must however be settled is the appointment of a local representative. Everything points to the necessity of having someone there with a general knowledge of our business methods, and one whom we can trust.

As a result a Limerick wholesale news branch was opened in 1929 with the needs of news alone in mind, rather than any other wider development: 'For the moment, news alone counts'.

In Waterford, Croker & Co. as well as owning a substantial retail newsagency and bookshop carried on a wholesale agency in the 1920s and 1930s for Sunday newspapers, which probably included a small amount of English daily newspaper and periodical distribution. In 1933 Eason's purchased the wholesale part of this business and thus for the first time entered the Sunday wholesale market, although in a very limited way, at the same time establishing a wholesale branch in Waterford for periodicals. In Dun Laoghaire a wholesale news branch was opened in 1937. Cork was left severely alone, suggesting a reluctance to attempt the potentially destructive competition that would result with a small but entrenched rival. In the 1930s limited wholesale business in books was carried on from the news branches in Limerick and Waterford.

Newspaper circulations are always difficult to measure, and even more difficult to estimate in a period of fierce competition, because newspaper managements were apt to encourage grossly exaggerated reports of their circulation. Although they were at the heart of the trade, Eason's themselves experienced difficulties in estimating the market accurately, and were not always clear about the extent of distribution through other sources. This difficulty increased in the period after 1920 because the channels of trade had become even more fragmented. In Northern Ireland local newspapers were sold directly by the publishers to the retailers, and the cooperation of the local wholesalers was never sought. Likewise in Cork the *Examiner* did its own distribution of the morning and evening paper and, with some exceptions, of its weekly.'

As we have seen earlier Eason's distributed a quantity of the *The Irish Times* and *Irish Independent* in the inter-war years. This amounted to perhaps a quarter of the circulation of the *Irish Independent*, and a smaller fraction of the *Irish Times*. As circulations grew, both publishers tended to open new newsagents whom they supplied directly. When the *Irish Press* began publication in 1931, it relied mainly on establishing its own distribution network in order to compete with the two established dailies, and while it used Easons' services as wholesalers to an extent similar to *The Irish Times* it was as a matter of policy, indifferent to the services which the wholesaler provided. This was particularly so in periods of sharp competition when availability was all-important, and the costs of distributing and accounting for unsold copies was disproportionately high.

In 1926/7 the circulation of the *Irish Independent* was reputed to be 90,000.[1] Eason's were handling 28,000. Unlike its rival, *The Irish Times* did not publicise its circulation, but the number of copies handled through Eason's fell from 14,900 in 1926/7 to 10,800 in 1930/31. In 1948 J.C.M. Eason reckoned that Eason's were wholesaling between one quarter and one third of Dublin dailies in the Dublin area, although the figure was inflated somewhat by the inclusion of supplies to the bookstalls. The expansion of the *Irish Independent* helped to boost supplies through Eason's, even though the trend in the trade as basically toward direct supplies. The number of copies of the *Irish Independent* handled by Eason's rose from 28,000 in 1925/6 to 44,000 in 1930/31, while the total number of Dublin dailies handled by the house rose from 42,900 to 54,800 in the same years.

At the outset of the century English morning newspapers did not arrive in Belfast or Dublin until the late afternoon. In fact the time of arrival of news in Dublin or Belfast was a function of the relationship between the time of going to press and the departure time of the Irish boats from British ports. Then in an effort to capture extra circulation in the Irish market, the *Daily Mail* went to press sufficiently earlier to catch the Irish night trains. From 1905 the *Daily Mail* was coming to the Belfast house via the Stranraer boat which left at 6.50 am and arriving at Larne at 8.30 made it possible to put the paper on sale in Belfast at 9 am. For Dublin, supplies came by the 10.45 pm train from Euston to Holyhead and arrived at the North Wall in Dublin at 8.00 or 8.30 am.[2] On arrival, the paper

1 As far back as 1917, the *Irish Independent* claimed that its circulation was three times that of any other Irish morning paper.

2 The departure of the mail train for Holyhead, leaving London at 7.45 pm, was timed too early for the next day's daily newspapers.

was distributed by cyclists. The *Daily Mirror* seems to have responded quickly to the competition of the *Daily Mail*, and can be traced as arriving on the morning boat at the North Wall as early as February 1909. With the shortest sea crossing — 20 miles — and the latest hour of departure of all the Irish boats — 6.50 am — Stranraer had many advantages for catching a wide range of morning news as competition sent papers to press earlier. Easons' Belfast branch in 1923 noted that 'the greater number of English newspapers are now coming by this route', and supplies included both the *Daily Mail* and the *Daily Mirror*.

In the 1920s other popular newspapers such as the *Daily Express* and *Daily Herald*, taking advantage of high-speed telegraphy, followed the example of the *Daily Mail* in establishing printing centres in Manchester in order to get earlier delivery to the northern English and Scottish market. This meant that by going to press earlier they were able to catch a 10.20 pm train from Manchester to Holyhead to connect with the Dun Laoghaire mailboat which at that time arrived at Dun Laoghaire at 5.45 am. This was of course too late for the Dublin wholesalers' first and main deliveries of Irish newspapers and periodicals, and although the wholesalers made a second delivery in the city which consisted solely of the English newspapers, the publishers, in order to get immediate sales in the city centre, established a comprehensive system of supply to street sellers through their own local sales representatives. Belfast supplies arriving via Holyhead could catch the 6.40 am train ex Dublin which once again in Belfast required a second delivery by the wholesalers, Eason's and Porter's, as well as an extensive street vendor network in the centre of the city served directly by the publishers' sales representatives.

Much weekly news reached Belfast at 6.30 am via Fleetwood in the early 1920s. The boat left too early to take daily news printed in London. Sales in the Belfast area in the inter-war years eventually reached a level which made it practicable for the newspaper publishers to hire a special newspaper train from Manchester to Heysham to catch the Belfast mailboat; this enabled them to be in Belfast soon after 7.a.m. This step not only improved sales in Belfast itself, but also enabled the newspapers to catch early buses and trains to the relatively densely populated hinterland of Belfast and developed for the first time sales through newsagents outside Belfast. Thus in Northern Ireland the English newspapers presented an appreciable competitive threat to the local newspapers, even though the main appeal of the popular English newspapers was not so much the news they contained as their coverage of sport, particularly racing and football.

For newspapers entering Ireland via Dublin development was much slower and no improvement in the arrival time was achieved. Except in Dublin, the main appeal of English newspapers to readers was in their features and treatment of sport, so that they did not provide an alternative to locally published newspapers. In Dublin the papers had already missed the early country trains. In order to catch later morning trains and buses to county towns, many parcels for county newsagents were packed by the individual publishers in Manchester, as there would not have been time to have these packed by the wholesaler in Dublin. The wholesalers' function in this case was limited to collecting the parcels at the mailboat and putting them on the earliest available train or bus. It was usual for such parcels to be charged by the publisher to the wholesaler who in turn charged the newsagent. However it is evident that arrival times in many county towns were measured not so much for world news brought in as for the tips for that day's racing which might be of value to the reader. A single copy of the *Sporting Chronicle* printed in Manchester and addressed to a country newsagent who had an order for it from the local bookmaker could cause a volume of correspondence for the wholesaler if it got lost in transit.

TABLE 30 *Circulations of Irish and English dailies through the Belfast house (February figures)*

	English Dailies	Irish Dailies
1928	22,059	7,174
1932	25,726	7,950
1939	33,601	7,954
1946	18,896	11,370
1949	27,118	13,052
1959	39,112	9,288

Eason's sales in Northern Ireland of Irish dailies largely reflects the distribution of Dublin dailies in the north and some country distribution of Belfast dailies, as the Belfast publishers arranged their own distribution around Belfast. Dublin dailies only penetrated the northern market to a limited extent. The rise in sales in the 1940s was due to the shortage of English papers in war time. The total circulation of English dailies in the north was probably three times Easons' circulation in the early 1930s. A rough estimate suggests a market for 200,000 English dailies in the south in the early 1930s and 100,000 in the north. Of the total market of 300,000 dailies, approximately one third was held by the two leaders, the *Daily Mail*, the more established paper, and its more recent rival, the *Daily Express*.

In 1933 the introduction of protection brought to an end to the growth in cross-channel newspaper sales on the southern market. A duty of ¾d per copy was imposed on newspapers with a surface area of less than 320 square inches in the 1932 budget. This was intended to apply to weekly reviews or periodicals. J.C.M. Eason reckoned that it cut down sales by 50 per cent. In the following year a duty of $\frac{2}{5}$ d. was imposed on dailies, leading to an addition of ½d to the selling price. The impositions were welcomed by the Gaelic League, some nationalist opinion, and many clergymen, who approved of the exclusion of alien literature, and who looked forward to the growth of the Irish publishing industry. The measures caused consternation among wholesalers and retailers in Ireland, where it was claimed that 80 per cent of the newspapers and periodicals handled came in from England. After 1933, when duties on imported newspapers had restricted their sales, the English dailies reduced the allowances made to the wholesalers in the competitive 1920s. In 1934/5 the *Daily Mail* eliminated its subsidy of £1 per week to the Dun Laoghaire service, and the *Daily Express* halved its former subsidy of £300 pa to the bare carriage costs.

The circulation of English newspapers was reckoned in 1934 to have fallen by 30 to 40 per cent. On the other hand there was a rise in the circulation of Irish dailies. The *Irish Independent* increased from 90,000 copies in 1927 to 140,000 in 1939, and the *Irish Press* claimed a circulation of 110,000 in the latter year. English Sunday papers were duty free, and did not suffer from the same inhibition as the dailies, but as we have seen[3] problems with censorship increasingly harrassed the circulation of the most successful Sunday papers. The only Irish rival in this field was the *Sunday Independent* whose net sales had risen to 180,000 in 1939. It is interesting to note that the Fianna Fáil government of that time did not give the protection of an import tariff to the *Sunday Independent* in the same way that protection had been given to the daily newspapers, the *Irish Independent*, the *Irish Press* and the *Irish Times*.

3 See Chapter 13.

Chapter 19 The 'Emergency': crisis years 1939-47

THE IMPACT OF WAR ON BUSINESS is always sweeping, but for Eason's the effects of the second world war years were more severe than 1914-18. In large measure this was because the two key elements in their business, newspapers and transport, were both severely hit. There was a scarcity of newsprint and other printing papers — newsprint consumption in the UK fell from 1,243,000 tonnes in 1938 to 255,000 tonnes in 1942.[1] At the same time British book publishers were cut back to 60 per cent of their previous paper usage. Fuel shortages cut back transport savagely, creating for the sensitive newspaper division problems which had no parallel in the first world war. Despite increases in prices, turnover fell, and the auditor's report in July 1941 noted that 'the main falling off in the gross profit has occurred in the wholesale news department where there has been a substantial decrease in turnover accompanied by a fall in the margin.'

Turnover in Dublin, which had exceeded £200,000, fell by £15,000, but the fall was made up of two contrasting components. Sales of Dublin dailies went up by £13,000, but this was offset by a dramatic decrease of £28,000 in newspapers and periodicals other than Dublin dailies. The fall in turnover was only part of the problem. Profit margins had always been lower on Dublin dailies than on other newspapers, so the switch in emphasis from the cross-channel products depressed the overall margin in wholesale news disproportionately. From August 1940 Eason's were obliged to pay newspaper and magazine publishers on a weekly instead of on a monthly basis, which meant that a larger working capital was necessary for the turnover. As a result trading profits were severely reduced in 1940/41, and even in 1941/42 they were only a little higher than they had been in 1939/40. In news however both gross profits and net margins continued to decline. Net profit as a percentage of wholesale

1 *Royal Commission on the Press, 1961-2* Cmnd. 1811, p. 202

turnover was 1.5 per cent in 1939/40, falling to 0.6 per cent in 1940/41, and 0.3 per cent in 1941/42, recovering to a bare 0.9 per cent in 1942/43, far from the pre-war figures of around 3 per cent.

As net profits in news shrank, profits in books and stationery increased. In 1943/4 stationery accounted for one-third of the profits, wholesale books and the retail shop for another £12,000 and even the bookstalls temporarily returned to profitability. The traditionally small Retail department began to make a larger contribution to profits. The wholesale stationery and book departments had entered the war holding substantial stocks which appreciated in value. Later on, the continuing shortage of supplies of books and stationery meant that the small supplies procurable could be sold without high selling costs, and these departments took on a new importance. Trading profit improved modestly in 1941/42 and more substantially in 1942/43.

By the outset of 1940 the mailboat no longer arrived in time to connect with the morning trains. The Dublin dailies were still distributed by trains leaving at various times from 3 am onwards as before the war. However by July, the mailboat was arriving between 1 and 1.30 pm and the cross-channel papers were being despatched on the afternoon trains. From September 1940 the scheduled time of arrival of the mail boat was put back to 6.55 pm and became increasingly irregular. Some papers were now routed through Belfast. Occasionally these were greatly delayed. On sixteen days in November 1940 papers via Belfast arrived at Amiens Street after 5.30 pm. For a while some papers were delivered in the Dublin area by a special service but later, because newspaper publishers were not prepared to make a payment for this work, the service was discontinued and papers arriving after 5.30 pm were held for distribution with the Dublin dailies on the following morning. As a result the sale of English papers fell off, and circulation fell to between 15 and 20 per cent of the pre-war level. By late 1940 papers had been made non-returnable, so the public had to become used to a system of fixed orders, and special deliveries were cut out altogether.

During the period of the second world war, all supplies were rationed, although not severely as in the United Kingdom, Éire being treated as an export area by the British government. However business was severely limited in all departments and staff had to be laid off. By the end of the war the wholesale news department, including branches and van drivers, was down to 76 men. During the first few months of 1941, following the continued downward movement in the volume of newspapers and periodicals, many of the staff were put on half-time.

Supplies from publishers were constantly cut back. In March 1941 both the *News of the World* and the *Daily Express* discontinued supplies to the south, and other papers temporarily or permanently discontinued Irish parcels. The *News of the World* discontinued its Irish edition.[2] The withdrawal of the *Daily Express* was considered by some to have been a political decision of Lord Beaverbrook as a means of showing his dislike of the Irish policy of neutrality. Be that as it may, the cost of the Irish distribution to the publisher must have been considerable in comparison to the revenue from sales. As a result the *Daily Mail* improved its share of the Irish market, and when the *Daily Express* returned to Ireland after the war its sales for many years were less than the *Daily Mail*, whereas in England the *Express* had established a much higher circulation than the *Mail*. At the end of February 1941 J.C.M. Eason crossed over to England to see Bernard Alton, secretary of the Newspaper Proprietors Association, in the hope of securing an increase in supplies from the national daily publishers, but he found that little could be achieved. He also saw Nicholas Mansergh, who was in charge of the section dealing with Ireland at the Ministry of Information, and who, though anxious to help, was unable to do anything. With a shortage of newsprint, costs of distribution of reduced supplies became more onerous, and for publishers were a stronger determining factor than the shortage itself.

In 1942 there was a further small drop in supply of cross-channel newspapers, though as J.C.M. Eason observed, it was 'felt to be severe because of the loss of regular readers for by that time casual purchase of cross-channel papers had practically disappeared.' The fall in wholesale news sales was accentuated by the conversion of some weeklies into fortnightlies or monthlies. In the autumn of 1942, however, there was some improvement in cross-channel weeklies. Eason took this to be a consequence of a reduction in export business from England to other destinations.

From an early stage in the war the transport problems it would cause were painfully evident. In 1941 the late arrival or disruption of the mail boat became more frequent, and the train service between Belfast and Dublin also deteriorated. Problems in distribution were further increased when double summer time was introduced in Northern Ireland and Great Britain in the summer of that year. This further disorganised the train services between Belfast and Dublin. The Dublin dailies went to press

2 The Irish edition, introduced in 1937, was technically a Saturday edition, i.e. it was a weekly, but it sold in competition with true Sundays.

an hour earlier to match the change, and a special 2.37 am newspaper train from Amiens Street to Belfast started on 5 May 1941. Fuel shortages had not so far seriously disrupted train services, but the effects of coal shortages began to be evident in July 1941. In mid-July the 3 am and 3.30 am newspaper trains were cancelled. The earliest train times from Amiens Street and Kingsbridge were now 5.55 am and 7 am respectively. Parcels for the west were sent by Great Southern Railway lorries. By the end of May parcels for Limerick were also being carried by lorry, and for a time Cork parcels were routed by the *Cork Examiner* lorry on its return journey from Limerick. From 8 October there was only one passenger train daily for Cork. A goods train carrying perishables was also put on, but the services were interfered with in November by the pressure of work in carrying turf, and more newspaper parcels were transferred to buses.

Early in the war period, the company had joined a group of firms called the 'Guild of Goodwill', which came together to lease peat bogs and to store and distribute supplies of turf to members of their staff. In Easons' case volunteers from the staff bagged the turf, and Frederick Nixon, one of the directors, acted as the cashier and accountant of the enterprise. The factory in Sean McDermott Street, which had been closed in 1941, was used for two or three years as a store for turf. Lorries bringing the turf to the factory normally telephoned Robert White, the garage superintendent, to say they were on their way. This would enable him to have the main door of the factory open so that the lorry could drive straight in. If the lorry had to wait for the doors to open, the boys from the nearby streets swarmed up and threw down as much turf as possible to the roadway, where it was rapidly collected by friends and neighbours. These storage arrangements were terminated shortly before the end of the war, when Dublin Corporation had built up reserve stocks of turf in the Phoenix Park.

The year 1942 saw several changes in the Holyhead to Dun Laoghaire service, and the times of the Belfast trains which carried much of the cross-channel newspapers were very irregular. The situation darkened as the year wore on. An indication of the incidental trouble in train services is that for three days in succession a goods train from Kingsbridge to Tullow was held up owing to the failure of engine power. The passenger journey to and from Cork frequently took from twelve to eighteen hours for the same reason. Lorry dispatch of newspapers increased.

In anticipation of a scarcity of petrol, the first of several electric vehicles had been ordered by Eason's immediately on the out-break of war. In all, four electric vehicles were in use for Dublin city deliveries by 1941.

At the beginning of 1941 there were acute restrictions on the use of petrol and an experiment was made by fitting gas bags to vans. Three vehicles were converted, and this reduced petrol requirements. From September 1941 when coal became scarce, the use of gas for haulage purposes was prohibited. By that time, however, the volume of news to be distributed had fallen so much that Eason's were able to work on their petrol ration.

By this time even Irish newspapers had become scarce. In February 1942 newsprint for the Dublin dailies was cut by the Department of Supplies. Reflecting these restrictions, retail prices were increased: *The Irish Times* to 3d, the *Irish Independent* and the *Irish Press* to 2d. The *Irish Independent* cut supplies by 12½ per cent, the *Evening Mail* by a third and the *Evening Herald* by a quarter. For *The Irish Times* the price was a sufficient measure of rationing, and the *Irish Press* allowed demand to find its own level. In October the *Irish Independent* cut supplies by one-sixth. J.C.M. Eason recalled: 'This was the heaviest single reduction which the News Department suffered, and it gave rise to much correspondence and protest; it was done on the instructions of the Department of Supplies.'

The plight of the Irish dailies reflected a scarcity of newsprint which had become critical by 1942. Apart from September 1941 when some small cargoes were delivered, there had been a complete stoppage of newsprint imports. In April 1942 an emergency order on the use of paper for magazines and weeklies provided that they should not exceed 25 per cent of their 1940 standard weight and no new publication could appear without special authorisation. Dailies were cut down to 15 per cent of their standard number of pages and in August this was reduced further to 8 per cent. Special steps were taken to secure a supply of newsprint from Sweden, and in the late autumn of 1942 this began to arrive through Lisbon. There was also an easement from September in the pressure on cargo space from North America, when the priority for foodstuffs became less pressing. Supplies of newsprint began to come through; and at the end of the year a year's supply had been built up.

By 1943 regular daily trains from Dublin to the south and west were maintained, although departure times were altered, but many bus services in country areas were suspended. From time to time the receipt of cross-channel newspapers to Dublin was switched between Dun Laoghaire and Belfast. In July 1943, according to J.C.M. Eason's recollections, the shortage of coal and petrol reached its nadir. From that time on, the time-table provided for a single scheduled service each way to seven destinations from Dublin (apart from the north). In April 1944 the cross-channel service deteriorated further. The mail boat service was reduced to three days a week, country passenger railway services were reduced to two days a week (Mondays and Thursdays) and goods services were reduced to four days a week, including Mondays and Thursdays. From 31 March 1944 there was a security ban which prevented all cross-channel newspapers, except dailies, from coming over. Telephone services for Britain were also cut off. This ban affected Northern Ireland as well as the south, and was more significant in the north, where papers such as *Thomsons Weekly News* had a substantial circulation. Sales of British newspapers in the south were now of negligible proportions, so the consequence was not serious. In July 1944 the number of days on which scheduled services ran was doubled, and thereafter the distribution system remained unchanged throughout the year.

After April 1945 there was an improvement. In October British double summer time was discontinued, but in Southern Ireland the extra hour was maintained, with the result that the Manchester papers arrived an hour later, and deliveries had to be extended in the evening. English publishers began to be able to buy more newsprint, and so increase supplies of newspapers. Cross-channel publishers began to look again to the Irish market and its problems of distribution. Representatives of the *Daily Mail* and the *Daily Express* both visited Dublin, but it was found that little improvement could be hoped for as long as the time of arrival of cross-channel newspapers in Dublin remained the same. Arrangements were made at one stage for the delivery of dailies from Manchester to Dublin by air. The plan was to bring them to Dublin Airport (Collinstown) and have them in O'Connell Street shortly after midday. This arrangement was cancelled without ever having been given a trial. Eason commented: 'In fact the weather shortly afterwards was very adverse, and the Collinstown Aerodrome was out of action for some days showing clearly that complete regularity could not be counted on.'

The harsh weather of early 1947 and the state of the English economy combined to bring about a crisis more severe than any experienced in the war years themselves. Train services were curtailed for want of fuel from 20 January 1947 and scheduled passenger trains were totally suspended from 24 February. Even goods trains ran only on three days a week. In February cross-channel weeklies were suspended for a fortnight because of a fuel shortage in Britain. The situation for the scheduled railway services remained unchanged until 24 May when operations were resumed on four days a week, and this was extended to six days a week from 16 June.

The short-term consequences of these years of difficulty are self-evident. There was a fall in turnover, partly concealed by a rise in prices, and poor profit margins. Furthermore, rises in profits in the wholesale stationery department and in the Dublin shop, which helped to make the house viable, were subject to legal controls in the later stages of the war. The auditors' report in July 1944 noted that 'the profits in both departments would be affected in the future by an agreement to be entered into with the Department of Supplies (Prices Branch).' The auditor's report of the following year makes it clear that this agreement restricted the rate of gross profit in the stationery and retail departments to 19 per cent and 27 per cent respectively.

The difficulties of the war years would have been even more serious if wages had not also been held down by controls. In January 1939 a new sliding scale had been agreed with the Irish Transport and General Workers Union (ITGWU) giving 60s at age 25 for males, and a similar scale was agreed in Belfast in July 1939. This was only a modest increase over the wage levels of the 1920s. Wages were in fact frozen during the emergency period, subject only to small adjustments. In Dublin in December 1941 the board decided to make a payment of £1 per month to senior men and 10s per month to senior women, at the end of the months of December, January and February following, to be treated as a payment out of past profits for good service to senior staff who had had no increase during 1941. 135 members of the staff benefited from this scheme. Wages rose less rapidly in Dublin than in Belfast, where they rose in 1941 and 1942 in particular. In 1943 a joint application was made by the firm and the ITGWU for a bonus payment of 5s a week for adult male packers and shop assistants, and an order was granted to this effect by the government. A supplemental agreement with the union provided for 2s 6d to all juniors. Subsequently bonus orders allowed for the spread of bonus payments throughout the rest of the house, and these were doubled later in the same year to 10s a week and 5s a week. The next bonus increase was authorised in 1945, and raised the total bonus payment to 15s a week. A new wage scheme was agreed with the ITGWU only in November 1946, providing for 90s a week for males aged 25. Before this rise, wage increases had fallen far behind the rise in the cost of living, a factor which explains the impetus behind wage increases once war-time controls were eased in 1946 and later removed.

The problems so far described were primarily due to the economic consequences of the war. Administrative problems, particularly those caused by the censorship, were also pressing. Because of the sensitive nature of the country's neutrality a very strict censorship was imposed. The first measure taken by the government was an order under the Emergency Powers Act, known as 'No.5 order 1939, S.R.O. No. 244' dated 13 September 1939. It provided for powers to deal with both news and posters, and affected both the home press and the foreign press circulating in the state. The first controller of press censorship was Joseph Connolly, who had been chairman of the Board of Works. In the early stages of the war these powers were used to exclude references to Poland, and particularly to an appeal on behalf of that country. News of incidents such as the arrival of seaplanes at a harbour on the east coast was also suppressed.

As early as 2 November 1939 J.C.M. Eason wrote to Wallace, the circulation manager of Odhams Press Ltd, that 'there are some other papers where the propaganda is very vigorous, regarding which we have felt some apprehension.' Posters raised the propaganda dimension in an acute form, and Eason wrote to Michael McGrath, Manager of Eason's wholesale branch office at Waterford, on 5 December 1939:

> .... It may not always be obvious whether a poster is objectionable or not. For instance, there was some query raised over the *Universe* poster for last week. We had it on the vans here. The headline — MURDER MINES — was criticised in certain quarters, but I did not take it off the vans. In that case, of course, we are directly responsible, and naturally our responsibility is greater if we put the posters on our own premises or vans. At the same time, we wish to prevent annoyance and trouble, and would suppress posters which we felt were unsuitable.

As far as Eason's were concerned they were advised by the Chief Censor, Michael Knightly, on 1 December 1939 that:

> The Press Censorship is somewhat embarrassed by the type of poster which is being displayed from time to time in connection with one or other of the English newspapers or periodicals which are being handled by your firm. Some of these posters are simply anti-German, and carry slogans which, however apt from the Englishman's point of view, cannot with propriety be allowed to be displayed on the public streets of a neutral State. Others are more subtle (or, perhaps, more ingenuous) and seem to take it for granted that we in Ireland are participating as belligerents in the war with Germany and thus give offence to our own people. An example of the latter type was provided last Sunday by the *Sunday Chronicle* with a poster bearing the slogan: HOW HITLER HOPES TO WIN US OUT. Note the US which

> could not have failed to give offence to a great many people here, and did in fact do so, to judge from the protests I have received. Of the former type the *Sunday Chronicle* also provided an example last week with the slogan: HUNS AT SEA. On the same lines were recent slogans of the *Daily Sketch:* NAZI SEA MURDERS, and in *Cavalcade:* HUNS MUST HANG. The latest poster of *Cavalcade* is no less objectionable with the following slogan; DO YOU HATE THE HUNS?

J.C.M. Eason was asked to write to the offending publishers and later he noted that:

> As a result a circular was sent by us to the cross-channel papers calling attention to the matter, and on the whole, there was very little difficulty arising after that time, but the situation was chiefly relieved by a reduction of posters during war time with a view to saving paper.

On January 10 1940 Michael Knightly wrote to J.C.M. Eason again:

> While I do not wish to cite any particular newspaper by name, I may say that the occasion of this communication is the appearance in an English newspaper of a story in regard to the alleged movements and activities of our troops with respect to a 'mystery ship' which is supposed to be manned by members of an illegal organisation who were planning to use it for dumping arms and ammunition. If this story was true its publication would, or might, have endangered the armed forces of the State or prevented the success of their operations; if it was not true, it was simply mischievous; and unfortunately mischief of this kind is often only aggravated by official denials.

On his own initiative Eason immediately wrote to the *Daily Mirror* and also to two periodicals which commented on news events and were becoming a source of concern, *News Review* and *Cavalcade*. On 25 January 1940 Knightly commented in a letter that:

> Generally speaking, the trouble with the English journalists is that they do not seem to appreciate Irish national sentiments. We have ceased to expect the average English journalist to deal either intelligently or sympathetically with the problem existing here. There are, of course, a number of honourable exceptions.

Other journals offended as well. In the case of *Picture Post* copies had to be submitted to the Censor before distribution. Eason wrote to the Circulation Manager at great length advising him of the position, and in a letter of 9 January 1940 he commented to him that: 'I genuinely believe you are wrong in your attitude.'

The first direct experience of censorship encountered was in March 1940 when copies of *News Review* were seized by the police. This occurred after it had been distributed, and with considerable trouble Eason's were able to get the covers in order to claim a refund of the duty. Again in April this periodical was seized, and it was subsequently banned for a month.

English papers tended to be insensitive to Irish security problems. The circulation manager of the *Daily Mirror* wrote to J.C.M. Eason on 12 January 1940 after talks with his editor:

> He is a little mystified in regard to your apprehension. The IRA being the illegal body that it is lends itself to such a story, and also is it not a fact that the *Irish Press* itself castigates them in much stronger fashion than we did in our issue of the 5th inst.?

To this letter Eason replied: 'I believe that your Censorship would exclude any such reference to similar incidents within your own quarter. The article is not in the slightest degree a criticism of the IRA. I cannot see a trace of castigation in your article from beginning to end.'

The *Daily Mirror* was in trouble again in April when two issues were banned. Assurances were given to play down reports of the hunger strikes by republicans, following the death of a hunger striker. Budden of the *Daily Mirror* wrote on 22 April:

> Like you I was pleased at the quick lifting of the ban and I have every reason to suppose that this was due to the fact that I prevailed upon the Editor to send two copies of the Irish edition of the issue which contained the offending cartoon, because it showed how quickly we acted on the Censor's request the previous evening not to make a large story of the 'Hunger Striker's death'. The one issue showed how we had indeed made a full back page story, and the other how this story was replaced by other matter, and quite obviously it was done in double quick time. Indeed, to be quite frank, it was due to this rush that this cartoon was overlooked, for which matter our editor expressed his regrets.

Despite apparent good intentions, problems quickly arose again, and the *Daily Mirror* was finally prohibited on 11 May 1940 and ceased to be imported. *News Review* continued to come under scrutiny from time to time. *Picture Post* also continued to give problems, *Cavalcade* was banned in July for having news unsuitable to a neutral country, and the *News Chronicle* was banned in October, although this ban was lifted a fortnight later. The reasons for banning were not always evident. On 30 October 1940 Eason advised the *News Chronicle* that 'something has been published to which great exception is taken and knowing so little about the subject as I do comment would be inappropriate and misleading.'

In December 1940 and January 1941 prolonged discussions on

censorship took place in the Senate. There was great criticism of the application of the powers to home papers, and more particularly to the reporting of domestic matters. In May 1941 *Picture Post*, unable to meet demand in England, held back supplies from the south, and cut supplies to the North of Ireland by 25 per cent. J.C.M. Eason commented that 'the natural conclusion therefore is that the publisher was not willing to take the risk of his paper being stopped on either of the two grounds of censorship in connection with which he had experienced difficulty.' It was a severe blow. *Picture Post* had the largest circulation at that time of any illustrated general interest weekly. Even when a ban was lifted, Eason's did not necessarily seek or get fresh supplies. In August 1941 Eason was unofficially informed that the ban on the *Daily Mirror* was lifted. He recalled later that:

> We did not take any action towards getting supplies because at that time there were several difficulties in the way of distribution; the publishers were short of paper; the papers were non-returnable; they were arriving later, and as a result of that the circulation had dwindled to about one-tenth of the pre-war figure.

The ban on *Cavalcade* was lifted in October 1941. After receiving some enquiries Eason's communicated with the publisher, but the latter did not see fit to take any action.

After 1941, at least until the end of the war, censorship of the press did not pose many problems. The biggest political event as far as Eason's was concerned were the scenes in O'Connell Street when the Six County Prisoners Reprieve Committee called for all premises to close from 11 to 12 pm on 2 September 1942, as a mark of respect for the memory of young Williams 'who had been executed in the North.' William Calwell, the senior director present, decided not to close. A crowd gathered outside, and an attempt was made to rush the door, which was closed just in time. The guards advised the Eason's not to open till some time after noon, and the house in fact did not open till 1.45 pm.

Publications other than the daily press continued to cause concern to the Censor, and T.J. Coyne, who had succeeded Connolly as controller of censorship, had an interview with Robert Eason and Eoin O'Keeffe of the Irish branch of the Booksellers Association on 7 November 1941. Robert Eason, director in charge of wholesale books, made a note of the censor's views:

> There is a certain type of propagandist publication to which no great exception is taken, this might be described as propaganda pro-something, as compared with propaganda 'anti' publications, and

> display within reason would not be objected to, but if a bookseller filled his window with a publication telling of the exploits of the 'Luftwaffe' or 'R.A.F.' then objection would be taken. This would mean that there would not be any objection to reasonable display and free sale of publications such as the British Government publication *Coastal Command* and *Battle of Britain* and also such publications as *R.A.F. Parade*. It would appear throughout the whole interview that there was no desire on the part of the authorities (Censorship Authorities) to deprive the public entirely of the opportunity of reading propagandist literature, but there is an objection to such literature being given prominent window display or undue display in the shops. The worst type should be excluded from stock altogether, but there will be no prohibition of copies of such books being procured and supplied to the order of any customer.

Towards the end of the war, 'offensive' articles on the subject of neutrality began to appear. When *Everybody's Weekly* was banned, J.C.M. Eason reminded the editors in April 1944 that on a previous occasion when the *Sunday Dispatch* was banned, the ban was withdrawn after a later issue carried an article setting out the position from the Irish point of view. On 14 June 1944 Eason wrote to the publishers of *Strand Magazine* justifying the operation of Irish war-time censorship and advising them of the error in confusing a war-time ban on the publication with the Censorship Act:

> The Editor of the *Strand Magazine* has chosen to insert political propaganda against this country of a type which, as has already been indicated by action taken in the case of *Everybody's Weekly* and the *Sunday Dispatch*, causes great resentment here. In one respect I think the particular article in question is even worse than its predecessors. I called your attention to the drawing at the head of the article — the implications are definitely false.
>
> In addition, the article is in many respects unfair and unbalanced. Moreover, it does not appear to me to attempt a criticism of our position here. There have been many papers circulating here which have contained criticisms, but I am afraid this does not come into that category.

This letter brought a retort from Duncan Lush, the circulation manager of the publishers, George Newnes Ltd. on 19 June 1944 that 'I did not ask for your political opinion. As our principal wholesale agents in Eire I sought your advice as a businessman.' Eason replied to this: 'I can find no business solution to a political difficulty.' Later Eason sent Duncan Lush some material on the Irish point of view on neutrality which elicited a friendly but somewhat uncomprehending letter in September stating that 'it is a great pity that there is not a little more sympathy in Ireland for the English point of view.'

The war years and their immediate aftermath were probably the most difficult in all the firm's history. As such a large proportion of the news handled by the firm came from Britain, that business was particularly vulnerable. Difficulties in cross-channel sailings and in train services exacerbated the problems, and the fact that many of the staff were on half-time illustrates how acutely the difficulties were experienced throughout the house.

A major and longlasting effect of the war, however, was a dramatic shift from rail to road news distribution as fuel shortages worsened. This was consolidated in 1945, when the bulk of distribution was switched permanently into lorries. At this time other factors were present, and a railway strike was the immediate catalyst, but the suitability of road transport for long-distance transport of news had been proved. The indirect consequences of the change were considerable. Road transport was a flexible operation in which direct costs predominated, in contrast to railway operation, where the fact that many of the costs were fixed overhead costs was reflected in rates determined by the transport company or by the state. As long as Dublin daily news was distributed by train, the publishers had nothing to gain by taking country distribution into their own hands, and the convenience of leaving country distribution in the hands of the wholesaler outweighed any direct savings. With the advent of road transport, and the disproportionately high rise in distribution costs over the next decades, newspaper proprietors had the alternative of either allowing larger margins to the wholesaler or taking distribution into their own hands. As wholesale margins became less and less attractive, and consequently profits fell, the attractions of customer-tailored transport (and ultimately 'house' transport) grew. Between 1945 and 1964 the distribution of Dublin daily news to the provinces was increasingly taken over by the publishers.

Chapter 20 ❧ Reconstruction

AFTER THE TRAUMA OF THE EMERGENCY PERIOD, and the difficulties caused by the harsh winter of 1947, the company was faced with a serious situation. Profits in the early 1950s were at a disturbingly low level. Labour costs as a percentage of turnover were 6.3 per cent in 1947/8. They had soared to 7.5 per cent by 1954/5. Even with a larger turnover and an assured competitive place in the distribution of monthly magazines, profits declined throughout the 1950s.

DEVELOPMENTS IN WHOLESALE NEWS

For some years after the end of the war, newsprint continued to be rationed and the supply of newspapers and periodicals, both Irish and from overseas, was severely restricted. In addition there was a shortage of petrol and other fuel. Later the Republic of Ireland was treated by the British publishers as an 'export area' and not subject to the continuing rationing which was a feature of publishing in Britain and in Northern Ireland in the years immediately after the war.

The distribution services of the wholesale news department continued in a pattern similar to the war period, and the department in Dublin was accommodated in the premises it had occupied since 1920 on the ground, basement and first floor of 80 Middle Abbey St. Virtually all publications were on firm sale and the 'returns' section of the department occupied an area on the fifth floor of the same building. The ground floor was used at night for the packing and despatch of the Dublin daily newspapers, and, during the day, for weekly periodicals. The 'Dublin daily' staff packed two editions each night of the Dublin papers, the country edition leaving from about 1.30 am, and the city edition being received from the publishers about 4.30 am and despatched an hour later in Easons' vans.

These vans also carried parcels of weekly and monthly publications that had been prepared during the previous day, and some weekly publications, mainly provincial newspapers that the night staff had packed between the two daily editions. Soon after the war ended, the mailboat service was improved, and this enabled the English daily newspapers to arrive at Dun Laoghaire by 6.30 am. These were immediately delivered to Dublin city and suburban locations on the 'Sketch run' as it was called, from the principal component. For the country generally, morning buses and trains left Dublin between 8.00 am and 9.30 am. Country sales depended on lunchtime business, and were small, with high unit costs.

From 1946, News Department staff who had been laid off during the war and had gone to work elsewhere, many in England, began to return and were re-appointed to their old jobs in the expectation that with peace, sales would increase and the extra staff would be needed. By 1949/50 the wholesale news staff had built up to 180. However the depressed state of the Irish economy was such that the easing of supplies had only a limited effect; staffing costs increased more quickly than sales with the result that throughout the 1950s the department had a struggle to survive.

Net profits in wholesale news in Dublin fell below 1 per cent of turnover in the 1950s, and as low as 0.4 per cent in 1955/6. This is not much different from the very low ratios experienced in the difficult war years: 0.6 per cent in 1940/41, 0.3 per cent in 1941/2 and 0.9 per cent in 1942/3. At such low levels, net profitability in news was erratic, sensitive to the impact of newspaper or transport strikes on either side of the channel. Caution was the prevailing outlook of the house in the 1950s. During this period also, the Dublin newspapers were themselves experiencing difficult trading conditions, and were unwilling and probably unable to improve the narrow margin on which Eason's operated as a wholesaler.

During the war the wholesale news division in Dublin had contributed very little to the business which was sustained by the wholesale stationery department centred in the Middle Abbey Street building. Soon after the end of the war, supplies of stationery and other goods became more plentiful, stocks increased, and more space was needed. As a first step, the small news 'returns' department was moved to part of the building, now empty, in Sean McDermott Street which had been occupied by the factory, which was closed in 1941. By 1950 it was clear that both the stationery and the wholesale news departments needed more space. It was decided to move the entire wholesale news department, with the exception of the Trade Counter, to the factory building which was renamed 'Diamond House', one corner of the site being on the Gloucester

Diamond at the junction of Sean McDermott Street and Gloucester Place. This move began in August 1950. The 'night work', consisting of the despatch of the Dublin daily newspapers, remained at Abbey Street for a few months longer to enable the newspaper publishers to be reassured that vans could get to Kingsbridge goods yard, the collecting point for the country lorries, as quickly as before, so that the country deliveries would not be delayed. This lorry service was operated by CIE on behalf of the three Dublin newspapers, and all Dublin newspaper parcels were carried by them, including Dublin newspapers for newsagents supplied by Eason's.

The move of the department to more suitable premises, allowing more and better working space, did not achieve the savings in operating costs in relation to turnover that had been hoped for. Work practices which had evolved in a department spread over four floors in the crowded Abbey street building were to a considerable extent carried over to Diamond House. The packing system required three people for each parcel, one to call out the titles and quantities from the newsagent's invoice, one to put the magazines in the labelled wrapper, and a third to tie the parcel and put it in a barrow for despatch. Newsagents' parcels of newspapers and magazines could only be made up on the day of despatch, so that an irregular work pattern, derived from traditional publishing days was caused through the week and through the month.

The difficult trading conditions throughout the 1950s also affected other wholesalers. In 1958, George Tivy, the managing director of News Brothers in Cork, approached James Walmsley to find out whether Eason's would be interested in taking over their business. After some negotiation, this was done; a major concern to the Tivys was that the pension arrangements of their staff, which the firm paid out of current revenue, should be continued. The year 1959 was one of poor business; a long British printing strike lasted through June and July, affecting most of the cross-channel weeklies and magazines. Despite the loss in revenue, expenses ran at the same level, to deal with the Irish and Scottish publications unaffected by the strike. On a turnover close to £1 million, net profit was less than £8,000.

The gradual rise in the sales of weeklies and magazines over the 1950s, and the consequent improvement in margins was eventually responsible for halting the deterioration in profits which had taken place. The success of women's weeklies, more than any other feature, contributed to this. In 1950 English dailies in the Republic of Ireland (on the basis of import figures) averaged 19,660 per day, whereas the 1952 census of production figures gave a total of 730,000 Irish dailies per day.[1] In April 1957 Eason's handled an average of 93,292 Irish dailies, and 18,429 English dailies. The Eason figure for dailies in 1957 compared with the 1950 figure for the whole market gives an impression of a real though modest rise in cross-Channel news.

By the early 1960s it was clear that the Dublin daily newspaper distribution had probably not made a profit for Eason's for ten years. On the other hand it was felt that the overheads, such as the provision of premises and the van delivery services would only be marginally reduced if the Dublin dailies were given up. Repeated attempts were made in the 1950s to increase the wholesale discount, which was 10 per cent for the *Irish Independent* and *Irish Press* and 8 per cent for *The Irish Times*. Eventually it was the *Irish Independent* rather than Eason's which precipitated events. In 1964 their General Manager, John Dunne, concluded that if their costs were to be contained they must either reduce their distribution staff or handle a greater volume with their existing personnel. He no doubt estimated that their existing staff, with only marginal adjustments, could distribute the share, about 20 per cent, of their sales which were sold to newsagents through Eason's. Once he had given notice to Eason's to this effect it was apparent at once, so far as Eason's were concerned, that the remaining Dublin daily distribution, accounting for an even smaller share of *The Irish Times* and *Irish Press* sales, was totally uneconomic. The result was the inevitable closure of this part of the business which took place on 1 June 1964.

Towards the end of 1965 publishers printing English daily newspaper editions in Manchester decided that the time had come to use air services instead of the mailboat for the transport of their dailies to Dublin. The papers printed in Manchester now arrived in Dublin airport at 2 am, in time to be despatched to the country by lorry. Deliveries in the Dublin area of British newspapers were now made at the same time as the Dublin newspapers, instead of by a late morning delivery between nine and ten-thirty, depending on the time the mailboat arrived in Dun Laoghaire. In the country van delivery from the airport ensured morning delivery in all but the most remote areas of the south and west. In Northern Ireland the effect was similar, the country outside the Belfast area being covered by delivery services jointly provided by Eason's of Belfast and their principal competitor. The British publishers hoped to build up sales throughout the country and not merely a concentration in the Dublin area.

1 This figure appears high because it includes evening papers as well as morning papers.

For this purpose, the wholesaler provided a service which could not easily be provided in any other way. The trend emphasised the shift in the company's distribution to a wide range of English dailies and weeklies whose higher margins admitted of a recovery in the house's profits and profit ratios beginning in the late 1950s. This development also profited from better economic conditions in Ireland in the 1960s.

THE END OF THE BOOKSTALL CHAIN

During the war years the position of the Belfast bookstalls had greatly improved relative to neutral Dublin. In the post-war period, Dublin's position improved somewhat, but the longterm trend was similar north and south: virtual stagnation in gross receipts. A tendency to fall became evident in the late 1950s, and the run-down of the bookstall network accelerated over the next two decades. The final break-up of the bookstall network came in the late 1970s.

The post-war period saw some contraction in the northern bookstalls, down to 26 in 1950. A further reduction of 3 bookstalls took place between 1956 and 1957. There were still 18 bookstalls in 1960, but the run-down of the rail system, and the losses sustained, combined to reduce the bookstalls further again in the next few years of two bookstalls in Belfast termini and one at Bangor. The Dublin bookstall network, though it was pruned, held out much longer in the end, mainly because the railway network was not reduced to the same extent. Conditions were increasingly unfavourable, and the network of bookstalls in the Republic was virtually ended in the 1970s with the closing of what had been the major bookstalls on the railway system (some of them substantial revenue earners in earlier years): Bray and Kilkenny in May 1972, Westland Row in April 1975, Drogheda and Tralee in 1977, Athlone, Galway, Killarney and Waterford at the end of 1978.

It was indeed the end of the era which had opened in 1856 and reached a high point in the heady days before the first world war when the bookstall network had spread across the country, and when bookstall sales for a short period accounted for over 40 per cent of the entire news sales of the firm. The bookstalls provided not only a service to the traveller, but also played an important role in opening up retail sales, when the habit of regular news buying was in its early stages. It is no accident that the high point of the bookstalls in terms of number, turnover and perhaps profit was concentrated within the first two decades of the twentieth century, when mass readership began to make its appearance. In turn it was inevitable in the long term that readers would seek more convenient outlets than the bookstalls, and the loss of local customers, even more than the shift of travellers from rail to road, was decisive. The better performance of the Belfast termini compared with their Dublin counterparts seems to owe something to their more central position for servicing passing town trade. Although the military establishment at the Curragh was much reduced, as compared with the British one prior to 1922, the resilience of the Curragh bookstall is an interesting illustration of the fact that it was on regular customers and not on passing travellers that the news retailer depended on for profitability in the twentieth century.

ADVERTISING

Once the railways ceased to be the dominant mode of mass transport, it was inevitable that advertisers would look at other media. Mass readership newspapers and magazines were the obvious solution. As a result Easons' revenue from railway advertising never recovered the buoyancy it had achieved at the end of the nineteenth century. The inevitable run-down of the railway advertising revenue would have happened much more slowly but for the brutal curtailment during the war of railway services in the south. Bus revenue held up, while railway income was halved, even with revenue from roadside sites included. In 1944/5 railway advertising revenue for the Dublin house was £8,927 compared with bus advertising at £5,982. In 1946 CIE, the newly-formed state transport company took over directly all advertising and brought railway, bus and tram advertising by Eason's to an end. In Northern Ireland it lasted a few more years.

By 1952 J.C.M. Eason had agreed that 'the advertising department can be dropped at any time without affecting the business as a whole'. Even if an active interest in advertising was retained, it was now changing greatly in character. Newspaper advertising had been a modest activity, handled through the Retail department in Dublin, usually at a net loss. It expanded dramatically in turnover in the years following the second world war, so that its turnover equalled that of the outdoor advertising department. The logical step was to combine both activities into a single department, and this took place in the year ended March 1952. Thereafter advertising continued as a successful general agency, always on a small scale; since 1965 it has operated as a separate company.

WHOLESALE BOOKS AND STATIONERY

The contribution of non-news activities on the wholesale side, of which books and stationery were the significant components, ran at about 30 per cent of turnover during the 1950s. Stationery had originally been the more active of the two, particularly in the 1920s and 1930s, a trend which was carried, though less strongly, into the 1950s. Costing, and therefore a precise allocation of profit and overhead, always presented problems in stationery, both in the division of sales and an exact attribution of costs in what was the most capital intensive department of the firm. J.C.M. Eason was always aware that the costing remained inexact. During both world wars profits in wholesale stationery rose sharply. Between 1941 and 1944, when poor delivery and shortage of supplies led to merely nominal profits in the wholesale news department, wholesale stationery was the main constituent of net profits in the firm.

The war and the shortage of outside material may have been responsible for a boost to the local publishing interest. In the late 1940s there was a significant increase in the number of weekly or monthly journals published in Ireland. The number of book publishers increased and in addition to the existing houses, Metropolitan Publishing House, Browne & Nolan, Dundalgan Press, M.H. Gill and the Parkside Press, Clonmore & Reynolds made their promising but short-lived appearance, and the Mercier Press published its first title, on church music, in 1944. Fallon's also published some books, and if the appearance of Club Leabhar and the establishment of Sairseal & Dill is included, the Irish publishing scene had developed a great deal. The demand for Irish-published or Irish-related material was strong. In 1943 Eason's reported on Gerard Lee's *Murder and Music*, a detective story set in Dublin, that 'there has been steady demand for copies, and the Talbot Press have now issued a cheap edition.... It will keep its place as a good selling story for some years to come.' John Harvey's *Dublin*, published by Batsford in 1949 is an interesting example of a successful serious book. It held its place in the best sellers' list during five two-monthly issues of the *Monthly Bulletin*, including the hectic period of the Christmas sales. In 1956 Eason's said that 200,000 copies of the works of John D. Sheridan had been sold. The dearth of books published in Ireland was not because of a lack of demand, because good books on Irish themes published either in Ireland or abroad sold well. It was either a failure of publishing houses, or a slowness on the part of authors in coming forward. In fact, it was as much a failure of authors as of anything else, a circumstance illustrated, for instance, in the shortage of books on Irish history. Easons' *Monthly Bulletin* had observed in 1925 that 'M'Gee's History of Ireland has been for many years the staple history of this country.'

Books like Lynn Doyle's *Spirit of Ireland* and Aodh de Blacam's *Gentle Ireland* both sold out in 1936, and given the success of such books as appeared, it is surprising how few efforts were made to take advantage of this market. Magazines also proved the existence of such a market, as for instance in the large circulation of *Dublin Opinion* and *Our Boys*. It might even be argued that the number of successes on their merits was large in relation to the number of books, and that the Irish market was starved of distinctly Irish literature. Whatever the reasons, the increased activity of the 1940s, though it faltered in the difficult economic climate of the early 1950s, was the beginning of an upward trend which has culminated in the comparatively flourishing Irish publishing industry of the last twenty years, and especially since 1975.

In the 1960s the paperback revolution made a major change in the book market. Paperback publishers such as Corgi and Arrow produced a much more popular kind of book than the somewhat middle-class paperback pioneers such as Penguin and Pan. At the same time the new Censorship Act, 1967, allowed books that had been banned for twelve years to be sold. The general climate became considerably more liberal. Donleavy's *Ginger Man* was only one of the titles that benefitted. Books became an increasingly important product, both in the retail shops and in wholesaling. By the end of the 1970s, Eason's was the fourth biggest customer in the world for British popular paperback publishers, and booktrade estimates suggested that 40-50 per cent of the popular book trade in Ireland passed through Easons' hands.

THE RISE OF THE RETAIL

Apart from the bookstalls, the retail business at the end of the second world war was small and virtually unchanged since the beginning of the century. It consisted of the small shop in the portion of the main Eason building on O'Connell Street, Dublin and the shops at the Curragh Camp and in Donegall Street, Belfast; the last two being little more than bookstalls. J.C.M. Eason's attitude to the retail department in 1952 was still dismissive: 'as long as we hold 40/41 Lower O'Connell Street and they are clearly needed for services to wholesale, there is no point in weighing up the pros and cons of the retail department. It exists.'

The fundamental reason for J.C.M. Eason's lack of interest in the retail side was his anxiety that developing their own retail side would conflict with the interests of the customers of the firm's wholesaling service — the retail newsagents and stationers. When he had assumed central responsibility for the management of the firm in the early 1920s it had been the recipient of bitter criticism because it combined its wholesale business with a retail business through its own bookstalls. In Belfast this had been Porter's selling point against Eason's, proclaiming themselves as the 'newsagent's wholesaler', and in Dublin Dawson's had also emphasised the fact that they did not conduct a retail business.

The move of the wholesale news department to Diamond House in 1950 virtually cleared the basement and ground floor of the Abbey Street building. These floors adjoined the O'Connell Street shop area. However in the light of the relative success during the war of the wholesale stationery department under William Calwell, and its immediate need for space, it was reasonable to allow it to expand into the space made available. The wholesale book department under Robert Eason also took over a large part of the ground floor in Middle Abbey Street. At this time the needs of the wholesale departments were paramount, and the shop was left virtually unchanged.

Up to 1951 the shop (the house term was 'the retail') was managed by William Hassell, a senior member of the staff with previous experience in the shop and in the factory, and also at the Curragh, which he had managed from 1916 to 1921. The shop received little central attention before the 1950s; unlike other departments it had no real departmental structure, and no director was given a clear-cut responsibility for its operation. Hassell reported to Calwell for his stationery requirements, to Robert Eason for books and to J.C.M. Eason for staff and personnel matters.

The key to the subsequent development of the shop, and the retailing aspect of the firm generally was the appointment in 1957 of E.J. Kelliher as a director with full responsibility for its running. Kelliher was an accountant brought into wholesale stationery under William Calwell in 1952. When appointed manager in the retail he took over a ground floor shop of about 1,700 square feet devoted to books, news and stationery. There were also about 1,000 square feet in the basement below, housing among other things the second-hand book department. Kelliher recalled the appearance of the shop when he took it over: 'the ground floor was rather gloomy, with massive mahogany wall shelves, glass cases and in the centre of the floor a large horse-shoe magazine counter. The books were on open display as was customary, but other products such as stationery were served from behind the traditional counter.' The symbolic first step was to remove the horse-shoe counter and replace it with stepped newspaper and magazine racks. Open display was to be provided for all items.

At this time a substantial part of the retail activities, with a long history of being run almost independently of the shop, was the retail news subscription department, which was in the charge of John O'Donnell. This was one of the range of activities which had been lumped together as a Retail department, not all of which were profitable. Newspaper advertising had made consistent losses during the 1920s and 1930s, and the library and the subscription departments had not been much better. The losses incurred in the news subscription department increased after the war. The department's main feature was a delivery service to offices and addresses in the central area of Dublin. This was highly labour-intensive and required a substantial despatch area in the main building. In 1952 J.C.M. Eason noted that 'the Subscription Department is ancillary to our general news service, but it has shown very bad results because we have not charged appropriate prices, and endeavoured to compete with publishers. That factor and the labour costs force revisions. If there must be a loss we can keep it down to smaller proportions.' John O'Donnell did his best to follow this policy until he was promoted to be Manager of the News Department; when Edward Kelliher took over in 1957 he closed down the department altogether.

A large area was now made free, into which the shop could expand. In later years the wholesale departments were moved to other buildings in Dublin. Thus was made possible a massive reconstruction of the basement, ground, first and second floors of the O'Connell Street/Abbey Street building, in the process of creating a large modern retail store. Following the new policy oriented towards high street retailing, shops were opened in Cork (1963), Dun Laoghaire (1966), Limerick (1970), Belfast — Ann Street (1971). With the opening of the Dublin — Mary Street shop and new shops in Belfast — Ann Street and in Lisburn in 1986, the firm in 1987 had fourteen such shops. Aided by the boom in general retail trade in the 1960s, these developments changed the firm beyond recognition. By the late 1970s retail sales accounted for nearly half the firm's total turnover. The boom meant that shops in central locations, carying a wide range of news, books and other requirements and having good connections with publishers and other manufacturers enjoyed strong growth.

Despite this change of emphasis, the firm still handled the same range of goods as in the past. Its comparative advantage in the retail trade lies essentially in the skills previously acquired and in the knowledge of selling books and other goods that had been manufactured and sold as wholesale items. It has been characteristic of the firm's history that the emphasis has changed from generation to generation. Even where comparative advantages were slight, the ability of the firm to change quickly could in itself confer advantage over potential competitors whose knowledge was less intimate. In its evolution during the 1960s and 1970s Eason's represents an example both of the exploitation of traditional know-how and of a sweeping change in the attitudes brought to the business. The firm is less wedded to activities apparently for their own sake, and is more open to new concepts. Even J.C.M. Eason, acute businessman as he was, did not see the potential of the retail trade, and it was the new generation of such men as James Walmsley as managing director of the firm from 1952 with Eddie Kelliher in charge of the retail who conceived and put into effect the major developments of the 1960s.

Chapter 21 J.C.M. Eason — managing a changing business

J.C.M. EASON WAS THE FIRM'S DRIVING FORCE during the years between 1920 and 1950. These were years in which a wholesale firm could never hope to achieve again profits such as it found in pre-1900 advertising, or to enjoy the assured position which the firm had held in news, first through its bookstalls and again in its dominance in wholesaling before 1914. When he joined the company in 1901, its advertising was becoming unprofitable for the first time in its history. When he became head in 1926 the bookstalls were declining. By the end of his active life wholesaling, which he liked better than any other activity in the house, and whose place in the firm he jealously protected, was on the verge of revolutionary change. In retiring, he told the board:

> It would be inappropriate for me to be over critical regarding your reference to my part in helping to keep the business going. In fact I was unsuccessful in several directions, but I must point out that there were many favourable factors (external) and that others — not indeed the Board members alone — contributed to such results as emerged.

A period of such sweeping change required a more flexible approach than that of any of his predecessors. The rise of trade unions, shifts in the structure of the firm, the change of government in 1922, aggressive press lords who bypassed the wholesaler to sell direct to the retailer, the novel problems of press censorship and of tariffs — all these factors not only marked a sustained change in the environment in which the wholesaler operated but required quick responses. In fact, Eason's own impression of business was of a difficult milieu in which toil was unremitting and the returns were finite. Not only were returns on capital low — they were much lower than before 1910 — but they were seen to be low. J.C.M. Eason was seventy in 1950. He had been managing director for twenty-four years at that stage, but he had effectively been in charge of the key wholesale news department since 1916 and of the business as a whole since 1920. It is clear that he was already thinking to the future, and that he was well aware of the growing limitations of age, as he set out in his letter of resignation to the board on 29 June 1950:

> The simple and adequate reason is that I am now not in close enough touch with the day-to-day details of the business to enable me to take the necessary immediate decisions: this is particularly applicable to the engagement of staff and regulation of their duties and as regards interdepartmental working.

His careful notes on profits continued well into the 1950s, but by 1958 he was seventy-eight, and he resigned as chairman in that year with effect from 31 March. He had completed 57 years within the firm, a longer association even than that of his grandfather. His resignation as chairman was followed in 1960 by a refusal to go forward again for election to the board:

> It is no doubt difficult to convey in simple form the chief reason or reasons for my leaving: but the main factor was that at all times my judgement and decisions were based upon knowledge I possessed from daily contact with all details in all sections. That was changed by the process of time — necessarily — the sources of inspiration were no longer available, or at any rate so greatly diminished as not to be of any force.

One of J.C.M. Eason's achievements was the opening up of the management of the firm. It was a tightly-knit family business in its management up to 1925, when Eason introduced William Calwell from the Chamber of Commerce, expressly to bring in outside expertise and to develop the wholesale stationery department. When Eason resigned as managing director in 1950, he was succeeded by Calwell, the memory of whose high reputation lingers on within the firm. Calwell had all the traits of a good soldier: an upright carriage, an integrity that rarely yielded to compromise and the capacity to inspire great loyalty in some and fear in others. He had won the Military Cross in the first world war, and personal friends referred to him as Captain Calwell. He was however essentially a very private man who had few interests outside the firm. It was he who introduced the one major diversification which Eason's was to have outside its traditional product range in the first half of the century: the toiletry department, later re-named the hairdressing department. This was later established as a subsidiary company in 1965. Calwell's authority in the stationery department was absolute; in time he recruited William Robertson who became head of the department and was appointed to the board in 1961 and remained a director until his death in 1967.

Later on (c.1944), J.C.M. Eason brought in J.J. Walsh, a bright young graduate of University College, on the recommendation of Professor George O'Brien. Walsh was made a manager and quickly a director. Eason had high hopes of him, and a later undated note recalled that:

> He grasped detail rapidly; but was not adverse from handling it in early days; but his rather prolonged academic work gave him no early knowledge of business and I think he was drawn away by the attractive offer from Government to work which may have been more congenial, and which provided a more rapid rise than we could hold out.

The appointment of a catholic to senior rank in what was at the time regarded still as a 'protestant' family business was unusual. In an obituary notice in the *Irish Times* on 29 September 1976 R.C. Geary recalled of J.C.M. Eason: 'I was particularly struck by his appointing a young Catholic graduate friend of mine to executive rank and later to a directorship in Eason's. That would occasion no comment now; it did then.'

Calwell's succession as managing director marked a significant transition in the nature of the business, as the major post in the firm for the first time in its history passed out of the hands of a member of the family. However, two of the four managing directors who succeeded Eason have had a family connection by blood or marriage, so that the family association is still very much a live one. Eason's concern to build up the senior ranks of the house can be seen in the bringing in of J.J. Walsh, and in the appointment of James A. Walmsley, who became assistant managing director to Calwell in 1950, and almost immediately assumed responsibility for the news department, then at the nadir point of its profitability.

James Walmsley himself had joined the company in 1948, a year after his brother Basil had started to work with George Best in the Belfast company. After a First Class Moderatorship in mathematics at Trinity, he had gone to University College, Oxford and then to the Indian Civil Service, where he reached the rank of deputy secretary to the Government of India. Walmsley was made joint managing director in 1952 and for the next twenty-five years he shaped, encouraged and led the firm. Although essentially a 'News' man his wide range of interests meant that he was at home in any department. His ability to command respect and affection in equal measure from all who worked with him was his most distinctive quality. Under his guidance Eason's acquired a less stern image while at the same time it expanded at both wholesale and retail levels. He became sole managing director in 1957, and on J.C.M. Eason's retirement in the same year also became chairman.

Married to one of Eason's daughters, Walmsley was a further case of an outsider brought into the business at this level.[1] One can speculate that some of Eason's concern for the future management was stimulated by the fact that he had no son to succeed him. In 1952 Edward J. Kelliher, from a Tralee family firm, was put in charge of the stationery division. Eason had been impressed by Kelliher's application for the headship of the Irish Management Institute, and offered him a managerial job in the firm. He was given a key post, as profits from the stationery division were more than ever important in the 1950s, as news profits sagged. In the 1960s, Kelliher played a major role in the development of the retail business. Later he was to become successively managing director and chairman of the company.

Another aspect of Eason's openness was in the matter of shareholding. Even as early as the 1930s George Best had become a shareholder in the Belfast company, and when J.C.M. Eason reviewed the situation in 1944, he noted that: 'there can be no expectation of any return to the old conditions of ownership. It is very desirable that directors should hold an interest in ordinary shares.' This change in direction acquired a greater momentum subsequently. By 1987 only three of the directors have a family association with Eason's and 120 members of the staff are shareholders in the firm.

During his period one of his greatest concerns was a close attention the analysis of departmental profits. Under him the stationery business was nursed back to profitability in the 1930s and the factory, which had run up large losses, was finally closed in 1941. The profits from stationery were to be invaluable in the post-1945 period in supplementing the wholesale news profits which had lost their former strength. Perhaps even more important for the company as a whole was the expansion of the Belfast business, where Eason's monopoly was being challenged even before 1900, and where it was much more seriously at risk in the 1920s. The profits of the Belfast house became a vital component of the general profitability of the firm.

Eason lived on for another sixteen years after his retirement from the board, dying at 96 years of age, the second longest lived of a family characterised by longevity. He remained fit and active almost to the last,

1 Albert Brunton was married to a member of the family, but he had worked his way up in the firm and did not represent therefore an outside influence brought in.

and though no longer guiding the destinies of the firm, he was a witness to the transformation during the 1960s and 1970s. During these years, in the recollection of one of his sons-in-law, he could, almost to the end, '.... be found in the College Park or Lansdowne Road on many a wintery Saturday, or in the Pavilion in Trinity watching cricket on summer afternoons.'

He still took an interest in the business, although he had no sympathy for the new emphasis on retailing. Eason never did appreciate the full potential of the retail, and it would in fact have been hard for him to have done so, as the depression of the 1950s in the south seemed to be a prolongation of the extraordinary economic difficulties of the 1930s and 1940s. His last active interest in the house turned towards the past, and towards a pursuit which he had followed intermittently over the years (notably at the time of the fifty year anniversary in 1936) the gathering and saving of some of the historical information relating to the firm. Ironically, though he was frequently solicitous in his days as managing director about saving or listing the pre-1916 records, or those of the early 1920s, he had never done much about preserving the papers or accounts created under his own management. Nonetheless, more of his own papers and those of his grandfather survive than of his own father. This may be fortuitous, but it approximates to the relative imprint of the three successive generations on the firm's character.

J.C.M. Eason had a very ordered mind, and he mentally marshalled the arguments for and against a case clearly. The way in which his mind worked can be followed from odd scraps of paper which survive in files on which he had jotted down in logical form the main points to be made in an interview, or had summed up the points at stake in some contentious issue. The cast of his mind is very evident in his correspondence with George Best, whom he had brought into the Belfast house. His mind ran in the well-ordered, disciplined way of a barrister or higher civil servant. The long and exhausting correspondence with the eccentric and difficult editor of *Our Boys*, which was, given the strange moods of Ireland in the 1920s, somewhat delicate, provides a good illustration of his consummate skill, tact and logical force.

Despite being intended for business, Eason and his brother Keith received an academic education. Eason graduated at TCD, with a senior moderatorship in logic and ethics and a gold medal, in 1901, and at Cambridge Keith was bracketed Wrangler[2] with two others in 1907. The

2 That is, a First Class Honours in Mathematics.

third brother, Alec, also graduated from Cambridge, with a first class Mechanical Science Tripos in 1908, and entered the Post Office in London as an engineer in the Telegraph Department. It is not possible to trace the impact of his father on J.C.M. Eason in the way that the first Charles Eason can be seen to influence the second. However the impact must have been substantial, and the fact that he chose the theme of 'A Philosophy of Social Reform' as the subject of his presidential address to the College Philosophical Society in November 1902 seems to spring directly from interests acquired from his father, who was deeply involved in the housing scheme.

> The topic is not only one of present public interest and enduring public importance, but also of interest to many graduates and undergraduates of this university, who have manifested their recognition of social reform by the formation of a company to manage tenement houses here in Dublin.

A generation later, however, within the Chamber of Commerce in the 1920s, on social matters or in his monetary outlook in the 1930s, his outlook was ultimately as conservative as was that of the powerful Secretary of the Department of Finance, J.J. McElligott, with whom he developed a close rapport. Though an extremely good businessman, Eason also represented an old-fashioned outlook, in which a businessman was attached to the activities in which he was engaged for their own sake as well as for the profits they conferred. But he was a modern man in his openness to all ideas which would help business or society operate more effectively.

Like his father, J.C.M. Eason took a great interest in Trinity College, even if he did not return as his father had done to its library and books. For many years after graduation he appeared at dinners of the Philosophical Society. During the 1930s, the magazine *T.C.D.* was printed by the firm, and for many years he was the President of the Dublin University Commerce and Economics Society. Some of this activity stemmed from an interest that both he and the Chamber of Commerce shared in improving commercial education. When Trinity College introduced honorary degrees in commerce in 1930, Charles Eason junior, his father, was honoured with an honorary M.Comm., and in 1960, J.C.M. Eason received a like honorary degree, the citation specifying that: 'He has done so much to bridge the gap between the business and academic worlds in Ireland.'

He was prepared to envisage a larger role for the state as a young man than later as a successful businessman, but his undergraduate interests were the start of a lifelong study of social and economic issues. Through the Chamber of Commerce he was brought into contact with the Civics Institute, in which he participated actively and on whose Council he sat. The Civics Institute arranged the first lectures in social science, which led eventually to the teaching of that subject in Trinity College. It sponsored the first playgrounds in Mountjoy Square, and opened the first day-nursery. All this was in the pattern of his father, as was his active participation in the Statistical and Social Inquiry Society of Ireland. He contributed thirteen papers to the journal of the Society between 1925 and 1945.

The Society has had a fluctuating career, alternating between periods of decline and activity. He was its President between 1930 and 1934 and Treasurer from 1944. His active association with the Society was during a period of revival in its affairs, and during his presidency the lectures financed under the Barrington Trust were extended in consultation with the trust by the appointment of three or four lecturers annually. Eason was in fact the only twentieth-century Dublin businessman who played a prominent role in the Society, and it was important in bringing him into contact with civil servants such as McElligott, and university professors. He was on cordial terms with Barney Shields and George O'Brien of University College.

Eason took a keen interest in the first census of distribution. The Irish census was one of the pioneers in this field, and he corresponded with experts outside Ireland, as well as with civil servants and university people in Ireland, and took pains to analyse it carefully. Eventually he read a paper to the Statistical and Social Inquiry Society on the subject of the census, and his views are doubly interesting, as they combine the perspective of a practical man of business with that of a student of social issues. His contact with these circles was of course reinforced by his prominence in the Dublin business community, which led to his being appointed to government committees and commissions. His appointment to these bodies was a function of his intellectual interests, his prominence as a businessman, and his support of the Irish Free State. Not only was the future of the new state uncertain in the early 1920s, especially when the civil war cast its shadow over its future, but many protestants and big business men generally were reluctant to take a part in its life and institutions. Charles Eason junior was one of the five signatories of a circular in 1925:

> ....strongly of opinion that candidates pledged to support the Government and the maintenance of the Constitution should be

> assisted both financially and by votes at the coming Elections. It has been suggested, however, that there are many persons who are desirous to support the Government Candidates, but who hesitate to send subscriptions direct to Cumann na nGaedheal, as they do not wish to be identified definitely with any organisation....

The signatories indicated that they would receive subscriptions and undertook to see that the funds would be used only for stated purposes. In November 1931 J.C.M. Eason replaced his father as the signatory of a similar circular issued in anticipation of a further election, to which a number of known unionists were prepared to lend their signatures. This circular leaked into the press. Eason himself ran for the Senate in 1925, although he failed to get elected. He ran for the Senate on an independent list, 'which is formed wholly without regard to party.' The other eleven included Samuel L. Brown KC, a Senator since 1923, and a major political influence on the Easons; Sir Arthur Chance of the Royal College of Surgeons: John J. Horgan, Chairman of the Cork Harbour Board; Henry Harrison, journalist; Charles K. Howard-Bury, landowner, George Crosbie, editor of the *Cork Examiner*, John T. O'Farrell, leader of the Labour Party in the Senate, John H. Pigot, an ex-county Court Judge; and three other professional men, Sir Edward Lacy Bigger, a doctor who had served as Medical Commissioner on the Social government Board; John W.F. Garvey, a solicitor, and Patrick Brady, an ex-President of the Incorporated Law Society. Eason's direct political interest was non-party. Although his father's and his own support could be interpreted as fear of the 'republicans', its purpose was to induce businessmen to back firmly what was at the time the government party in the state, and hence to commit them to its institutions.

After 1931 Eason never seems to have taken an active interest in politics, although he maintained a purposeful interest in improving relations with catholics. He was a member of the Contemporary Club in which Noel Harnett was active. The surviving correspondence of his father throws some light on the probable political outlook of the Easons: fearful of the republicans in the 1920s, and pragmatically quick to identify de Valera's conservatism in the 1930s. In a note written in 1942 J.C.M. Eason commented that, 'de Valera had wide support and it has been consistent.'

The identification of the Easons with the new state was important in the climate of the times. J.C.M. Eason was scathing afterwards about the older unionist businessmen like the Gouldings and the Arnotts. In playing a prominent role in the Dublin business community in the 1920s, and identifying themselves publicly with the new state at its outset, the Easons had a significance in reconciling the city's business community to the new state. It was the first occasion on which the Easons played any role in Irish political life, either discreetly or publicly. Before this time, the closest association with public notoriety was J.C.M. Eason's joint secretaryship of the War Savings Committee in Southern Ireland for 1918, for which he received an OBE in 1920. Even in business circles the Easons had played a minor role, although Charles Eason junior was a member of the Chamber of Commerce at least from 1881.

The involuntary involvement of the firm in the 1913 dispute had brought them into a more central role among businessmen, and J.C.M. Eason became president of the Dublin Mercantile Association in 1922 and of the Dublin Master Printers Association in 1923-4. He was already a Council member of the Chamber of Commerce in 1924, and participated in no less than 44 meetings or deputations, a degree of involvement which was equalled or exceeded in following years. He was President of the Chamber of Commerce in 1927, and by coincidence this happened to be the year in which electricity supply became a matter of concern to the Chamber. Ostensibly revolving around the implications for the three existing municipal plants in Dublin of setting up a new supply board, it was really a test of the Chamber's relations with the new state, and the Chamber's views were followed closely by the government and the public. During Eason's term of office as president, both Cosgrave and McGilligan addressed the Chamber, and Eason's crowning achievement was an unanimous vote by the Chamber on a resolution which both covered the Chamber's concerns and gave its support to the proposals for setting up the Electricity Supply Board.[3] In all, as president, Eason attended no less than 71 meetings and deputations in 1927.

These were the peak years of J.C.M. Eason's career. He had succeeded to the managing directorship in 1926. In 1927 he was the first member of the firm to become a president of the Chamber of Commerce, and he was publicly identified with the new state and its institutions. Through the Chamber, he was to become a member of two committees of enquiry, one on bankruptcy law, the other on workmen's compensation, and in 1927 he was appointed a member of the newly created Currency Commission, a position which he was to hold for six years. All this activity was combined with a very demanding role in the business, and several visits a month to Belfast. In 1934 he was appointed a member of the commission to investigate banking, credit and currency, a demanding and

3 See L.M. Cullen *Princes and Pirates* (Dublin 1983), p. 98.

time-consuming task spread over four years. He missed few meetings, and took an active part in questioning witnesses before the commission. He read Keynes' *General Theory* shortly after it appeared, understanding much, although not all, as he admitted himself. He was especially stimulated by the presence of Per Jacobson of the Bank of International Settlements who was one of the outside members, and a warm rapport developed between the two men.

He could fairly be described as the first 'modern' member of the family. By the time of the first world war, he had already learned to drive a car and had bought the firm its first delivery van — in marked contrast to his father who, even in the 1930s, did not own a wireless. His interests were many and various. As a student, he was a member of the Dublin University Harriers and a successful cross-country runner as well as an active member of the University Philosophical Society. His intellectual approach to the social problems of his day, to war and peace, to christianity and the human predicament, was matched by practical support of charitable organisations and learned societies and of church and local government. His taste in books was wide, ranging from biography, history and travel to detective fiction. With his wife, who was one of the first woman graduates and scholars of Trinity College, he shared an extensive knowledge and enjoyment of the English classics. They both loved reading, though not it must be said, to the exclusion of other favoured pastimes, such as a weekly game of bridge with friends or visits to the theatre with the family and, on Sundays, *the* crossword (Torquemada, later Ximenes).

His home life seemed a necessary complement to the business life which inevitably occupied so much of the daily 24 hours. His leisure time was scant by present-day standards and was largely devoted to family activities. As the family grew, he gave up competitive sailing in Dublin bay and parted with his yacht in favour of a motor car. Through the 1920s and 1930s he spent much of his free time, at weekends and on holiday, taking family or friends on drives through the countryside of Ireland which he loved dearly or on visits to places of particular interest in the country's economic development, such as the Carlow sugar factory and the Shannon hydro-electric scheme. Not surprisingly, he found little time to indulge his love of sport, though he contrived to play golf regularly, at Dollymount and Delgany, right up the age of 70; his 'spectator' interest — in rugby and cricket, in particular — stayed with him to the end of his long life.

If he had ambitions for his four daughters, he never let it be known, but, clearly, he and his wife subscribed to the doctrine of equal opportunities for the sexes. Three of their daughters graduated from Trinity; all were equipped to earn their living and to recognise that the world didn't owe them one. They were encouraged to travel abroad, as their parents had so enjoyed doing. Eason himself was taking frequent holidays in Madeira in his eighties.

As to his personality, his reserve was proverbial, but it masked a formidable self-confidence as well as an inner warmth and human understanding which those who knew him learned to trust. William Cunningham, former senior partner in Craig Gardner, the firm's auditors since 1917, remembers his kindness to him as a young man 'so that it was always a pleasure to meet him as one was always at one's ease.' Others whom he went out of his way to help on to the first rung of the career ladder endorse this sentiment. Dr Geary may well have put his finger on it when he said that Eason had 'that rare gift of making his friends feel important'.

With J.C.M. Eason's retirement from the board in 1960 at the age of 80, an era had come to an end in the history of the house. The very nature of the business was changing. Eason was the only one among the directors who had grown up in the old world in which railways dominated the business at large, and in which the wholesale department was planned around the arrival of mail boats and the departure from Dublin termini of early morning newspaper trains. As the firm responded first to the difficulties and then to the opportunities of the decades after his departure, its activities bore less and less resemblence to the house which the first Eason had developed after 1856, and which had flourished first on railway business in stalls and advertising, and then on wholesaling news.

Chapter 22 ❧ Conclusion

THE DISTRIBUTION OF NEWS, in the form of newspapers and magazines, became a major activity over the last century and a half both in Ireland and Britain. To a greater degree than on the continent, wholesalers played a large part in this. Smith's in Britain and Eason's in Ireland are household words in their respective markets. Wholesaling created a national press: the existence of a national distributive network gave London or Dublin news a prominent place in the nation-wide news budget. But national distribution of newspapers was quite expensive. Publishing margins in fact were low, and worse for daily newspapers than for weeklies. Efficiency was therefore crucial, the maintenance of a large turnover equally so, and as rates and margins varied a good deal from item to item, an ability to identify the profitable and unprofitable was vital.

Total distributive margins for newspapers were broadly the same as in the distributive trades at large, but after the retailer's margins were allowed for, the wholesaler's share was modest. On the other hand the wholesaler's broader economic interest was opposed to excessively large margins, as J.C.M. Eason realised, because they would attract more wholesalers into the business, to the long-term detriment of the established wholesalers' profitability. Wholesalers were also opposed to too great an expansion of retail outlets because they pushed costs up. This put them in conflict with publishers, who because so much of their revenue depended on advertising which in turn depended on circulations, were eager to expand outlets. Thus wholesalers did not derive the full benefit from the expansion in circulations in the 1920s. Compared with pre-1914 days, they were distributing a growing amount of publications, which were often bulkier than they had been, at falling real cover prices, to an increased number of outlets. The cumulative results of these changes were fully evident only from the outset of the 1930s when wholesalers' profits fell from the high level they had held up to the end of the 1920s.

In the house at large the rates of net profit were probably at a peak in the late nineteenth century; in the early twentieth century, there was a contrast between falling profits in much of the house, and a rise in the wholesale news department. This rise concealed different returns from daily and weekly newspapers. Dailies were expensive for publisher and wholesaler alike because of the high costs of getting the papers to the reader with a minimum of delay. The wide range of weekly material was a more decisive factor in determining the profits of wholesalers. Weeklies frequently had a higher cover price, were delivered ahead of the date of issue and hence avoided the high cost involved in the hectic morning or early afternoon distribution of daily news, and also offered larger trade margins.

The rise in net profits in the 1900s in the wholesale division seems to have been a once-for-all event brought about by the high margins attained by switching from supplies from Smith's to direct purchases from publishers in 1905. News profits as a proportion of turnover appear to have fallen over the period 1906-1928 as a whole. This is particularly striking because publishers had actually widened their margins in the 1920s in the effort to push circulation. Indeed, as observed elsewhere, profits probably fell in real terms.[1] Moreover, if daily and weekly publications could be isolated the position would almost certainly be that daily news became progressively less profitable, while the house relied more and more on weeklies. The fact that the rise in news profits was not progressive, and that they compensated for a dramatic fall in profits elsewhere in the house, especially in advertising and later in bookstalls, points to a less-assured business environment at large for the house. As pointed out earlier, returns on capital in the early twentieth century were distinctly lower than in the Victorian era. Returns on capital were lower again in the 1920s. There is little doubt that the pre-1914 years were a golden age, and business prospects were never to approach the same heights again. The capitalisation of the house — and hence the fall in profits — had of course been magnified by the post-1916 rebuilding.

In the early 1920s the changing fortunes of business — a reduced net profitability on an expanded turnover — seemed attributable to the trials and tribulations of the painful years from 1916 to 1923, but taking a long perspective of trends, the underlying reasons ran much deeper and were more fundamental. From the point of view of profitability the greatest days of the wholesaler were the Victorian era when news range and circulation was widening and the wholesaler had few rivals. Prices were high, the outlets comparatively few and wholesalers were catering to a

1 See p. 184.

regular and compact market for a limited number of titles, entailing few returns, compared with the larger, more varied, highly competitive and often over-sold markets that emerged over the 1910s and 1920s.

In the Irish market the Dublin wholesaler was even more dominant than the London wholesaler in the British market, where the north of England and especially Scotland had vigorous local traditions in wholesaling. This was due to the fact that in Ireland carriage rates were flat rates for the whole country, whereas in Britain, rates became higher over long distances. Hence a provincial wholesaler in England had some protection in transport costs whereas in Ireland he had no advantage over a wholesaler in Dublin. Indeed the only local monopoly in Ireland developed in County Cork where the Tivy family ('News Brothers') were able to create a monopoly in news redistributed in the extensive area in west Cork served by the local railway network which was not connected with the mainline system, and on which through rates did not apply. Eason's would have had to pay two sets of freight charges. In the north, too, where Porter's developed as rivals, railway rates were altered in the 1920s and thus helped the growth of the only other stable and successful rival which Eason's faced in news wholesaling at large. Wholesaling however was never a secure monopoly since wholesalers enjoyed no long-term contracts with publishers. The distributor's imperfect control could be challenged in certain conditions. The increased margins offered by direct purchases from news publishers in 1905, while they enhanced the profits of the news division, also helped to attract and retain rivals in the business. It was obviously a factor which helped Porter's to establish a successful business despite the presence of an established firm. The London house of Dawson's were attracted to set up business in Dublin in 1911, the sole incursion into the Irish market by a British house since Smith's had taken over Johnston's business in 1850.

The wholesaling of Sundays in the early decades of the century is an interesting illustration of the economics of distribution in Ireland. As they became popular, Sundays were retailed to news buyers who did not at this stage buy other newspapers and who were prevailed on to buy by direct solicitation i.e. sales outside churches, and street hawking. This entailed a broadening of marginal channels of distribution, a process unattractive in cost terms to the wholesaler who drew profit from supplying a wide range of publications to regular outlets. Established wholesalers had little to gain and much to lose in supplying a few titles on one single day a week to outlets which took little else from them. Hence Sunday newspapers, massive in circulation though they became, relied for expansion in the 1910s largely on newer and less experienced distributors and a whole range of new and frequently unorthodox retail channels.

In Irish dailies too the position of the wholesaler was insecure, as there developed an increasing tendency for the publisher to involve himself directly in distribution. The Dublin dailies departed from the exclusive reliance on the wholesaler which had emerged in the 1860s. In Belfast and Cork the local dailies sold direct extensively to city retailers. Hence, important though they were in the wholesale business of the 1850s and 1860s, they did not remain in the long-term with the wholesaler. Though London or Manchester publishers did rely largely on national wholesalers, the urge to push sales in the 1920s made them impatient with the reluctance of the wholesalers to open new retail outlets.

Dailies on their own or combined with a handful of widely circulated weeklies were not in the late nineteenth century sufficient to make a wholesaling business profitable. With low cover prices and high costs in distribution the net margins were modest. From the time that the penny daily appeared in the 1850s, profitability in news wholesaling as a whole depended on weeklies other than news weeklies. This was a market which in the early decades of the twentieth century was given tremendous boosts by a combination of women's magazines and radio and later TV magazines. In wholesale news itself the aggregate net margins of the 1920s were not approached again for half a century. How they compared with pre-1914 margins is not perfectly clear for want of data. The publisher of a weekly was moreover under no temptation to sell direct to a multiplicity of retail outlets, especially as retailers also preferred to get their supplies from a single source rather than to run accounts with innumerable publishers. Established wholesalers were much more secure from challenge for their distribution of weekly news than they were for the distribution of individual mass circulation dailies or Sundays. The small or emerging wholesaler who could take on the distribution of a Sunday newspaper was not usually tempted to enter the field, because a broader distributive function required both an existing national network of retail outlets and a large investment in wholesale premises.

The railway bookstalls afford a striking example of the economics of distribution. At the bookstalls, book sales subsidised news sales in the middle decades of the nineteenth century. In turn the bookstalls were to prove the spearhead of the provincial service of the metropolitan news wholesaler. Because the sales of magazines and newspapers were as yet relatively small, there were few retail newsagents, and Smith's and Eason's in their respective countries were able to offer a larger demand than any rival. The railway bookstalls were thus, in the early years, a crucial feature in establishing the commanding presence which both houses enjoyed. The dominant position of both houses on the railways depended on the successful negotiation of contracts with the railway companies, and this itself linked up advertising with railway bookstalls and the carriage costs of their wholesale business: the terms of the contracts usually applied to all three dimensions of the wholesaler's activities.

Irish wholesaling profitability, by extrapolation from later data, must have been lower than in Britain, because weekly sales were smaller, and the amount of news per retail outlet was much lower. This reflected the circumstances of a smaller, declining and more rural population. Hence, the profits derived from the railway connection, through the bookstalls and advertising, were crucial to the profitability of the business, as its news business towards the end of the nineteenth century reached out from the more lucrative centres to more marginal ones. The railway contracts ceased to be lucrative from 1900 onwards because of more onerous terms. The timing of the negotiation of direct terms with the news publishers in 1905 was a response to this situation. Profits in wholesaling to an increasing number of independent retail outlets compensated for falling profits in advertising and rising costs at the stalls. A retail market in depth was beginning to grow, and the wholesale side of Eason's was for the first time becoming the man thrust to expansion. At the same time these retail customers began to resent Eason's competing with them through the bookstalls. Although it was not realised at the time, the bookstalls were on the eve of contraction. The rise in costs during the first world war was the final blow. Wage costs had almost doubled, and the bookstalls, usually on the periphery of towns, faced with the competition of new outlets within the towns, were especially vulnerable. The process of closing them began.

The ending of the increasingly unprofitable wholesaling of Irish dailies helped in 1964 to improve the profitability of the wholesale news department which had become precarious in the 1950s. The increased sale of English daily newspapers, the original base of the wholesale function of the distributor, is fascinating. The mainstay of wholesaling in the 1850s, it was then eclipsed by Dublin dailies. It returned in 1905 with the aggressive selling of the *Daily Mail* followed by other papers to win a large place, north and south, in the enlarged market of the 1920s. Cross-channel dailies virtually disappeared in the Free State under the protectionism of the 1930s and then slowly but steadily expanded their share of the market in the last three decades, largely as a result of the use of air transport from 1965.

CONCLUSION

The habit of buying newspapers and other publications has permeated Irish society. Most Irish adults now buy several news items a week. The circulation of dailies, weeklies and periodicals within Ireland (excluding local press) probably averaged one third of an item per household per week in the early 1880s; it had already reached six items by 1930, and this figure has been greatly exceeded in recent decades. Neither radio nor television, despite their efficiency as purveyors of news and entertainment, have undermined the printed word. The experience of the 1920s was that radio helped to sell magazines and even created a demand for new ones. This was most evident in the case of the radio guides in the 1920s and 1930s whose circulation within the British market reached phenomenal proportions. The cinema helped to sell books which became the subject of films, and radio and cinema also spawned weeklies for both adult and juvenile readerships. The role of television has been no different, although of course it has increased the demand for visual content in presentation. But this was a trend already evident in the 1890s which has been helped by technological changes in improving the quality and lowering the cost of illustration.

The dramatic increase in disposable incomes, combined with the variety of publications, has ensured that distribution has become more rather than less indispensable. Today's great wholesale-and-retail businesses are very different from their counterparts of Victorian times — and this is reflected in lower returns on investment — but they are an essential pivot in linking a wide range of publishers with a retail market geographically and socially wider than ever before. Without distributive businesses like Eason's or in Britain Smith's or Menzies the reader would not have ready access to the vast range of periodical literature, and either small markets or high costs in distribution would restrict publishers' ventures and both literally and figuratively narrow the readers' horizons.

Appendix

GENEALOGICAL TREE

No.	Name	Born	Died	Cross-Ref.[1]
1.	**Eason** George	1782	31.8.1828	
	married 15.1.1821			
2.	**Tucker** Rebecca	31.7.1795	4.1.1856	
	Children			
3.	George	4.11.1821	6.6.1880	
4.	Charles	11.5.1823	5.11.1899	8
5.	Mary	16.9.1826	22.2.1907	
6.	Emma	14.1.1828	26.9.866	
7.	William Tucker	1824		
8.	**Eason** Charles			
	married 2.5.1851			
9.	**Birks** Caroline	22.2.1828	18.12.1908	
	Children			
10.	George	17.2.1852	25.6.1882	
11.	Charles	10.4.1853	5.8.1941	18
12.	William Waugh	30.11.1856	8.1.1908	
13.	Alfred	3.5.1859	25.5.1936	
14.	Emma	26.9.1861	20.12.1940	24
15.	Fanny	17.12.1863	21.5.1955	30
16.	Frederick Tucker	12.2.1865	13.4.1964	32
17.	Benjamin	11.10.1868	5.3.1949	36
18.	**Eason** Charles			
	married 9.2.1876			
19.	**Thomson** Anna Maria Selina	26.6.1855	8.9.1929	
	Children			
20.	Edith Anna	20.9.1877	2.1962	
21.	John Charles Malcolm	22.6.1880		44
22.	Edward Keith	8.5.1885	5.1.1960	
23.	Alec Birks	18.3.1887		
24.	**Eason** Emma			
	married 14.7.1891			

1 Cross-references refer to the subsequent entry for the same person.

25.	**Carpenter** George Herbert	17.11.1865	22.1.1938	
	Children			
26.	Mary Birks	10.5.1895	25.4.1896	
27.	George Kingsford	2.3.1897	18.8.1970	50
28.	Sidney Birks	17.9.1900	24.8.1985	
30.	**Eason** Francis			
	married			
31.	**Brunton** George Albert Edward	15.4.1868	6.7.1921	
32.	**Eason** Frederick Tucker			
	married 5.4.1905			
33.	**Burrows** Evelyn	18.4.1880	6.3.1949	
	Children			
34.	Freda Caroline Isobel	22.6.1907		
35.	Thorold Evelyn Burrows	22.1.1910		
36.	**Eason** Benjamin Macfarlane			
	married 11.1.1894			
37.	**Richardson** Henrietta Jane			
	Children			
38.	William George	31.5.1896		
39.	Caroline Vida	31.8.1899		
40.	Charles Henry	23.7.1901		
41.	Robert Birks	1.1.1904		
42.	Elizabeth Dorothy	5.3.1907		
43.	Winifred Mary	6.8.1910		
44.	**Eason** John Charles Malcolm			
	married 30.1.1908			
45.	**Douglas** Eliza Beck		21.6.1950	
	Children			
46.	Jessie Douglas	18.11.1908		
47.	Edith Mary	13.3.1914		60
48.	Elizabeth Caroline	12.4.1917		
49.	Joan Penelope	22.11.1919		
50.	**Carpenter** George Kingsford	2.3.1897	18.8.1970	
	married 8.2.1926			
51.	**Phillips** Constance Kathleen	8.2.1897	4.10.1978	
	Children			
52.	Sidney David	29.12.1926		
53.	Jean Mary			

54. Ian Hugh

55. **Eason** Robert Birks
married 2.6.1937

56. **Davis** Eileen
Children

57. David Robert Sydney 1.1.1940

58. Joyce Caroline 1.3.1945

59. **Eason** Edith Mary
married 30.9.1937

60. **Walmsley** James Andrew 4.10.1912

Bibliography

THE STORY OF EASON'S DEPENDS ON THE records of two houses, those of W.H. Smith's and its own. Unfortunately little survives in W.H. Smith's for the period before 1900, and in the case of Eason's the premises were occupied by the rebels in Easter Week 1916 and destroyed in the holocaust of O'Connell Street and neighbouring streets.

The main series of accounting records, customer ledgers, letter books, wage books, correspondence received, did not survive the fire. How much of the accumulated records of the preceding century actually remained intact on the eve of the fire is not clear. A reference within the surviving sources suggests that letter books from the 1880s onwards existed in 1916. This would suggest that earlier letter books (and much else besides) already no longer existed in 1916. The 1880s are a significant period in the history of the house. They mark the end of the major period in the physical expansion of the house since its inception as Johnston's in 1819: massive expansion in both Sackville Street (O'Connell Street) and Abbey Street and the consequent move of departments was likely, as any archivist knows, not only to disturb but to result in the loss of many routine and apparently no longer relevant records. In addition the ownership of the firm was transferred in 1886 from W.H. Smith's to the Eason family, in itself merely a legal break but one which may have had an effect on the relevance of past records to future activity.

Some isolated documents and bound volumes have survived from the pre-1916 period, but it is clear that the practice must have been to leave old records, to the extent that they accumulated or were not destroyed, in the departments that created them, and hence they fell prey to the flames which consumed the house in 1916. In the event not a single series of primary documents (barring the minute books of the board and railway contracts) survived 1916.

However, even if the basic series of records were destroyed in 1916, much archival material survived the holocaust. This is thanks to the three-storey block of strong rooms designed by Ruthven, who acted as architect for the house, and which stood intact after the fire. It is possible of course that some older series of records had been stored in the strong rooms, and then were destroyed when the firm faced the task of sorting the strong-room material and transferring records to the scattered and cramped premises in which it was forced to operate for the years from

1916 to 1920. However, this seems to be ruled out because of the survival of a small number of primary books of the pre-1916 period, which give the impression that routine records can only have been haphazardly and rarely transferred to the strong rooms. If whole series had been stored in the strong rooms, either more or still less should have survived a sorting process in 1916. Moreover, for the reasons set out below it seems certain that no records of the most important department of the house, the News division, had been moved out of the division itself, not only before but even after 1916.

For the pre-1886 period only a handful of primary items survive. So haphazard are the survivals that it is clear that there was no systematic interest in retaining records. A few very early items survive, including a few sheets of accounts between the London house and the Dublin house in the 1850s, copies of some letters to W.H. Smith, and some letters from the London end, from Smith, Lethbridge, White and Kingdom, both before and after 1886. There is some evidence of systematic interest later in the surviving correspondence, and some of it was typed and bound together. This endeavour seems to have been prompted by J.C.M. Eason, who in the interwar years collated the early items, and also compiled notes on the troubled 1910s and early 1920s.

Of the surviving records from the early period the most substantial are a remarkably detailed 'Wages book: index — J. Dewar, 1872-1886', which seems to have survived because it was associated with various wage analysis books, and a memorandum book for the late 1880s and 1890s on wholesale news in the hand of Charles Eason I. The latter book is interesting because it coincides with the break with W.H. Smith's and with the incorporation of the firm as a private company. In fact these events account for the most significant accumulation of surviving files of correspondence in the house. These are labelled as 'Board Room Files' because prior to finding their present berth they were accommodated in the board room. However, originally they were held in the strong room: otherwise they would like so much else in the house have gone up in flames in 1916. Essentially they are eclectic in nature, relating to major topics such as libel and war-time conditions as well as more mundane issues: in other words they contain anything which went beyond the internal routine of supervising departments, corresponding with customers and disciplining staff. Unfortunately all the latter files were held within departments, and were not, before or after 1916, kept in the strong rooms in the manner of important but less routine files which like the sacred minutes constantly made their way to and from the strong rooms. At some date after the reconstruction of the house in 1920, they were transferred to the board room, and were added to as in the past by new files as issues arose into the 1950s. They provide for a period of seventy years quite a remarkable range of information on many topics which preoccupied the senior management of the firm. Unfortunately, they have no later systematic sequel.

The other major category of record to have survived the fire, because of the haven of the strong room, were various analysis books of turnover and wages which run from 1856. They reflect the impact on the firm of Charles Eason I, because there is no pre-1856 precedent, and they all start abruptly in 1856 or soon after. The analysis books of turnover, either in the firm as a whole or in individual departments, ensure that from 1856 to 1916 though the basic records are gone, figures of turnover can be established. Unfortunately, except with the help of stray documents, accounts or bound volumes, very little can be done in the way of analysing the business within departments in detail. However, compared with the parent house in London, much more is known about the turnover of the Dublin house in the pre-1900 period. From the 1870s to after 1900 these records are mostly in the copperplate hand of E.W. Hallett. They are in fact very numerous, and are an interesting illustration of early methods of analysing the turnover of a large and complex business. Annual figures often appear to differ in the overlapping volumes. This is due to the fact that departmental totals were accumulated for each quarter, and the years in the individual analysis books are sometimes based on different quarters for their terminal date. The series were continued in the post-1916 period, but from 1917/8 audited accounts provide for many purposes a more convenient and more sophisticated source of information.

Wage summary books from 1856 also exist. These are not strictly speaking the actual wage books, but are essentially record volumes to indicate wage increases and promotions. Hence they have a double value; they both record the names (and numbers) of staff and indicate wage increases. However, almost no records exist for the railway bookstall staff. The surviving pre-1916 books were essentially summary records, and increasingly as time passed were intended to guide the head of the firm in the operation of the informal promotion or incremental salary structure which had come into existence well before the end of the nineteenth century. In the case of railway bookstall staff, the records were in the province of the railway bookstall superintendent, and as such they were within the large wholesale division.

A large amount of material exists from 1916 onwards: ledgers, analysis books, various forms of departmental records. Unfortunately, with the exception of some individual files, scarcely any correspondence survives (outside the Board Room files), and the surviving series are also poor in what might be described as 'customer'-related documents. There are only two important exceptions to this: among the great accumulation of post-1916 accounting records, there exist three bulky files, one of the long and sometimes exasperated correspondence with the Christian Brothers in the 1920s, and two of the correspondence in the 1930s between George Best in Belfast and J.C.M. Eason in Dublin. The fact that these files, in isolation from departmental files at large, found their way into the mass of routine general records and survived is something of a comment on the interest of both topics. Though neither fell into the category of board room file or were ever held with them, they were kept apart from or were at some stage separated from the files in their parent department, books or news, and in consequence survived.

The wholesale news division was always the prime division of the house. It remained a separate department, directly under the supervision of the head of the business (even if a formal manager existed under him), and was distinct and even secretive in its ethos. Little information on wholesale news circulated readily through the house. One employee, James Dignam, in News, for instance, noted in his diary in 1864 that some matter must have been of weight, as Charles Eason left in secrecy for London. The pre-1916 analysis books for instance while they provide details of total turnover do not give specific details of the wholesale turnover in news (they do for bookstalls), and wholesale turnover has to be calculated simply as a residue. Only with the audited accounts from 1917/8 did the wholesale news function acquire a statistical existence in its own right. For the entire period before 1917, a single sheet survives giving details of wholesale turnover in a single month in 1877. Clearly such records existed but never found their way into the general records of the house. Despite innovation in accounting procedures, the old tradition continued to flourish after 1916. In the large accumulation of post-1916 records in the house, few files and account books relating to wholesale news are included. Wholesale news continued to run its own affairs, and to dispose of its records in its own manner, apparently uninterferred with.

Some records of newspaper circulation survive, but only from the 1950s. The isolated scraps of accounts, and the three large files of correspondence with the Christian Brothers and with Best, which survive, do so, one must assume, because in some way or other their importance transcended the department. Some memoranda and working sheets of figures of wholesale news turnover by J.C.M. Eason are personal papers and not strictly speaking departmental records. The bookstalls, though under the general umbrella of news, are somewhat better served by survivals. Pre-1916 figures exist, there is some internal break down by category and by individual bookstall, and some fragmentary correspondence or copies of correspondence also exist. Likewise, a small amount of detail survives for advertising. After 1900 stalls and advertising became the subject of greater scrutiny. Some results of this survive, though the bulk of the items analysing trends are in J.C.M. Eason's hand or are in typescript. They are mostly from the 1920s and later, and reflect the much more advanced level of analysis adopted by him.

The Belfast house, though its business was smaller than Dublin's, is much better served from c. 1900 by the survival of accounts and correspondence. For instance, all or almost all the correspondence about news matters Best exchanged with Dublin over a period of more than thirty years seems to survive, and there is also a wider range of miscellaneous or routine items from the early decades of the twentieth century. The Belfast house records include a private letter book kept by Brunton in 1905-6 for letters which he seems to have regarded as too secret to direct in routine fashion to Dublin. Though dealing with competition from Porter's and the advent of the *Daily Mail* they hardly seem very confidential to modern eyes, but the book does illustrate the obsessive secrecy in which the wholesale business was shrouded. Brunton subsequently added in copies of a few personal letters to Charles Eason II. For some reason he seems to have left the book behind him in Belfast after the house had come to terms with the new competition. That has ensured its survival. In Dublin no comparable records survive, nor would Brunton's letter book, had it rested there, have passed either into the strong room or on to posterity. Scarcely any documents in Brunton's hand, or in that of McDowell, manager of the wholesale house in the two decades before 1916, exist, although both men were key figures in the business.

A fair amount of family papers survive. They are invaluable both in throwing light on the family background, and often on business. The latter comments are especially invaluable because they afford revealing glimpses of how members of the family actually saw the situation, without the interposition of the historian's interpretation of events. Some early legal documents survive of the family in Somerset before Charles Eason's coming to Ireland, and some of the letters of Charles Eason I at various stages of his childhood and youth, together with a few letters from his mother, one of his sisters and John Toms, exist. Through the good offices of Robert Eason, it was possible to see the commonplace book of Charles Eason I, last in the possession of the late Caroline Vause Eason in Sheffield. From this source also came copies of the letters of Charles Eason II to his clergyman brother Benjamin MacFarlane Eason for the period, c. 1895-1920. These are a remarkably interesting series of letters, ranging widely over business and non-business items. Robert Eason very kindly transcribed much of the commonplace book and made extracts from the letters, and I am much indebted to him for his painstaking work. Equally interesting in their light on Charles Eason II are his letters to Daphne Clare, an Australian cousin who eventually came to London to make a career in journalism. They range over almost three decades from 1914: in other words the correspondence must have continued until near Charles Eason II's death, and together with the letters to Benjamin MacFarlane are a testimony to his intellectual vitality and epistolary energy.

Other family correspondence includes some private account books of Charles Eason I, correspondence with the two sons who emigrated to Canada, and some documents and letters from the Birks family (into which Charles Eason I married) both in England and Australia. Charles Eason II wrote an interesting surviving account of his family background and youth; later he compiled in the immediate aftermath of the 1916 rebellion a highly interesting diary of the week, revealing not only in its account of the impact of the rebellion on the premises, but in its view of the rebellion as seen by a remarkably detached businessman living in the outer suburbs of the city. The board room files also reveal the cast of mind of Charles Eason II. The much more impersonal and reserved character of J.C.M. Eason is reflected in the total absence of personal items in the surviving files (if we take an exception of some items relating to his activities in the Statistical and Social Enquiry Society of Ireland) and in the highly impersonal tone of his correspondence. However the documents bear ample witness to a total grasp of the business and to a highly analytical cast of mind.

W.H. Smith's records in London are very slight for the nineteenth century, smaller in quantity and less revealing than the records surviving in Dublin: even aggregates of turnover of the business do not exist for most of the period, and the breakdown of the business into its broad components is almost always impossible. The Manchester Accounts from 1863 (A22) are among the rare sequences of turnover aggregates surviving before modern auditing began at the end of the century and provided the basis for a surviving series. For the second half of the nineteenth century, C.H. Wilson's account in *First with the News* very ingeniously compensates for the meagre crop of data within the firm, by a very thorough use of railway company board minutes. Inevitably this tends to overstress the railway context of the business, but the approach was unavoidable, given the slight record within the firm from the 1840s to the 1890s.

However, the individual items which survive are intrinsically interesting, and doubly so, because some of them cover the early years before 1856 when only a few stray items survive in Dublin. Most important in this pre-1856 category are the Coach book 1840-42 (A16) dealing with subscriptions service by coach, two letter books, 1852-3 (A1) and 1852-6 (A2), and Solicitor's bills of costs 1846-73 (A41). In addition some letters survive from Eason to Smith and from Smith to Eason for the late 1850s and early 1860s (Series 16, 17, 18, 19, 20, 22). These relate to the only period when the Dublin business was in the forefront of Smith's mind, and are therefore particularly informative. A few letters from White to Smith (series 14) and from Lethbridge to the house (series 110) survive. A small number of letters from Smith touch on the Irish business, and a few from Charles Eason I relate to a proposed acquisition of the Belleek China Co. in the early 1880s (series 121).

The deficiency is in part compensated by the Hambleden Papers, held within the house, which include W.H. Smith II's personal and family papers. While his political life tends to predominate inevitably in this collection, some of the paper are informative on the Irish business. This is so particularly of his letters written in Dublin to his wife (series A), and to his sister Augusta or Gussie (series B). The small number of letters from Lethbridge to Smith are also informative (Series DD). The Irish influences on Smith's outlook are reflected in the letters from Irish correspondents (series N), and his involvement in Irish political issues is documented in letters mainly in the several series PS 7, 8, 9, 12, 13, 14, in correspondence from his Irish agent Pattison (series KK), and in communications from Smith himself in Dublin in 1886 (series BB).

The records in Eason's were listed by the Irish Manuscripts Commission Survey of Business Records in the 1970s, and with the help of that list individual files can be traced without undue difficulty. A separate check list exists for records in the strong room, only a small portion of the total but including most of the early material. W.H. Smith's records are very well-organised. It was felt that it was not necessary to multiply footnotes as the bulk of the records are stored in two locations, and from the list in Eason's or the good arrangement in W.H. Smith's series and documents alike can be identified with comparatively little difficulty. For the most difficult or more isolated sources in either house, footnote references to the document or series are provided.

Other manuscript sources quoted in the text include Public Record Office of Northern Ireland D2458/2, account book of John Lee, a Dundalk newsagent, late 1830s and 1840s, and T3221/1/134-144, transcripts of letters written from the west of Ireland by George Wyndham to his wife, 21-31 October 1890.

An unusual and interesting personal diary survives for one employee, James Dignam, who became prominent in the News Division, for the year 1864 (in the Kenneth Spencer Research Library, University of Kansas). It mainly relates to his courtship and marrying in October 1864 of a girl named Jane, and ends with "a review of 16 months". It has little reference to his work at Eason's where at the time he earned £1-6-0 a week. Two comments were revealing however. When "an English chap" in the firm absconded with some cash, he noted that "it is flattering to us to know that he is not Irish but a protegé of the Protestant Association" (May 16), and a month later be recorded "the mail late. The Lord Lieutenant threatens to complain of papers being late" (27 June).

Among books the following items are the most relevant:

M. Adams, *Censorship: the Irish experience* (Dublin 1968)

[G. Clear] *The story of W.H. Smith & Son* (W.H. Smith & Son, privately printed, London 1949)

Anon., *The Menzies Group* (Edinburgh 1965)

Chilston, Viscount, *W.H. Smith* (London 1965)

B. Farrell (ed.) *Communications and community in Ireland* (Cork and Dublin 1984)

J. Feehan, *An Irish publisher and his world* (Cork 1969)

J.J. Hart, 'The early history of the Irish Retailers' national association', *Irish retail newsagents gazette*, 1943-4

B. Inglis, *The freedom of the press in Ireland 1784-1841* (London 1954)

F.S.L. Lyons, *A handlist of Irish newspapers* (London 1960)

H. Maxwell, *Life and times of the Right Hon. William Henry Smith, M.P.* (Edinburgh and London 1893), 2 vols.

R.L. Munter, *A handlist of Irish newspapers* (London 1960)

C. Wilson, *First with the News* (London 1985)

Index

INDEX